THE ... L

THE POLITICS OF SCANDAL

Power and Process
in Liberal Democracies

EDITED BY
ANDREI S. MARKOVITS
AND
MARK SILVERSTEIN

HOLMES & MEIER
New York   London

Published in the United States of America 1988 by
Holmes & Meier Publishers, Inc.
30 Irving Place
New York, NY 10003

Book design by Dale Cotton

The paper used in this publication meets the requirements of the
American National Standard for Permanence of Paper for printed
Library Materials, Z39.48-1984.

Library of Congress Cataloging-in-Publication Data

The Politics of scandal : power and process in liberal democracies
  edited by Andrei S. Markovits and Mark Silverstein.
    p. cm.
  Includes bibliographies and index.
  ISBN 0-8419-1097-9 (alk. paper). ISBN 0-8419-1098-7 (pbk.: alk.
paper)
    1. Corruption (in politics) 2. Comparative government.
3. Democracy. I. Markovits. Andrei S. II. Silverstein, Mark,
1947– .
  JF1525.C66P67   1988   88-11045
  351.9—dc19   CIP

MANUFACTURED IN THE UNITED STATES OF AMERICA

Contents

Foreword

THEODORE J. LOWI

Scandal is corruption revealed. Scandal is breach of virtue exposed. Apparently of religious origin, scandal literally referred to the conduct of a religious functionary that tended to discredit the religion itself. Scandal also referred to the effect on the communicant, as to the confusion of conscience produced by the scandalous conduct.

Scandology should be the proper name for the serious study of political scandals, and, given the opportunities provided by modern politicians, scandology ought to be a large and thriving subdiscipline of political science, sociology and anthropology. Yet there are surprisingly few bona fide scandologists, and most of them are contributors to this book. Many serious social scientists study particular scandals, but mainly because the exposure of scandal, with all the leaks, formal investigations, and printed reports, provides outside observers with unusually good opportunities to get data on the internal political processes that are not routinely available. To the serious observer, politics under conditions of scandal is comparable to cells under the microscope. Scandals, in other words, are a useful exaggeration of reality. But that's not scandology. Scandology is all that, plus the opportunity to compare and to judge political systems.

There are other observers who do make scandals their special universe, but these people are attracted only to the prurience of the conduct, not to the lessons to be learned. The editors and writers on the infamous *Enquirer* in the U.S. and the typical British daily newspaper are serious students of scandal and good sources of information about scandal, but they aren't serious scandologists. There are scandal mongers. There is money in scandal and the journalists on the staff of the *Enquirer* are really not much worse than the journalists on the staffs of the more responsible newspapers. Responsible journalists are just as hungry as the *Enquirer* journalists for any tidbit of scandal—albeit of a more political character—and when they can't find an intrinsically scandalous item, they are not above trying to pump up (without literally inventing it) a minor indiscretion into a major crisis. Timothy Crouse in his widely read book of fifteen years ago, *The Boys on the Bus,* described the powerful columnists Evans and Novak in the following way: "Of course, it was close to impossible to dig up sufficient inside dope to make five significant pieces a week. So they were part-time hoke artists. They would take a small incident (which they and they alone had discovered by prodigious digging) and they would blow it up into a campaign crisis." News is money. If the story is contrary to factual expectations, it's a scoop, worth even more money. If the story is contrary to ethical expectations, it's not merely news but scandal, and that's worth a lot more than a scoop. More precisely, a scandal is worth at least four times more than a mere scoop. First, there is a breach of morality which is a news break. Second, there is the denial. If the scandal is real, then the denial is what Woodward and Bernstein referred to as the "non-denial denial," which tends to invite suspicion of cover-up. Third, there will be one or more news breaks over revelations of the cover-up; if the guilty party or parties owned up immediately to the original indiscretion, it would quickly become mere news, or worse, past news (olds?), which is worthless, except perhaps in the *New York Times.* But if there is a cover-up, that is not only the third news opportunity but a series of new scandals of a different, but almost equally valuable character. The first news break is usually a *substantive* scandal, in which there is a breach of an actual norm, such as taking the money, giving the money, invading some- body else's country, or entering into a conspiracy to gain or maintain power without playing by the rules. But once the substantively corrupt conduct has been revealed, and while it is still in the realm of accusation and before there is incontrovertible proof, the original scandal will be extended and sustained by what we call a cover-up, which is actually a whole series of second level actions that go well beyond the effort to keep the substantive conduct concealed. Rather than cover-up this phase is better understood as *procedural* scandal.

The distinction between substantive and procedural scandals is important. Even though the substantive scandal must take place before the procedural one, and though the substantive scandal produces the procedural scandal, the procedural aspect can and often does outweigh the substantive. It is fairly obvious that the Profumo affair in England was far more important for the procedural aspects of the cover-up than for the original substantive indiscre- tion, which was nothing more than an affair with call girls who responded to the calls of Britain's enemies as well as her friends. And, although the substan- tive scandal that came to be called Watergate was a burglary combined with a conspiracy to violate various campaign laws, these were petty in comparison to the procedural scandal that eventually brought Richard Nixon down and doomed his administration to disgrace. This amounted to a virtual coup d'état against his own administration. Foreigners find it difficult to understand why we treated Richard Nixon so harshly because the substantive scandal of Water- gate was simply not very important.

When the substantive scandal involves national security, the accompanying procedural scandal is likely to be all the more important. In the Iran/Contra affair, the Lavon affair in Israel, and in the RCMP affair in Canada, the pro- cedural matters were far more sustaining and intensifying than the substantive, mainly because most of the opposition people and parties either agreed on the national security goals or were fearful of opposing the goals or the means utilized. Procedural niceties like the failure to use proper procedure or the attempt to lie or otherwise try to conceal what really happened are welcome ways of skirting the substantive issue almost altogether. The Tower Commission hit President Reagan not for (substantively) dealing with Iran terrorists and mercenaries but for secretly disregarding a perfectly good foreign policy structure provided for the president. If the RCMP trampled civil liberties for a good cause, then they should not have appeared ashamed by trying to cover it up once it was, alas, revealed.

Distinctions like these are important, but for serious scandologists they are important only to the extent that they serve the higher cause of political theory. For example, Markovits and Silverstein open their inquiry with assertions that amount to an article of faith that by studying scandals we will improve upon our grasp of the society at large and how or by what means society goes about maintaining itself. A general theory of scandals becomes an integral part of political theory itself. Scandology moves beyond the study of particular scandals through two motivating questions, which tie together all the case studies in this book. First, how and why does an event become a scandal? Second, what is the aftermath; i.e., of what consequence is the scandal to the system?

First, then, how to explain the scandal. Culture is the patently obvious starting point. Since politically relevant moral values vary from culture to culture and country to country, conduct that offends values deeply and widely enough to become a serious scandal will vary accordingly. On the other hand, since political values—e.g., standards about due process or the rules of the game—are likely to be common among countries with comparable political systems, conduct that is a scandal in one country ought to be a scandal in the others. This is the basis for the tantalizing observation made by Markovits and Silverstein that political scandal is only possible in liberal democracies. Liberal democracies, the reasoning goes, are grouped together precisely because they share so many political values even if their institutions are not precisely the same; most importantly, they share "rule of law"—the belief that there should be one system of laws for every citizen and that it should apply equally to officials as well as to citizens at large. Because liberal democracy rejects the distinction between ruler and subject, then there can be a standard of conduct *independent of the ruler* by which that ruler's conduct can be judged.

But a cultural approach, or a more narrowly defined political culture approach, would be the death blow to scandology or any other political phenomenon if taken too far. It becomes merely a way to beg the question. Scandology would go nowhere if all it could say were that there are sex scandals in Britain because the British have an aristocracy, pecuniary scandals in the U.S. because the U.S. is more truly capitalistic, or conspiratorial in Italy because of the diffuseness of its democratic politics. In the first place, scandals don't neatly distribute themselves cross-nationally according to the substantive morality breached by the conduct or the moral values that are cross-nationally shared. In the second place, countries may be culturally so different from one another that the same type of scandal can produce quite different reactions. No one would want to explain the Tanaka/Lockheed scandal, the Giscard scandal, the American share of the Lockheed scandal and the Iran/Contra scandal as though they reflected the same cultural context. Cultural factors are important; each author presents a rich and instructive cultural background for the case study in each country.

Another factor of profound importance in scandology is the presence of competitive political parties. On the basis of the empirical studies in the book Logue in his concluding chapter observes that there is no major scandal without party. Revelation of scandal is healthy, and parties have incentives to reveal the indiscretions of the opposition party or parties.

Since the primary political element of scandal is concealment and its exposure, surely we can state as a theorem that society will have few if any scandals unless there are institutionalized means of exposure. Thus, even if culturally the conditions for scandal are present—i.e., the actions in question are truly and genuinely breaches of the values of that society—the scandal will not occur spontaneously but will require attention and incentive to reveal and to sustain it long enough and intensely enough to obtain public attention. A free press is essential, but a free press needs inside information, and that requires institutional capacity and incentive—most likely to be provided by opposition parties. Thus, there is great plausibility in the governing proposition of this volume, that political scandals occur only in liberal democracies, with free presses and competitive parties.

But still, as the cases show, and as Logue admits, the opposition parties do not always exploit the scandal. And he should have added that parties don't necessarily succeed even when they do make the attempt to exploit the opportunity.

This leads directly to the second theoretical question, which concerns the aftermath of the scandal: Why is it that a political scandal in one country will make hardly a ripple, even when fully exposed and defined as a scandal, when in another country it is treated as an event of regime-shattering importance? Why, indeed, do the U.S., British and Canadian cases show a nearly regime-shattering aftermath while the Austrian, the German, the French, the Italian and the Japanese cases display hardly any aftermath at all, despite sustained exposure and proven public awareness? These cases provide ample data to permit all readers to pursue this fascinating question in their own way. In fact, these cases are so interesting and informative that they make theorizing about consequences almost impossible to resist.

To me, the theoretical answer to the question of aftermath will be found in an extension of Tocqueville and Hartz through Edmund Burke. According to Tocqueville and Hartz, since Americans were "born free" and had no feudal system and *ancien régime* to stage a revolution against, we became a liberal society, with a small state, a tradition of real self-government, and a consensus about the rules of the game. Now, a direct extension of this hardly fits England, against whose old regime America fought its own war for independence, nor does it exactly fit Canada, which remained a colony until its peaceful transition to commonwealth status in the 1860s. But one very important fact *is* shared by the three of them and not by the other liberal democracies. This is where Edmund Burke comes in. The U.S., Britain and Canada are the three liberal democracies *without a formative experience in revolution*. As for the so-called American revolution, we all know it was a rebellion, not a revolution. It was precisely on this basis that Burke could support the American war for independence against his own country and could vehemently oppose the French revolution. Americans, according to Burke, were actually fighting to maintain a society already close enough to perfection, while the French were at war against their society, trying to create a new society from an abstract design based on abstract ideas about a perfect society. America was, to Burke, following the

English tradition even while at war with the English. This points to the essence of the difference between revolution and rebellion—and to the trait that distinguishes the U.S., Canada and Britain from the others: There are two different formative experiences in the histories of liberal democracies—rebellion and revolution. The first is shared by the U.S., Canada and England. The second is shared by the others.

Revolution is an organized effort to change *by force* the regime, the rules by which the regime operates, and the social class structure and social values that prevail in that regime. Organized radical activity should be called revolutionary only if the clear intent and theory of the group is revolutionary in the sense defined here. To paraphrase Lenin, there is no revolutionary party without a revolutionary theory. Because the important revolutionary parties in Europe have been relatively quiet and obedient in recent years, some observers have been led to speculate upon the "twilight of revolution." However, these parties of the extreme left and the extreme right maintain the original revolutionary experience or experiences, not only among their own members but also among centrist people and parties. The contemporary Left and Right in the European democracies can be understood only by reference to original revolutionary experiences, extending for the French back to 1789 and for the others to more recent but quite poignant revolutionary, state-transforming experiences.

Rebellion, like revolution, is an extreme reaction against authority. Rebellion also involves disobedience and is a violent political activity. But rather than using violence to displace one regime with another and one dominant class and dominant set of rules with another, rebellion seeks to use violence and disobedience to *change the behavior of the existing regime.* If a rebellious group or movement has a theory at all, that theory will be aimed at bringing elite behavior into closer proximity with existing rules rather than changing those elites or rules. It will be oriented toward joining the ruling class rather than displacing it. The Declaration of Independence was, after all, a long bill of particulars against the *mis*behavior of the British monarchy, not an appeal for its overthrow.

If Tocqueville and Hartz are correct about the force of formative experience, we can say that the revolution and rebellion experiences are likely to have produced two quite different contemporary models of political behavior: The revolutionary experience gave rise to a *radical* model and the rebellion experience gave rise to a *reform* model. I call them models, but they could probably better be understood as screens through which specific political events are received and evaluated. And note well that these models or screens are formative in the political values of moderate and inactive citizens as well as extreme and militant citizens.

Both models are actually imbued with hope and optimism. Each has some Utopian goals. But there the similarity ends. The radical model holds no hope for the existing political order; it is optimistic only in its belief that organized actions can eventually eliminate injustice by creating new institutions and a new ruling class. Radicals may look for the worst but only because the worst provides the opportunity finally for the best to win out. Adherents of the reform model are also optimistic but in fact are optimistic that the existing political order can be changed. It is optimistic that institutions are reformable and rulers are redeemable. When a reformer is forced to resort to extremes, the extreme is likely to be civil disobedience, and the purpose of civil disobedience is to remind the ruling class that it is not behaving according to their own values, and that as a result of civil disobedience, the existing system can be everything it claims to be.

These models or screens can go a long way toward explaining why a scandal in one country can be of regime-shattering proportions and hardly cause a ripple in another. One of the most striking things about ordinary French or Japanese or German citizens, the proverbial "man on the street," is their tremendous tolerance for contemporary injustices and inconveniences. It is as though they don't really care. They seem to be terribly cynical, while the typical American citizen is intensely indignant over the same state of affairs. I think the difference lies in the distinction between two traditions, two models, two screens—the radical model and the reform model. To a person with a radical screen, even if that person is of moderate temperament with no orientation toward political action, things simply have to get worse before they get better. Corruption in high places, personal indiscretions, and political or economic conspiracies are likely to be taken as evidence of the corrupt society or regime. To the reformer, every such corrupt action or indiscretion is a cause of action. "There oughta be a law." "Get the rascals out." Just as the radical screen produces the appearance of cynicism, the reform screen produces the impression of naïveté.

Finally, there is a third model, the analytic model, and this describes the authors of this book and identifies their extraordinary contribution. For them, the scandal is an opportunity, an opening neither to the Left nor to the Right but to the political system. If I were qualified to teach comparative politics, which I am not, this would be my text, because each author, like Candid Camera, is catching each country in the act of being itself. And if I were qualified to direct research, which I am, I would, and will, use these chapters as a model, not of radicalism or reform, but of good method. The most difficult problem in political science is that all our facts are commonplace. The facts are known already or they become commonplace the moment they become familiar. Good political science must cultivate the knack of being surprised—how to locate the few significant commonplaces from among the million ordinary commonplaces. Scandology is a lever worth its weight in gold if it can lift political science out of the trenches of the commonplace.

Introduction: Power and Process in Liberal Democracies

ANDREI S. MARKOVITS
MARK SILVERSTEIN

The study of scandals, particularly political scandals, is barely in its infancy: as one German sociologist aptly remarked "there hardly exists any research about scandals which itself would not be scandalous."[1] A thorough literature review of the German and English scholarly output, combined with a more limited perusal of the French, points to the dearth of academic interest in the topic.[2] While studies of the history and anatomy of particular political scandals are quite numerous—Watergate in the United States being an excellent example[3]— only rarely does one find comparative work that attempts to understand political scandals in the larger context of social and political structures as well as of human behavior. The very concept of "scandal" seems to lack scholarly acceptance.[4] This is particularly surprising in sociology, which has produced superb analyses of fashion, rumor, humor, gossip, hobos, and a number of other "ordinary" phenomena influencing social life.

Yet the study of political scandals provides a unique opportunity for both macro and micro analysis. Across a broad spectrum of time and place, scandals have toppled governments, challenged established elites, and created controversy with clear lines of partisanship. Few subjects of scholarly pursuit appear to have the explanatory potential of scandals, despite their exclusion from the purview of all the social sciences.

One explanation for this exclusion is that scandals seem frivolous and trivial. The very mention of the term evokes a Molière farce. As the great and powerful make fools of themselves, their idiocy rubs off on contact—and few scholars care to take that risk. Political scandals are short, often intense affairs, which capture the public's attention for brief periods, only to vanish with hardly a trace. And while political scandals may seem momentarily amusing or even important, they appear in the long run to be irrelevant, or at least too

1

transitory to contribute to a deeper understanding of politics and human behavior. To political scientists engaged in the weighty study of "real" conflicts—like wars, revolutions, elections, and class struggle—scandals barely reach the level of fluff. Thus, even if certain scandals are worthy of case study, their wider explanatory significance is seen as negligible. This being the case, many in the academic community believe scandals are best left to the prurient pages of the yellow press rather than the rigorous investigations of scholars.

Although scandals appear in so many forms and guises that they defy categorization and challenge the parsimony of scholarly explanation, the neglect of political scandals in the social sciences has not been complete. In 1986, Anthony King provided a systematic comparative study of British and American political scandals, from which he developed some interesting comparative observations about the political realities of Great Britain and the United States.[5] Noting the absence of other studies of political scandals, King suggested—only partly tongue in cheek—that the new discipline of "scandology" be recognized in the social sciences.

Elsewhere, two German sociologists also suggested the term *Skandalogie* for the systematic study of what each believed to be a completely neglected topic, perhaps, as Manfred Schmitz suggested, within the larger sociological literature on deviance.[6] Certainly, the best scholarly work on scandals has been produced by sociologists and social anthropologists, a point that holds true even for the few essays devoted explicitly to political scandals.[7] Sociologists and social anthropologists working within the context of norms, values, and the cohesion of social life provide us with an important framework for the analysis of political scandals. Political science, with its focus on institutional analysis, has, for the most part, neglected the extrainstitutional mechanisms that help to integrate a society. As a result, such critical aspects of everyday life as dress codes, speech, dialects, gossip, friendships—and scandal—have remained the concern only of sociologists, social anthropologists, and some innovative social historians, often inspired by the pioneering work of the *Annales* school.

Within sociology, research building on Emile Durkheim's work in social integration has dominated studies dealing with scandals. Durkheim argued that even the most asocial, amoral, pathological actions (e.g., murder, theft, suicide) are ultimately functional to the integration of society.[8] By violating a shared belief, sacred or profane, such a transgression helped to reaffirm not only the belief itself but the social collectivity that upholds and sustains that belief. Hence for Durkheim, transgressions are not only normal in everyday life but necessary for the maintenance of any social order.

Scandals fit this model perfectly. Invariably, scandals serve to strengthen the community's *conscience collective*.[9] In addition to reaffirming and ultimately strengthening the bonds of a common morality, scandals help to create the scapegoats, enemies, and pariahs needed by all communities. This, in turn, aids the social processes of legitimation and mass mobilization. While a scandalous act invariably challenges the norms and values of the community, the public ritual of investigation, discussion, and punishment ultimately serves to reinforce the primacy of those shared norms and values. According to Durkheim, criminal behavior and subsequent punishment serve much the same function. As many of the essays in this volume forcefully illustrate, the ritual of scandal and punishment provides social systems with a means for self-legitimation and purification. Scandals, in short, constitute an important opportunity for re-affirming the social order.

Therefore while every scandal is unique, political scandals share important characteristics which serve to reaffirm the *conscience collective*. Both the cast of characters as well as the basic plot outline are virtually interchangeable. Despite the existence of a specific victim, political scandals rarely produce martyrs because the transgression is redefined as against the public interest rather than an individual's private interest. The result is that the transgression must be punished for violating the public trust despite claims that the scandalous acts were simply the means to lofty goals. Completing the cast is the purifier who may discover or investigate the scandal and thus assumes the role of the public's defender.

While the duration of most scandals is relatively short, especially as far as their acute phase is concerned, their impact may have a considerable duration, as witnessed by the Watergate scandal in the United States and the Profumo affair in Great Britain. Whereas the legacies of scandals are often considerable in creating major temporal divides, lending names to particular historical epochs (e.g., "post-Watergate" America or "post-Lockheed" Japan) the actual events—just as is the case with social upheavals—are of relatively short dura-tion. Typically, a period of normalcy is disturbed by an unusual event. Initially confined to a small circle of active participants, the transgressor and the immediate victim, the event "takes off" through the efforts of a third party, often the purifier. In the third stage, the event becomes public and demands are made for punishment and restitution. Stage four comprises the process of reaffirmation in which transgressors are punished and reforms are instituted. The cycle is completed when normalcy is again restored, incorporating the reforms designed to safeguard the system from similar transgressions in the future. The reforms are only successful in preventing very similar events from recurring shortly after the initial transgression. Different transgressions, how-ever, are bound to occur later; as the essays in this volume strongly suggest, scandals are inherent in the very structure of politics and confirm Durkheim's point that each social system needs pathologies for its successful reproduction. In short, political scandals constitute important ingredients in the maintenance and development of political life.[10]

Of course, political scandals are also marked by variety. The role of purifier, for example, has been historically performed by Cassandras, seers, prophets, political parties, investigatory committees, and, most recently, the media. Fur-thermore, there is what one might call the *Zeitgeist* factor. What is considered a scandal at one point in history is considered normal in another. The Romans did not find the fact that their empress Messalina had sexual intercourse in public with twenty-five men as part of a contest with a leading courtesan as cause to challenge the legitimacy of the ruling elite. In recent years, political careers in the United States have been severely impeded, sometimes destroyed, by even the suggestion of a sexual adventure on the part of the politicians concerned. The shared experiences of one generation produce a set of beliefs and norms of behavior inevitably unique to that generation. Moreover, contem-porary events that produce a scandal in one culture might be considered perfectly normal in another; what is scandalous in Japan may be business as usual in France. Because both the *conscience collective* and public morality vary considerably over time and space, the *Zeitgeist* factor plays a major role in the production and assessment of political scandals.[11]

Political scandals are social events and are thus very much determined by their social milieux. Men and women, young people and old ones, may perceive the same "scandalous" events very differently. While sex scandals, for example, may appear primarily to involve issues of gender politics, Robin Gaster's essay illustrates the extent to which the Profumo scandal rested on class values and the changing dynamics of British society. Conversely, financial scandals involving bribes, kickbacks, and irregularities in campaign funding may well be more prevalent in societies dominated by personalistic political parties, where the candidates are largely responsible for the financing of their own campaigns—as demonstrated by Terry MacDougall in his discussion of the Lockheed scandal in Japan—than in political systems with the well-organized and highly bureaucratic mass parties typical of the political landscape of Western Europe. However, as Aline Kuntz's study of the Flick affair in West Germany and Anton Pelinka's analysis of the AKH scandal in Austria amply illustrate, even these party-dominated liberal democracies remain far from immune to scandals involving what is conventionally known as corruption. Moreover, many members of an ethnic "outgroup" will hardly be perturbed if one of their own advances by means that are defined as scandalous by the dominant segment of society. As the essays in this volume illustrate, political scandals must be understood within their social context.

Nevertheless, these essays also illustrate an important element missing from a Durkheimian analysis: the exercise of, and struggle for, political power. Durkheim's framework misses the single most important ingredient in any political scandal: the central role of power in the construction of social reality, public morality, and the *conscience collective*. Durkheim demonstrated the significance and the social function of norms in developing a cohesive and integrated social order. Within that context, crimes (or scandals) and their subsequent punishment serve as a means of reaffirming that social order. But a framework that simply concentrates on the social function of norms cannot, in our opinion, provide a satisfactory analysis of scandals in the modern polity.

Power and modern political life are tightly intertwined and often indistinguishable, and nowhere is this more apparent than in liberal democracies.[12] We define liberal democracy as a political system in which the application of state power is curtailed in several specific ways. The first, most important constraint is the clear separation of the private and the public realms. Any explicit attempt to merge the two is considered illegitimate. Liberal democracies are also political systems in which any application of political power must be sanctioned by law and a certain degree of equality before the law is accorded all citizens. Furthermore, political power is subject to popular control through regular, open, and reasonably fair elections in which at least two parties compete for power. Finally, while there may not be a constitutional separation of secular and clerical authorities, the former has prevailed over the latter, at least in recent times.

If liberal democracies can be defined quite easily, this obscures the fact that the liberal and democratic traditions often form a rather uneasy alliance. Political philosophers of the eighteenth and nineteenth centuries would have considered the two traditions antithetical, principally because each tradition understood and employed political power in a fundamentally different way than the other. The modern liberal democracy merges these two traditions, and, in doing so, evidences both a fear of and an acceptance of state power. Liberal democracies are ambiguous constructs: While they need power like any other kind of state, they also curtail this very same power in order to maximize the individual's autonomy from the state. There thus exists a constant tension that is inherent in liberal democracies. Political scandals in the modern world can be understood only by developing an appreciation for this ambiguity concerning the use of political power—an ambiguity present to varying degrees in all liberal democracies.

Historically, liberalism connoted a set of radical ideas that liberated individuals from a hierarchical, feudal society, where one's position in the social order was preordained, to a modern world in which personal achievement and ability, particularly in the marketplace, defined an individual's station in life.[13] The liberal battle was a celebration of the individual against the confining norms of custom, tradition, and religion. As a result, the liberal inherently distrusted the imposition of any authority over the individual and the forces of the marketplace. Although classic liberalism could accept limited state power to ensure the protection of property and the fruits of one's labor, it was, at heart, an essentially antistatist philosophy.

With its deeply entrenched suspicion of coercion by the state, liberalism clashes with virtually all other arrangements and philosophies in modern political life. This is certainly the case with democracy, because the democratic tradition champions participation and equality, often at the expense of individual freedom from state compulsion. Only recently has democracy been redefined as simply a process for choosing political leaders.[14] In its most radical and pristine form, democracy is a means by which members of a community could ensure equality while working to achieve common goals and aspirations. Thus Rousseau articulated a basic democratic aspiration when he proclaimed that the general will of the community could force men to be free. Far from seeking to defend the liberty of the individual from the power of the state, the essence of democratic thought is to capture and employ the power of the state to benefit the community as a whole. Phrased another way, if liberalism proclaims the primacy of the individual, democracy demands the subordination of the individual to the collective welfare of the whole.

The net result of these contradictory mandates is that all liberal democracies exhibit a deep-seated schizophrenia over the uses of political power. The liberal seeks to separate state and society, with primacy accorded to the former and strict limitations placed upon the latter. The democrat blurs the distinction between state and society in the name of communal equality.[15] These contradictions become all the more apparent in the management of the modern nation state, as the demand for state action and the deployment of political power increase dramatically, be it in the name of social welfare or national security.

It is within these inherent tensions of liberal democracies that we locate political scandals: political scandals are the manifestations of an ever-present, tension-laden balancing act between the incompatible ingredients of liberal democratic rule in the modern, industrial state.

Fundamentally, we believe that political scandals can only occur in liberal democracies. In no other political arrangement is the separation of the public and private realms so essential to the vitality of the political system. Certainly, the separation of the private from the public has marked the modernization of politics; liberalism was revolutionary precisely because it sought to separate the private and the public in a way that "premodern" politics did not. Today, the distinction between public and private realms distinguishes the liberal democratic state from all others. Such "modern" regimes as National Socialist Germany, Soviet Russia, and Fascist Italy all shared one common trait: the obliteration, in theory and practice, of the line between the public and private. Indeed this separation forms the basis for Americans' normative assessment of virtually any other nation's political arrangements. If a state maintains a more or less functioning separation of the public and private, Americans—joined by most citizens of all liberal democracies—categorize it as a "democracy" and worthy of support. If this separation is flawed in practice, or worse yet, if its absence is theoretically or constitutionally mandated, the nation is labeled a totalitarian, communist dictatorship, if it opposes American global policy, or an authoritarian dictatorship, if it is an American ally or at least does not contest America's global role.[16]

Liberal democracies seek both to ensure the separation of the private and public realms and to overcome (or hide) their ambiguity over the use of political power. They perform these miracles through a faith in process. It is only via the firm institutionalization—almost sanctification—of due process that liberal democracies can legitimately curtail the randomness, secretiveness, and exclusive character inherent in the exercise of political power. Any violation of the formal arrangements of due process is tantamount to a frontal attack on the very nature of the liberal democratic system proper. Crucial to this system is the public character of politics: politics is only legitimate if it takes place in public. Anything latent, hidden, or not readily apparent is dismissed by liberal theory as nonexistent, or as a matter to be relegated to the private, nonpolitical, realm of social life. To the liberal, the political game must be open and accessible. The liberal's inherent distrust of political power is lessened by a political process defined by strict rules, procedures, and public scrutiny. The liberal *conscience collective* extols process; in fact, the celebration of process is perhaps the only "collective" value in a political arrangement founded on a profound individualism and commitment to personal freedom. To the liberal, the process *is* the public interest and hence any attempt to escape from the strict rules of the political process—regardless of the ultimate goals—is contrary to the common good. Just as all that is political can, for the liberal, only legitimately occur in the public realm, so too must the private sphere be protected from the political one, i.e., the state. This strict separation of private and public entails two different sensibilities and legitimation mechanisms that for the most part are mutually exclusive of each other.

It is precisely this clash that lies at the heart of many of the ten scandals presented in this volume. Central to each scandal is a violation of process, often perpetrated in the name of the more effective use of political power. Yet in liberal democracies, a more effective use of political power by its very nature borders on the scandalous. In our view, the critical feature of any political scandal is not the degree of personal gain involved nor is it the normative merit of the ends sought, but rather it is the presence of any activity that seeks to increase political power at the expense of process and procedure. As depicted in Figure 1, political scandals occur at the intersection of power and process. This, in a nutshell, is why political scandals can only take place in liberal democracies.

FIGURE 1.1

The realm of scandals in liberal democracies

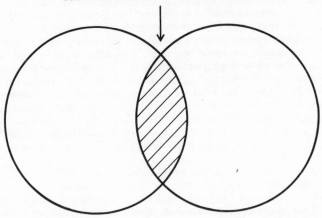

The logic of power

By its very nature:
—*Privatizing*
—*Secretive*
—*Exclusive*

The logic of due process

By its very nature:
—*Public-oriented*
—*Open*
—*Inclusive*

The cases in this volume have convinced us so forcefully of the primacy of the problem of power and process in political scandals that we view all other manifestations of scandals in the political world as epiphenomenal. Thus we differ from many who classify scandals in terms of sex, money, corruption, spying, and so forth.[17] In our view, the Profumo case was only secondarily a sex scandal and the Lockheed affair in Japan was not merely a tale of greed and corruption. The destruction of the Greenpeace ship *Rainbow Warrior*, discussed by Stephen Bornstein in this volume, was not simply a problem of the French security forces run wild. At the core of each scandal was the quest for political power at the expense of due process and procedure. Obviously, we do not deny the existence of sex or money scandals; indeed they are probably far more prevalent than political scandals. Our point is simply that not all sex scandals are best understood as examples of the human libido at work nor are all money scandals best understood as expressions of human greed. The controversy surrounding Gary Hart's presidential campaign in 1988, for instance, was the product of a classic sex scandal.[18] A public figure violated the sexual mores of his particular society and the public exacted punishment and restitution. The fact that Hart was a politician did not, in our view, make this a political scandal.[19] There was no abuse of power at the expense of process and procedure. One can easily imagine a corporation's stockholders or board of directors removing a corporate officer for sexual adventures that placed corporate profits or the corporation's image in jeopardy. On the other hand, had Hart used women to gain political advantage for himself or others, we would have witnessed a political rather than a sex scandal.

To continue on this point, we should contrast the Hart affair with the Profumo case. Much of the interest in the Profumo affair derived from the thrill induced by anything sexual in the largely bourgeois cultures of all liberal democracies. In this regard, the Profumo and Hart cases are similar. The Profumo incident, however, was a political scandal because there was a genuine fear that Britain's security would be jeopardized when it was revealed that Her Majesty's minister of defense was apparently sharing a young woman of ill repute with a Soviet intelligence officer based in London. Furthermore, Profumo lied to Parliament. His behavior violated the moral code of Britain's most venerated institution, and his lying undercut the public's faith in the sanctity of Parliament. On several dimensions, Profumo's activities violated the *conscience collective* of British liberal democracy at a time when Britain was undergoing major social and cultural upheaval. None of these factors were present in the Hart scandal.

The political nature of the scandals described in this volume can therefore be gauged by the extent to which they are a product of the inherent tension between the morality of liberalism and the requirements of governing and statecraft. In a sense we observe the clash of two contradictory values of the *conscience collective:* the liberal ethic that celebrates process as the means to control and limit power; and the democratic statist philosophy that demands the effective formulation and deployment of political power to further the communal good. Conservative critics of liberal democracies inevitably point to the liberal democrat's obsession with process to the exclusion of the effective use of state power.[20] Too great a concern with process, the argument goes, results in a weakened state, one unable to compete effectively in an increasingly dangerous world. The fact that the majority of scandals described here rests, in one way or another, on fears for national security tells us much about liberal democracies. The protection of the state and citizenry from foreign threats calls for the decisive application of state power; the liberal element in liberal democracies fears this state power and seeks to confine it by means of tying it to process and procedure. Paranoia is a fact of political life; only in liberal democracies, however, do fears for the national security appear inevitably to trigger political scandals.

Most importantly, process provides liberal democracies with the legitimacy to rule. In other states, for example, that legitimacy might be provided by forces such as religion. Much of the power of Ayatollah Khomeini's rule in Iran is derived from the linkage of the state and radical Islam. In other regimes, the forces of hypernationalism and anticolonialism may serve the same purpose. The push for modernization in developing nations often triggers a sense of social solidarity and cooperation toward the achievement of common goals that results in individual aspirations being linked to those of the state. Government in liberal democracies plays a far more abstract role and the question of why the citizen should obey government becomes far removed from immediate needs and desires. In the final analysis, process legitimates political power for the citizen of the liberal democracy.

The conclusion that a faith in process is a central element in the *conscience collective* does not imply that this core liberal value is above conflict, controversy, and political struggle in liberal democracies. The essays in this volume graphically illustrate that struggles over the conflicting demands of liberal democracy vary from country to country. In the United States, where a particularly strong faith developed in the liberal process as a curtailment of statist power, Watergate was a scandal of major proportions. At the other end of the spectrum lies France, where the *raison d'état* subsumes the liberal ethic to such an extent that the state's illegal destruction of a ship and the murder of an individual, all performed in the name of state security, barely engendered any debate. Considered from this perspective, the careful study of political scandals allows us to appreciate how existing regimes strike a balance between the conflicting demands of liberalism and democracy.

Political scandals play yet another contradictory role in all liberal democracies. While by their very nature they are clear manifestations of a clash between the system's public and private realms and are thus evidence for what one commonly calls a political crisis, they also build support for the system by concretizing its overall legitimacy. It is simply harder to maintain citizen support and loyalty for abstract values such as due process and equal protection under law than it is for more concrete, or discrete, national, religious, and ethnic identities. The rituals of political scandals and their resolutions take the abstract values of liberal democracy and make them tangible and visible. They reaffirm for the citizenry that the process does work, that it does curtail the arbitrary exercise of political power, and that the political system by and large deserves the support and loyalty of all citizens.

There is, then, a wonderful irony in each of these political scandals. From the conspiratorial activities of the P–2 Masonic lodge in Italy to the zealotry of the Canadian Mounted Police, each of the events recounted in this volume constitutes a betrayal of the public trust in terms of the accountability and process of the liberal democratic state. Indeed we believe that this kind of breach is the very mark of a political scandal; what is a political scandal in a liberal democracy is often business as usual in other political systems. What each of these essays also reveals, however, is that the resolution of the scandals' challenge to the system is a reaffirmation and strengthening of the public's faith in that system. What begins as an abuse of the liberal tradition inevitably culminates in a celebration of the values of that tradition. Clearly, differences on this issue are enormous among the liberal democracies discussed in this volume. In countries such as Italy and France, where political scandals have become so common that they define political normalcy, this constancy of crisis has led to a cynical attitude on the part of the citizenry vis-à-vis all political arrangements and institutions. For historical reasons, this contrasts with the situation in Great Britain and the United States, for instance, where the absence of constant scandals has permitted their respective systems to attain a greater legitimacy in the eyes of their citizens, who hold less cynical attitudes vis-à-vis politics and the exercise of power than has been the case in Italy and France. Ultimately, the irony as well as the impetus for the study of political scandals is the inescapable conclusion that if political scandals did not exist, liberal democracies would have to invent them.

The essays that follow suggest that political scandals provide an important and exciting means for the comparative study of the political systems of liberal democracies. In times of normalcy, which constitute the background for most comparative studies, the inherent conflicts and contradictions within each system are often obscured from view. Because political scandals represent a challenge to the very legitimacy of liberal democracies, their study provides a starker, more precise picture of the political and social system than may be afforded by the more traditional subjects of case studies. Simply stated, the goal of these essays is not to bring to light previously unknown facts concerning particular political scandals, but rather to use each scandal as a vehicle for improving our understanding of the particular country and its political system.

The essays are presented in three groups, based upon shared temporal traditions and historical experiences. Under the heading of "The Anglo-American Experience" Mark Silverstein discusses the Watergate scandal in chapter 1. Reg Whitaker presents the Royal Canadian Mounted Police scandal in chapter 2 and Robin Gaster analyzes the British experience of the Profumo affair in chapter 3. The second group, entitled "The Continental Experience," comprises four scandals that have taken place in European liberal democracies: In chapter 4, Stephen Bornstein presents the Greenpeace scandal in France, which is followed in chapter 5 by an analysis of a number of Italian scandals surrounding the P–2 Masonic Lodge, authored by Judith Chubb and Maurizio Vannicelli. The *Spiegel* affair and the Flick scandal highlight the West German situation, as written by Aline Kuntz. Finally, Anton Pelinka presents the Austrian case by analyzing a far-reaching scandal involving the construction of a hospital in Vienna. The book then concludes with two cases under the rather cumbersome title of "The Non-European Experience." In addition to this geographic description, the relative novelty of functioning liberal democracies in the case of all three countries warranted these studies being grouped together. In chapter 8, Terry MacDougall discusses the Lockheed scandal in Japan. In chapter 9, Mitchell Cohen details the Lavon affair in Israel. In the volume's concluding essay John Logue provides insightful commentary on the cases presented in this volume by discussing themes addressed in this introduction in analyzing the study of political scandals in a comparative context.

NOTES

1. Niklas Luhmann, as cited in Sighard Neckel, "Das Stellhölzchen der Macht. Zur Soziologie des politischen Skandals," *Leviathan* 14, 4 (1986): 584.

2. A number of authors such as Anthony King, Sighard Neckel, and Christian Schuetze introduce their respective studies by bemoaning the dearth of scholarly literature on the topic of scandals.

3. See e.g., Ronald Pynn, ed., *Watergate and the American Political Process* (New York: Praeger, 1975); Leo Rangell, *The Mind of Watergate: An Exploration of the Compromise of Integrity* (New York: W. W. Norton, 1980).

4. See Christian Schuetze, *Die Kunst des Skandals: Über die Gesetzmäßigkeit übler und nützlicher Ärgernisse* (Munich: Scherz Verlag, 1967), p. 9.

5. Anthony King, "Sex, Money and Power," in *Politics in Britain and the United States: Comparative Perspectives*, ed. Richard Hodder-Williams and James Ceaser (Durham, N.C.: Duke University Press, 1986), pp. 173–222. King linked the prevalence of sex scandals in Great Britain compared to the money scandals in the United States to the different party structures in each country.

6. See Christian Schuetze, *Die Kunst des Skandals*, p. 11; Manfred Schmitz, *Theorie und Praxis des politischen Skandals*, (Frankfurt: Campus Verlag, 1981), p. 125. While it seems Schmitz uses the term *Skandalogie* in a more systematic fashion than Schuetze, both authors clearly imply that the establishment of such a scholarly subdiscipline would

undoubtedly help to systematize the hitherto rather haphazard and virtually nonexistent study of scandals.

7. See Maxime Rodinson, "De l'histoire de l'antisemitisme à la sociologie du scandale" in *Cahiers Internationaux de Sociologie* 49 (July 1970): 143–50 and Max Gluckman, "Gossip and Scandal" in *Current Anthropology* 4 (1963): 317–16. We would like to make special mention in this context of Sighard Neckel's superb article, cited in note 1. It provides the most interesting theoretical framework for the study of scandals in general hitherto encountered by us anywhere in the political sociology literature. As to an essay devoted to a discussion of political scandals in particular, see Klaus Laermann, "Die gräßliche Bescherung: Zur Anatomie des politischen Skandals" in *Kursbuch* 77 (1984): 159–72.

8. The literature by and about Durkheim is enormous. See the following for a summary of Durkheim's approach to sociology. Jeffrey Alexander, ed., *Durkheimian Sociology* (Cambridge: Cambridge University Press, 1987); Steven Lukes, *Emile Durkheim—His Life and Work: A Historical and Critical Study* (Harmondsworth: Penguin Books, 1975) and Anthony Giddens, *Capitalism and Modern Social Theory: An Analysis of the Writings of Marx, Durkheim and Max Weber* (Cambridge: Cambridge University Press, 1971). Specifically on Durkheim's emphasis on integration, see Andrei S. Markovits and Warren W. Oliver III, "The Political Sociology of Integration and Social Development: A Comparative Analysis of Emile Durkheim and Karl W. Deutsch" in *From National Development to Global Community: Essays in Honor of Karl W. Deutsch*, ed. Richard Merritt and Bruce Russett (London: George Allen & Unwin, 1981), pp. 165–83.

9. We prefer using the French because it includes in its meaning aspects of both of its English cognates, i.e., "collective conscience" and "collective consciousness," thus expressing an element of integration more powerfully than either one of the English versions.

10. In this regard see Carl J. Friedrich, *The Pathology of Politics* (New York: Harper and Row, 1972).

11. Such a *Zeitgeist* analysis lies at the heart of a very perceptive analysis comparing the public indignation in American opinion at the Watergate abuses with the relative public complacency in connection with the Iran-Contra scandal. See Jeffrey Alexander, "Constructing Scandal" in *The New Republic*, 8 June 1987, pp. 18–20.

12. For two of the most perceptive analyses of power in modern politics, especially in the context of the contradiction between liberalism and democracy, see Steven Lukes, *Power: A Radical View* (London: Macmillan, 1974) and Alan Wolfe, *The Limits of Legitimacy* (New York: The Free Press, 1977), pp. 1–10.

13. See Isaac Kramnick, "Equal Opportunity and the Race of Life," in *Dissent* 28 (Spring 1981), p. 178 for a highly literate account of this development.

14. See, e.g., Joseph Schumpeter, *Capitalism, Socialism and Democracy* (New York: Harper and Row, 1950).

15. See Carole Pateman, *Participation and Democratic Theory*, pp. 20–22 for an excellent essay on the differing views of participation held by liberals and democrats.

16. This phenomenon is illustrated by Franklin Roosevelt's characterization of Nicaraguan dictator Anastasio Somosa García: "He may be a son of a bitch but at least he is our son of a bitch." Suffice it to say, had the regime respected the distinction between the public and private, Garcia would not even have been a son of a bitch. It is obvious that the partisanship of the beholder will strongly influence perceptions of a political regime regardless of the characteristics defining that regime. For example, President Reagan has repeatedly referred to Saudi Arabia and Brunei—probably as feudal and undemocratic nations as can be found at the end of the twentieth century—as "democracies" in his defending these countries' support of the contras in Nicaragua. For President Reagan, as well as other American conservatives, any nation supporting America as a global power—not the United States as a representative of liberalism—constitutes, by definition, a "democracy."

17. See for example Werner Klose, *Skandal und Politik: Ein Kapitel negativer Demokratie* (Tübingen: Katzmann Verlag, 1971); and Dietrich Thraenhardt, *Skandale und Affären in der Bundesrepublik Deutschland* (Münster, unpublished manuscript, 1986).

18. For those with short memories, Senator Gary Hart was the leading contender for the Democratic nomination well prior to the start of the primary season. Plagued with a reputation as a "womanizer," Hart eventually challenged the media to prove that he was anything but a happily married, faithful husband. The *Miami Herald* "staked out" Hart's Washington, D.C., townhouse and alleged that Donna Rice, a young actress, spent the weekend with Hart while his wife was in Colorado. Within days, Hart withdrew from the presidential race, only to rejoin it six months later. His poor showings in a number of Democratic primaries compelled him to withdraw from his party's nomination race by the spring of 1988.

19. Thus we differ from Schmitz and Schuetze, both of whom define a political scandal as involving someone from the political and/or administrative arena. For these two authors, the Gary Hart–Donna Rice episode would be considered a political scandal.

20. See, for example, Samuel Huntington, *American Politics: The Promise of Disharmony* (Cambridge: Belknap Press, 1981); and The Trilateral Commission, *The Governability of Democracies* (New York: Trilateral Commission, 1975). The first draft of this introduction was written during the joint House-Senate Iran Contra hearings in the summer of 1987. Almost every witness justified his actions as necessary steps in defending the interests of the United States, thus making all illegal involvements morally acceptable because they were performed in the name of "national security," hence protecting the public good.

THE ANGLO-AMERICAN EXPERIENCE

The Anglo-American experience represents to some degree the epitome of liberal democracy. With its birth in seventeenth century Great Britain and its early export to the North American continent, the liberal ethos has continued to flourish in Great Britain, the United States, and Canada. In contrast to virtually all other societies, the liberal democratic tradition has reigned supreme in these countries over the last two hundred years. The tension between power and process, inherent to all liberal democracies, is most pronounced in these cases. Testimony to the uninterrupted hegemony of liberal democracy in these three countries is that the scandals depicted in the following three chapters—all serious crises to the nations involved—would have been of far lesser significance in countries with weaker liberal democratic traditions.

1 · Watergate and the American Political System

MARK SILVERSTEIN

Faustus: Come, I think hell's a fable.
Mephistopheles: Ay, think so still, till experience change thy mind.
—Christopher Marlowe, *The Tragedy of Doctor Faustus*

In the Court of the Borgias

To Ron Ziegler, White House press secretary, it was simply a "third rate burglary attempt." An apt characterization, perhaps, if the Watergate scandal was confined to the bungled June 1972 break-in of the Watergate headquarters of the Democratic National Committee by four Cuban Americans and James McCord, security coordinator for the Committee for the Re-Election of the President (CREEP). Suspicion may have mounted that something more was involved when E. Howard Hunt and G. Gordon Liddy, men with direct links to the White House, were implicated in the crime, but throughout much of the summer and fall of 1972 it all seemed so implausible. Even before the Democratic convention, the incumbent Richard Nixon stood almost twenty percentage points ahead of any Democratic rival. The likelihood of the nomination of George McGovern, considered by many the weakest of the Democratic hopefuls, coupled with the general disarray of the national Democratic Party, made continued Republican control of the White House a virtual certainty. One had to suspend logic and belief to link the president or the president's men with the transgressions at the Watergate.

To comprehend the events of the next two years, however, often required the suspension of logic and belief. By 1974 the word "Watergate" had been transformed. No longer representing an address or even petty criminal activity, the word had become part of our political lexicon, connoting a level of official corruption and malfeasance in office hitherto unknown in the American experience. Throughout 1973 and 1974, the revelations of perjury, obstruction of justice, conspiracy, misuse of authority, and common criminal behavior at the highest levels of government numbed the mind. Instinctively we might have known that the significance of Watergate extended beyond any specific event or individual, but in the sea of detail and scandal few could gain the necessary perspective. Blame had to be fixed and the scoundrels of the Nixon administration evoked little sympathy. The fall from grace of Nixon and his cronies provided a needed catharsis, but Watergate cannot be explained and dismissed simply in terms of individual culpability. With the wisdom provided by hindsight, we can say with some certainty that Watergate was not merely the product of men blinded by ambition and the hunger for power; nor was it the result of public servants who permitted their zeal to serve to obscure reasoned judgment. The root causes of Watergate were systemic, not personal, and the value of reviewing the scandal of Watergate, years after the fact, lies in the perspective it provides for separating the myths from the realities of American politics.

It began, not surprisingly, in paranoia.[1] Early in Richard Nixon's first term, an interagency task force was established to formulate plans for strengthening domestic surveillance. Almost a decade of serious domestic unrest had convinced the men of the White House that draconian measures were needed to ensure order and domestic tranquility and to protect the Nixon administration from its "enemies." The resulting report (the Huston plan) recommended to the president the adoption of a program of illegal intelligence-gathering on American citizens. The fruits of this surveillance would be used to plug leaks of information embarrassing to the administration and to attack political enemies. Although originally approved by the president, the plan never formally went into effect because of the objections of the director of the FBI J. Edgar Hoover. Nevertheless, the paranoia and quest for control that prompted the Huston plan persisted; the Nixon White House, distrustful of the FBI and other established law enforcement agencies, wanted an investigation unit of its own. The unit would be secret, controlled by the White House, and responsible only to the president's men. John Ehrlichman, the chief domestic affairs adviser to the president, placed his top aide, Egil Krogh, in charge. Krogh immediately recruited new staff members, among them David Young, a former assistant to Henry Kissinger, E. Howard Hunt, a retired twenty-one-year veteran of the CIA, and G. Gordon Liddy, a former FBI agent and unsuccessful candidate for Congress. Their offices were in the basement of the Executive Office Building, and because one of their primary tasks was to plug leaks to the press, they were called the "plumbers." The plumbers would engage in a broad range of espionage and surveillance activities on newspaper reporters, bureaucrats, and political opponents. With the coming of the 1972 presidential election, the plumbers unit was transferred to CREEP. The bungled break-in at the Watergate was merely one small event in a larger effort to spy on enemies and to ensure the reelection of Richard Nixon.

Paranoia generated the moral tone of the White House. Loyalty to the president was equated with loyalty to the nation and the reelection of the president became synonymous with the public good. Threats, unspecified and often imagined, warranted repression. Freedom became secondary to order because people were either for Nixon or against America. In the same bizarre and tragic logic that justified the complete destruction of Vietnamese villages to save them from communist control, the Nixon administration began a systematic, clandestine attack on the constitutional rights of the citizenry in the name of preserving the republic.

At first, the enormity of it all escaped even the most perceptive observer. Stories in the *Washington Post* authored by two then-unknown reporters, Carl Bernstein and Bob Woodward, began to trace responsibility for the break-in at the Watergate first to CREEP and then eventually to the White House. Within weeks of the break-in, we learned of a secret slush fund kept in the safe of Maurice Stans, the secretary of commerce during Nixon's first term and chairman of the Finance Committee to Re-Elect the President. With money laundered through Mexican banks, the secret slush fund was used to finance, among other things, campaign dirty tricks and widespread intelligence-gathering. Control of this fund was quickly linked not only to Stans, but also to John Mitchell, the former attorney general of the United States and director of the Nixon reelection campaign. Nevertheless, although Mitchell and Stans had been part of the Nixon cabinet and among the most powerful men in the country, the initial stories of campaign dirty tricks and slush funds centered on the Committee to Re-Elect the President. We were assured by the president himself that the corruption did not taint those in the White House. As long as this remained the case, Watergate was not a direct threat to the regime; the business of government could proceed as usual and Watergate could be dismissed as the work of overzealous campaign officials. There were, of course, indications that the malfeasance did not stop with CREEP. Anyone familiar with the Nixon campaign operation understood that CREEP was controlled by the White House. Moreover, in the days before the 1972 election, the *Washington Post* ran a story linking H. R. Haldeman, assistant to the president, to the slush fund at CREEP. Although the story was technically incorrect and the White House vehemently attacked the *Post,* on the eve of Richard Nixon's reelection the stain of Watergate was spreading.[2]

Rejoicing in the White House over the president's resounding electoral victory would prove to be short-lived. On 8 January 1973, the criminal trial for the original Watergate break-in began before Judge John J. Sirica. Almost immediately E. Howard Hunt entered a guilty plea, stating to Judge Sirica that to his knowledge no "higher-ups" were involved. Within days, four of the other defendants followed suit, each denying that he had been paid "by anybody for anything." The remaining defendants, McCord and Liddy, proceeded to trial and were found guilty on all counts. Sirica, frustrated in his belief that the full story of Watergate had not been developed at trial, criticized the prosecution and set bail for Liddy and McCord at $100,000 for each man.

In January and February of 1973, it appeared that the Nixon administration had survived the threat of Watergate. A Gallup Poll conducted toward the end of January 1973 showed presidential popularity at a high of 68 percent. Indictments and convictions for the original break-in had stopped with Liddy, Hunt, and McCord; no one with significant ties to the administration had been implicated. Although there was increasing evidence in the media that Watergate was more than the work of a few overzealous individuals, the story had obviously not captured the minds of most Americans. There had been no break in the administration's story; none of the participants had implicated higher-ups. But in March of 1973 there were two major developments. James McCord, one of the convicted Watergate conspirators, wrote Judge Sirica charging that White House officials had worked to cover up the true dimensions of Watergate and that he and his codefendants had been pressured into remaining silent. Three days later, L. Patrick Gray, the acting head of the FBI, testified in Senate hearings on his confirmation as director of the FBI that White House Counsel John Dean had "probably lied" during the Watergate investigation. These were major developments; within days the original Watergate grand jury was reconvened to continue its investigations. Moreover, the Senate had already voted for a special committee to hold hearings to investigate campaign abuses. With the excitement generated by the McCord letter and the Gray testimony, attention was directed toward the upcoming Senate hearings.

The spring of 1973 brought a torrent of new developments, each seemingly striking away another layer of the White House's defenses. John Dean, White House counsel, was cooperating with investigators and Jeb Stuart Magruder, deputy director of CREEP, confessed that he had lied to the grand jury. On 17 April, Nixon reported that "serious charges" had been brought to his attention and announced a new investigation; his press secretary stated that all previous White House statements concerning Watergate were "inoperative." Within ten days a seemingly unrelated event became a major development in the ever-expanding scandal. In Los Angeles, at the trial of Daniel Ellsberg concerning the release of the Pentagon Papers, the trial judge announced that the Watergate prosecutors had informed him that Hunt and Liddy had supervised a break-in at the office of Ellsberg's psychiatrist in 1971. Fixated about leaks, the plumbers had sought damaging information about the man who had leaked the Pentagon Papers in the offices of his psychiatrist. Within days, the trial judge dismissed all charges against Ellsberg, citing "government misconduct." Once again the malignancy of Watergate had spread. For months the White House had dismissed the break-in at the Democratic headquarters as the work of misguided underlings magnified by hostile media. The break-in at Dr. Fielding's office, planned and supervised by the president's men, shattered the credibility of the White House. Days later the president accepted the resignations of Haldeman, Ehrlichman, Dean, and Richard Kleindienst, John Mitchell's successor as attorney general. In an address to the nation, Nixon stated that in March of 1973 "new information . . . came to me . . . suggesting there had been an effort to conceal the facts from the public . . . and from me." The president assured us that he was now taking responsibility for the Watergate investigation.

Thus began what might be seen as the second phase of the Watergate scandal. From the date of the break-in through the first few months of 1973, Watergate remained a fascinating but complicated tale of intrigue in high places. The efforts of investigative journalists to unearth the story necessarily resulted in sporadic and piecemeal revelations. Names like McCord, Stans, and Magruder pointed to faceless individuals linked in a web so complex that it mystified even investigators and prosecutors. Watergate was an important story and by May of 1973 even the most casual observer of the American scene was aware of the widening scandal. Nevertheless, in a media age this was a story that lacked easily recognizable symbols and images. With the convening of the televised hearings of the Senate Select Committee on Presidential Campaign

Activities (better known as the Ervin Committee, after its chairman, Senator Sam Ervin of North Carolina) on 17 May 1973, the situation dramatically changed. In a few short weeks, Watergate became what the administration most feared: a media and public relations event.

With the passage of years, it is difficult to recreate the grip the Watergate hearings had on the American public during the summer of 1973. A few weeks earlier the Senate had passed a resolution calling for a special prosecutor to investigate the widening Watergate scandal and to prosecute wrongdoers. In the days before the Watergate hearings opened, Attorney General Elliott Richardson named Archibald Cox, one of his former professors at Harvard Law School, to the post. Cox unsuccessfully sought to stop the televised hearings, citing possible prejudicial effect on future criminal trials. Although the office of the special prosecutor was to play a critical role in the developing story, the spotlight, nevertheless, shone on the Ervin Committee hearings. As the men of the Nixon White House were called to testify, the audience exceeded all expectations. A Gallup poll showed that almost 90 percent of a cross-section of the United States population watched at least some of the proceedings; total exposure (which included a rebroadcast in the evening hours by PBS) was estimated to be thirty hours per television home.[3] No longer was Watergate a simple burglary; we were exposed to the Ellsberg break-in, the plumbers, the wiretapping, the enemies list,[4] and a host of illegal or unseemly activities. No longer were the participants merely names without faces or personalities; we would now sit in judgment of the character and veracity of Haldeman, Ehrlichman, Dean, Magruder, Mitchell, and a host of others. Indeed the only figure missing was the president himself, and this was a significant omission. In testimony given over the week of 25 June 1973, John Dean directly implicated the president in the Watergate scandal. Dean testified that as early as September 1972 Nixon was aware of and involved in the cover-up. According to Dean, Nixon was pleased that the grand jury indictments had reached no higher than Liddy and Hunt, and he said he had discussed with Nixon the possibility of clemency and of making payments to the convicted Watergate defendants to buy their continued silence. In addition to linking the president to the cover-up, Dean told of White House involvement in other illegal activities, including the plumbers' intrigues and the break-in at Ellsberg's psychiatrist's office. If believed, Dean's testimony was political dynamite.

Dean, however, was the only one of the president's men to break rank. Other witnesses were vehement in denying presidential culpability, although they had little hesitancy in implicating former friends and associates. Indeed, two themes emerged from the testimony of Nixon's closest advisers. The first was that Richard Nixon was completely innocent of the crimes committed by his underlings. The second was that these crimes were not really crimes because they were committed in the name of national security. For example, John Ehrlichman maintained that the burglary of the office of Ellsberg's psychiatrist was legal because of national security needs. The reason he did not want the break-in linked to the White House was simply, he stated, a matter of public relations.

By the summer of 1973, few could doubt that officials in CREEP and the Nixon White House had engaged in, at best, unethical and, at worse, criminal activities. But what of Richard Nixon himself? John Dean had been an impressive witness, but his words, unsupported and contradicted by almost every other witness, would never topple a president. Committee member Howard Baker's question "What did the President know and when did he know it?" expressed the issue, but one certain to remain unanswered, to be debated for generations but never to be resolved. At least that appeared to be the case until 16 July 1973 at approximately 2:00 in the afternoon.

The surprise testimony of Alexander Butterfield, a former White House aide, that Richard Nixon had recorded all his conversations in the White House and the Executive Office Building was a stunning development. By the summer of 1973 we had become immune to a merely startling development; the news that a high-ranking official had resigned or had implicated another one was politics as usual. But we were unprepared for the revelation that tapes existed of all presidential conversations and that we could thereby test the veracity of Dean and Mitchell, Haldeman and Ehrlichman, and the president himself. The political world had been turned upside down. From the date of Butterfield's testimony through the summer of 1974, Watergate became the battle for possession of the White House tapes. The Ervin Committee hearings would continue (indeed some of the most important testimony came after the disclosure of the tapes) but attention now shifted to the protagonists in the battle over the tapes. Within days Special Prosecutor Archibald Cox requested access to them; when the White House refused, Cox, acting on behalf on the Watergate grand jury, issued subpoenas to the president of the United States directing him to turn over the relevant evidence in the grand jury's Watergate investigation. The White House, citing presidential privilege, refused to comply. On 22 August 1973, Cox, contending that discussions of criminal activity were not protected by executive privilege, squared off against White House Counsel Charles Alan Wright[5] in Judge Sirica's courtroom. The issue had been joined and the outcome would ultimately determine the fate of the Nixon presidency.

Thus began the third and final phase of the Watergate scandal. The battle for the White House tapes would involve the three branches of the American government in an unprecedented constitutional and political drama with the citizenry a spellbound audience. When we believed that nothing more could surprise us, that we were immune to further revelation, we would wake to an event that would shake the very foundations of our faith. Consider for example:

In early August we learn that the vice president of the United States is under investigation by federal prosecutors. Spiro T. Agnew, the darling of the silent majority, is alleged to have taken kickbacks from building contractors during his days as executive of Baltimore County and while governor of Maryland. Even more startling is the allegation that the payments continued during his term as vice president. Publicly Agnew proclaims his innocence and vows to fight; privately he and his lawyers scramble to make a deal. On 10 October, Agnew pleads *nolo contendere* to a single count of tax evasion and resigns as vice president. As part of the plea bargain, the prosecutors are permitted to release the wealth of evidence linking Agnew to the corruption. Within a matter of days, Nixon nominates Congressman Gerald Ford to be vice president.

On 20 October, Nixon's press secretary announces that Special Prosecutor Cox has been fired, the office of special prosecutor abolished, and that Attorney General Richardson and Deputy Attorney General William Ruckelshaus are discharged of further duties in light of their refusal to fire Cox. The "Saturday Night Massacre" grew out of Cox's pursuit of the Watergate tapes. In response to Cox's subpoena of the tapes, Judge Sirica had earlier ruled that the White House must deliver the tapes. The White House appealed and on 12 October, the Court of Appeals had upheld Sirica's order. During the ensuing week, the administration sought a compromise; Cox refused to budge, demanding that the tapes be provided to the court. The White House, then elected to fire Cox and immediately a political "firestorm" erupted. So great is the public outrage that within days the White House produces the nine tapes sought by the subpoena and a new special prosecutor, Leon Jaworski is appointed.[6]

On 21 November, the White House reveals an unexplained eighteen-and-a-half minute gap in one of the subpoenaed tapes. The tape is referred to a panel of experts who report on 15 January 1974 that the gaps were the result of five separate, intentional, manual erasures.

On 1 March 1974, seven former Nixon aides and government officials including Mitchell, Haldeman, and Ehrlichman are indicted by a federal grand jury, charged with conspiring to cover up the Watergate burglary. Much later we would learn that the grand jury had named Richard Nixon as an unindicted co-conspirator. Less than a week later, Ehrlichman and six others are indicted for the break-in at Ellsberg's psychiatrist.

The Internal Revenue Service announces on 3 April, that Richard Nixon owes $432,787 plus interest and penalties in back taxes. This is mainly the result of an IRS finding that Nixon took a deduction for the gift of his vice presidential papers after the date on which such contributions were prohibited and that the deed of gift had been backdated to make it appear as if the gift had been timely.

Throughout the summer of 1973, Carl Alpert, the Democratic Speaker of the House, had avoided a confrontation on the many calls for the impeachment of Richard Nixon. The firing of Cox, however, compelled the speaker to act. Refusing to establish a special committee to conduct an impeachment inquiry, Alpert elected to turn the matter over to the House Judiciary Committee and its chairman, Peter Rodino of New Jersey. As the battle between the new special prosecutor, Leon Jaworski, and the White House over expanding requests for additional tapes occupied public attention through the winter of 1973–74, the staff of the Judiciary Committee quietly began its investigation. Quickly the Judiciary Committee joined in the quest for the tapes. In February the committee requested access to tape recordings of forty-two presidential conversations. The president responded on 29 April. Rather than continue to fight the committee requests, in a bold stroke he voluntarily turned over transcripts of the conversations. Almost immediately, his remaining support crumbled.

In four consecutive issues the *New York Times* published the 1,308 pages of transcript. Within a week, publishers had printed paperback copies and the transcripts became an instant bestseller. And the impact was even greater than the firestorm over the Saturday Night Massacre. "If this is what he thought he *could* release," said one congressman, "I'd like to hear what else is on those tapes." What did appear throughout the transcripts, beyond the obvious vulgarity ("expletive deleted"), the meandering conversations, the dearth of intellectual content, the hostility, suspicion, and double-dealing, was cold, cynical contempt. The transcripts exhibited the Nixon White House's contempt for the judiciary and for Congress, contempt for due process, contempt for other leaders, and, indeed, contempt for the American public. Thus we were exposed to the president of the United States instructing his aides on how to "stonewall" a grand jury without committing perjury; planning how, with his White House counsel, to "screw" his political enemies using the FBI and the IRS; developing public relations "scenarios" to explain possibly illegal actions with the constant and only question being "will it play?"

Nixon had released the transcripts because, at least in his view, he had committed neither a crime nor an impeachable offense. Furthermore, transcripts, unlike the original tapes, could be doctored. Thus, for better or for worse, the transcripts released by the White House were ambiguous; the president might appear to be an amoral scoundrel, but direct evidence of criminal acts was missing. The transcripts were a public relations disaster, but Nixon was now fighting for survival and public outrage was, of course, not grounds for impeachment.

The House Judiciary Committee quickly issued a statement stating that a majority of the committee remained unsatisfied with the release of transcripts rather than the original tapes. The committee, however, would do little to force the president's hand. The same could not be said for the special prosecutor. With the indictment of Haldeman, Ehrlichman, Mitchell, and others in the Watergate cover-up, Jaworski had subpoenaed additional tapes to be used in preparation for the criminal trials. Unverified transcripts coupled with refusal to provide access to additional tapes would seriously prejudice both the prosecution and the defense (material on the tapes, for example, might provide exculpatory evidence for some of the defendants). The White House objected to providing additional evidence on the ground of presidential privilege. Judge Sirica had upheld the claim of the special prosecutor and the White House sought appellate review in the Court of Appeals. Faced with the inherent delays of the federal appellate procedure, Jaworski responded by successfully petitioning the United States Supreme Court to take the extraordinary step of bypassing intermediate appellate review and agreeing to hear the case immediately.

Stage three of the Watergate scandal was now quickly drawing to conclusion. After weeks of secret deliberations, the House Judiciary Committee was preparing to hold public debate on whether to recommend to the full House that articles of impeachment be brought against Richard Nixon. The special prosecutor's quest for evidence had now reached the United States Supreme Court. For several weeks in late July and early August of 1974, business, indeed life, as usual was suspended as we watched, transfixed by the final act in a constitutional drama.

On 23 July, the Supreme Court announced its decision that the president must comply with the request for the tapes. The next evening, the House Judiciary Committee began televised debate. Four days later, the committee was prepared to vote on the first article of impeachment, that the president of the United States had committed high crimes and misdemeanors by engaging in a course of conduct designed to obstruct justice. The vote was twenty-seven ayes and eleven nays. In the ensuing days, additional articles citing Richard Nixon for abuse of power and refusing to obey congressional subpoenas were approved by similar margins. Richard Nixon vowed to fight, but it was an empty threat. He knew that among the wealth of tapes ordered produced by the Supreme Court were a series of conversations that took place on 23 June 1972, several days after the original Watergate burglary. Appearing on that tape was the voice of the president of the United States ordering the CIA to halt the FBI's investigation of Watergate on counterfeit grounds of national security. This was it, direct evidence that Richard Nixon, the president of the United States, had engaged in the obstruction of justice. On 8 August 1974, Richard Nixon announced his resignation from the office of president. Later the Republicans on the Judiciary Committee who had voted against the articles of impeachment of Richard Nixon before they knew of the contents of the 23 June tape filed a minority report. It read in part:

> We know that it has been said—and perhaps some will continue to say—that Richard Nixon was "hounded from office" by his political opponents and media critics.

> We feel constrained to point out, however, that it was Richard Nixon who impeded the FBI's investigation of the Watergate affair by wrongfully attempting to implicate the Central Intelligence Agency.

> It was Richard Nixon who created and preserved the evidence of that transgression and who, knowing that it had been subpoenaed by this Committee and the Special Prosecutor, concealed its terrible import, even from his own counsel, until he could do so no longer.

> And it was a unanimous Supreme Court of the United States which, in an opinion authored by the Chief Justice whom he appointed, ordered Richard Nixon to surrender that evidence to the Special Prosecutor, to further the ends of justice.[7]

"If men were angels. . . ."

A common thread that united the extraordinary group of men who met in Philadelphia during the summer of 1787 to fashion a new republic was the understanding that all governments are tyrannical. All governments demand that citizens cede a measure of personal freedom to the state to ensure order and domestic tranquility. The problem becomes one of balance. To concede too much freedom to the state is to create the tyrannical Leviathan; to deny to the state sufficient power is to ensure the tyranny of anarchy. Madison put the problem neatly in *Federalist* No. 51:

> But what is government itself but the greatest of all reflections on human nature? If men were angels, no government would be necessary. If angels were to govern men, neither external nor internal controls on government would be necessary. In framing a government which is to be administered by men over men, the great difficulty lies in this: you must first enable the government to control the governed; and in the next place oblige it to control itself.

In the hearts and minds of these men, as well as of future generations of Americans, lay a profound ambivalence about the nature and uses of political power. As the intellectual beneficiaries of Locke, Hume, and Adam Smith, the founders had a deep distrust of state power, choosing to make the individual rather than the communal will the cornerstone of the new republic.[8] As pragmatic realists, however, they understood the value of state power in maintaining order. The new government they created reflected this ambiguity. It was potentially powerful, but it was a government in which institutional checks and balances and the fragmentation of authority made decisive governmental action the exception rather than the rule. Only measures enjoying the most widespread and sustained support could successfully tap its vast reservoir of power. The delegates to the Philadelphia convention feared government as the greatest threat to personal freedom, and the system they produced reflected their commitment to moderation and balance.

Their primary concern was less with the untrustworthy and despotic leader than with the tyranny of the masses. In the years following the Revolutionary War, representative and powerful state legislatures had enacted an extraordinary volume of often-radical legislation in response to the shifting demands of constituents. The confiscation of private property, paper money laws, and debtor relief statutes were, in the minds of many of the framers, symptomatic of the evils of too much democracy. The men who came to Philadelphia in 1787 were firm in their belief that government must rest on the consent and participation of the governed. Nevertheless, the experiences of the past decade had made manifest to them the evils of democratic tyranny. The primary task in establishing a new government was to unite popular consent with a system of governing designed to avoid "the turbulence and follies of democracy."9

One step was to ensure that only the best and brightest would be chosen to govern. The ideal representative would be a man of property and education, capable of acting to further the public good while screening the selfish, short-sighted demands of his constituency. Here the enormous size of the republic, once thought to be a substantial obstacle to republican rule, could be made into a virtue. In a small republic (and here the example again would be the state legislatures of the day) a greater proportion of citizens could achieve public office, hence increasing the likelihood that the less talented would find themselves in positions of responsibility. By enlarging the republic, only the most distinguished could appeal successfully to the larger numbers necessary to achieve election to the national government. As Madison characterized the situation in *Federalist* 10, "as each representative will be chosen by a greater number of citizens in the large than in the small republic, it will be more difficult for unworthy candidates to practice with success the vicious arts by which elections are often carried and the suffrages of the people being more free, will be more likely to center on men who possess the most attractive merit and the most effusive and established characters." Moreover, a large republic, with diverse interests and cleavages, made unlikely the emergence of an enduring majority; narrow, and often diverse interests rather than broad-based class consciousness would dominate American politics. In the large, commercial republic envisioned by the Federalists, a potential majority would always be fragmented, with particularized and selfish interests neutralizing each other, thereby freeing government from the demands of an overbearing majority.

To limit further the efficacy of majority will, the framers developed a government in which a complex web of institutional checks and balances resulted in moderation. The cumbersome legislative process, for example, in which prospective legislation had to secure majorities in both the Senate and the House, was designed to ensure that most measures would fail to become law. The staggered terms and differing constituencies of elected representatives guaranteed that no single election could transform the government. Groups seeking access to power would soon be frustrated by the fragmentation of authority that marked the new republic; the new system quite openly favored minorities opposed to change rather than transient majorities in favor of it. Judicial review, the power of an unelected judiciary to declare acts of the representative branches null and void, fit easily within the system as perhaps the ultimate hedge against majority rule. It was, in short, a form of government in which decisive, quick action would be the exception to the general rule of inaction. The framers had performed the extraordinary feat of establishing a system that rested on the consent of the governed while at the same time making majority rule in day-to-day politics a virtual impossibility.

Modern America's often-expressed frustration with its national government is the legacy of the framers' choice to separate Congress from the president and to diffuse power through a federal system. What today may appear as inefficient and indecisive was then celebrated as a model of moderate government. Indeed, while we venerate both the Constitution and its creators, a good deal of the history of American politics may be viewed as a continuing effort to avoid the institutional and procedural impasses created by the founders. On several occasions we have employed the amendment process to expand suffrage or to remove institutional checks on popular democracy.[10] For the most part, however, the formal structure of the national government has remained inviolate, with evolutionary adaptations altering the functions and practices of the institutions.

One of the first steps was the development of a party system. Almost to a man, the founders disapproved of political parties, characterizing them as factions that elevate self-interest and greed over the common good. Nevertheless, despite Washington's farewell warning of the "baneful effects of the Spirit of Party," parties did develop, in no small part in response to the institutional fragmentation of power that marked the American political system.[11] The inevitable demand for legislation invariably imposes on a legislative body the discipline of a rudimentary party system, and, in the case of the United States, an expanding electorate necessitated permanent organizations within the body politic to channel and to moderate constituency demands. Moreover, even a relatively weak party system could serve as a bridge to link the constitutionally severed executive and legislative branches. Hence the 1830s and 1840s saw the emergence of the American party system, as first Jacksonian Democrats and then the Whig opposition put together the grass-roots organization necessary to sustain a national political organization. The growth of political parties changed the face of American politics. In the quest for supporters, parties extended the franchise and assimilated new social groups seeking access to the political arena. The importance of Congress relative to the presidency during much of the nineteenth century was in no small measure due to the power of political parties to link Congress to a rapidly changing and expanding electorate.

Political parties posed a significant threat to the Madisonian model of government; by encouraging cooperation among interests, a two-party system would inevitably produce the majority factions the system was designed to forestall. This is precisely what took place during much of the nineteenth century. With state governments assuming the burden of the day-to-day regulation of citizen affairs, the national government set about the task of distributing public lands, financing internal improvements, and providing subsidies to further development. Theodore Lowi has characterized this as "the patronage state," in which a party-organized Congress distributed particularized benefits to local constituencies.[12] The party system not only organized these legislative activities but also structured the demands of diverse constituencies and served as a conduit linking the electorate to the legislative branch. Within this system, the presidency was a second-line institution with little responsibility and less power.

The turn of the century witnessed the demise of the patronage state. The significance of political parties was undercut by a series of reforms triggered by a Progressive movement that saw partisanship, the political machine, and the manipulation of the urban, immigrant vote as a threat to enlightened government. The direct primary, voter registration laws, the civil service, nonpartisan elections, and a host of other measures seriously weakened the party system.[13] At the same time, the responsibilities of the national government were increasing. The growth of industry triggered demands that government control the harsh realities of unregulated capitalism. As the size and power of the organized private sector grew, the focus of regulatory efforts shifted from the individual states to the national government. The nationalization of economic and social problems and the expanding international role of the United States combined to upset the old model of politics and to generate a new one. To many, the twentieth-century world required an efficient, expertly administered state capable of both speedy responses to changing conditions and the development of long-term, coordinated national public policy. This realization produced, in the early twentieth century, a generation of reformers who broke with the traditional Jeffersonian faith in limited, decentralized government and called for strong, centralized national government led by a powerful chief executive.[14] The fragmentation of power and institutional noncooperation, however, were the key characteristics of the constitutional system. The genius of the framers, keyed to the problems of an eighteenth-century world and informed by the Anglo-Scottish Enlightenment, increasingly appeared to be out of joint with the reality of a modernized, industrial state.

The New Deal and the presidency of Franklin Roosevelt marked the passage of the patronage state into the modern regulatory, welfare state. Federalism in the United States was redefined; the locus of power in American politics was no longer diffused throughout the several states but centralized in Washington, D.C. With the regulatory state came the expansion of the executive branch and the narrowing of congressional influence. Expert administrators were the symbol of the new state, as Congress gradually abdicated control to a growing bureaucracy. To oversee this growing state, the presidency grew dramatically. The White House staff, nonexistent throughout much of the nineteenth century, numbered 51 in 1943. By 1971, the president's immediate staff had grown to 583. In 1939 Congress, responding to pleas that the president needed help, approved the Executive Office of the President, in effect creating a mini-bureaucracy to help the president administer a growing bureaucracy. The emergence of the presidency and the retreat of Congress highlighted America's institutional adaptation to the social and economic changes produced by a growing urban and industrial society.[15]

Roosevelt also transformed the very nature of presidential power. The linkage between an elected official and his or her constituency is the key to political power in the modern democratic state. For the first one hundred fifty years of its history, the presidency remained remote and the president required the cooperation of party leaders and supporters in Congress to establish constituent support. During this period, comparatively few could see the president or even hear his voice, a fact difficult to appreciate today when the president is a ubiquitous presence in the lives of most Americans. Franklin Roosevelt dramatically altered the president's relationship with his constituency. A master of the press conference, Roosevelt, with the aid of the presidency's first official press secretary, Steve Early, succeeded in seeing that the White House position on any issue was thoroughly reported, despite the fact that the nation's newspapers were overwhelmingly Republican. Of far more significance, however, was Roosevelt's appreciation of the power of the mass media. "Time after time," he wrote of his days as governor of the state of New York, "in meeting legislative opposition in my own state, I have taken the issue directly to the voters by radio, and invariably I have had a most heartening response."[16] Whereas other politicians simply gave political speeches over the radio, Roosevelt used the radio to establish direct links with a national constituency, free from the mediation of party, Congress, or the print media. With Roosevelt, the president became the living symbol of the nation, reifying the very will of the American people. The modern presidency had been born, powerful, dynamic, and the centerpiece of American politics.

The economic and social dislocations that gripped America during the first third of the twentieth century forcefully highlighted the fact that Americans were confronting the problems of an industrial, technological society with a form of government responsive to the concerns of an eighteenth-century world. The eighteenth-century liberal mind feared government and for good reason sought to confine its reach and to moderate its influence. The twentieth-century liberal, for equally good reason, saw government as the necessary response to the nationalization of social and economic problems and to the growth of private power. Nevertheless, this transformation of the very idea of government produced not even the hint of formal institutional change; the New Deal, for example, did not produce a second constitutional convention. Rather than grapple with the difficult task of constitutional reform, we begged the question and simply turned to the office of the president. The Roosevelt presidency suggested that a forceful, dynamic president, skillfully employing the media to mobilize the electorate, could overcome the institutional stasis created by the framers. The executive branch could provide speed, expertise, innovation, and administration, continually powered by the president's increasingly intimate and direct relationship with the mass electorate. Stated simply, America adapted to a changing world by making the presidency the focal point of the American political universe, and in so doing, it relegated other national as well as state and local institutions of governance to democratic irrelevance.

Shake Hands with the Devil

The fact was that in the name of progress we had struck a Faustian bargain. We had agreed to sell our democratic souls to the president, to make him the center of our aspirations and to transform, through the power of our collective will, his limited constitutional power into a broad political mandate. In return, the president assumed the responsibility of governing, of professing fealty to an eighteenth-century divided form of government while centralizing the operations of state within an ever-expanding executive branch. Because we believed that in a modern world only the executive had the capacity to govern effectively, we bargained away the heart of the Madisonian system for a plebiscitary presidency. The terms hardly seemed onerous: the imperial presidency would solve the problem of governing while permitting us to remain seemingly faithful to a constitutional regime frozen in time. While other industrialized systems modernized through the emergence of ideological parties, particularly on the Left, posing alternatives to existing arrangements, our bargain freed us from contemplating new alternatives and principles and made identification with personalities rather than programs the cornerstone of our politics. While other societies confronted sharp political clashes over the very nature and direction of the state, we merely equated the president with the state and proceeded with business as usual. For years we reaped the benefits of the bargain as the United States emerged from World War II as the most productive and stable industrial society in the world. Within a generation, however, the costs of this bargain both to the presidency and the polity would become uncomfortably clear.

Considered from this perspective, Watergate is hardly the tale of the fall from grace of a single man. Certainly the paranoia, anger, and mistrust that were Richard Nixon played an important role. Character flaws aside, however, Richard Nixon understood the modern presidency and the implications of its Faustian pact with the American people far better than most. With the presidency the "center of action" (John Kennedy's words), it was hardly surprising that Nixon (as well as all other modern presidents) would seek to free the presidency from the constraints of the Constitution. Nor were Nixon's efforts to diminish legislative interference with his programs or to reorganize the bureaucracy and centralize control in the White House out of step with our understanding of the modern presidency. Because public opinion constitutes the vital component in the presidential quest for power, it was perfectly predictable that public relations, manufactured events, and media images would obsess the president and his most trusted advisers. To produce the public support on which the modern presidency rested, however, required continual promises of a better life and, more often than not, the result was heightened public expectations beyond the president's institutional capacity to meet. The cruel irony of the Faustian pact between the president and the American people is that *all* modern presidents are destined to fail. Watergate was simply Richard Nixon's futile battle to escape his fate.

Consider from this perspective the very existence of CREEP. Richard Nixon had been elected president of the United States in 1972 with the largest popular vote recorded in American history. More remarkable than the scope of his victory was the fact that it was achieved by means of an organization totally independent of the Republican Party. Because the modern presidency is founded upon popular support rather than constitutional power, the candidates in presidential elections seek not simply victory but an overwhelming personal mandate. Thus CREEP, over-zealous as well as over-financed, was an organization whose sole purpose was the personal victory of Richard Nixon. Mindful of the need to add Democrats to his electoral mandate, Nixon eschewed party labels throughout the 1972 campaign, preferring to appear simply as the president of the United States, above mere partisan politics. This strategy produced a huge electoral majority for the president, while both houses of Congress remained in Democratic hands, and many congressional Republicans were embittered over the president's lack of support during the 1972 campaign.

Nixon thus faced the uniquely American task of transforming an election victory into a tool for effective governing. Despite his overwhelming victory and success in appealing directly to the individual citizen, the Madisonian system circumscribed his presidential perogatives. Stasis was, of course, unacceptable; the nation demanded of the president effective leadership even if the constitutional means for it were not readily available. Hence all presidents seek control over the apparatus of governing. What Thomas Cronin has characterized "the swelling of the presidency" is but one example of this quest for control.[17] Up to the time of World War II, presidents lacked the means to bypass the existing bureaucracy to implement presidential decisions. The growth of the White House Staff and the EOP provided the executive with the opportunity to carry out certain policy directives without the intervention of a cumbersome and quasi-independent bureaucracy. In the view of many, the president not only needed his own source of expertise for policy formation but he also needed a coterie of administrators and experts with unquestioned loyalty to the president's program in order to control policy implementation. Richard Nixon encouraged this development, creating a counter bureaucracy in which White House aides bypassed cabinet secretaries and subcabinet officials to control and oversee vital agencies and bureaus.[18] In a 1971 speech, Senator Ernest Hollings described this development:

> It used to be that if I had a problem with food stamps, I went to see the Secretary of Agriculture. . . . Not anymore. Now, if I want to learn the policy, I must go to the White House to consult John Price [a White House aide]. If I want the latest on textiles, I won't get it from the Secretary of Commerce, who has the authority and responsibility. No, I am forced to go to the White House and see Mr. Peter Flanigan. I shouldn't feel too badly. Secretary Stans [Maurice Stans was then Secretary of Commerce] has to do the same thing.[19]

The goal was to centralize control over the bureaucracy within the White House. Nixon assumed office in 1969, expressing, as do all presidents, great hopes for his cabinet. Very quickly the men of Nixon's White House found that cabinet secretaries were men of divided loyalties, torn by the demands of their departments, constituent groups, and the White House. John Ehrlichman complained that cabinet secretaries "soon go off and marry the natives."[20] The "natives"—the career staff of the departments—typically have an agenda and an outlook that may not square with that of the president. When, for example, Nixon perceived this to be the case with the State Department, the National Security Assistant to the President, Henry Kissinger, became the prime foreign policy actor, while the Secretary of State, William Rogers, faded into virtual obscurity.[21] In the quest for control, presidents inevitably turn to close friends and personal advisers who see issues and policy solely in presidential terms.

For Nixon the issue of control was magnified by the war in Indochina. His particular pact with the American people included a promise to end the war in Vietnam. To achieve "peace with honor" required not only intensified efforts in Vietnam but expanding the theater of operations to neighboring Laos and

Cambodia. With Congress unlikely to provide the necessary support, Nixon called upon his inherent powers as commander in chief to carry on military operations, including strikes across the borders of South Vietnam into North Vietnamese sanctuaries in Cambodia. The war could not be won—in private moments even Richard Nixon might have conceded as much—but the modern presidency could hardly afford to preside over military defeat. The bargain that forged the modern presidency made the occupant of the White House responsible for results, regardless of the scope of his constitutional powers. Thus Nixon proceeded without direct congressional approval.[22] In 1970, with the invasion of Cambodia, the college campuses of the nation exploded. Nixon fought back, arresting thousands of demonstrators, plugging leaks about supposedly secret bombings of Cambodia, wiretapping his own aides, and eventually appearing in court to stop the publication of the Pentagon Papers. Challenges to presidential power were easily transformed into threats to the nation. As one White House aide put it: "It was a question of whether anybody could govern the country with the machinery he had."[23] Outsiders could not be trusted; only the men of the White House understood the bargain that existed between the American people and the president.

Within weeks of the Cambodian invasion and the resulting domestic upheaval, a committee was formed at the White House to coordinate American intelligence-gathering. One product of this committee was the Huston plan. To the men in the White House, the welfare of the nation and the welfare of the presidency had become indistinguishable; challenges to presidential policy were considered nothing less than challenges to the state and an ordered society. It was not that the president was above the law; more insidiously, the president had become the law. The Huston plan was the inevitable result and Richard Nixon and the American people began their collective descent into the hell of Watergate.

The Illusion of Power

Watergate was the product of a political system that increasingly focused upon the president the hopes and aspirations of a nation without providing the lawful means of satisfying those expectations. Phrased another way, Watergate was simply one indication of the price we pay for an eighteenth-century system of checks and balances in a twentieth-century world. Indeed, this may well represent the ultimate irony of the Watergate scandal: a system designed to foster moderation and inaction not only failed to prevent, but indeed produced, a presidency that engaged in illegal surveillance, dirty tricks, secret bombings, cover-ups, enemies lists, and a host of other abuses.[24] In short, suggestions made after the resignation of Richard Nixon that the lesson of Watergate was that the "system works" should be viewed with more than a trace of skepticism.

Despite continual allusions to the national interest, politics in the United States is essentially local. The structure of Congress limits the power and incentive of party leaders to enforce discipline on their members. With funding for election campaigns often outside of party control,[25] congressional careers are built upon satisfying local interests rather than furthering the agenda of the national political parties. As long as the representative returns the necessary particularized benefits to his district, he remains relatively autonomous. In a system in which the executive is constitutionally divorced from the legislature, the natural outcome is impasse. When such a system is marked by the absence of an effective party system, the result is often virtual paralysis. Even a president blessed with a Congress controlled by his own party is not guaranteed the means to govern. CREEP, we must remember, was designed to permit Nixon to conduct his campaign free from the "stigma" of political party. This produced not only a presidential campaign run by amateur zealots, without the (presumably) sage and moderating presence of party professionals, but one that encouraged ticket-splitting by the electorate and little loyalty to the president on the part of congressional Republicans. The end result was a party system too fragmented and divided to enforce the discipline and control necessary to overcome the separation of powers.

This absence of accountability and discipline produces a politics centering upon personalities rather than policies and programs. Party platforms in the United States are relegated to obscurity within hours of their creation. Candidates avoid discussion of specific programs in favor of catchy slogans and thirty-second spot commercials attacking opponents. Hence elections in the United States often stand for little more than a reaffirmation of the electoral process itself.[26] A vote is, at best, the expression of support for someone and not something. In a political world in which elected officials are not linked with particular policies, voting ceases to be a means by which the citizenry intelligently communicates with government. The fact is that voting in the United States has become a civic obligation with little or no impact on the formation of the nation's public policy.

Moreover, the resignation of the president can hardly be considered an example of meaningful political accountability. Throughout the ebb and flow of the Watergate scandal, impeachment was viewed by most Americans as an act of parricide, when indeed it could have been considered an act of political regeneration designed to further the constitutional system.[27] The first resolution for impeaching the president was offered by Father Robert Drinan, a Democratic representative from Massachusetts, in July 1973 during the Ervin Committee hearings. The resolution was dismissed by congressional leaders of both parties as an irresponsible act, despite the abundant evidence of possible criminal activity in the Nixon White House and the erosion of public support for the president. Earlier, parliamentary manuverings had prevented Representative Paul McCloskey, a Republican, from even holding a one-hour discussion of impeachment on the floor of the House. The actual "process" by which Nixon was removed from office consisted in fact of two years of extraordinary events and tortuous proceedings leading to the resignation of a thoroughly discredited president. During Richard Nixon's last year in office—certainly during his last six months—the presidency ceased to operate and subordinates worked simply to keep the ship of state afloat. Not only does this represent a travesty of accountability, but one might be excused for harboring doubts as to whether a modern world power can afford months of drift while a president, to borrow a phrase of John Ehrlichman, twists slowly in the wind, devoid of public support and all capacity to govern.[28]

Ensuring the accountability of the executive branch for the transgressions of Watergate became, to an extraordinary degree, the responsibility of the judiciary. That it was the judiciary that ultimately called the president to task must have been particularly galling to Richard Nixon. During the 1968 presidential campaign, Nixon had stridently attacked the "liberal" decisions of the Supreme Court under Chief Justice Earl Warren, promising, if elected, to employ the appointment power to reshape the Supreme Court as well as the lower federal courts. Despite the opportunity to appoint four new Supreme Court justices and numerous lower court judges, Nixon found the judiciary to be suprisingly (and distressingly) independent of his executive will. Throughout a good deal of American history, the federal judiciary had normally aligned itself with the political agenda of the executive; Nixon, however, confronted a more independent judiciary, one less amenable to presidential control.[29] His frustrations with the judiciary continued throughout his term in office, the denouement being the refusal of a unanimous Court to uphold the president's claim of privilege in his attempt to avoid producing the incriminating tapes.[30] Nixon was thus confronted with the distinctly unpresidential choice of complying with a decision of the Supreme Court that in his view seriously compromised presidential power or asserting executive independence and facing certain impeachment.

Although Watergate produced numerous reforms of the political system, none are cause for great optimism. Perhaps the best known is the War Powers Resolution, passed in 1973 over President Nixon's veto. The purpose of the resolution was to limit the president's ability unilaterally to commit American troops to hostile action. The resolution provides that the president may commit troops to combat only in the event of a declaration of war, specific statutory authorization, or in response to a national emergency produced by an attack on the United States or its armed forces. Section 3 states that the president will "in every possible instance" consult with Congress prior to the instigation of hostilities. Absent a formal declaration of war, the president must report to Congress within forty-eight hours of the ordering of military operations and such operations cannot continue for more than six months without specific congressional authorization. While proponents have asserted that the measure ensures the "collective judgment of the Congress and the President," opponents of the measure contend that the resolution severely handicaps the president's ability to protect national security; the impact of the measure has been negligible. It has proven ineffective in limiting the initial commitment of troops by a president and every administration since its passage has violated the intent if not the letter of the resolution.[31]

In 1974 Congress passed the Budget and Impoundment Control Act, which sought both to control the presidential impoundment of appropriated funds and to provide Congress with a comprehensive budget process to balance executive control of the budget. On the impoundment issue, the act has been relatively successful, and none of Richard Nixon's successors has attempted to use the impoundment of funds as a means of establishing executive policy goals. The verdict on budget reform, however, is not quite so clear. Although the Congressional Budget Office (established by the act) has substantially improved the quality of information furnished to Congress in budget deliberations, the formal structures imposed by the act have not diminished the power of the president in the budget process. At times the process has worked as designed, with Congress dominating a procedure reflecting orderly, top-down budgeting. In 1981, however, President Reagan pushed through budget cuts of $35 billion and dominated the process in precisely the manner the authors of the act had hoped to avoid.[32] More often than not, the budget process, despite the recent reforms, simply reflects the interest group bargaining of American politics, with Congress unwilling to make the hard choices necessary to produce rational spending priorities. The budgetary system remains chaotic; the president and Congress respond to different constituencies and interests. Tinkering with changes in the process may have certain appeal, but the defects are structural and for the most part beyond band-aid remedies.[33]

These and a host of other "reforms" were predicated on an optimistic understanding of the American political system. Any particular problem was inevitably attributed to an "imbalance" in the system; if only the president would cooperate with Congress, the great constitutional design could function in the modern world. The suggested reform would promote the necessary cooperation. Once in place, however, the reform inevitably resulted in another perceived overload and the call would go out for Congress to cooperate responsibly with the president. Thus, for example, when confronted with evidence of the Nixon administration's clandestine activities, Congress sought to reform the intelligence system by reasserting a semblance of control. The Hughes-Ryan Amendment of 1974 required the president to inform eight different congressional committees of clandestine operations.[34] Responding to revelations of widespread abuses, the Senate and the House each set up a select committee on intelligence activities to exert legislative and budget control over the CIA and other intelligence organizations. Many critics contended that this was an overreaction, endangering the effectiveness of the president in matters of national security; the obsession with the abuses of the Nixon years had resulted in a pendulum swing too far toward congressional government. The balance, it was asserted, must be reset.

Or, perhaps, balance is part of the problem. Deep in the political souls of all Americans is a fear of government; hence the promise to "get government off our back" has been a sure-fire campaign theme for politicians of both parties, despite steady public support for a myriad of government programs and subsidies. For Americans, government is both the problem and the solution and we pay dearly for this political schizophrenia. Clinging to the structures of the eighteenth century, we nonetheless demand the services expected of modern governments. Professing faith in balance and countervailing powers, we nonetheless are contemptuous of a government of inaction. Unwilling to accept the inherent limitations of the venerated constitutional system, we turn to the president as the solution to our woes. Small wonder that our presidents have become masters of the media, expert at campaigning and manipulating the symbols of government but sadly lacking in the skill or power to govern effectively.

Watergate was a scandal motivated by the quest for political power. Although Richard Nixon left the office of the president a far wealthier man than when he entered it, Watergate is not a tale of personal aggrandizement. For the most part, money was simply a means to an end. Politics without parties is an enormously expensive undertaking and American candidates are continually beholden to the rich and powerful. From the perspective of the rich and powerful, buying a politician in the United States is a sound investment. Freed from the constraints of party discipline, the votes and influence of congressmen and senators are up for grabs. Buying consideration within the executive branch makes even greater financial sense, and the list of corporate officials found guilty of violating the restrictions on corporate campaign contributions during the Nixon years reads like a corporate Who's Who in the

Fortune 500.[35] The money generated, however, did not line pockets but rather funded the crimes of Watergate. In the eyes of the president's men, it was simply the cost of securing power in a system designed to forestall effective governing. To even the most jaded of citizens, however, the actions of the Nixon administration constituted crimes against the very integrity of the constitutional system. From either perspective, Watergate was the product of a bad bargain. Until that bargain is renegotiated, Watergate will tell us as much about our future as it does of our past.

Postscript—Iranian Arm Sales

The initial years of the Reagan administration were celebrated by many as the revitalization of the American presidency. The legacy of Watergate, as evidenced by the administrations of Gerald Ford and Jimmy Carter, appeared to be a presidency of diminished stature and political power. Institutional deadlock, the legacy of the framers that the proponents of the strong presidency had sought to overcome, settled in. The election of Ronald Reagan in 1980, however, reawakened the vision of the president as the white knight of the American constitutional system. The battles over the budget early in Reagan's first term once again demonstrated that a politically skillful president, armed with the support of the electorate, could overcome the demise of party and the fragmentation of power. Proclaiming a new vision and pride in America, the Reagan administration, powered by the extraordinary personal appeal of the occupant of the White House, set about the task of governing.

Six years later, the presidency of Ronald Reagan is in ruins. Inspired by the desire to secure the release of American hostages as well as by an obsession with the overthrow of the Sandinista government in Nicaragua, the White House of Ronald Reagan dealt arms for hostages, directed a secret and almost certainly illegal campaign to aid the contra insurgents, and, in response to public inquiries, sought to cover up the scope of both operations. To generations of Americans with poignant memories of Watergate, there is a distressing sense of *dèja vu* to the whole sordid affair.

Despite obvious differences, the Iran-Contra scandal and Watergate share common roots. Constrained by the very process of government and yet responsible for results, Reagan sought, as did Nixon a decade earlier, to circumvent the checks and balances of the Madisonian system. The NSC staff, ever loyal to presidential goals, was used not simply for policy formation but policy implementation as well. The institutions with traditional responsibility for implementing policy were seen as too slow, too public, and too hesitant about placing presidential aspirations above those of the institution. The net result was foreign policy initiatives carried forth by ideological zealots freed from the constraints of a professionalized bureaucracy and a system of electoral control.

Rather than a rebirth of executive skill and dominance, Ronald Reagan's presidency exposed—for those willing to look—the facade of light and shadows that characterizes so much of modern American government. Better than any of his immediate predecessors, Ronald Reagan *performed* as a president must. Anecdotes were substituted for facts, ideology for analysis, rhetoric for reality. Reagan effectively symbolized the myths of America and this became the source of his power. Efforts at governing became, in effect, performances with standings in popularity polls the measure of their success. The fact that Reagan was by profession an actor only made the performances that much more effective. Each issue and each initiative demanded a new performance and the success of the White House rested on the "power" of the performance and the illusion created.

Thus the Iran-Contra affair is best understood as an abuse not of power but of popularity. The men of Reagan's White House apparently believed that even the most outlandish policy could ultimately be sold to the public by the Great Communicator. Their arrogance lay in the belief that public support would sanction *any* presidential policy and that Ronald Reagan had a lock on that public opinion. Their understanding was that Reagan had overcome the constraints of the political system through his unique relationship with his constituency. In one sense they were not far from wrong; what they failed to perceive was how truly ephemeral the power of the presidency has become. Symbols are too easily tarnished. In a government of light and shadows, the penetrating glare of reality cannot long be tolerated.

As of this writing, the testimony of Lt. Col. Oliver North before the joint congressional committee investigating the Iran-Contra affair has just concluded. Although he professed the love of both his country and its constitution, the reality of North's words and deeds evidenced a profound contempt for the Madisonian system. Expressing only disdain for those constrained by the rule of law, the self-righteous North steadfastly maintained that aid to the Contras in Nicaragua and his international battle against the menace of communism justified the use of any means. What North apparently failed to grasp was that for liberal democracies in general, and for the United States in particular, ends can never justify the means. It is faith in process that distinguishes liberal democracies from other political regimes. The fact that during the bicentennial celebration of the United States Constitution, Oliver North became, even for a fleeting moment, a national hero is testimony to the surreal nature of American politics in the final quarter of the twentieth century.

The reports of the various investigatory committees have yet to be written. Unquestionably their conclusions will mirror that of the Tower Commission, that the fault lies not in the process but in the men and women who are part of that process. In a liberal democracy like the United States, there really can be no other conclusion. To fault the process is to call into question the legitimacy of the state itself. Hence the rituals of the investigation and redress of political scandals are another way in which we assert the primacy of the system. But in a larger sense, the system is at fault. For Reagan, like the men who preceded him, confronted a political structure in which governing is made next to impossible. Reagan, like Nixon, was destined to fail. Indeed the same fate awaits future presidents unless we are willing to confront the reality of a government of light and shadows.

NOTES

1. Henry Steele Commager traces the roots of Watergate to America's post WWII obsession with communism. Commager, "The Shame of the Republic," in *Watergate and the American Political Process*, ed. Ronald Pynn (New York: Praeger, 1975).

2. The *Washington Post* reported that Haldeman's name had been mentioned as one of the people controlling the fund in grand jury hearings investigating the original

break-in. This was incorrect; Haldeman had not been directly linked to the fund in the testimony given at the grand jury. Nevertheless, the gist of the *Post* story was correct; Haldeman did control the use of the slush fund.

3. See Kurt and Gladys Engel Lang, "Televised Hearings: The Impact Out There" in Pynn, *Watergate and the American Political Process.*

4. In his testimony John Dean revealed that the White House kept a list of political enemies that the administration hoped to punish—principally through the use of the IRS—after the 1972 election. Names on the list ranged from actor Paul Newman to football star Joe Namath to the president of Harvard University.

5. Charles Alan Wright, a professor at the University of Texas Law School, was a prominent constitutional scholar brought to the White House to argue the president's constitutional case. Wright returned to his law school position in the fall of 1973.

6. A former president of the American Bar Association and personal friend of Lyndon Johnson, Jaworski had been approached about the job of special prosecutor prior to the appointment of Archibald Cox. He had declined the position at that time because of a perceived lack of independence of the office from presidential control.

7. Report of the Committee on the Judiciary, House of Representatives, 93 Cong. 2d sess., R. 93–1305.

8. See Gary Wills, *Explaining America: The Federalist* (Harmondsworth: Penguin Books, 1981) on the impact of the Scottish Enlightenment on the founders. The emphasis on the individual and individual rights in the American context can be contrasted with those nations that drew inspiration from the French Revolution and from the communal spirit of the Continental Enlightenment.

9. Quoted in Gordon S. Wood, *The Creation of the American Republic* (New York: Norton, 1972), p. 22.

10. Amendments 15 (1870), 19 (1920), 26 (1971) explicitly expanded suffrage. Amendment 17 (1913) provided for direct election of senators, and Amendment 24 (1964) outlawed the poll tax.

11. See Richard Hofstadter, *The Idea of a Party System* (Los Angeles and Berkeley: University of California Press, 1969) for a description of the birth of American political parties.

12. Theodore Lowi, *The Personal President* (Ithaca, N.Y.: Cornell University Press, 1985), pp. 22–43.

13. Concerning the decline of political parties as well as other aspects of the American party system, see Gerald Pomper, ed., *Party Renewal in America* (New York: Praeger, 1980); William Chambers and Walter Dean Burnham, eds., *The American Party Systems,* 2d ed. (Oxford: Oxford University Press, 1975). These reforms, coupled with the fundamental fragmentation of power devised by the framers, have resulted in a far weaker party system than is found in almost any other liberal democracy.

14. See e.g., Herbert Croly, *The Promise of American Life* (New York: E. P. Dutton, 1963); Walter Lippmann, *Drift and Mastery* (Englewood Cliffs, N.J.: Prentice Hall, 1963).

15. For an excellent essay treating this development, see Samuel Huntington, "Congressional Responses to the Twentieth Century," in *Congress and America's Future,* ed. David Truman (Englewood Cliffs, N.J.: Prentice-Hall, 1965).

16. Quoted in Godfrey Hodgson, *All Things to All Men* (New York: Simon and Schuster, 1980), p. 64.

17. Thomas E. Cronin, *The State of the Presidency,* 2d ed. (New York: Little Brown, 1980).

18. The best account of these developments appears in Richard Nathan, *The Administrative Presidency* (New York: John Wiley, 1983).

19. Quoted in Thomas Cronin, "The Swelling of the Presidency" in Pynn, *Watergate and the American Political Process,* p. 208.

20. Quoted in Frank Kessler, *The Dilemma of Presidential Leadership: of Caretakers and Kings* (Englewood Cliffs, N.J.: Prentice-Hall, 1982), p. 93.

21. Such advisers are not subject to congressional approval and because they act in the

name of the president, they can invoke executive privilege when called to task before Congress. The result is that foreign policy decisions are shielded from congressional as well as public scrutiny.

22. In the domestic arena, the impoundment of funds was the functional equivalent to the unauthorized bombings in Indochina. Unhappy with many of the programs supported by Congress, Nixon simply refused to spend funds authorized by Congress, in effect giving the president a line item veto on domestic programs. See James P. Pfiffner, *The President, the Budget and the 1974 Budget Act* (Boulder, Colo.: Westview Press, 1979).

23. Quoted in Theodore White, *Breach of Faith: The Fall of Richard Nixon* (New York: Atheneum, 1975), p. 130.

24. The belief that Watergate is best understood as a systemic crisis is not intended to excuse Richard Nixon or the political thugs that were his closest advisers. The venality that Richard Nixon brought to American politics can never be excused and should never be forgotten. While his lieutenants in the White House and in CREEP received substantial prison terms, Nixon "suffered" on the shores of the Pacific at his estate (improved with substantial expenditures of taxpayers' funds). To many, Gerald Ford's full and complete pardon of Richard Nixon made a mockery of any claim that the law must apply equally to all. The fact that, as of this writing, Richard Nixon enjoys "elder statesman" status suggests we have collectively forgotten that justice, like mercy, must be evenhanded.

25. See Michael Malbin, ed., *Money and Politics in the United States* (Chatham, N.J.: Chatham, 1984) for a series of essays on the growth of political action committees and the effect of money on American politics.

26. Benjamin Ginsberg, *The Consequences of Consent* (Reading, Mass.: Addison-Wesley, 1982).

27. See Raoul Berger, *Impeachment: The Constitutional Problems* (Cambridge: Harvard University Press, 1973).

28. The selection of Gerald Ford as Vice President further illustrates the weakness of the system at work. On the eve of his appointment as Vice President, Gerald Ford was an undistinguished member of the House from Grand Rapids, Michigan, who had become House Minority Leader on the basis of his party loyalty. Said one Democratic senator during the hearings on the Ford appointment: "Nixon can't last. Jerry Ford President? There are other Republicans we could agree to—Nelson Rockefeller, even Barry Goldwater. We know who they are. Who is Jerry Ford? If we had a parliamentary system, he wouldn't be President." Quoted in Elizabeth Drew, *Washington Journal: The Events of 1973–1974* (New York: Vintage Books, 1976), p. 92.

29. For a description and explanation of this independence, see Mark Silverstein and Benjamin Ginsberg, "The Supreme Court and the New Politics of Judicial Power," *Political Science Quarterly* 102 (Fall 1987): 371.

30. See United States v. Nixon, 418 U.S. 683 (1974). Justice Rehnquist, a Nixon appointee, did not take part in the decision.

31. E.g., the Ford Administration and the *Mayaguez* incident, the Carter administration and the attempted rescue of the hostages in Iran, and the Reagan Administration in Granada, Lebanon, and El Salvador.

32. And in so doing generated one of the finest studies of American politics. See, William Greider, *The Education of David Stockman*, rev. ed. (New York: New American Library, 1986). On the Budget Reform Act, see Howard Schuman, *Politics and the Budget* (Englewood Cliffs, N.J.: Prentice-Hall, 1984).

33. The passage of the Gramm-Rudman-Hollings Deficit Reduction Act, a mandatory balanced budget plan providing for automatic spending cuts in the event Congress failed to reach agreement on cuts, is testimony to this inability and the failure of Gramm-Rudman meaningfully to alter budget priorities is testimony to the inability of the executive and the Congress to work together toward common ends.

34. In 1980 the number of committees was reduced to two.

35. See e.g., Leon Jaworski, *The Right and the Power* (Pleasantville, N.Y.: Reader's Digest Press, 1976) pp. 283–92.

2 • Canada: The RCMP Scandals

REG WHITAKER

On the morning of 5 October 1970, a group of intruders armed with revolvers and submachine guns broke into the Montreal home of James Richard Cross, the British trade commissioner. Cross was dragged into a stolen taxicab that sped away. Shortly after, a Montreal radio station was contacted by telephone and police directed to a communiqué from a cell of the Front de libération du Québec (FLQ), an urban terrorist group seeking the independence of Quebec from the Canadian federal state. A set of political demands was made in exchange for Cross's life. This kind of event, familiar enough in the contemporary world, was unprecedented in Canada. From it a series of events,[1] dramatic and tragic, unfolded over the next weeks that were to entail certain long-term consequences for a country whose self-image was best described in the title of an anthology that appeared at the same time as the October Crisis was unleashed: *The Peaceable Kingdom.*

Tensions between English- and French-speaking Canadians had been an ever-present theme in Canada's "peaceable kingdom" throughout its history, but the decade of the 1960s had witnessed a sharp escalation of demands for the autonomy of Quebec, the one province with a Francophone majority. In the 1960s Quebec experienced a so-called Quiet Revolution of rapid modernization. A broadly based and self-confident Quebec nationalist movement was given political expression by Quebec provincial governments, which assumed wide new economic responsibilities and made far-reaching demands for greater provincial powers within the Canadian federation. At the same time there emerged a small but highly visible radical separatist movement, passionately seeking national independence for Quebec, which included some elements willing to use the violent methods of urban terrorism to force the issue.

The terrorist element, grouped under the banner of the FLQ, made its major bid to precipitate a "revolutionary" crisis in October 1970.

Six days after the Cross kidnapping, the crisis escalated when another FLQ cell kidnapped the Minister of Labour in the Quebec provincial government, Pierre Laporte. The air was rife with rumors of mass mobilization of students and workers by the FLQ, of further violent actions, of the possible collapse of the Quebec government. The Canadian Army was ordered into the streets of Quebec, and the War Measures Act (a draconian emergency powers act employed by the national government during two world wars to quell internal dissent and command civilian mobilization) was invoked on the grounds of an "apprehended insurrection." Extraordinary powers of search, arrest, and detention were given the police, and selective press censorship was imposed. One day later Pierre Laporte was murdered by the FLQ. Some five hundred persons were detained over the next few weeks. In December the cell holding Cross was discovered and the kidnappers surrendered their hostage in exchange for safe passage to Cuba. Later the members of the other cell were captured and charged with kidnapping and murder. The emergency powers were allowed to lapse in the spring of 1971. There were no further acts of separatist terrorism and the FLQ eventually faded into memory.

Canada appeared in the aftermath of the October Crisis to have awakened from a brief but intensely vivid nightmare. During the peak of the crisis, public support for the federal government's tough and extraordinary actions, both in English Canada and in Quebec, had hit commanding heights of approval rarely if ever achieved by governments in peacetime. Yet second thoughts were not long in coming. Opposition parliamentarians, who had lined up to pass the emergency powers, began to talk of how they had been stampeded by unfounded scare tactics. Books and articles appeared that suggested that the magnitude of the crisis had been much overblown, that the FLQ had been a tiny organization without mass support that was not worth the steamroller that had been applied to it.[2] The realization that basic civil liberties could be swept away, even if only temporarily, by a state invoking a threat to national security, which that government itself defined, on the basis of information kept secret from the public as well as its political opponents in Parliament, grew into a reproach against the government that had unleashed these special powers under what many now felt was a dubious pretext. Separatist sentiment did not diminish but went into a new and more serious phase, that of a legitimate parliamentary challenge to the existing constitutional basis of Quebec's provincial status. In 1976 a provincial party dedicated to achieving legal sovereignty for Quebec, the Parti Québécois (which had contested its first election in 1970), swept to office in a convincing victory. The federal government and its internal security agency, the Royal Canadian Mounted Police (RCMP), were faced with more difficult and complex questions of dealing with legitimate dissent seeking the same formal goals as the violent terrorist movement had sought with very different means.

The RCMP Scandals of the 1970s

The October Crisis, dramatic as it was, is only the background to the RCMP scandals of the 1970s. There was no public scandal, as such, associated with police behavior during the crisis. There was a perceived lack of competence exhibited, but there was no public evidence of the security forces taking the law into their own hands or of their running out of political control. Some—though a very few—Canadians said at the time that it was scandalous that such excessive arbitrary powers of seizure, detention, and censorship could be invoked in peacetime, and their ranks grew modestly in the next few years. By 1977–78, however, a series of revelations of RCMP illegality, violence, agent provocateur tactics of infiltration, and the disruption of political parties and groups, and highly questionable methods of wiretapping, electronic surveillance, mail-opening, coercive enlistment of informers, and unauthorized access to confidential government files on private citizens, burst onto the public agenda by means of sensational media reports. Two rival government commissions of inquiry, one in Quebec and one in Ottawa, took thousands of pages of evidence, as the revelations continued into the early 1980s. There was no central focus to these scandals, except that they all involved accusations of unlawful activity on the part of the RCMP and they all involved the question of the government's knowledge and approval of these activities in excess of statutory authority. Most, although not all, of the illegal activities seemed to be centered on Quebec. This is in fact the thread that connects the events of the October Crisis to the later RCMP scandals. In the wake of the crisis, machinery was set up at the highest levels of the federal government to coordinate an attack on separatism. The RCMP either was told or assumed (the point was later to be a matter of much dispute) that "counterterrorism" might involve actions that went beyond the law.

The first public intimations of trouble came in the summer of 1974, when it was revealed that an RCMP constable had been injured when a bomb that he had been attempting to plant at the Montreal home of an executive of a major supermarket chain had exploded prematurely. This was not a political bombing; rather the constable was apparently doing freelance work for a local mafioso. At his trial, however, he hinted darkly that he "done worse things for the RCMP than plant bombs." Charges were made that the Mountie was linked to an earlier unsolved break-in at a left-wing Quebec news agency where files had been stolen. Little came of this until the Quebec government (after 1976 under the direction of the Parti Québécois) began a criminal investigation. In 1977 three RCMP officers pleaded guilty to a charge of failing to obtain a search warrant. The Quebec government decided to pursue the matter further and appointed a special commission of inquiry (the Keable Commission, named after its chairman). The federal government consulted with the RCMP and declared that the news agency break-in was an isolated act. Three weeks later a chagrined minister responsible for the RCMP discovered that the force had been less than forthright with him and announced that a federal royal commission (known as the McDonald Commission) would investigate growing allegations of RCMP wrongdoing. The floodgates were open, as revelation after revelation poured forth. Among acts for which the RCMP were found responsible were the following:

(1) In 1972 the offices of a left-wing Quebec news agency were illegally broken into and over two hundred files were stolen.

(2) In 1970 the Toronto offices of a left-wing group organizing a national conference of poor people had been broken into, its files stolen, and a fire lit. The files mysteriously fell into the hands of the RCMP.

(3) In the wake of the October Crisis, false communiqués purporting to issue from the FLQ had been written and distributed by the RCMP. One in particular had urged further violent action and denounced a former FLQ leader who had turned away from violence. In addition, the RCMP had been aware that a number of communiqués from one cell of the FLQ had in fact issued from an undercover agent being run by the Montreal police, but they did not inform the federal authorities of this fact in their reporting on separatist activity.

(4) Informers within the FLQ had been enlisted by coercive, gangster-like, tactics in 1971.

(5) In 1971 an "enemies list" of twenty-one federal civil servants, compiled by the RCMP, said to constitute an "extra-parliamentary opposition," was circulated to cabinet ministers by the solicitor general with the advice that they not be employed or promoted.[3] The list was also forwarded to four "friendly" foreign intelligence agencies.

(6) A privately owned barn had been burned in 1972 to prevent a meeting between the FLQ and the U.S. Black Panthers.

(7) Dynamite had been stolen in 1972 in an attempt to discredit a political group.

(8) An ongoing operation had enlisted postal workers in unauthorized mail openings.

(9) Access had been illegally gained to government files on private citizens and these were used against them.

(10) "Dirty tricks," including the circulation of forged letters and documents, had been carried out to disrupt the activities of left-wing groups and to discredit certain individuals.

(11) Wiretaps had been used in excess of the relatively tolerant limitations imposed on such activities under Canadian law, and electronic surveillance devices ("bugs") had been surreptitiously planted in places where dissident political groups met. In one case a paid RCMP undercover agent had secretly bugged the solicitor general, the cabinet minister "responsible" for the RCMP, on his superiors' suggestion that the minister was "leaning too far to the left."

(12) Civil servants and applicants for civil service positions had been security screened in the early 1970s to keep out those with "separatist sympathies, associations and activities," even though the security agency had no authority to apply these criteria.

(13) In 1975 the Montreal offices of the Parti Québécois had been broken into and the computerized membership lists of the party had been stolen and copied.

(14) The RCMP had amassed a vast amount of material on Canadians engaged in legitimate political activities whom the police suspected might be undercover Soviet agents. These included members of the New Democratic Party, which was the party with the third largest Parliamentary representation and which from time to time held office in various provinces; senior civil servants; and, most unsettling of all to the government, prominent members of the perennially governing Liberal Party.[4]

The above list is not exhaustive, but it gives some idea of the dimensions of the problem posed by the RCMP, which was unfolding before the public in the 1970s. To compound matters, the information did not come out all at once but in fits and starts, the process often being characterized by a federal government that first denied, then admitted the allegations, which fought (sometimes successfully, sometimes not) to prevent evidence from being made public, and which seemed at times to be covering up for the RCMP, and at other times to be denying responsibility for their actions. A bitter rivalry was struck between the Ottawa government and the Keable Commission in Quebec, owing to the federal perception of the Parti Québécois government as the separatist enemy: the federal government's constitutional powers were exercised to impede and diffuse the Keable inquiry. In short, revelations of wrongdoing were spilling out in a somewhat chaotic political and administrative atmosphere. The dimensions of the scandal seemed elastic and obscure.

What was clear was that the RCMP had obviously and repeatedly violated the laws of the land and engaged in activities that could be the subject of criminal proceedings, and which certainly constituted subversive (to put an old term to new use) intervention in the political life of the nation. The common thread running through all the RCMP actions in question was the invasion of the private realm by an agency of state power—in an illegitimate manner. When the state had invoked the powers of the War Measures Act during the October Crisis, it radically extended the scope of public intrusion into the private sphere in a manner that was procedurally legitimate, although politically suspect. With the lapse of the emergency powers, the surreptitious extension of police activity within the private sphere raised serious questions for liberal democracy, questions of a different order than those raised by the use of emergency powers. Inevitably, the questions became those associated with scandal, in the sense that the editors of this volume have specified in the introduction: "the presence of any activity that seeks to increase political power at the expense of process and procedure."[5]

While there is no evidence that the police had engaged in such activities for the purposes of private gain or enrichment, there was apparent reason to believe that the private ideological standards of the secret police were being imposed upon the community. Either the RCMP considered itself above the law—in which case the government had, through negligence or incompetence, allowed its security agency to go out of control—or the RCMP was reflecting the wishes of its political masters, in which case the government itself was out of control. Either outcome was scandalous in a liberal democracy.

To understand the manner in which the RCMP scandals were handled, and to what effect on Canada and Quebec, it is perhaps useful first to survey briefly some of the salient points of the Canadian constitutional and political system.

The Canadian Constitutional and Political System

In formal terms, the Canadian constitutional system is a hybrid of British parliamentary government and of the American federal division of powers. When the governing elites of the British North American colonies commenced negotiations in the 1860s to arrive at a constitutional settlement upon which a political union could be founded, it became apparent that two divergent tendencies had to be reconciled. The first, stemming from imperial loyalism, the need for economic consolidation, and fear of the military power of the victorious forces of the Union in the American Civil War, pointed to a strong central authority. The second arose from the desire for local autonomy and the need to accommodate the coexistence of two cultural and linguistic communities, English and French, and two religious communities, Protestant and Catholic (largely, but not entirely, overlapping with the linguistic communities). The compromise finally arrived at in the British North American Act of 1867 (the constitutional basis of the Canadian Confederation until 1982) was to graft together parliamentary government with federalism. Powers were divided between federal and provincial jurisdictions, but at each level there was no separation of powers between the executive and the legislature. Centralism and decentralism are the persistent constitutional antinomies of this system.[6]

The national government was given constitutional and fiscal powers decisively superior to those of the provinces, yet despite the centralist efforts of national governments in the first decades of confederation, the actual practice of Canadian federalism has evolved toward one of the most decentralized models to be found in the world today. There are many complex reasons for this evolution, but for the purposes of this study, the importance of Quebec and/or French Canada may be particularly cited.

The original confederation "bargain" struck between the English and French Canadian elites—which itself reflected an earlier bargain arising out of the conquest of New France by the British in 1760—involved a trade-off of linguistic, religious, and cultural autonomy for the French Canadians for economic freedom for the English-speaking commercial class to pursue continental development. By the early 1960s this ancient bargain had collapsed as new nationalist forces in Quebec sought economic powers for a modernized provincial state (the so-called Quiet Revolution). The 1960s witnessed a series of victories for the Quebec government in relation to Ottawa over the control of pension funds, taxation, medicare, and so forth. Some of these battles resulted in a broader diffusion of powers to all provinces, some led to de facto "special status" for Quebec. At the same time, a violent extraparliamentary separatist movement was growing on the fringes, which burst into a full-scale explosion with the October Crisis of 1970 and the invocation of the War Measures Act. During the 1970s the issue was polarized between a faction of the Quebec elite under Liberal Prime Minister Pierre Trudeau, which opted for "French Power" by means of a federal government pursuing aggressive policies of bilingualism and widened career opportunities at the national level for Francophones, and another faction that opted for a parliamentary road to Quebec independence, under the Parti Québécois, which was elected to provincial office in 1976. In 1980 the question was finally resolved when a referendum on sovereignty proposed by the PQ was defeated by 60 percent of Quebec voters. The backdrop to the RCMP scandals of the 1970s reviewed in this article must thus be seen as a very serious crisis of national and state legitimacy, deepening throughout the decade. Quebec nationalism, which for over a century had been a factor driving the Canadian system toward decentralism, was by the 1970s a force threatening the continued viability of the federal state itself.[7]

Quebec was not the only force leading toward the attenuation of federal power. The wealthier English Canadian provinces traditionally had been forces for decentralization as well, and this tendency had become very pronounced during the 1970s in the course of rancorous federal-provincial struggles. Although they posed less of a legitimacy challenge than did the independence movement in Quebec, the emergence of rival provincial states with semi-autonomous economic bases and extensive and sophisticated bureaucracies transformed federal-provincial relations into something almost akin to international diplomacy between sovereign states.[8]

Relations between governments and interest groups tend to be rather diffuse in Canada, with neither the state nor capital or labor possessing concerted voices to bring to the negotiating table. Instead of broad sectoral bargains, there is a welter of special interest deals, often negotiated directly between middle-level bureaucrats and particular interests. Power thus tends to be fragmented in the Canadian system.[9]

Yet paradoxically there is another, apparently contradictory, tendency that is central to the Canadian experience: executive dominance. Even by the standards of British parliamentary government, legislatures have been weak historically in relation to the executive arm. Both conservatives and reformers in the nineteenth century were contesting the same prize: command over the executive, with accompanying control over extensive patronage powers. One-party dominance in Ottawa was checked not by strong opposition in parliament but by the growth of rival strong executives in the provinces commanding their own extensive patronage networks.[10] In the twentieth century, patronage redistribution has been giving way to bureaucratic redistribution, but one-party dominance of rival bureaucratic states has been just as characteristic. The Liberal Party has been in power in Ottawa for approximately 80 percent of the years since the end of World War I; the Conservatives have governed the largest province, Ontario, uninterruptedly from 1943 to 1984. So enduring and so close have been the relations between governing parties and their permanent civil services that some observers have pointed to a virtual fusion of party and state. The division of these powerful executive-dominated bureaucracies into federal and provincial spheres has called forth "executive federalism" as a mechanism for coordination. Crucial decisions for the political system are decided in direct negotiation between representatives of the various governments; legislatures, opposition parties, the press, and the public are at best peripheral to this process of executive diplomacy. The Canadian federal system is thus a "government of governments" in a much more effective sense than it ever has been, as a former prime minister claimed, a "community of communities."

This curious combination of executive domination and fragmentation is explicable within the broader context of the heavy reliance the Canadian system has placed on elite accommodation as the means of integrating the two national communities. Resting comfortably within a dominant antidemocratic political discourse in the last century, and rather less comfortably within an increasingly democratized discourse in the latter half of this century, the theory of elite accommodation suggests that a nationally segmented people will tend to fall into communal conflict (once involving religion, now language) if they are not kept relatively separate at the mass level. Integration then falls to the respective elites on whom the nation-saving burden rests.[11]

Since this theory is notably weak in empirical support, its practitioners may be ideologists as much as analysts: Canadian variants of the elite pluralist theorists of American political science. There is, however, no gainsaying the degree to which elite accommodation describes a certain reality concerning the way Canadian politicians have traditionally operated and how political institutions have reflected and reinforced this elitist style. Yet elite accommodation has been coming under increasing strain in Canada, from two separate directions.

First has been the breakdown among elites themselves, who have become increasingly competitive rather than cooperative: the adherence for a time of significant sections of the Quebec elite to a rupture with English Canadian elites is the most spectacular sign of this change. On the other hand, there have been growing demands for greater popular participation in government and more bypassing of traditional elite "representatives" and "spokesmen" in favor of direct participation by previously unrepresented or underrepresented groups.[12]

The uneasy dominance of elite accommodation is illustrated by the process of constitutional revision in 1980–81. In the aftermath of the defeat of the sovereignty referendum in Quebec, Prime Minister Trudeau launched a protracted and bitter federal-provincial struggle to achieve a "made-in-Canada" constitution.[13] The final result—the Canada Act of 1982—was a compromise thrashed out between the prime minister and the nine Anglophone provincial premiers (the Quebec government refused to sign). It has never been submitted to ratification by the people, and indeed a provision for constitutional amendment by popular referendum was dropped at the insistence of the premiers. Elite bargaining continued to rest at the heart of this fundamental process of constitution-making. Yet the most important change in content in the revised document was the addition of a Charter of Rights, which is already altering the balance of legal power between the state and the individual and thus the procedural basis of politics. Moreover, the hermetic process of bargaining was accompanied by sometimes passionate popular movements to strengthen elements of the Charter of Rights on behalf of certain groups, especially women and native peoples.[14]

Even while elite dominance has been attenuated under the pressure of democratization, the weight of the past continues to be felt in the institutional apparatus of government and in a political culture in slow transition. There is an ongoing tradition of scholarship, especially among Americans looking at Canada from the outside, which stresses the greater elitism and conservatism of Canadian values as compared to those of the United States—a thesis restated many times by Seymour Martin Lipset and given recent voice by the sociologist Edgar Z. Friedenberg under the title *Deference to Authority.*[15] Certainly deference to authority is a value appropriate to a political system featuring a high degree of executive dominance and stressing the importance of elite accommodation and limited popular participation. It is not an unchanging characteristic of the political culture, however, but one in a certain decline during the period of this study. The course of the RCMP scandals is best understood against this changing backdrop.

National Security and the RCMP

Executive dominance has played an especially important role in relation to the particular subject of the RCMP scandals—national security. If liberalism seeks to protect the individual from the power of the state, it is not only democracy that tries to "capture and employ the power of the state to benefit the community as a whole."[16] Canada illustrates the conservative uses of state power in the name of the community.

It is perhaps odd that a country that has never been imminently threatened by foreign armies (at least since the American invasion in the War of 1812) and has never been confronted by a serious revolutionary or insurrectionary movement from within should have placed such a high premium historically on the defense of national security. The exercise of a high degree of administrative discretion (Crown prerogatives) by the national government has rarely been challenged by provincial governments when it is invoked in the name of national security, even when this involves infringements on provincial jurisdiction or interventions in the private sector. "National security" has usually conjured up the nearly unanimous consent of all governments and all corporate interests: especially in so far as it has generally been invoked against a left-wing threat (real or imagined) to capitalist hegemony or against unpopular ethnic minorities such as the Japanese-Canadians during World War II. Until the entrenchment of the Charter of Rights in the new constitution in 1982 there were few protections for the civil rights of individuals affected by the often arbitrary and sometimes brutal exercise of extraordinary powers under the rubric of national security.[17] And criticism was stilled by shrouding actions in a thick fog of administrative secrecy. In this area, executive dominance has tradionally been exercised with a vengeance.

The role of the RCMP has been crucial. Anomalously both a regular police force (employed in eight of the ten provinces and within direct federal jurisdiction) and an internal security and intelligence agency, the RCMP approached its role in national security with a paramilitary discipline and with the benefit of the near-mythical legitimacy of the Mounties—perhaps the most quintessential symbol of Canada itself in the popular mind.[18] Buttressed by innumerable romanticized depictions in popular fiction and Hollywood movies, the RCMP traded on its iconographic image to consolidate the position of its security service as Canada's secret police. Within the structures of government, the Mounties exploited the advantages of administrative secrecy and their privileged international links to American, British, and other foreign intelligence agencies to deflect civilian control over their activities and even on occasion to compel the elected politicians to refrain from projected courses of action of which the Mounties disapproved.[19]

During World War II, Canada not only mobilized for total war but built a formidable national security state for internal control. Under the authority of the War Measures Act—an emergency powers law that far exceeds in scope similar powers in either the United States or Britain—newspapers and magazines were censored, banned, or shut down; political parties and private associations were declared illegal; and large numbers of persons were rounded up and thrown into internment camps. Most notoriously, the entire Japanese-Canadian population of the West Coast was forcibly removed to camps in the interior, but German and Italian Canadians, Communists, Nazis, trade union officials, and many others found themselves behind barbed wire. It is interesting that even after Canada had become an ally of the USSR in the war against fascism, the Communist Party and its front organizations remained major targets upon which the RCMP focused much of its antisubversive effort.[20]

The war had no sooner ended than the cold war began, and in Canada it began with greater alacrity than in other countries. In September of 1945, a cypher clerk in the Soviet Embassy in Ottawa, Igor Gouzenko, secretly defected with documents implicating a number of Canadian Communists and sympathizers in Soviet espionage. Under the authority of the War Measures Act, still in force, a secret order in council was enacted, with the knowledge of the prime minister and only two other cabinet ministers, under which predawn raids were carried out in February 1946. Thirteen persons were detained incommunicado, without charges and without counsel, and interrogated night and day in the RCMP barracks. They were subsequently hauled before secret hearings of a royal commission, still unrepresented by counsel. This commission eventually published a lengthy report, widely distributed in Canada and abroad, which named twenty-six persons as spies or agents.[21] In subsequent legal proceedings, five people were never charged, ten people were convicted in Canada, one person was convicted in Britain, and ten people were either acquitted or had the charges withdrawn. It is instructive to contrast these events with the later anticommunist congressional investigations in the United States. In Canada control was exercised decisively by the executive.

This tendency can be seen even more clearly in the establishment of the machinery for a permanent national security state to conduct the domestic cold war. The hunt for alleged communists and fellow-travelers within the civil service that so convulsed Washington in the late 1940s and early 1950s was conducted in Ottawa under the quiet and effective control of the executive, using the RCMP as its investigative agency. Would-be McCarthyites in the parliamentary opposition and the media were simply denied information on the grounds of administrative secrecy. Yet a purge was taking place, based on anonymous informers and undercover agents and most of the paraphernalia familiar to McCarthy-era America.[22] The ruling elites in Ottawa were, however, careful not to allow matters to get so far out of hand as to endanger their own positions, as had happened to the Truman Democrats in the United States whose public fanning of the flames of anticommunism had served only to engulf themselves. So the purges and blacklists were administered behind the scenes from the top down, and the Ottawa elites successfully rode the tiger without ending up inside.[23]

Civil servants became primary targets of RCMP investigation and surveillance, but there was another huge class of persons who also fell under the jurisdiction of the secret police: immigrants and would-be immigrants. A vast operation to screen out communists and left-wingers among the millions of postwar applicants for immigration was set in motion in the late 1940s, and this effort drew the RCMP into close liaison with security forces abroad, including those of some repressive right-wing regimes. Those who filtered through could be denied citizenship on the basis of RCMP reports and deported. Checks were also made on the Canadian relatives who sponsored immigrants.[24] Extensive lists were compiled and maintained by the RCMP on persons to be interned in the event of war or national emergency. Added to the business-as-usual activities of Mountie surveillance of trade unions, ethnic organizations, peace movements, civil liberties associations, and youth groups (among others), security dossiers on individual Canadians in the files of the secret police grew over the cold war era to the point where a Royal Commission of Inquiry found that they covered some eight hundred thousand persons in the late 1970s (quite a handsome catch out of a population of just over twenty-two million!) Very little interest was ever shown by the Mounties in right-wing groups, but for a quarter of a century after the war, communism was their primary, if not exclusive, obsession. In this the RCMP was reflecting the pervading concerns of the American, and to a lesser extent, the British, security and intelligence networks. The cold war era has seen the ever-closer integration of Canadian national security policy into that of the United States; the Mounties were willing conduits for the importation of U.S. concerns and U.S. standards.

By the time of the October Crisis in 1970, the exercise of wide administrative discretion by the federal government in the name of national security and the place of the RCMP as the primary agent of security policy might have seemed fairly secure. In fact, the basis of postwar internal security policy was eroding beneath the surface. During the 1960s the cold war consensus, which in the 1950s had united Liberals, Conservatives, and social democrats, had undergone a considerable fragmentation. Disgust at the Vietnam War and fading faith in U.S. stability and purpose were not perhaps characteristic of the majority of Canadians, but they were expressed by a vocal and articulate minority. Political dissent on the left widened well beyond the Communist Party—into New Left manifestations, peace movements, student protests, and, most significantly of all, a strident and aggressively radical separatist movement in Quebec. The RCMP were singularly ill-prepared to tackle these anarchic manifestations, given their time-honored obsession with communism (itself an aging victim of the new radicalism). The October Crisis threw the RCMP's inadequacies into sharp relief. Always a predominantly "Anglo" force, they had few resources to call upon in French-speaking Quebec; indeed, they had few francophone officers in the security service. The intelligence that they could offer to the government on the terrorist *Front du Libération Québécois* when the kidnapping crisis broke was not apparently very impressive.

At the height of the crisis, the federal cabinet had assembled for a two-hour briefing by the RCMP about the FLQ and its "apprehended insurrection." Ministers (many of whom, starting with Prime Minister Pierre Trudeau, were themselves experienced and intelligent observers of Quebec political life) later described the RCMP briefing as "pathetic," "a farce," and "unbelievable."[25] RCMP intelligence was very poor on Quebec, despite the fact that there had been seven years of bombings and other terrorist activities on the part of the FLQ prior to the October Crisis. Relations of the RCMP with the Quebec police were poor. But there was a deeper problem. As the closest journalistic observer of the RCMP security service has written: "The situation was aggravated by the fact that the WASPish RCMP was not at home in Quebec. Information was gathered (partly) by Anglophones in Montreal and analyzed (almost exclusively) by Anglophones in Ottawa. It was not the best way to probe French-Canadian nationalism in Quebec."[26]

A cartoon in a Quebec newspaper at the time showed a federal cabinet minister carrying the telephone directories of all the major cities in the province. "Nous avons maintenant," he was explaining, "des listes de suspectes!" ("At last we have some lists of suspects!")

More than this, the RCMP were to find that investigating separatism in Quebec raised a very different response than investigating communism: important and articulate sectors of Quebec society were sympathetic to the idea of independence and resentful and suspicious of a federal government agency attempting to infiltrate and disrupt groups seeking to further the idea. Finally, and broadly across the country, there was a growing civil libertarian tendency in public opinion coming out of the 1960s. Governments were beginning to feel pressures to recognize individual rights as against the arbitrary actions of the state. The American experiences of Watergate and the congressional investigations of the CIA, extensively reported in Canada, also served very importantly to demystify hitherto sacrosanct conceptions of national security. The climate in the country was becoming less conducive to the unimpeded pursuit of national security at all costs.

The position of the RCMP had been eroding within the government as well. A Royal Commission on Security had reported to the government in 1968 and recommended the transfer of the security service out of the RCMP, to be placed under civilian auspices. This recommendation drew fierce and frantic resistance from the Mounties. Eventually, they were able to cash in their credits with the bureaucrats and politicians with whom they had worked so closely for so long. The "civilianization" proposal was shelved. As a compromise, a civilian with hard-line views and many years of experience in security was put at the head of the security service. For the RCMP, however, the handwriting was on the wall. Thus on the eve of the public disclosures of the RCMP follies of the 1970s, the once unassailable position of the force in the Canadian political system had already been undermined. All that was needed was a strong push: ironically it came from the force itself.

How the Scandals Were Handled

There is little reason to believe that similar excesses of the security service had not been committed in earlier years when the Communist Party was its major target under the legitimating cloak of the cold war consensus. Although that consensus had broken down by the 1970s, for reasons suggested in the previous section, it seemed that many actors in the political process in the late 1970s continued to behave as if little had changed since the 1950s. The immediate response of each of the three major national political parties to the scandals was instinctively to follow through traditional patterns set in the early cold war era.

The party system in Canadian national politics is something of a hybrid of the brokerage-style American party system with elements of the European class-politics model grafted on. The two main parties, the Liberals and the Progressive Conservatives, make broad cross-class appeals to the electorate on relatively nonprogrammatic but pro-business platforms and both tend to govern from the center. The New Democratic Party (NDP) is a social democratic party dependent organizationally and financially on trade unions belonging to the Canadian Labour Congress, the largest union federation, but it has never yet been able to better its third-party status in Parliament.[27]

The governing Liberals had been in national office, with two brief exceptions (1957–1963 and for nine months in 1979–80) since 1935. They were the party that had built and defended the national security state during World War II and the cold war. Senior civil servants closely identified with Liberal governments over the years have been intimately involved in the liaison between the RCMP and Liberal politicians in relation to national security arrangements. Moreover, in the context of the 1970s, the Liberals, headed by a strong Quebec Prime Minister, Pierre Trudeau, backed by a powerful team of pro-federalist ministers from Quebec, had every apparent reason to defend a security service that was finally directing its attention to the separatist threat. In 1975 the Liberal government issued a secret cabinet directive laying out guidelines for the security service's mandate, which permitted it not only to investigate but to "deter, prevent and counter" persons and groups about whom it entertained reasonable doubts: a very broad mandate indeed. The Liberals were also worried that any deep investigation of the scandals might turn to the events of October 1970, which they wanted to remain a closed book for a good long time.[28] Consequently, the Liberals often appeared to be covering up the scandals as they broke, particularly when successive solicitors-general first denied, then shamefacedly were forced to admit damaging allegations. At times leading Liberal spokespersons, including the prime minister (who had a previous reputation in Quebec as a philosophic liberal and formidable civil libertarian) issued off-the-cuff *obiter dicta* on the role of the police in national security matters that seemed to suggest a quasi-authoritarian mentality.

Yet despite appearances, the Liberals were more ambivalent about the issue than might have been expected. Regardless of the long and intimate association between the Liberals and the security forces, there was also some distance and even coolness and suspicion. The RCMP, like all western security and intelligence agencies, was permeated with a hard-line anticommunist ideology, which tended to place its members on the extreme right of the political spectrum. The Liberals, despite their lengthy record as cold warriors and ready allies of the United States in the western bloc, were seen by many of the security police as "soft on Communism." A former Prime Minister, Lester Pearson, had been the subject of allegations of pro-Soviet activities leaked to the press by the U.S. Senate Committee on Internal Security in the 1950s.[29] Pierre Trudeau was definitely viewed by many in the Mounties as a security risk, if not a closet communist (he had been involved in left-wing causes in the 1950s and had made visits to Russia and China during the coldest days of the cold war; he had even been barred at one time from visiting the United States under the antisubversive clauses of the McCarran-Walter Act). In 1974 the Liberal government had brought in specialists from the military to sweep the offices of cabinet ministers to determine if the RCMP had been planting listening devices. Since one of the important results of the scandals of the 1970s was the chasing of the RCMP out of the security field in 1984 by a Liberal government, this distance between the party and the force must be taken into account in the analysis. It did manifest itself from early on in a convenient fallback position, which the government could adopt when faced with irrefutable evidence of police wrongdoing: lawbreaking was unfortunate but it had not been authorized by the politicians.

This must also be balanced against the obvious fact that sections of the Liberal Party did not share some of the leaderhip's coolness toward the RCMP. Many perceived that public opinion was predominantly favorable to the police. This indeed was believed by all parties and was supported by polling results; even though specific sections of the public were now critical of the Mounties, the majority were still strongly in support of them. Finally—and this facet of the question must be faced—there were Liberal cabinet ministers who were simply afraid of the secret police. It had become publicly known that the RCMP had been accumulating dossiers on ministers that might include personally embarrassing material.[30]

If the Liberals were highly ambivalent about handling the affair, the official opposition in the House of Commons, the Conservative Party, could afford the luxury of playing both sides of the issue. The Tories took the politically expedient view that the RCMP were blameless and that what had gone wrong had gone wrong because the Liberal government had misused the police. This allowed them to criticize the scandals while maintaining the RCMP as a sacred cow. This did have the effect of reinforcing the resort by the government to a royal commission as a policy instrument, since it tended to remove the issue from partisan contention.

The NDP should have been the one party with every reason to direct hostile attention at the security police. As social democrats, they had often fallen afoul of the bizarrely right-wing standards employed by the RCMP. Indeed, a number of members of the NDP had been targeted in one of the operations that had come to light with the revelations. And the union movement, structurally linked to the NDP, had always been a prime target of RCMP surveillance and infiltration. To an extent, the NDP did play a role in parliament as the left-wing voice of conscience. But only to a point. When reports were made public that an adviser to the NDP leader in the early 1970s had been an RCMP informant, the party was reluctant to make much of it. "We don't want to look like a bunch of Pinkos," a party spokesperson explained off the record. The NDP and its predecessor party before 1961 had fought a cold war of its own in the past against the communists as electoral rivals and competitors for influence within the union movement. During the late 1940s and 1950s it had offered support for anti-Soviet external and defense policies. In short, social democrats played much the same role in Canada as the "cold war liberals" had played in the United States. Now they were anxious not to appear too far out in left field, especially in light of the continued popularity of the RCMP. They could, however, be expected to offer measured support for any moderate and respectable solution, especially one that had the imprimatur of an official, nonpartisan inquiry. Once again, a royal commission offered the government the route with the broadest ultimate consensus.

Parliament, as such, has generally been weak and dominated by the cabinet in Canada. Moreover, in matters of national security, there has been a longstanding usage that the crown prerogatives and administrative discretion must prevail ("in the national interest"). Faced with this tradition and with the strong public image of the RCMP, the opposition parties were on the whole ineffectual critics. Neither of these parties had any intention of trying to make the RCMP scandals an element in an election attack on the Liberal government. Neither in the 1979 nor 1980 general elections did the scandals figure as an issue. It was left to other forces in Canadian society to carry the burden.

The press played a crucial role. At first it seemed reluctant to get involved at all, which would have been in keeping with its traditionally deferential place in the Canadian political system. When the story first began to emerge of the involvement of the RCMP in the break-in at the Quebec news agency, there seemed to be a conspiracy of silence on the part of the press. When an investigative reporter drew some crucial linkages in a story appearing in the *Vancouver Sun,* the Canadian press wire service refused to carry the story. When a question was raised in the House of Commons, not a single reporter in the parliamentary press gallery reported it.[31] Soon, however, the story took on a momentum of its own, and with growing enthusiasm elements of the press began to join in. Hard-hitting investigative journalism does not have a long history in Canada, but the reporting of the RCMP scandals was, by the end, a chapter in the emergence of a new tradition of investigation. Press vigilance did also ensure that the government was unable to sweep the story under the rug with the passage of time. It also helped foster a climate of public opinion that made it impossible for the government to undermine its own royal commission at a crucial juncture, which will be discussed shortly. Finally, media coverage of the scandals did much to undermine the popular legitimacy of the Mounties. From a revered national symbol, the force was transformed into an object of derision in countless editorial cartoons. Doubtless this delegitimation was of limited purchase on the Canadian people. Yet contempt for the RCMP, even if it remained a minority opinion, was a new factor in the political culture. This changing attitude certainly greased the skids on which the RCMP was eventually forced to make an exit from security work.

As has already been indicated, the major policy instrument employed to resolve the crisis was the royal commission of inquiry. Royal commissions have been a favorite instrument of governments in Canada, offering besieged governments a quasi-judicial justification for removing controversial or scandalous matters from partisan contention. In the case of the RCMP scandals, the appointment of commissions fulfilled this task only in part. For one thing, reporting of testimony ensured that the interested public was kept tuned in to the issues. More importantly, the commissions themselves became rival bones of contention in a Canada-Quebec and federal-provincial struggle over constitutional jurisdiction. Finally, the federal commission came up against the hostility of the government that had appointed it and, in what amounted to a public showdown, the commission forced the government to back down.

The Keable Commission in Quebec gave every indication of being the real threat to the RCMP's position. Appointed by a Parti Québécois government—the archenemy of the federal Liberals—and operating in a province where the RCMP enjoyed very low public esteem relative to English Canada, the Keable Commission began by pursuing witnesses and documents aggressively and pointedly. Some of the damaging admissions made by the federal government were made because Keable was about to go public with the information, and the Liberals preferred to preempt the Quebec inquiry. The federal answer was to declare constitutional war on Keable's inquiry. Already reluctant to make some documents public out of fear that the federal government could invoke the Official Secrets Act against them, the Keable investigators ran into a major roadblock when the Liberal government won a decision in the Supreme Court of Canada, which declared that the Keable Commission was in violation of the division of powers between the two levels of government because it sought to investigate a federal police force. This effectively meant that the RCMP did not have to answer questions posed by Keable nor produce documents subpoenaed by the inquiry. This obviously reduced the effectiveness of the commission to a considerable degree. Yet the federal government's action in bringing this case did not rouse anything like unanimous support in English Canada. In fact, six of the nine English Canadian provinces joined Quebec in the case. Once it became a matter of federal-provincial conflict, Quebec could count on allies against Ottawa. The Supreme Court had the last say, of course, and that was on Ottawa's side. Yet the political alignment showed that Ottawa could not isolate Quebec in opposition to the RCMP. The sway of executive dominance that the Ottawa government had usually enjoyed in matters of national security could not be recreated politically in this instance, once it became a matter of federal-provincial contention: the other, decentralist pole of the Canadian system was also in play. The role of the judiciary was another matter, to which we shall return later.

When the Keable Commission reported early in 1981, it managed, despite the legal disabilities put in its path, to produce a relatively hard-hitting report that was damaging both to the RCMP and the federal government, and which called for criminal prosecution of police officers who had broken the law (the administration of criminal law is a provincial responsibility in Canada).[32]

The federal McDonald Commission started under a cloud. It was widely noted that the three commissioners were all associated with the federal Liberal party, and questions were raised about how energetic they were likely to be in pursuing the hard questions. What was not known publicly at the time was that the government acted to set up a commission at the direct request of four senior RCMP security officers, who argued that this would be the best way to defuse the uncontrolled bad publicity arising from press reporting and to avoid possible criminal charges—and that a "Federal Inquiry may well have the effect of limiting the current Quebec judicial enquiry."[33] Some observers quickly compared McDonald unfavorably to Keable.[34] The federal commission proceeded at what seemed like an excruciatingly slow pace. Slowly, however, the commission began to gain greater credibility as evidence was painstakingly amassed. Then in the fall of 1978 a confrontation developed with the Liberal government, which tried to invoke a Canadian variant of the executive privilege argument with which Richard Nixon had notoriously tried to protect himself during the Watergate scandal. On the question of ministerial knowledge of RCMP activities, the cabinet asserted the right to decide what evidence could be heard in public and which cabinet documents should be released to the commission. The press was indignant and the two opposition parties both sharply attacked the government. The McDonald Commission took a stand by asserting that if the government disapproved of the commission's independence and autonomy, it would have to change the terms of reference under which it had been set up. Watergate was cited as a precedent. The Liberal government sensed a political disaster and backed down.

The commission's work continued for another three years. When its report was finally published in 1981 (in incomplete form, at the insistence of the government) it encompassed three volumes, which totalled just under eighteen hundred pages. Despite its labyrinthine complexity, virtually all the sections upon which criminal charges might have based against individual RCMP officers had been removed at the command of the government. In this sense it might appear to have been a whitewash of the RCMP. Yet this criticism misses the larger point that the McDonald Commission was pursuing. Its real thrust was to recommend a major overhaul of the entire national security machinery. Central to this purpose was the removal of the security service from the RCMP and the establishment of a new civilian agency operating under a strict and explicit legislative mandate specifying what the agency could legally do and not do. This agency's activities were, moreover, to be subjected to the scrutiny of a parliamentary oversight committee, and a review board would be established to hear appeals from individuals who felt injured by the activities of the security agency. These recommendations together called for a structural overhaul of the national security machinery and process. McDonald was concerned more with changing the rules of the game than with punishing individuals. The same might be said concerning the commission's findings with regard to ministerial knowledge of wrongdoing, which were rather diffuse and opaque. Again, however, it might be said that the commission was seeking a favorable response from the government to its structural recommendations.

Put within a broader context, the McDonald Commission's structural recommendations reflected the changing political culture of Canada. The report was released just as the constitutional debate was approaching its climax. The new Charter of Rights, with its constitutionally grounded limitations on state intrusions into the private sector, embodies a changing balance between the public and the private sectors. In invoking limitations on government by means of mechanisms of accountability, the McDonald Commission was appealing to a more appropriate method of legitimating state activities in the name of national security. Given this backdrop of changing values, the conclusion of the editors of this volume that in political scandals "what begins as an abuse of the liberal tradition inevitably culminates in a celebration of the values of that tradition,"[35] requires some further clarification in relation to the Canadian case. More precisely, an abuse of liberal values culminated in a resolution of the scandal that helped strengthen and consolidate newer liberal values, even at the expense of some elements of the older tradition.

The more immediate context was also favorable. By the time the commission's recommendations had been made public, the political environment had altered drastically. The threat of terrorist separatism had receded into memory. In 1980 the Quebec referendum on sovereignty had resulted in a decisive rejection of separate status; even the parliamentary road to independence had vanished from the agenda. The existence of the clamorous and active extra-parliamentary left wing in English Canada, which had so disturbed the security forces in the late 1960s and early 1970s, was by now barely discernable. There was thus a moment of some calm in which the question of the role and nature of an internal security service might be discussed in relation not to the excited exigencies of the moment but to longer-range considerations of principle. The McDonald report, weighty yet understated as it was, did provide the basis for such a debate. Its recommendations were by no means radical, but in the context in which national security issues had usually been discussed in Canada, they were certainly liberal. The commission had, moreover, targeted for reform the major institutional manifestation of the national security state, the RCMP.

The Liberal government appointed a transition team to draft legislation to establish a civilian security agency and to become the nucleus for the new organization. This team included two principal figures: one a veteran Mountie from the security service with wide contacts in the western intelligence network, the other a civilian security establishment type who eventually became the first head of the civilian agency. The government was committed to civilianization of the security service as a means of establishing political control over its activities, but it was entrusting the process to men who were themselves an integral part of the national security club.[36]

Predictably, when draft legislation was finally presented in 1983 it was heavily loaded in favor of the new agency, called the Canadian Security Intelligence Service (CSIS): the definition of threats to security in the agency's mandate was broad enough to allow it to harrass, infiltrate, and disrupt legitimate dissenting groups, just as the RCMP had always done. The powers granted CSIS were, if anything, broader yet than the powers under which the RCMP security service had operated. And the provisions for independent review and oversight committees were much watered down from the McDonald Commission's recommendations. What the security establishment types had not perhaps counted on was the public reaction. The years of scandals and sordid revelations had created a body of opinion deeply suspicious of the whole national security business. This was a body of opinion that was articulate, sometimes well-placed, and not easily ignored. As a recent analyst of the process that brought CSIS to birth has written, the bill

> received a disastrous reception from the public. . . . Within days it had generated a storm of controversy. The bill was attacked not only by civil libertarians, but also by labour leaders, church leaders, and provincial Attorneys-General. Roy McMurtry, the Progressive Conservative Attorney-General of Ontario, summed up the views of many of his colleagues when he said that "the federal government has produced a legislative monster which places freedom in actual jeopardy by threatening to stifle the ordinary debate and discourse which is at the very foundation of freedom itself."[37]

The exact motives of the Trudeau government at this stage remain unclear, but a partial retreat was clearly in order. Such a retreat was in fact executed, and in a rather elegant fashion. The bill was sent to the Senate, the upper house of parliament that under normal circumstances does little other than rubber stamp government legislation emerging from the House of Commons. This time the Senate directed a committee to consider seriously improvements to the bill that had roused such public disapproval. The committee was under the chairmanship of a recently appointed Senator, Michael Pitfield. Pitfield had been a powerful figure in Trudeau's Ottawa as clerk of the Privy Council, the highest civil service post, and he was known to have personally close ties to the prime minister. He had also been the chairman of the interdepartmental committee on security and intelligence, the senior public service coordinating body in the area, from 1977 to 1982. The Pitfield Committee heard numerous witnesses and made suggestions for over thirty changes to the bill.[38] Most were accepted by the government, which reintroduced a revised bill in the House in 1984.[39] The most important changes were in the definition of the threats to security that were within CSIS's mandate to investigate. Actions "intended to lead to the destruction or overthrow of the constitutionally established system of government" was changed to read "destruction or overthrow *by violence*" (emphasis added). And a clause was strengthened indicating that "lawful advocacy, protest or dissent," unless carried on in conjunction with the improper activities specified as threats to security, would not constitute legitimate grounds for investigation. Thus CSIS was given a mandated limit on what it could investigate and what it could not. There were still complaints about the revised bill, but they were more muted. The Conservative opposition was happy to have left liberal revisions to the Pitfield Committee, and happy to leave the Liberals with the responsibility for driving the RCMP out of the security field just prior to an election that the Conservatives were confident of winning. The CSIS Act was given final approval in June 1984, the last legislative act of the government before Pierre Trudeau stepped down after sixteen years as prime minister.

The Long-Term Effects of the Scandals

The RCMP had been driven out of the business of national security. In this sense they were the ultimate losers from the scandals they had initiated by their own overzealousness and disregard for the law. Under a relatively precise legislative mandate, a new civilian security agency had been created that might be expected to be under the closer control of elected governments. A review committee was established that could offer a permanent forum for public assessment of CSIS's performance and a body to hear appeals was set up, particularly appeals from civil servants and immigrants who believed themselves to have been victimized by security screening decisions.

Second thoughts were not long in coming, however, once CSIS had set up shop.[40] Ninety-five percent of the original CSIS agents were recruited from the old RCMP security service. Thus individual Mounties could continue in the same line of work, albeit without their old uniforms and under somewhat different rules. Their behavior in their new organizational guise appears remarkably consistent with their past record. CSIS agents have been publicly reprimanded by the solicitor general for surreptitiously taping conversations with civil servants.[41] The review committee began making public warnings about the inability of CSIS to distinguish between threats to security and legitimate protest and dissent, including the improper targeting of a left-wing magazine.[42] Then in the fall of 1987, a series of new scandals broke: a union strike organizer in Quebec convicted of conspiring to plant bombs in hotels admitted to being a CSIS agent whose services dated back to the mid-1970s; separate investigations were launched of CSIS infiltration of a number of leading Canadian trade unions; it was revealed that CSIS agents were engaged in surveillance and infiltration of the peace movement. Most spectacularly, the head of CSIS was forced to resign when it was revealed that a wiretap application to a judge had been falsified by CSIS. Ten years after the creation of the McDonald Commission to deal with the RCMP follies of the 1970s, the RCMP's successor agency seemed to be caught in an instant replay of history. Late in 1987, the government ordered CSIS to close its countersubversion branch. Its targets were to be merged with those of the counterespionage and counterterrorism branches.

It might well be that the Canadian fixation on the problem of the paramilitary RCMP had led to an overemphasis on civilianization as a solution. Other western countries have always entrusted their security work to civilian agencies. It is not clear at all that the civilian status of the FBI, MI5, Australia's ASIO or Israel's Shin Bet has impeded them from committing the same (or, in some cases, worse) excesses than those committed by the RCMP. For instance, the British government continues to attempt to prevent the publication of the memoirs of former MI5 officer Peter Wright; among Wright's revelations are an alleged plot by a cabal of MI5 officers to "destabilize" the Labour government of Harold Wilson in the 1970s.[43]

The Canadian solution did not come to terms with the deeper problem of national security in a democracy, with the cancer of official secrecy in an open society, with the scope for repression and lawlessness inherent in the institution of the secret police (whether or not they call themselves police). At best it merely nibbled at the edges of these problems. Scandals have already returned. This time, however, there is one difference from the past, which may be seen as a definite legacy from the scandals of the 1970s. CSIS, unlike the RCMP, has no public legitimacy, is surrounded by no mythic aura, and sets off no ingrained positive responses among Canadians. What notice CSIS has been given in the media has been generally unfavorable: an image somewhere between amateurish incompetence and dangerous meddling. As scandals recur, CSIS can count on little instinctive public or political backing. That is some change from the past.

There is another change in the environment in which CSIS operates, although this has little to do with the issue of the scandals, as such. In 1982 the constitutionally entrenched Charter of Rights came into effect, giving Canadians for the first time something like the U.S. Bill of Rights. A number of security-related cases have begun coming before the courts based on charter claims. This may have some bearing on future security scandals, depending upon how the courts adjudicate the conflicting claims of national security and individual rights. There is an escape clause in the charter that states that the enumerated rights and freedoms in it are guaranteed "subject only to such reasonable limits prescribed by law as can be demonstrated in a free and democratic society." Given past patterns of judicial deference to the state's invocation of national security, there is little cause for confidence that the charter will affect the exercise of national security powers in any profound way. Nevertheless, there is a new context of accountability in security matters, and a greater prominence given to process and procedure than in the past. The new rules for security activities are both a reflection of and a modest contribution to this changing climate.

If accountability has been realized it is largely in abstract legal and institutional terms. Accountability in a more direct sense—the individual accountability of RCMP officers who exceeded their legal mandate—has not been realized at all. Here the judiciary, with political support, has played a conservative role in protecting offending state officials from the consequences of their actions. Many of the specific incidents involved criminal acts by individual members of the RCMP, as the Keable Commission made very clear. Under the Canadian constitution, criminal prosecutions are normally undertaken by the provincial attorneys-general. Despite their stated objections to the excesses of the federal security force, these provincial officials have proved remarkably reluctant to undertake the prosecution of individual Mounties, except in Quebec. Here, however, after prosecutions were undertaken, the judicial system proved just as reluctant to convict (the justices of most of the important courts are appointed by the federal government). Where prosecutions were not undertaken, the recourse of injured parties was to seek damages in the courts: such actions have all failed. The judicial system has not only failed to respond to this challenge brought about by police who break the law, but has in effect slapped the victims of police lawlessness in the face. The startling fact is that not a single officer implicated in the illegal acts has ever been punished. At best, suspended sentences have been handed down, but in most cases the offending individuals have been acquitted—despite the facts not being in dispute. Just as the judiciary intervened to cripple the Keable inquiry, it has consistently protected individuals within the security service.

The role of the judiciary was dramatized in extraordinary fashion as late as November 1986. One of the dirty tricks operations had been against Ross Dowson, veteran leader of a Trotskyite group centered in Toronto. Two RCMP operatives had forged and circulated false documents making allegations about Dowson's mental health, among other things, which succeeded in bringing about such division within the group's ranks that it eventually collapsed. For years Dowson sought redress in the courts against what amounted to slander by agents of the state. The facts were undisputed, but the damage claims failed in court after court. In the Ontario provincial court in late 1985, a judge dismissed the claims once again, stating that "even if the defendants could be said to have acted wrongfully, they were clearly acting in the performance of their functions or role." Dowson's lawyer, Harry Kopyto, was quoted in the press as commenting that "this decision is a mockery of justice. It stinks to high hell. . . . We're wondering what is the point of appealing and continuing this charade of the courts in this country which are warped in favor of protecting the police. The courts and the RCMP are sticking so close together, you'd think they were put together with Krazy Glue."[44] Kopyto, whose law office was earlier infiltrated by an RCMP informant, was then cited for contempt of court, convicted, and ordered to apologize to the court. If he refused, as he indicated forcefully that he would, the judge decreed that he should be barred henceforth from appearing in court. In short, for making a statement that was manifestly true, Kopyto had been punished by denying him the right to practice his profession—an almost Soviet-style "sentence." The sentence was later reversed on appeal to a higher court, but as a final comment on the RCMP scandals, it is both deeply ironic and at the same time redolent of the essential meaning of the scandals in Canadian society.

The conservative weight of institutions is a powerful force of inertia against changes brought about by basic conflicts within the society. This is particularly true when national security offers a legitimating cloak for conservatism—even in a broader context of a growing liberalism in the society and the constitutional and political framework. Apart from pure legitimation, some change was brought about as a result of the scandals, although the depth of the changes is open to question. Yet even these came only as the result of an agonizingly lengthy process and the expenditure of many political and other resources, often to very little visible effect. Perhaps the ultimate lesson of the Canadian experience is that even when the state is itself divided, control over the processes of investigation and reform of the activities of agencies of the state affords the executive and judicial branches of government the capacity to diffuse and limit the challenge to state legitimacy that the revelations of scandal pose. "National security" remains a powerful card to be played by the central government in a situation of the division of authority and decentralized political conflict. More than a powerful card, it was ultimately a trump.

NOTES

1. The events of the October Crisis are described in a number of contemporary accounts: see Ron Haggart and Aubrey Golden, *Rumours of War* (Toronto: New Press, 1971); Denis Smith, *Bleeding Hearts . . . Bleeding Country: Canada and the Quebec Crisis* (Edmonton: Hurtig, 1971); the view of a federal cabinet minister from Quebec is Gérard Pelletier, *La Crise d'octobre* (Montreal: Editions du jour, 1971) and the view from the other side of the barricades is in Jean-Marc Piotte et al., *Québec occupé* (Montréal: Editions parti pris, 1971).

2. It was revealed, for instance, that the two FLQ cells had had no communication with each other, and that the cell that kidnapped and later killed Laporte had only thought of

the idea when members heard about the first kidnapping over a car radio while driving in Texas, from where they rushed back.

3. The sources for this list of scandals are many: Government of Canada, Commission of Inquiry Concerning Certain Activities of the RCMP, *Second and Third Reports* (Ottawa: Government of Canada, 1981); Gouvernement du Québec, Ministére de la Justice, *Rapport de la Commission d'enquête sur des opérations policières en territoire québécois* (Québec: Government of Quebec, 1981); *La police secrète au Québec* (Montreal: Black Rose, Editions Québec-Amérique, 1978); Robert Dion, *Crimes of the Secret Police* (Montreal: 1982); Jeff Sallot, *Nobody Said No* (Toronto: Lorimer 1979); William Edward Mann and John Alan Lee, *The RCMP vs. the People* (Toronto: General Publishing, 1979); *Ross Dowson v. RCMP* (Toronto: Foreward Publications, 1980); Richard Fidler, *RCMP: The Real Subversives* (Toronto: Vanguard Publications, 1978); John Sawatsky, *Men in the Shadows: The RCMP Security Service* (Toronto: Doubleday, 1980).

4. This list was extraordinarily ineffective: of the twenty-one civil servants, four have since risen to the rank of assistant deputy minister (the second executive position in a government department) and one became the youngest ever deputy minister in the Canadian government.

5. See Markovits and Silverstein, Introduction to this volume.

6. Donald V. Smiley, *The Federal Condition in Canada* (Toronto: McGraw-Hill Ryerson, 1987); Garth Stevenson, *Unfulfilled Union: Canadian Federalism and National Unity*, rev. ed. (Toronto: Macmillan, 1982).

7. Kenneth McRoberts, *Quebec: Social Change and Political Crisis* rev. 3d ed. (Toronto: McClelland and Stewart, 1988); William D. Coleman, *The Independence Movement in Quebec: 1945–1980* (Toronto: University of Toronto Press, 1984).

8. Richard Simeon, *Federal-Provincial Diplomacy: the Making of Recent Policy in Canada* (Toronto: University of Toronto Press, 1972).

9. A. Paul Pross, *Group Politics and Public Policy* (Toronto: Oxford University Press 1986).

10. Gordon T. Stewart, *The Origins of Canadian Politics: A Comparative Approach* (Vancouver: University of British Columbia Press, 1986).

11. Kenneth McRae, ed., *Consociational Democracy: Political Accommodation in Segmented Societies* (Toronto: McClelland and Stewart, 1974); Robert Presthus, *Elite Accommodation in Canadian Politics* (Toronto: Macmillan, 1973).

12. Reg Whitaker, "Federalism, Democracy and the Canadian Political Community," in *The Integration Question: Political Economy and Public Policy in North America*, ed. Jon Pammett and Brian W. Tomlin (Toronto: Addison-Wesley, 1984), pp. 72–94.

13. The 1867 constitutional document was an act of the British Parliament that had never been "patriated" to Canada because the federal and provincial governments had never been able to agree upon an amendment formula.

14. Reg Whitaker, "Democracy and the Canadian Constitution," in *And No One Cheered: Federalism, Democracy and the Constitution Act,* ed. K. Banting and R. Simeon, (Toronto: Methuen, 1983). In 1987, another set of negotiations resulted in a further package of revisions including the constitutional recognition of Quebec as a "distinct society"; again, the bargaining was conducted strictly among the political elites and no changes whatever were made at the urging of nongovernmental groups.

15. Seymour Martin Lipset, *Revolution and Counterrevolution* (New York: Basic Books, 1970), pp. 37–75; "Canada and the United States: The Cultural Dimension," in The American Assembly and Council on Foreign Relations, *Canada and the United States: Enduring Friendship, Persistent Stress* (Englewood Cliffs, N.J.: Prentice-Hall, 1985), pp. 109–60; Edgar Z. Friedenberg, *Deference to Authority: The Canadian Case* (White Plains, N.Y.: M. E. Sharpe, 1980).

16. Markovits and Silverstein, Introduction to this volume.

17. There was a Bill of Rights passed as an act of parliament in 1960 but it lacked constitutional entrenchment and was generally disregarded by the courts.

18. Keith Walden, *Visions of Order: The Canadian Mounties in Symbol and Myth* (Toronto:

Butterworths, 1982); Sawatsky, *Men in the Shadows;* Lorne and Caroline Brown, *An Unauthorized History of the RCMP* (Toronto: James Lewis and Samuel, 1973).

19. I have reported an instance when the RCMP forced the prime minister of Canada to change his policy on a matter of the highest international significance by citing the authority of J. Edgar Hoover and the FBI: see Reg Whitaker, "Spy story: lifting Gouzenko's cloak," *The Globe and Mail,* 6 November 1984.

20. Reg Whitaker, "Official Repression of Communism During World War II," *Labour/ le Travail: Journal of Canadian Labour Studies* 17 (Spring 1986): 135–68.

21. Royal Commission to Investigate the Facts Relating to and the Circumstances Surrounding the Communication by Public Officials and Other Persons in Positions of Trust of Secret and Confidential Information to Agents of a Foreign Power, *Report* (Ottawa: The King's Printer, 1946); Robert Bothwell and J. L. Granatstein, *The Gouzenko Transcripts* (Ottawa: Deneau, n.d.); the Gouzenko affair will be assessed at length in the light of recently declassified documents in a forthcoming book that I am coauthoring with Gary Marcuse, *Cold War Canada.*

22. Reg Whitaker, "Origins of the Canadian Government's Internal Security System, 1946–1952," *Canadian Historical Review* 65, 2 (June 1984): 154–83.

23. Reg Whitaker, "Fighting the Cold War on the Home Front: America, Britain, Australia and Canada," in *The Uses of Anti-Communism,* ed. Ralph Miliband et al. (London: Merlin Press, 1984), 23–67.

24. Reg Whitaker, *Double Standard: The Secret History of Canadian Immigration* (Toronto: Lester and Orpen Dennys, 1987).

25. Richard Gwyn, *The Northern Magus: Pierre Trudeau and Canadians* (Toronto: Mc-Clelland and Stewart, 1980), p. 122.

26. Sawatsky, *Men in the Shadows,* pp. 261–62.

27. M. Janine Brodie and Jane Jenson, *Crisis, Challenge and Change: Party and Class in Canada* (Toronto: Methuen, 1980).

28. The Liberal justice minister during the October Crisis, later to become the Liberal leader and prime minister, indicated at one point that the records of the crisis should remain closed until the twenty-first century.

29. The FBI accumulated a file on Pearson, the releasable portions of which constitute close to three hundred pages. FBI files, Lester B. Pearson 65–60356, FOI request #262,554.

30. When a Liberal solicitor general was forced to resign, when information that he had forged the signature of a woman's husband on an abortion consent form was leaked to the press by a "concerned citizen" some time after the event, speculation about how the RCMP might use personally damaging material took a dark, but unresolved, turn.

31. Sawatsky, *Men in the Shadows,* p. 279. Sawatsky is himself perhaps the best example of the new generation of investigative reporters to emerge from the 1970s.

32. *Rapport de la Commission d'enquête sur des opérations policières en territoire québécois* (Québec: Government of Québec, 1981).

33. Commission of Inquiry Concerning Certain Activities of the RCMP, *Second Report,* 3 vols., v. 1 (Ottawa: Government of Canada 1981), pp. 8–10. To make matters even more suspicious, the key drafter of the letter to the government from the RCMP was later a key member of the transition team appointed to implement the recommendations of the McDonald Commission.

34. Robert Dion, *Crimes of the Secret Police,* pp. 145–84; Edward Mann and John Alan Lee, *The RCMP vs. the People,* pp. 214–31.

35. See Introduction in this volume.

36. James Littleton, *Target Nation: Canada and the Western Intelligence Network* (Toronto; Lester and Orpen Dennys, 1986), pp. 148–52.

37. Littleton, *Target Nation,* p. 152.

38. Special Committee of the Senate on the Canadian Security Intelligence Service, *Delicate Balance: A Security Intelligence Service in a Democratic Society* (Ottawa: Government of Canada, 1983).

39. 32–33 Elizabeth II, 1983–84, C–9, *An Act to Establish the Canadian Security Intelligence Service.*

40. Murray Rankin, "National Security: Information, Accountability, and the Canadian Security Intelligence Service," *University of Toronto Law Journal* 36, 3 (Summer 1986): 249–85.

41. Reg Whitaker, "Witchhunt in the Civil Service: Ottawa's New Security Force has Taken the Role of an Orwellian-style Thought Police," *This Magazine* 20, 4 (October/November 1986): 24–29.

42. The Security Intelligence Review Committee has issued three annual reports by the spring of 1987, each of them successively more detailed and more critical of the shortcomings of CSIS. The head of SIRC, Ron Atkey, a former Conservative cabinet minister, has been a highly visible public critic of CSIS.

43. Peter Wright, *Spycatcher: The Candid Autobiography of a Senior Intelligence Officer* (Toronto: Stoddart, 1987); Richard V. Hall, *A Spy's Revenge* (Harmondsworth: Penguin, 1987).

44. Kirk Makin, "Ex-RCMP Officers Only Doing Job, Ontario Judge Decides," *The Globe and Mail,* 18 December 1985.

Sex, Spies, and Scandal: The Profumo Affair and British Politics

3 •

ROBIN GASTER

From loving girls, ye wise, refrain;
'Tis little pleasure, longer pain.
But love three females none the less,
Compassion, Wisdom, Friendliness.
For swelling breasts of lovely girls,
Trembling beneath their strings of pearls,
And hips with jingling girdles—well,
They do not help you much in hell.
                    —Bhartrihari (ca. 50 B.C.)

In the summer of 1963 Britain finally discovered sex. From across the English Channel, observers saw a century of stiff upper lips and stiffer Victorian underwear suddenly fall away, revealing all manner of strange and sometimes wondrous sights.

During that summer, as revelation followed rumor, even the French and Italians (acknowledged experts in matters of the heart) were amused by a classic British sex scandal. As John Profumo struggled with his conscience, the press, and his enemies, flashes of illumination lit the darker corners of the British polity—light that showed traditional strengths to the full, but also exposed some unpleasant and even sordid characteristics.

The Scandal: A Tragicomedy in Five Acts

ATTRACTION

The story began one day in July 1961, at Cliveden, the famous country residence of the Astors, one of the great aristocratic families of Britain. On the grounds there was a swimming pool, enjoyed by a wide array of friends and acquaintances. That day these included two minor figures from the emerging world of "swinging London," Stephen Ward and his friend Christine Keeler.[1]

While in the pool, Christine Keeler was playfully stripped of her bathing suit by Ward, just as other guests arrived, including Jack Profumo (the minister of war) and his wife. They saw an attractive sight indeed: almost all of a gorgeous nineteen-year-old blonde with long legs and a pretty face. Profumo called her the next day.

Their affair was, at best, a mere summer fling; no grand passions and little enough romance intruded. Profumo took some risks, using his official car and perhaps even his own house, but sex rather than love was clearly the issue. Keeler's own account emphasizes this somewhat gritty reality: "We didn't see each other many times. I was impressed when I found out that he was a Minister, and overwhelmed by his domineering character, but I didn't like him that much."[2]

What turned the affair into an eventual catastrophe was the fact that Keeler had not limited her attentions: in July, she had slept at least once (and possibly more often) with the Russian naval attaché, Eugene Ivanov.[3] And while this promiscuity eventually brought its own problems, the Ivanov-Keeler-Profumo triangle also had obvious security implications.

In the end, the affair with Profumo lasted only a month. Stephen Ward was fashionably political as well as Bohemian, and he had become friendly with Ivanov. In July 1961 MI5 (Military Intelligence, the security service in charge of counterespionage) had warned Ward about Ivanov, and now in early August they warned Profumo about Ward. Though Profumo's affair with Keeler was still unknown, Profumo nonetheless ended it at once. Rather unwisely, he did so by letter, eventually a key piece of evidence in his fall.[4]

And that appeared to be that.

DECEPTION

A year later, in December 1962, Johnny Edgecombe (a jilted West Indian lover of Keeler's) appeared at Ward's flat (where she was staying) and fired several shots from a gun. This generated major press coverage at Edgecombe's trial in March 1963, and it also led to Keeler's first contact with the police in January, when she made a statement revealing a good deal of her private life. The police called in MI5, who for unknown reasons refused to pursue the matter.

New sources of information now emerged. By late January, rumors had reached the chief legal officers of the government, the attorney-general and the solicitor-general. They confronted Profumo for the first time, and for the first time, he denied having had an affair.

Next, in early February the *News of the World* took its evidence to officials very close to the prime minister. Confronted now by the chief whip, Profumo once again denied the affair, knowing that the truth would end his political career.[5]

Press interest in the Edgecombe case increased when the chief prosecution witness, Keeler, vanished abroad, apparently on funds provided by "others" (rumored to be Profumo). And Profumo's letter to Keeler was now in the hands of the *Sunday Pictorial*, while Ward, Keeler, and their mutual friend, Mandy Rice-Davies simultaneously tried to sell their life stories.[6] A wild melange of truth and fiction flooded London's "high society": senior members of the government apparently held naked candlelight dinners, waited on by an important politician clad only in a mask and a sign saying "Whip Me." Orgies, whipping parties, and drug-taking seemed widespread, though no one had yet identified either the naked politician or the nine High Court judges allegedly involved.

On 21 March a pale version of these rumors was raised in the House of Commons, which gave Profumo a chance to deal with them publicly. Colonel Wigg, a Labour M.P. who had clashed bitterly with Profumo over military issues, now used his House of Commons privilege to protect himself against libel actions while he attacked Profumo.[7] That night, Profumo met with five senior government ministers and his own lawyer to prepare his defense, a personal statement for the House of Commons.[8]

On 22 March, Profumo was almost completely truthful. He denied several current rumors—but also included the fateful words "There was no impropriety whatsoever in my acquaintanceship with Miss Keeler." Cloaked by the prestige of the personal statement, his innocence was largely accepted by the House and the press. The statement was printed verbatim in all the newspapers, and the government aligned its prestige behind Profumo: Macmillan and other senior ministers ostentatiously sat next to him while he made the statement. A month later, Profumo successfully extracted token libel damages from *Paris Match* and *Tempo Illustrato*.

But his successful defense was only temporary. In mid-April Keeler was again assaulted, this time by a different jilted West Indian lover (Lucky Gordon). As Gordon's trial approached in May 1963, the police began an extremely thorough investigation of Ward, with whom Keeler and Rice-Davies had stayed off and on after they had arrived in London.[9]

Ward now emerged onto the larger stage for the first time. Originally from a relatively poor background, he had by this time become a confidant of important members of the aristocracy and was keen to enter the magic world of politics. He used both his osteopathy practice in London's best medical district and his skills as a portrait painter of royalty to enter "society." And he also found that his skill in picking up girls helped him everywhere, from aristocratic and political circles to less reputable clubs and dancing halls, all the way to the prostitutes' hangouts in lower Picadilly. His charm and glibness made him a universally welcome visitor.

The police now began interviewing his patients. As this drove them away, Ward first complained to the home secretary, and then attempted to blackmail the government by threatening to reveal Profumo's lie. At the same time, possible security problems were emerging: the Profumo-Keeler-Ivanov triangle was obviously explosive, opening Profumo directly to blackmail, but now the Profumo-Keeler-Ward relationship also became important. Three times in March, and once in her police interview in January, Keeler mentioned a request from Ward that she ask Profumo about a "nuclear secret." This had enormous security implications given Profumo's job as minister of war (though even at the end, few ever believed that Profumo's pillow-talk with Keeler was indiscreet, and she certainly never passed any information to Ivanov). Specifically, Profumo was wide open to blackmail while the affair remained a secret—and one known by Ivanov.

Once Ward's claims about Profumo reached the ears of Harold Wilson (the leader of the opposition), he used the security issue to pressure Macmillan privately, with little initial effect. But the official silence was finally broken when Ward wrote to the home secretary, to Colonel Wigg, to the prime minister, and to several major newspapers. Macmillan conceded a further investigation on 28 May and then displayed his well-known nonchalance by disappearing to Scotland on holiday.

DENOUEMENT

On 5 June Jack Profumo returned from holiday to resign from both the government and the House of Commons; a full-scale debate was set for 17 June in the House of Commons. In the interim, Ward was arrested on a variety of morals charges, but that had to wait. Politicians were jostling for the spotlight.

Morality was not the central issue in the House of Commons on 17 June. Harold Wilson opened the debate, translating the affair into party politics by emphasizing the national security problem. He argued that either the security services knew about the affair, and hence knew that Profumo was wide open to blackmail, but had not acted; or that they knew nothing—a remarkable display of incompetence. Either way, surely the prime minister (in overall charge of national security) had failed to fulfill his responsibilities.

Macmillan's reply was barely satisfactory. He effectively defended his honesty if not his prestige by pleading ignorance. But this mattered less than his damaged reputation. Macmillan was "Supermac," the effective politician who ran a country that had "never had it so good" (his slogan at the last election); yet here he seemed out of his depth. Symbolic, perhaps, was his famous admission that he "did not live widely among young people," and hence could not judge the innocence or otherwise of Profumo's letter to Keeler.

The debate continued all day, but it proved nothing conclusive, except in relation to Lord Hailsham, a senior member of the government who had bitterly attacked Profumo on television. He was completely humiliated by Reginald Paget, who included him amongst those who "compound for sins they are inclined to by damning those they have no mind to," adding that "When self-indulgence has reduced a man to the shape of Lord Hailsham, sexual continence involves no more than a sense of the ridiculous" (Hailsham was rather overweight at the time).[10] Few could live that down, and they did not include Hailsham.

In general, the debate was embarrassing for the government, and it provoked a sustained rebellion within the governing Tory Party. Some twenty-seven M.P.s abstained rather than support the party, a large revolt in the context of British party politics. A few more and Macmillan's position would have been impossible. As it was, he hung on (with some luck) despite the damage. The debate also exposed the embarrassing gullibility of senior ministers who had failed to force the truth from Profumo, or even made much of an effort to do so. And the security services also came in for a pasting from Labour. But in the end the debate mainly paved the way for the concluding chapter, the official investigation by Lord Denning (a judge on the High Court). Before that, however, the trial of Stephen Ward took place.

TRAGEDY

Today, Ward's innocence of pimping charges is obvious. The evidence was absurdly thin, and two key prosecution witnesses claimed either during or after the trial that they had been put up to their testimonies by the police.[11] Other police behavior was also puzzling. For example, more than 140 interviews were conducted, at least twenty with Keeler, and Rice-Davies was threatened by the police while in jail on a minor unrelated charge.[12] Why were the police so determined to convict an essentially harmless, if charmless and sordid inhabitant of the demimonde?

Answers lie in the trial itself. Ward was tried not for his specific offenses, but for being, as the prosecutor put it, "a thoroughly filthy fellow." At the trial, the new 1960s world of sexual liberation collided hard with the Victorian values that had dominated public life in England during the 1950s. The prosecutor not only explained that the definition of a respectable girl was one who didn't want to sleep with anyone, but was also horrified that Rice-Davies should make love with Bill Astor while Ward was in the next room. Various other sexual practices and items, like the two-way mirror in one of Ward's bedrooms and Ward's indulgence in flagellation, also horrified the court. The fundamental conflict between traditional public puritanism and the new and increasingly defiant world of sexual freedom could not have been clearer.

The judge's summary indicated the world to which he belonged; and Ward did not wait for the verdict, which came while he lay in hospital dying from an overdose of sleeping pills. Guilty perhaps, but not as charged. He remained the one final, and in a large sense innocent, victim of the affair.

RESOLUTION?

The final official stamp followed in September, in the shape of Lord Denning's Report. Though snapped up by eager buyers, it was something of a disappointment, despite its journalistic, even racy, style. Rice-Davies calls it the Whitewash Report, with some truth.

Denning accepted that there was limited fire behind the smoky pall of rumor that still hung around London. There had indeed been orgies—but no Cabinet members (or High Court judges) had been involved. Profumo had had an affair, but Keeler had not slept with Ivanov (a conclusion later strongly disputed). Denning then examined security and surprisingly exonerated MI5. This despite Keeler's confession of the affair in her January statement to the police. When this news reached MI5, further action was specifically forbidden at the highest levels. No explanation was offered, then or in the report, and no refutation was offered to Wilson's accusations of incompetence. In the end, the security services simply slunk away into the sunset.

The government was less fortunate. Denning emphasized the gullibility of the five senior ministers, a judgment that did not help the general credibility of the government or of Macmillan. Indications of political decline had been growing for a year, and during the crisis Macmillan was reputed to have made a deal with critics in his own party that he would stay on for a few months and then gracefully leave before the next election.[13] By September, he had however apparently decided that his position was solid enough for him to stay on permanently, when he was suddenly faced with the prospect of immediate surgery. This led him to resign in October 1963. Macmillan certainly believed that while he had been damaged, he had survived, and we should probably believe him.

Some postscripts remain. Profumo himself was eventually rehabilitated after a second career devoted to social work. Keeler and Rice-Davies both entered show business, with varied success, and both published their stories. While Rice-Davies overcame or even exploited her notoriety, owning a successful nightclub in Israel and appearing in movies, Keeler was not so fortunate. Jailed for perjury after the affair, she now lives as a recluse in squalid public housing in a poor section of London. For her, the burden of adverse publicity generated by the trial and its conclusions was simply too heavy to bear.[14] Hailsham suffered a devastating decline in his political standing, which may have prevented him from becoming prime minister, while the unfortunate Ward has already been discussed. Perhaps the last word belongs to the voters. In the September by-election to fill Profumo's seat, Labour did indeed win, but by a margin no wider than that expected before Profumo resigned. It seemed that the scandal's effects, at least on electoral politics, were undetectable.

But twenty years later, the Profumo affair is still the benchmark of British political scandal. Why that kind of durability?

The Profumo Affair and British Politics

An affair or scandal lingers in the public mind not just because it was sensational at the time, but because it tapped some deep cleavage within the society. The Dreyfus affair is remembered not because an obscure Jewish army officer was framed at the turn of the century, but because it graphically illustrated the conflict then raging between church and state in France.

— The Profumo affair tapped a deep vein of confusion in Britain about the legitimate spheres of public concern: at what point could the state's interest in regulating the lives of its citizens be legitimately rejected in favor of individual liberty?

British traditions pushed in both directions: historically, English liberties had centered around the defense of the home from state authority; yet the state undeniably had the responsibility to regulate the life of the nation so as to defend it. That defense might include conflict with the peril within—decadence in all its forms—as well as the enemy without.

SEXUAL MORES AND PUBLIC LIFE

Most obviously, the Profumo affair is about a profound clash of sexual values. Ward, Keeler, and Rice-Davies found themselves in trouble because they openly transgressed the dominant rules of sexual conduct in Britain. And naturally, sex being such a powerful issue, this clash generated considerable heat. Following Jeffrey Weekes, the following points help to define that dominant tradition.[15]

The core of traditional British sexual ideology has been derived directly from the Christian, and specifically the Pauline, tradition. As Weekes notes, the strongest (most Puritan) defenders of this tradition had argued, with St. Paul, that sex was only permissible within marriage, and even here was strictly tied to reproduction. In any event, celibacy was undoubtedly the goal, and sexual pleasure verged on sin, even within marriage.

Of course, this ideal was rarely practiced, and as the Victorian age was left behind, even the ideal came under fire as attitudes toward sex within the family changed. But it was an Englishwoman who replied to her daughter's question about sex in marriage by advising her to "Lie back and think of England." And it was Ward's prosecutor who argued that the definition of a respectable girl was one who didn't want to go to bed with anyone. And it was British public schools that developed cold showers and massive exercise as a way of avoiding "impure thoughts."[16] Thus there is plenty of evidence for arguing that official British morality continued to reflect fear and distrust of sexuality altogether.

A second element in Victorian ideology was the sacred character of the family. With the codification of the marriage laws in the mid-nineteenth century, and the radical changes in the nature of work that first separated it from the home during the process of industrialization, the family began to resemble the "nuclear family" rather than its extended ancestor. It became, in Hobsbawm's words, a sanctuary: "Here, and here alone, the bourgeois and even more the petit bourgeois family could maintain the illusion of harmonious, hierarchic happiness."[17]

The newly separated middle-class family began to develop the idea of "respectability," an idea that turned out to have an enormous effect on British mores. Respectability was based on an absolutist notion of morality—the development of a rigid set of specific standards from which behavior should not deviate. Within the broad framework of Christian ethics, respectability emphasized both an increased distinction between the public and private realms and an increased need for the state to regulate that boundary.

> Victorian morality was premised on a series of ideological separations: between family and society, between the restraint of the domestic circle and the temptations of promiscuity; between the privacy, leisure and comforts of the home and the tensions and competitiveness of work. And these divisions in social organization and ideology were reflected in sexual attitudes.[18]

In practice, respectability adopted in particular the double standard: the expectation of female chastity and fidelity alongside new and more rigid definitions of manhood and masculinity.[19] Men were both freer to indulge their carnal tendencies, and more strictly measured against a standard of masculinity increasingly differentiated from femininity. At about this time, for instance, British men stopped crying in public.

At the extreme, this contradiction actually endorsed male promiscuity as part of the normal behavior of men. The double standard was attacked by both feminists and strict conservatives, whose sometimes similar arguments are summarized in Christabel Pankhurst's famous slogan "Votes for Women, and Chastity for Men."

Respectability was intimately intertwined with the rise of the middle class and its distinctive morality: "First and foremost, sexual respectability expressed the lives and aspirations of the middle class. Only secondarily was it for export to other classes"[20] (including both the working class and the aristocracy). Indeed the development of respectability was closely tied to a series of wider developments:

The ideology of respectability had been in the process of articulation throughout the century. Its stress on values such as self-help and self-reliance, the value of work, the need for social discipline, the cohering centrality of the family, were all challenged by public immorality.[21]

Thus the catchwords of respectability, prudence, and postponement were also the catchwords of the new capitalist ethos of the nineteenth century. And this linkage allowed the rapid penetration of the working class by this new morality, affecting in particular artisans and skilled workers. With upward mobility came the adoption of middle-class values:

> The hard-working, God-fearing, nonconformist working man and "labour aristo-crat" of the northern industrial cities, with his Sunday best, neat front parlour, non-working wife and high morality was to become the epitome of the respectable proletarian.[22]

Alternatives to respectability also developed in the nineteenth century, from the liberalism of Bentham and especially that of John Stuart Mill.[23] Mill argued that the determination of morality lay in the question of injury; harmless conduct should not be penalized, and participation in sexual activities was the exercise of free will. This defense was always important to homosexual and other "deviant" subcultures, which were coming under increasing state attack in the early and middle years of the twentieth century, but it made little formal headway before the 1960s.

Respectability thus emerged triumphant from the Victorian era as the norm of British sexual morality, and that norm was vigorously defended by public figures and institutions. The legitimacy of a public morality was argued by Sir William Joynson-Hicks, the home secretary from 1924 to 1929:

> The government has a general responsibility for the moral welfare of the community which is traceable partly perhaps to the peculiar relationship existing between the Church and the State, and partly also to the duty inherent in all governments of combating such dangers as threaten the safety or well-being of the state.[24]

And for most members of the government, the analogy with Rome in decline was always beckoning, always pushing the state to defend the traditional morality. But government action also contributed to another aspect of the double standard: the distinction between public and private morality. In other words, that well-known British hypocrisy:

> One of the outstanding features of the period is the continuing dominance of the formal standards of respectability. The mistresses of Lloyd George and the Prince of Wales were discreetly screened from the public view, while a prominent Liberal politician preferred suicide to the threat of a public accusation of buggery.[25]

The 1950s were both the epitome and the climacteric of the traditional morality. Male and female sexuality became even more distinctly defined, and female behavior was linked more clearly to "femininity" and the cult of the female as sexual object. The feisty movie stars of the 1940s were replaced by the sex kittens of the 1950s, as Bardot and Monroe replaced Bacall and Russell. But at the same time sexuality itself, and sexual pleasure, were increasingly legitimated, but only within the traditional boundaries of heterosexual marriage.

Thus the outlines of British sexual norms were clear enough: the 1950s were the last decade in which an absolutist standard could remain more or less unquestioned in British life, and that standard was directly descended from the Victorian invention of respectability. "Respectability" implied both real and ideal standards. The ideal included chastity and fidelity on both sides of a marriage, the absence of premarital sex, and the rejection of "deviants" like homosexuals or pederasts (together with anything "prurient" like *Lady Chatterley's Lover*). But in practice these ideals focused much more strongly on women, accepted that men somehow were more likely to fall from grace, and emphasized that even where ideals had failed, appearances had to be maintained. Hence the public display of vice was unacceptable, whatever the private reality: respectability above all.

THE CHALLENGE OF OPEN SEXUALITY

During the 1960s this dominant paradigm of sexual behavior faced several challenges. Sexual behavior itself changed rapidly. With the new affluence of the 1960s and the beginnings of a new youth culture (which quickly bloomed into full-scale rebellion during the decade), new sexual mores spread rapidly. Sex before marriage became increasingly popular and legitimate; sex outside marriage became the subject of jokes, not obloquy.

This new behavior was accompanied by a change in attitudes toward sex. The old Biblical mores themselves were under fire, even among those who were not participants in the sexual revolution. By the end of the decade, parents were suggesting trial, not shotgun, marriages (although as in most aspects of sexuality, the change occurred first in the middle class and was only gradually adopted by most working-class families).

Official standards of sexual behavior also started to change. Had Profumo's affair occurred today, or even at the end of the 1960s, this would be no one's affair but his own (and his wife's, perhaps). Measuring public officials by their private lives had become the preoccupation of increasingly marginal commentators (usually aligned with traditional religious organizations). And the measurements applied were in any case more liberal.

Most seriously of all, both aspects of the traditional double standard came under attack. Even before the women's movement burst onto the scene in the late 1960s, women's sexuality had begun the long trek out of the closet, out of the family, and into the public domain. The Profumo affair illustrated two key transitions. It publicized the change from sexual fulfillment within marriage to sexual availability outside. And it captured the first stage in a transformed interpretation of "respectability," which now translated as hypocrisy, not propriety.

The Profumo affair marked these changes. Most directly there was the extraordinary behavior of Keeler and Rice-Davies, who apparently slept with men simply because they liked to, thus embracing hedonism and rejecting Biblical puritanism. Ward too seemed alien: a man who could get girls apparently whenever he wanted to (and what envy *that* inspired), and who saw nothing wrong in "providing" girls for the rich and powerful. Even if no money changed hands, this too squared with neither Biblical morality nor the western tradition of romantic love. But of course, all this meant nothing without

Profumo. He provided the publicity that created a *cause célèbre,* while showing the dangerous attractions of the "new morality," even for defenders of the old.

During the 1960s, these changes coalesced into a fundamental rejection of traditional state prerogatives. Government intervention in private matters was challenged and found to be illegitimate. As church attendance plummeted, the old philosophical base of state intervention, the established religion, became increasingly irrelevant. And the laws relating to homosexuality, abortion, divorce, censorship in the theater and in print all changed in the 1960s, in every case radically reducing the state's right to intervene in "private" affairs. The Profumo affair marked and illustrated this change, and hence it channeled considerable public anger and confusion at both the participants and the political system itself.

SEX AND DECADENCE: POLITICS AND THE PRESS

The sexual ferment featured prominently in press treatment of the affair, treatment that illustrated both the caution and sensationalism of the British press as well as an extraordinarily British mixture of moralism and hypocrisy. But press treatment also indicated the prevailing tendency for all events to be viewed through the prism of British decline and its causes—a point to which we will return in a moment.

Certainly, the problem of the boundary between public and private, between matters open to press comment and those closed to it, was of central importance. Historically, that distinction—and the related boundary determining the state's own relationship to the press—have been defined rather differently in Britain than in most other democracies. As in so many other matters, Britain has relied upon the consensus available to a highly homogeneous nation with a tightly bound elite, rather than on the rules of law and process. This difference becomes very clear in the case of Profumo.

To begin with, the press showed caution verging on cowardice in refusing to publish what it knew. The *Sunday Pictorial* had had Profumo's letter for some months, but refused to print it on the grounds that it was ambiguous, and that Keeler's motives for selling it were not pure (an extraordinary comment coming from a tabloid). In the end it was returned to Profumo unpublished. There were certainly mitigating circumstances: two journalists were still in jail for having refused to reveal their sources in the Vassall affair, and that in itself had turned out very badly for the press, which hounded a completely innocent man into resignation from the government.[26] The press was reluctant to take that risk again, and it was also reluctant to take on the British libel laws, which are much stricter than on the European continent or the United States—as Profumo's successful libel prosecutions clearly show. John Freeman, the editor of the *New Statesman* (a left-oriented opponent of the government), claimed afterward that he had had the story all along but could not risk the possible lawsuit. This caution did not square very well with the heroic British tradition of "publish and be damned."

British laws have always been most protective of the Establishment so far as the press is concerned, even beyond the laws of libel. There is an extremely restrictive Official Secrets Act, still actively employed, which makes illegal the publication of any classified or even not unclassified information. This applies even if the information comes into the hands of a journalist from perfectly legitimate sources—which makes the Act almost the opposite of the American

Freedom of Information Act: it can be invoked with great ease to protect the government.[27] There is also the "D Notice," a notice sent from the prime minister's office to newspapers demanding the suppression of a story on national security grounds. There were rumors of a D Notice concerning the Profumo affair, but none was eventually sent out. This practice has no legal basis; it rests completely on the willingness of the press to suppress stories and hence indirectly on the Establishment basis of the national press. Once again, the generally conservative cast of newspaper proprietors places them firmly within, not outside, the ranks of the Establishment. Successful news media proprietors are often rewarded by titles or knighthoods, something that also tends to bind them into the tightly knit circles of the British political elite.

On the other hand, the press reveled in the seamier side of the Profumo affair. Keeler and Rice-Davies sold their stories to the papers where they were shamelessly edited (or rewritten) to focus on the most sexually sensational aspects. The *News of the World* provides a taste:

> Here was my perfect specimen of a man (Ivanov). And he wanted me. He couldn't have stopped now anyway. We crashed across the room. . . . From that second too I threw all caution to the winds. . . . I was afraid that he would hate me afterwards, because I knew that he was abandoning his principles. But he was like a god. . . . Clumsy perhaps, but only because he wanted me. He said so. . . . All I know is that when I allowed Eugene to love me I was young and free.[28]

This story appeared beneath a picture of Keeler astride a chair—and naked; Keeler's was indeed "the best documented body in the history of espionage."[29] While hard news was handled cautiously, the tabloids had a field day, and the editorial and letter writers were in full cry.

To many, the affair was much more than a simple tale of sexual incontinence, or even a security lapse. It was about the decline of Britain, captured by the decline of Britain's sexual and social code. As the British Empire dwindled and Britain sought a new role in the world, comparisons with Rome became ever more frequent. Nothing typified this comparison more than the Profumo affair, for here was living proof that decadence and decline went hand in hand.

> By far the greatest volume of Press comment generated by the Profumo Affair has been about sexual morals, and by far the greater part of that has been shocked, restrictionist, even demanding what the *British Weekly*, the Church of Scotland paper, called a "national act of cleansing and commitment that will lead Britain out of this mess to find a new purpose under God in the world and for the world." "Thus fell Rome," headlined the *New Daily:* "Corruption, Degeneracy, and Indolence in High Places."[30]

Most publicly, the editor of the London Times, Sir William Haley, let fly with an editorial headlined "It *is* a moral issue." In it he blamed Britain's problems directly on the Conservative government: Macmillan's "never had it so good" apparently epitomized a turn away from the old values of duty and self-sacrifice, toward self-indulgence and hedonism. The Profumo affair was both a symptom and inevitable outcome of this change.

Despite Britain's relatively early industrialization and the peaceful integration of the aristocracy into the ruling classes of capitalism, a strong strain of anticapitalist conservatism has always flourished. This message recurs in English literature from Coleridge to Dickens (see his *Hard Times*) and in Kipling (where it reappears as imperialism instead of feudalism). This strain of thought or ideology became more visible in the confusion of the early 1960s, when changes in sexual and moral values were mixed up with the decline of the Empire, as though the two were directly and causally related. The Empire and its values thus stood as a symbol and structural support for the tradition of "respectability."

Haley stood with the old, protesting the final victory of a capitalist, acquisitive ethos in Britain, even though that victory came neither so soon nor so completely as Haley imagined. Indeed, Britain's economic decline was very soon attributed precisely to the retention of values from the imperial period: specifically, to the refusal to accept money as the measure of man and morals and hence the refusal to accept the core of capitalist values. Mrs. Thatcher certainly believes that Britain's recovery depends specifically on the values so brusquely rejected by Haley.

But despite this continuing conflict, the 1950s marked an important turn toward materialism and away from the older verities of duty and empire. In focusing on this change, Haley tapped a critical question about the future of Britain. And it was partly the link between a challenge to sexual morality and the decline of Britain that accounts for the extraordinary power that infused the affair.

DECLINE AND FALL: PROFUMO AND THE LIE

But all these elements fused only when catalyzed by the lie. In this moment, Haley's defense of the feudal order meshed perfectly with Hailsham's outrage at Profumo's behavior to generate further powerful insights into British politics. This was partly because lying directly contradicted many elements of the prevailing moral code. Other aspects of these events, however, were also important.

Profumo resigned because he had lied to the House of Commons under circumstances that forbade it. While he would probably have been forced to resign for sexual misdemeanors anyway, the lie alone was enough. But the lie attracted opprobrium out of all apparent proportion, as Hailsham showed perfectly. In a BBC television interview,

> [a] count of the text shows that in one passage alone he called Mr. Profumo a liar seven times in ninety words, and the force with which he pronounced the word was such that it seemed, by some strange phonetic mutation, to be entirely composed of sibilants, so that it would not be too fanciful to say that he *hissed* it at his interlocutor and the unseen audience. . . . The final "liar," which occurred at the end of a sentence in which he was putting a very reasonable point—"A great party is not to be brought down because of a scandal by a woman of easy virtue and a proved liar"— was pronounced with such manic violence that those watching might have thought that he was about to go completely berserk.[31]

But lies are the very stuff of politics, as we know only too well. Why then was Profumo's lie so terrible?

What mattered was not the lie itself, but the rules that Profumo broke when he lied. When Macmillan defended himself in the House, he argued that Profumo's behavior made the British mode of politics impossible. If such things became common, British politics would become unmanageable.

I would ask the House to consider what alternative I had except to believe what I was told by Mr. Profumo. Here was a man who had been for a long time a Member of the House; who had a good war record; who had been appointed originally to a junior office in 1951 and had worked his way up the ladder. Why, then, should I disbelieve what he had told me? . . . The House will, therefore, realize what a terrible shock it was to me suddenly to be confronted with this dreadful admission, and all that it implied regarding his conduct towards us all.[32]

This is the crux of British politics. Unwritten rules operate not just in the constitution, but in the behavioral patterns of British politicians. Within the House of Commons, all business is conducted under the aegis of unwritten rules that control the behavior of all the parties and participants; conflict is limited by specific rules; parties are bound by the unwritten class ideologies from which they were created and to which they appeal; players must act both within the confines of their class character and also within the prevailing rules of political discourse.

There are a thousand illustrative examples available. But to understand the power and importance of unwritten rules in British politics, a closer analysis of British politics itself is necessary.

British Politics and Political Scandals

MECHANISMS OF POWER

Political power in Britain is unified, not separated on the American model. The legislative and executive powers are fused through the mechanisms of the Cabinet and of party politics: the party that controls a majority in the House of Commons forms the government. And the power to legislate is absolutely vested in Parliament, unrestrained either by the courts or a written constitution. Thus no law can be "unconstitutional."[33]

Inside Parliament, power today is predominantly held by the House of Commons (or the "House"), for although the House of Lords (the "Lords") can still modify, delay, or even introduce legislation, it cannot override the expressed will of the Commons.

One political party forms the British government because it is supported by a majority of M.P.'s in the Commons, and when a government loses that support, it is evicted from office. But support is based on the British system of very strong political parties, and rebellions by individuals or groups of M.P.s are extremely rare, which made the rebellion faced by Macmillan over the Profumo affair that much more threatening. Precisely because party control is so strong, party leaders fear their own supporters more than they do the opposition. Only his own M.P.s could bring Macmillan down.[34]

This party control is also *desirable* in the British view. In America, congressmen or senators are tightly bound to the specific needs and demands of their geographical districts, and are likely losers should these needs be forgotten. Their interests are deliberately parochial. In Britain, M.P.s represent the party and its policies to the voter, but are generally not held responsible for their ability to deliver on specific local issues. Thus while Americans have excellent representation for their local interests, British voters are offered two or three national-level alternatives.

But the benefit of less representation is more responsibility. In Britain, there is no shading of responsibility because the majority party in the House also provides the personnel for all the top jobs in the executive. The leader of the majority party becomes the prime minister. Other senior leaders in the Commons become ministers (e.g. of defense or education). This ends potential conflicts between the legislature and the executive. And as the judiciary is subordinate to Parliament, it too cannot challenge the supreme power of the party leadership. Thus policy outcomes are extremely clear: either the voters like what the *party* has done while in office, or they don't.

Responsibility is reinforced by two critical unwritten conventions of British politics. Under the doctrine of "collective Cabinet responsibility," Cabinet decisions are made collectively by the joint leadership of the majority party. All Cabinet ministers are responsible for all government decisions. This underpins government unity. And under the doctrine of "individual ministerial responsibility," ministers are also individually responsible for their departments; if a civil servant acts illegally (or just stupidly), his minister must take full responsibility for it, even including his resignation.[35] Hence the lines of responsibility extend directly from the lowest civil servant to the leaders of the majority party.

Power thus flows from the voters, through the political parties, into Parliament. Here majority leaders keep their supporters in line, giving many M.P.s jobs in the executive as ministers or their assistants. Control of the House allows both the ability to legislate (untrammeled by the courts), and the ability to execute (the power of ministers over their departments—where a professional civil service is theoretically bound to execute all policies impartially).[36]

Formal power is therefore almost unlimited. Control of Parliament apparently means the complete domination of government. But British governments are much better known for their failure to act and for their extreme caution than they are for the exercise of untrammeled executive power. Somehow, British governments are in fact restrained.

MECHANICAL/STRATEGIC CONSTRAINTS

It would be wrong to deemphasize completely all structural constraints; to begin with, governments must face electoral competition. Historically, the British electoral system has produced two large parties and some smaller ones. While one major party controls the government, the other becomes the "loyal opposition."

This is much more than a phrase. The "loyal opposition" captures both the concept of democratic competition and also the fundamental legitimacy attached to criticism in British politics. It is the function of the opposition to oppose, and hence to provide a constant constraint on the government: out of conflict comes truth. The Profumo affair demonstrates the double role of the opposition in Britain. The *loyal* opposition raised the security implications of the affair quietly, out of the public eye, seeking to defend British interests; the loyal *opposition* used the affair to attack the government, and Macmillan in particular.[37] And the opposition is trusted to determine, within the unwritten rules, which role is appropriate in any particular instance.

Voters support such opposition. Historically, voting in Britain has been strongly tied to class, and these alignments have left power balanced quite closely between the Labour and Conservative parties since World War II.[38] Governments thus face severe consequences should their popularity falter: losing parties are entirely ejected from power, because power is centralized.

Constraints also emerge from various players within the government. There is always a certain amount of infighting within the dominant party, based on a variety of ideological or even personal issues. In addition, civil servants may have their own agendas, dissimilar to the government's, and civil servants run British government because they are permanent, while ministers are lucky to last more than two years.[39]

Beyond the confines of the government itself, there are important interest groups to be placated. Both major parties have extensive connections with the interest groups that tend to support them (the trade unions for Labor and business for the Conservatives). But all interest groups must in some cases be consulted, in other cases used to implement policies, and in others simply dealt with before policies can be implemented.[40]

However, that raises some important questions, because interest groups do not have the organized access available to them in other systems. Indeed, British governments can, if they choose, effectively insulate themselves from any interest group demands. (Labour completely ignored its own trade union backers over wage policy in 1978, while even under Mrs. Thatcher, the Conservatives have sometimes rejected the claims of big business, e.g., the decision not to support the British defense industry during the Westland affair.) But British governments in general do not choose to ignore interest groups. And explanations for that are found in British political culture.

THE CONSTRAINT OF POLITICAL CULTURE

British politicians operate in a complex web of circumstances and conditions, of which only the most important can be discussed here.

To begin with, the British political elite is small and overwhelmingly concentrated in the House of Commons, where leaders steadily work their way to the top through years of service. Profumo was the youngest M.P. in the House in 1940. By 1963 he was a junior minister, not yet in the Cabinet, and he might have needed another fifteen years (and lots of luck) to become prime minister. More than twenty years in the House set the prevailing rules of politics deep in Profumo's character.

This proximity exaggerates one particular value: the British notion of fairness. Government officials are constrained in the way in which they do things, not by any defined legal notion of "due process" or by the specter of legal challenge, but by a shared vision of fairness.

Take the treatment of Profumo himself. He was given the benefit of every possible doubt. His colleagues were "fair" to the point of complete gullibility, refusing to accept the evidence that there was fire behind the smoke, and determined to accept that Profumo must be innocent until proven guilty.

Look at another example: the treatment of interest groups. Though British governments are structurally well insulated from interest groups, such groups end up with excellent access.[41] And when such access is denied, appeals can legitimately be based on a shared notion of fairness, rather than on legalistic rules.

On the other hand, the notion of "fairness" has distinct limits. Those defined as outsiders have lesser claims, as Ward's treatment shows. His sexual interests placed him outside the framework of society and he paid heavily for that. More generally, fairness works more in theory than in practice when class, gender, or racial differences are present. Britain is not only a class-ridden society, it is sexist and racist to boot. Had Profumo been from the working class, a woman, or black, the fairness extended to him and so strongly defended by Macmillan would have been conspicuously absent. But within the tight and homogeneous British political elite, fairness is an important influence on conduct.

We can take this argument a little further by resurrecting the now archaic word "honor." To connect the words "honor" and "politician" merely raises guffaws in America (with some justice). Yet honor is a word that still matters in some British circles, and it mattered more in 1963. Though ill-defined, "honor" can be recognized by the clichés that it spawned. Connoisseurs of older British movies may recognize some of them: "stiff upper lip"; "play the game"; "take one's punishment like a man"; "face the music"; "a man's word is his bond"; "it's not cricket". Aside from showing the English taste for unimaginative phraseology, these clichés capture some of the binding rules of the British political elite, rules that still held in the mid-twentieth century.

But neither fairness nor the elite itself appeared out of thin air. Aside from processes of socialization within politics, the great colleges and public schools were the wider socializing forces of the middle and upper classes—defending the moral rules that had developed during the period of imperial expansion. Hence those staple values of British nineteenth-century novels: duty and self-sacrifice, the necessity for leadership, King and Country, modesty, sexual conservatism, and a deep philistinism almost the equal of America's. It was therefore no coincidence that of the five senior ministers who interviewed him, Profumo had been in the same regiment as one, at the same college as another, and at Oxford with all five. Aspiring politicians go to Oxford as a matter of course; aside from James Callaghan, every British prime minister since Churchill has done so.

Most of the key rules defined by this culture were broken by Profumo, as he later acknowledged and for which he paid. But these values also congealed in a particularly British kind of conservatism, with a very small "c." Very pragmatic, very cautious, generally opposed to change not from philosophical but for temperamental reasons, the atmosphere of British politics becomes extremely clubby—the House of Commons is known as "the best club in London"—and for that reason very closed.

These then are some of the bases of British political culture and of the tightly closed world on which such unwritten rules must depend. But political culture does not exist simply as an artifact; above all it depends on support from the material structure of politics. While beliefs can motivate, their reproduction eventually demands some link to the structural bases of British politics—to the simple boundaries imposed by the rules of the game, the background of the participants, the nature of the electoral competition, and a multitude of other possible supporting factors. Should important material supports vanish or decline, the ideology that they support undergoes first strain and then extinction. The wider phenomenon of British political scandals allows us to examine some of these supports in greater detail.

BRITISH POLITICAL SCANDALS: SEX AND MORE SEX

The most remarkable thing about British political scandals, at least since World War II, is that they are almost exclusively about sex; and not just sex, but lurid, 3–D sex, featuring almost every gender and combination. The following list, adapted from Anthony King's path-breaking work, makes this abundantly clear:

BRITISH POLITICAL SCANDALS, 1959–1986

John Profumo, 1963. Resigned as M.P. and minister.

Reginald Maudling, John Poulson, 1972. Maudling, then home secretary, said while out of office to have accepted favors from John Poulson, a property developer. Charges denied successfully, but still resigned as minister.

Lord Jellicoe, 1973. Leader of the House of Lords. Admitted involvement with prostitutes. Resigned.

Lord Lambton, 1973. Air force minister, resigned as minister and M.P. after involvement with women and drugs.

Jeremy Thorpe, 1976. Acquitted of charges of murder conspiracy against his alleged homosexual lover. Resigned as leader of the Liberal Party, lost seat at next election.

Cecil Parkinson, 1983. Senior minister, resigned as minister after publicity surrounding his affair with his secretary.

Jeffrey Archer, 1986. Senior Conservative Party official, resigned post after apparent payment of blackmail to a prostitute.

Source: Adapted from Table 7.1 in Anthony King, "Sex, Money, and Power," in *Politics in Britain and America*, James Ceaser and Richard Hodder-Williams, ed. (Durham, N.C.: Duke University Press, 1986), pp. 180–83.

Profumo managed to compromise himself with Keeler while she entertained a Soviet officer; Lord Lambton and Lord Jellicoe had excessive (or excessively public) heterosexual predilections; Jeremy Thorpe was forced to resign the leadership of the Liberal Party after being charged with a bizarre conspiracy to murder his alleged homosexual lover; Cecil Parkinson resigned as chairman of the Conservative Party after first making his secretary pregnant and then reneging on his promise to marry her; and Jeffrey Archer resigned his position in the Conservative Party after arranging for what became an embarrassingly public pay-off to a possible prostitute. One must conclude that British politics makes for strange bedfellows.

Against this, money matters little—only the T. Dan Smith affair, which eventually involved Reginald Maudling, revolved around money. The affair primarily concerned municipal corruption in Newcastle and it was not a national scandal. And Maudling's involvement was, at worst, peripheral.[42]

This absence of money is a remarkable characteristic not shared by any other polity. Why? Some obvious possibilities can be ruled out. Surely British politicians cannot successfully conceal their financial scandals while miserably failing to manage their sex lives. Are they hopelessly oversexed? Are the British more severe than other countries on sexual misdemeanors? The evidence is against both: British uniqueness lies not in its sex scandals, which regularly occur elsewhere, but in the absence of money corruption. Only in Britain is money so divorced from politics, and this simple fact provides some powerful insights into the wider workings of British politics.

MONEY AND POLITICS

A comparison may help us explicate the links between money and politics. In the United States, money talks in many ways: through the needs of politicians;

in the supply of money from non-party sources; and in the motivations of the political players.

The Demand for Money

Why do American politicians need money, while British ones do not? The answer lies in the electoral system, where the American system places no final limits on spending: indeed, court decisions have enshrined the use of money as a First Amendment right.[43] Political Action Committees (PACs) and direct contributors alike have the right to their say, and they can have it through money as well as speech.[44]

There are now of course limits on individual campaign contributions—but in 1984 Alan Cranston and Ed Zschau nonetheless spent more than $27 million between them in California. Though such staggering sums are rare, all races are becoming increasingly expensive, as election or reelection increasingly demands access to staggering sums of money.

Why is so much money needed? Primarily, to operate the increasingly sophisticated electoral machinery necessary in any major American election. Politicians need media time and media advisers; organizations and the people to man them; political strategists and political consultants; direct mail specialists and stamps. In essence, they often need to create an organization from the ground up, and they do so primarily without the help of political parties. That is extremely expensive, even outside the big media markets, and there is also an element of competition here. A highly visible candidate still needs money to counter the organizing and media blitz of an opponent. As all American politicians have developed considerable media sophistication, they now know that however crummy they look in real life, make-up can do a lot. In other words, they don't need Ronald Reagan's media skills to be a good "media candidate." And unless they handle the media professionally, they will not win.[45]

Attention to the media is reinforced by the nature of the American electorate and by the limits of party identification. The American electorate is by European standards remarkably apolitical—and it sees politics in localized, rather businesslike ways. The electorate is also very mobile, which makes stable political organizations difficult to create today; this factor has contributed to the decline of the great city machines. Politicians must therefore go outside the parties to reach the masses, a process that demands huge sums of money.[46]

British politics is radically different. Here money and elections are almost completely divorced. From the politicians' perspective, the legal limit on campaign funding is so low that it pays only for a few posters: less than ten thousand dollars per candidate in a general election. Candidates, or their friends, are simply not allowed to spend money on their candidacies.

There is also less need to spend money. Impressive and effective party organizations know much smaller constituencies intimately. Candidates for the major parties will very quickly have in their hands a good idea as to exactly who will vote for them, down to their names and street addresses. Their main attention will go to marshaling their party organization to make sure that those inclined to vote for them will get to the polls to do so. Getting out the vote, not persuading people, is largely the extent of British electoral politics at the local level.

That is largely because people vote not for the individual candidate but for the party. Many British voters will undoubtedly go to the polls with little or no knowledge of the candidate for whom they intend to vote. It is enough that he or she represents the party of their choice—and it is the choice of party that determines the outcome of elections, not the choice of candidate. Even excellent candidates can mean an additional 1 percent of the vote in their constituencies, at best. That swings few elections.

Even if a candidate wished to publicize himself more effectively, there would be nowhere to do it. Neither radio nor television are legally permitted to take paid political advertisements. All television stations provide free time for politicians of all political parties (although the major parties get by far the lion's share), but advertising in the media is impossible for an individual candidate. Even the print media are impractical: most papers have a distinctive political cast and would either find it impossible to accept advertising from a political opponent, or else they would provide excellent coverage for their candidate or party even without money. Money therefore does not influence media coverage, and media coverage (at the local level) has little influence on the election.

Individual candidates cannot even spend money to make themselves acceptable to their own parties. The American system of primary elections is not used in Britain. Instead, candidates for a seat are selected by local party members from a list of potential candidates held by the central office of the party. Neither the central list nor local selection is open to monetary influence.[47]

Thus money has no place in British elections beyond the expenditures of the political parties—and even these are extraordinarily modest by American standards, partly because the campaigns are so short, partly because media coverage is intense and free, and partly because organizations are already in place and need not be created from scratch. Thus in 1983, British political parties needed only a total of £15 million for the campaign.[48]

The Supply of Money

Just as American politicians need increasing amounts of money, they can also perform the favors that will earn it. Frankly, from a European perspective, the sale of influence is an open scandal in America.

Politicians must curry favor with the dispensers of big bucks: the various industry lobbying associations in particular. And these associations go out of their way to find not only candidates that support their positions, but candidates uniquely qualified to affect their specific industries. Thus Congressmen sitting on committees whose legislation affects hospitals get substantial contributions from the AMA, if they vote "sensibly." If they don't, they may face an unusually well-financed opponent next time. This businesslike approach also means that PACs tend very strongly to favor incumbents—because incumbents (especially in the House of Representatives) get widely reelected, and it pays to back the winner. But this in turn makes the incumbent more powerful and hence more likely to be reelected.[49]

Lobbyists and their money are necessary because American politicians have enormous influence over legislation and the disbursement of public funds. In 1986, dramatic changes in the tax codes showed how powerful the lobbying process can be—the "transition" period opened up thousands of loopholes on behalf of specific industries or even specific firms: General Motors received tax breaks worth millions of dollars.

Now these tax breaks may be in the public interest, but they certainly link the benefits disbursed by politicians to those groups most capable of providing money. This reciprocal arrangement ensures that corruption will force its way into politics. Because the system of ethical enforcement within Congress is highly legalistic in its orientation, and because it is extremely difficult to find a legally acceptable "smoking gun" when charging corruption, full-blown scandals are unusual. But few observers of American politics would claim that influence is not, indirectly, sold by Congressmen to powerful lobbying organizations. Indictable evidence may be rare, but anecdote is all-embracing and heavily contributes to the generally low esteem of U.S. politicians.

Congressional influence is specifically based on the separation of powers, which specifies an area of dominance for the Congress insulated from the executive. The Congressional committee system then partitions that general territory into the specific preserve of particular Congressional committees. The separation of powers ensures that the oversight functions of Congress are not taken lightly. Congressional committees have enormous powers to investigate any area of government and society, publicizing their hearings and offering (or stopping) potential legislation. They can subpoena witnesses, and even provide legal immunity. And these committees are permanent, with large staffs and long-serving members. They form permanent structural links between the suppliers of hard cash and targeted politicians.

British M.P.s have much less individual influence. To begin with, the strong party system ensures that almost all of the Commons' business is conducted along party lines. And as we have seen, the penalty for stepping out of line is potentially devastating to a political career.

Rather than relishing the protection offered by a statutory separation of powers, British M.P.s are overwhelmed by the unity of powers. The House of Commons is run for and by the majority party, and M.P.s have a specific, reasonably effective, but distinctly limited ability to challenge the government, either over legislation or over its actions. Reacting to the challenge (especially during Question Time) is certainly one of the primary ways that an ambitious young politician like Profumo makes his reputation. But that ability is largely focused through the Opposition, not through individual M.P.s.

Backbench M.P.s introduce very little legislation—that is the prerogative of the government. M.P.s do not oversee the behavior of specific industries—that is the function of the government.[50] And M.P.s do not control the disbursement of government funds—that is the result of months of infighting within the government. The Budget comes to the House of Commons completely set; M.P.s do little more than provide the rubber stamp.

Thus in Britain there are neither institutional links between M.P.s and potential sources of money, nor mechanisms like powerful committees through which M.P.s can act to influence industry-oriented decisions. In essence, the supply-side of the money-influence link is broken.

MOTIVATION AND MONEY

Discussing motivations is tricky. Perhaps the British are simply less venal, less materialistic, more virtuous—or simply repressed sex maniacs with their minds on other things. None or all of these possibilities might be true.

Yet there are reasons to believe that money has less motivating power in Britain than elsewhere—especially in the social circles of most M.P.s. This rejection of money results both from the general structure of class stratification in Britain, and the specific socialization processes undergone by M.P.s.

Britain is not only an extremely class-ridden society, it is one where class does not directly relate to money—being rich in no way makes you upper class. As a consequence, it takes two or three generations to rise, as *nouveau riche* families seek to adopt the protective coloration of the life styles, education, accent, and taste accepted by the upper classes. It took Profumo's family three generations to produce a prime candidate for a Conservative seat.[51]

More to the point, in the course of building an empire, the British ruling elite very clearly adopted an aristocratic disdain for money, at least in the abstract. Though they are in practice no less venal than their counterparts elsewhere, it became "bad form" to discuss money—as a look at any classic 1920s or 1930s literature will show. Money was a problem for the lower classes. Those who discussed money were those who hadn't got it, and those who hadn't got it were clearly never part of the ruling class in the first place. Gradually, this attitude seeped down into the middle classes, and though the working classes always presented a healthy trade union skepticism to this ideological development, the middle classes were much less stubborn. It is still "bad form" to discuss one's salary in the British middle class, or indeed to discuss money in general. Bluntly, money is not the measure of success in Britain.

Thus the classes from which M.P.s are overwhelmingly drawn are those for whom money has developed the least legitimate value—a nuisance necessary for the pursuit of a civilized life, but uncivilized in itself.[52]

This is especially true for M.P.s. They may enter politics for a variety of reasons, but self-enrichment is not one of them: low salaries see to that. Because the party system is so strong, it selects candidates who fit into the mold of the party. And these molds are fundamentally ideological and social. People become M.P.s in general because they seek to push some specific set of public policies, be they conservative or radical. Or simply because they seek power. But this does not mesh with money motivation.

Thus the demand, the supply, and the motivation of money are all missing in British politics. That certainly explains why British scandals are so focused on sex, but there are other conclusions to be drawn as well.

Scandals and the Unwritten Rules of British Politics

The Profumo affair acted like other scandals as a catalyst, mutually adjusting public and private visions of appropriate morality. If the public was shocked or dismayed by the flow of revelations and rumors about the sexual proclivities of high-ranking politicians, a consequence was that high-ranking politicians were now known to have active sex lives. And in the succeeding decades, sex per se gradually faded from British politics. Thus the liberalization of public attitudes toward sex must have been encouraged by the affair, despite the torrents of sanctimony that it also generated.

But at a deeper level, the Profumo affair pointed directly to the primacy of unwritten rules in the British political system. The treatment of Profumo, of Ward, and of the government (and some of its members in particular) all reemphasized this point. Unwritten rules work however only when the community governed by them is sufficiently homogeneous—where all the players are sufficiently well socialized both to know what the rules are and to be prepared to accept them. Even Profumo, in his resignation letter to Macmillan, paid obeisance to these rules:

> I have come to realise that, by this deception, I have been guilty of a grave misde-
> meanor, and despite the fact that there is no truth whatever in the other charges,
> cannot remain a member of your Administration, nor of the House of Commons. I
> cannot tell you of my deep remorse for the embarrassment I have caused you, to my
> colleagues in the Government, to my constituents and to the party which I have
> served for the past twenty-five years.[53]

Profumo had broken no written laws and there were no criminal sanctions pending. Yet he followed the injunctions of the unwritten rules. By doing so, he showed his acceptance of the communal values that he had always supported.

Homogeneity in the British political world is reinforced by a variety of methods—but the most important is in the end the total domination of electoral politics by the party machines. And as we have seen, this in turn rests both on political culture and on the mechanisms of British politics, and in particular on the exclusion of money from politics. By excluding money, parties destroy the most significant viable lever by which independent forces can push themselves into electoral (and hence national) politics. And by ensuring that the media are also tied to the major parties, they make the world of British politics a closed one indeed.

In Britain, politics can be entered only through the political parties. And for that, the right sort of person is necessary, and the right attitude of dedication, and the right pattern of political positions, and the right period of socialization both within the party (before selection as a candidate) and after entry into the House (before selection as a member of the executive). Thus the predominance of unwritten rules is very strongly underpinned by the simple structure of British politics.

This closed circle certainly brings with it some of the traditional benefits of the British political system. British politics is known both for its ability to generate effective compromises and for its flexibility. Both are much more difficult to achieve within a more rigid set of political arrangements.

This flexibility and homogeneity should not be underestimated. Though Britain's economic failure has reduced its political prestige, and flaws in the Westminster system appeared with the 1981 riots and the miners' strike of 1984, it is not long since that system was being examined as *the* effective model of democracy. Britain's peaceful inclusion of the working class into politics and its relatively peaceful shedding of the Empire provided convincing evidence that this cosy model worked well. However, both homogeneity and the accompanying dependence on unwritten rules are now under substantial attack.

Despite the apparent successes, the older system gradually developed difficulties. Substantial segments of the population have been excluded from participation, either because of the prejudices of the dominant elites or because they did not fit into the class alignments that have dominated British political parties. Minorities and women have been particularly ill-treated (as elsewhere in British society), but their interests are not the only ones being ignored. British politics has very largely been organized around the cleavages generated by production: workers and managers. Not only has this cleavage begun to fall apart with the emergence of a dominant middle mass of white-collar workers, post-industrial cleavages have also developed that fit very poorly into the existing party structure. Who for example stands for a pro-ecology position? Or for the rights of the consumers of state services, given that the natural party of these people, the Labour Party, is dominated by the producers of those services, the public sector trade unions?

These problems, combined with the disastrous failure of the dominant parties to solve the British economic crisis, have led to some surprising and rather rapid new developments. First, the Labour Party has changed its selection rules, opening the party substantially to penetration from below. While this led initially to problems from the extreme left, in the long run Labour's change may break open the magic circle of British politics. Women, minorities, and the baby boom generation have all become substantially involved in internal Labour Party politics, and as they do so, they bring radical new perspectives to the party and to British politics generally. None of these groups have been effectively socialized as previous generations of political leaders have been—and all are eager to challenge one aspect at least of the unwritten rules: the widely shared perspectives at the top of what exactly is feasible within British politics, so far as policy decisions are concerned. Labour's increased internal democracy has also reduced the hegemony of the Parliamentary Labour Party, making the party leadership more responsive to pressure from below.

Second, the development of a new and potentially viable third party (the Social Democratic Party, the SDP) has also upset the stability of the party system, both by its own possibilities and by changing the balance of political power within each of the other parties. Thus the departure of its right wing has made Labour more radical. The advent of the SDP has made power a possibility for the Liberals, changing their self-perceptions. And the Alliance now lurks in the bushes should the Tories falter at the next election. New influences and new personnel now have an additional route into British politics.

Third, the Conservative Party itself is now undergoing one of its periodic metamorphoses. The new leaders of the party are no longer Disraelian (or pre-Disraelian) Tories, but harder, brighter, more ideological, and more middle-class. Mrs. Thatcher is the obvious example, but her chief lieutenant, Norman Tebbitt, is a better one. This is ideological Conservatism, along the lines of Reaganism or Thatcherism, not the gentler, more conservative tones of the old Tory party.

Profumo stood for the old order in many ways. His career hit every one of the notes appropriate to an old-fashioned Tory politician: country gentry, Harrow and then Oxford, with athletics but not too much academia at both. Charisma carefully developed (in due degree) by a keen interest in flying (then all the rage), and by the "grand tour," which Profumo took as a young man (after it had almost fallen out of fashion). Political posts in local politics followed immediately, based partly on the family's excellent political connections. Tory M.P. at twenty-five, followed by a "good war" (in Macmillan's telling phrase). And then the slow climb from the back benches. And of course, he accepted the cultural norms of the old Tory Party described above (breaking the rules does not mean a rejection of their legitimacy).

Profumo's kind have not dominated the Conservative Party since the eclipse of Alec Douglas-Home in 1964. Heath and then Thatcher took the party in a new direction, and in doing so broke the authority of the traditional Conservative Party elites. Today, the perfect Conservative candidate no longer looks much like Profumo. Norman Tebbitt went to no private schools, but made his way instead through academic brilliance from a lower-middle-class background to the heights of the party. And though there has been much wailing and gnashing of teeth in more traditional circles, the old Tory Party is being replaced by a more modern, and certainly more capitalist, Conservatism.

In one way, this change is part of a generational change that is transforming the structure of British elites in many areas: the generation that emerged from World War II was gradually replaced during the 1970s, and it is now under terminal attack from the baby boom generation. In that sense, Mrs. Thatcher is one of the last of the old cast, though her behavior is that of the new.

Thus, though the structural patterns yielded by the study of scandals remain, forces of change have developed along new dimensions, using alternative levers to force their way into the magic circle of politics. Whether the decline in pre-Commons socialization will be continued within the House remains to be seen. But as the composition of the parties, and the House of Commons, changes, this seems increasingly likely.

I suggested in the sections on the Profumo affair and British politics, and on British politics and political scandals, that the structural bases of the closed circle of British politics lay in the symbiosis of rigid party control and a traditionalist political culture. Recent events suggest that both of these elements are now in a state of flux, as parties are opened up from within and as the dominance of the old culture is challenged by the transformation of British society as new patterns of media engagement, work, lifestyles, and education emerge. One consequence of this change is that the longstanding British reliance on the culture to defend individual rights may indeed have to be modified in favor of a more rule-oriented approach, and the line between public and private may in the end have to be codified in law.

Perhaps all these changes mean that after 150 years of pondering the thought, Britain is beginning to adopt the Napoleonic ideal of "a career open to all the talents." But for Britain, that would be as revolutionary as an Italy without corruption or American politics without money. It is a tribute to the bankruptcy of the old order that British politics is undoubtedly the most likely of the three to change.

NOTES

1. Ward played a crucial role in the affair and consequently suffered a good deal of later analysis. A complicated man, he seemed driven by the need for recognition by the world in which he traveled, and in particular by "Society." This led him in several dangerous directions, ranging from the charges on which he was eventually convicted to an amateur interest as a player in the game of national security. He was undoubtedly a hedonist, whose tastes led him into the lower reaches of London life.

Keeler was only nineteen. Having left a poor and dull life in the provinces for the bright lights of London, she worked in a variety of nightclubs and as a model. Her inclinations too seemed geared to the new fun-loving character of "swinging London," although she never recovered from the notoriety of the affair.

2. Christine Keeler, *Sex Scandals* (London: Xanadu Publications, 1985), p. 15. Lord Lambton noted rather drily that the real security risk would have come if the two had not been sleeping together, for that would have given Profumo more time in which to divulge information.

3. Keeler, *Sex Scandals,* p. 14.

4. The full text of the letter read:

Darling,

In great haste and because I can get no reply from your phone—

Alas something's blown up tomorrow night and I can't therefore make it. I'm terribly sorry especially as I leave the next day for various trips and then a holiday so won't be able to see you again until some time in September. Blast it. Please take great care of yourself and don't run away

Love, J.

P.S. I'm writing this 'cos I know you're off for the day tomorrow and I want you to know before you go if I still can't reach you by phone.

5. The government official responsible for maintaining party discipline. In effect, Profumo's superior within the party. "The Chief Whip reassured him (about the need for resignation). If the rumors had any foundation *he had no alternative,* but if, as he claimed, they were false, then there was no reason whatsoever for his resignation." (My italics.) Clive Irving et al., *Anatomy of A Scandal* (New York: M. S. Mill and William Morrow and Company, 1963), p. 82.

6. Mandy Rice-Davies was a close friend of Keeler and Ward who eventually became fully embroiled in the scandal.

7. It is noteworthy that even with this protection, no one mentioned Profumo by name, evidence of the caution with which this whole affair was handled.

8. A personal statement is unique in the House of Commons: the M.P. (Member of Parliament) involved simply rises, makes a statement explaining his or her conduct, and no questions are allowed. In return, the member must be absolutely truthful.

9. Ward was a form of guru or father figure to Keeler and Rice-Davies. He let them stay at his flat, made contacts for them, occasionally slept with them, and used them as his entrée into the worlds of power and high society. In exchange, they paid him a few pounds toward the phone bill—and it was those pounds that convicted him of living off "immoral earnings."

10. *Hansard,* 17 June 1963.

11. Two prostitutes who "fortuitously" appeared to give evidence against Ward, neither of whom was in the slightest bit convincing.

12. Lucky Gordon's appeal took place at the same time as Ward's trial and was partly based on the same evidence from Keeler. Gordon was freed on the basis of Keeler's probable perjury—for which she was eventually imprisoned—but the judges allowed Ward's trial to proceed, based on that same testimony. See Bernard Levin, *The Pendulum Years* (London: Jonathan Cape, 1970) pp. 80–85.

13. Wayland Young, *The Profumo Affair* (Harmondsworth: Penguin Books, 1963), pp. 68–71.

14. Both Keeler and Rice-Davies were branded as prostitutes as part of the prosecution of Ward. They too suffered from the desire of the police for a conviction. *Washington Post,* 3 November 1986.

15. Jeffrey Weekes, *Sex, Politics and Society* (New York: Longmans, 1981).

16. The private boarding schools that train the British elite from seven to seventeen.

17. E. J. Hobsbawm, *The Age of Capital 1848–75* (London: Weidenfeld and Nicholson, 1975), pp. 230–31.

18. Weekes, *Sex, Politics,* p. 81.

19. Men gradually ceased to embrace physically, and tears ceased to be a manly response to stress. "Effeminate" behavior became increasingly tightly defined.

20. Weekes, *Sex, Politics,* p. 32.

21. Ibid., p. 86.

22. Ibid., p. 74. Of course, not all of the working class aspired to this ideal. Peter Gaskell for example noted that "the chastity of marriage is but little known or exercised amongst them: both husband and wife sin equally, and an habitual indifference to sexual vice is generated. . . ." (Ibid., p. 58). However, one could also argue that this contradictory tradition largely died out during the twentieth century under the impact of middle-class ideological dominance.

23. Interestingly, British socialists have always had a very hard time with the question of sexual values. There is a distinctive strain of Puritanism within the British socialist movement, perhaps stemming partly from its nonconformist background (cf. the links usually made between the development of British socialism and its roots in the Methodism of John Wesley). In this respect the British socialists fell far behind their German counterparts, where Kautsky, Bernstein, and their followers had all adopted notably progressive views on sexual morality before World War I.

24. In Britain, the Church of England is the official state religion, and the queen is the official head of the church. Thus church and state are combined in her person. Ronald Blythe, *The Age of Illusion: Britain in the Twenties and Thirties,* (London: Hamish Hamilton, 1963), chap. 2.

25. Weekes, *Sex, Politics,* p. 214.

26. Vassall was a clerk in the Admiralty caught spying for the Russians. He was on good terms with his superior, Lord Galbraith, and this was sufficient for the press to start an enormous witch-hunt against Galbraith. In the end, Macmillan accepted Galbraith's resignation and set up an inquiry (the Vassall Tribunal), which concluded that Galbraith was completely innocent. Macmillan was damaged by his own cowardice in sacrificing an innocent man to the wolves, and the press lost a great deal of credibility. Understandably, they were eager not to make the same mistake with Profumo only a couple of months later.

27. A classic element of official defensiveness can be found in the act itself. The act must be signed by all people accepting government employment, and it remains binding even after they leave. But it is also classified under the Official Secrets Act, which means that it cannot be revealed to the potential signatory until after he has signed the act. Hence one must sign the act *before* reading it.

28. Quoted in Young, *Profumo Affair,* pp. 37–38.

29. Irving, *Anatomy,* p. 90.

30. Young, *Profumo Affair,* p. 98.

31. Levin, *Pendulum Years,* pp. 63–64.

32. *Hansard,* 17 June 1963.

33. Phillip Norton, *The British Polity* (London: Longmans, 1986). This book provides an excellent introduction to the analysis of British politics.

34. Phillip Norton, *The Commons in Transition* (Oxford: Martin Robertson, 1981).

35. Hence the resignations of Lord Carrington (foreign secretary) and John Nott (minister of defense) during the Falklands War, on the grounds that their departments were unprepared for the conflict. Both ended major political careers in British politics by resigning.

36. R. H. S. Crossman, "Introduction" to Walter Bagehot, *The English Constitution* (Harmondsworth: Penguin Books, 1967).

37. See Phillip Norton, *The British Polity* for a general description of British constitutional practices.

38. See David Butler and Donald Stokes, *Political Change in Britain* (New York: St. Martin's Press, 1976).

39. See R. H. S. Crossman, *The Diaries of a Cabinet Minister,* 3 vols. (New York: Holt, Rhinehart and Winston, 1978), for numerous comments on civil service–politician relations.

40. See Michael Moran, *The Politics of Industrial Relations* (London: Macmillan, 1977) for a case study of government–interest group relations in a critical circumstance.

41. See Harry Eckstein, *Interest Group Politics* (Stanford: Stanford University Press, 1960) for the classic study of British interest groups, a case study of the British Medical Association.

42. The T. Dan Smith affair implicated several municipal officials in Newcastle in a kickback scheme in which Smith paid for being assigned public sector building contracts in the late 1960s and early 1970s.

43. In *Buckley vs. Valec,* the Supreme Court upheld the right of any candidate to spend as much of his own money on an election as he or she liked. The decision was directly based on the First Amendment.

44. Recent reforms have made limits on expenditures a prerequisite for candidates accepting public funds for elections. But they are still at liberty to refuse the funds and spend what they like.

45. Gary C. Jacobson, *The Politics of Congressional Elections* (Boston: Little, Brown and Co., 1983), chaps. 4–5.

46. Ibid. pp. 102–5.

47. See Jeffrey Archer, *First Among Equals* (New York: Bantam Books, 1985) for a fictionalized but accurate view of candidate selection, and indeed for a wider picture of life in the British political elite.

48. David Butler and Dennis Kavanaugh, *The British General Election in 1983* (New York: St. Martin's Press, 1984).

49. David R. Mayhew, *Congress: The Electoral Connection* (New Haven: Yale University Press, 1974) pp. 53–54.

50. The current Conservative government has expanded experiments with permanent oversight committees directed at specific government departments, and these committees now have more power than previously, including staff of their own and the power to compel testimony. As yet, however, one cannot conclude that there has been any major switch in the balance of power against the government because of these developments.

51. Irving, *Anatomy,* pp. 14–15.

52. *Times Guide to the House of Commons* (London: Times Books, 1983).

53. Quoted in Irving, *Anatomy,* p. 138.

PART

II •

THE CONTINENTAL
EXPERIENCE

While liberal democracy has dominated Anglo-American politics, it has failed to establish a similar governmental hegemony on the European continent. Liberal democracy has been forcefully challenged by both the Left and the Right. Historically, the Right has been particularly successful in establishing governmental authority at the expense of liberal democracy's concern with limited state power. Hence, the historical experiences of the four countries that follow are in marked contrast to those of the Anglo-American section. Although France, Italy, West Germany, and Austria have been successfully governed by liberal democracies since 1945, their earlier traditions still contribute to a somewhat more skeptical acceptance of due process and to a more tolerant view of state power.

4 • The Greenpeace Affair and the Peculiarities of French Politics

STEPHEN E. BORNSTEIN

Late on the evening of 10 July 1985, two explosions a few minutes apart ripped open the hull of a medium-sized trawler moored in the harbor of Auckland, New Zealand, sinking the vessel and killing one member of the crew. The boat was the *Rainbow Warrior*, flagship of the Greenpeace organization, a highly respected international association of ecologists and pacifists who, since the early 1970s, have been in the forefront of efforts to protect endangered species of wildlife such as the whale and to promote nuclear disarmament. The vessel had been on its way to Mururoa Atoll, a French colonial dependency in the South Pacific, to lead a protest against underground nuclear tests scheduled for mid-October. The dead man was Fernando Pereira, a freelance photographer covering the voyage for Greenpeace. Six days after the attack, two French secret agents, masquerading as Swiss tourists named Turenge, were arrested on suspicion of involvement in the bombing. They vehemently proclaimed their innocence, as did the French government once their real nationality had been revealed.

At the present writing, the more politically sensitive aspects of the attack still remain shrouded in a haze of official secrecy. There has not yet been any serious scholarly study of the events, nor is it likely that there will be one soon, since only a tiny number of very highly placed politicians and state officials know the whole truth and they are not very likely to wish to reveal it. Still, by carefully weighing press accounts against what we know about the workings of the French state, the past performances of the various actors involved, and the history of previous scandals in French political life, we can piece together a fairly reliable outline of what happened. Nonetheless, the reader must always keep in mind the fact that, particularly where questions of "who knew what and

91

when" are concerned, it is not really possible to move beyond the level of informed speculation.[1]

It is now entirely certain that the bombing had indeed been carried out by French military frogmen acting as part of a full-scale, covert military operation involving over twenty French agents, sophisticated electronic and aquatic equipment, explosives transported by boat from a French military base, and the participation of some of the top figures in France's intelligence agency, the DGSE.[2] There was nothing accidental or haphazard about the sabotage: it had apparently been four months in the planning and had been intended to sink the ship (though without hurting the crew who, it was assumed, would evacuate the vessel after the first relatively small explosion). Nor was it the handiwork of some sort of runaway faction within French intelligence, operating on its own or in collusion with military or political circles beyond the control of the Mitterrand government. The attack, we can now say with some certainty, had been authorized by the very highest echelons of France's military and civilian authorities: planning for the offensive had involved the defense minister, Charles Hernu, the director of the DGSE, Admiral Pierre Lacoste, and President Mitterrand's personal military attaché, General Jean Saulnier. It is likely that the president himself knew about and approved the operation, at least in general terms, from the very beginning.[3]

For about three weeks, very little was heard in France about the attack or the arrest of the "Turenges." The French press did not make very much of the incident, and the government did little more in public than continue to deny any responsibility, while dropping hints that the secret services of some other government were probably to blame. On the night of 8 August, however, the affair suddenly heated up and boiled over. As two French weekly magazines prepared to go to press with evidence that the "Turenges" were not merely French citizens but agents of the DGSE, François Mitterrand and Prime Minister Laurent Fabius exchanged public letters. Those who read the following day's newspapers would learn from this peculiar correspondence that there was indeed a "*Rainbow Warrior* affair," that the two people arrested were "suspected" of being French agents, and that the French government was going to ask an "unimpeachable figure" to conduct a "rigorous" investigation, leading to criminal charges and severe punishments should any French official be found to have been involved.[4] This exchange of letters and the press revelations of the following day marked the beginning of a scandal that would take President Mitterrand and his government two months to live down, and which at various points looked as if it might threaten their very political survival.

The "figure" chosen by Fabius to conduct the investigation was a veteran Gaullist public official, Bernard Tricot. His credentials were impeccable and he managed to interview all of the principals involved in the case, including Hernu, Lacoste, Saulnier, and many of the DGSE agents just back from New Zealand. The problem was that almost everybody lied to him, presenting a united front on behalf of Hernu's official version of the events: the DGSE's activities had involved only two "teams"—the Turenges, and another group of four men on a chartered sailboat named the *Ouvéa* who had just managed to evade the New Zealand police; their missions, undertaken completely independently of each other, had been confined to mere surveillance of the *Rainbow Warrior;* the sabotage was not the work of French agents but was probably done by a foreign intelligence service (the Soviets? the British?) to embarrass France and undermine its independent nuclear program.

On 25 August, Tricot issued his report, announcing his "certainty" that the French government had not ordered the attack and that "in the present state of [his] information," neither the "Turenges" nor the crew of the *Ouvéa* had been responsible for it. For the government, the report was a major disappointment. At the surface level, its total exculpation of the DGSE was too good to be true, or credible. At the same time, between the lines, Tricot had provided a number of "time bombs" that might very well blow the government up later on. He had made it clear that the financing of the very expensive "surveillance" operation had been specifically approved by General Saulnier and by the prime minister's staff: if it were ever to be established that the DGSE had done more than simply shadow the *Rainbow Warrior*, Fabius, Hernu, and perhaps even Mitterrand, would have a lot of explaining to do. Similarly, he had insisted that the DGSE officers he had interviewed were not the sort to undertake a major mission without official authorization: once again, if new evidence of DGSE complicity in the sabotage were found, Lacoste and Hernu (at the very least) would be in trouble. Moreover, at several places in his report and repeatedly in interviews upon its release, Tricot hedged his bets by allowing for the possibility that he had not been told the truth. In the report, he noted that he could "not exclude the hypothesis" that the DGSE officers "had got together to conceal from me a part of the truth." Speaking to the press, he repeated this point even more bluntly: "I do not exclude," he told a television interviewer," the possibility that I have been deceived."[5]

Rather than putting out the fire, Tricot's efforts caused the "affair" to burn even more brightly. The press, both in France and abroad, was highly skeptical of his conclusions.[6] New Zealand's Prime Minister, David Lange, branded it as "unbelievable"; and even Laurent Fabius found himself unable to endorse it explicitly, saying only that "at that stage" he did not possess any evidence that would allow him to contradict its author's "conviction."[7] What made the government's position especially difficult was that, while Tricot had been preparing his report, the press had been filled, day after day, with increasingly juicy stories, all of which pointed toward the guilt of the DGSE and the involvement of highly placed French officials. The real names of the "Turenges" had been revealed, and "Alain Turenge" had been identified as Alain Mafart, an expert frogman, formerly second-in-command of the DGSE's underwater combat base in Aspretto, Corsica; evidence had been provided that the "Turenges" and the crew of the *Ouvéa* had been in regular contact in the weeks prior to the attack; it was revealed that a DGSE "mole" had spent several months on board the *Rainbow Warrior* and had left shortly before the attack; a very high-ranking DGSE officer was revealed to have been present in New Zealand, under various pseudonyms, throughout the operation and was suspected of having directed it; the defense minister was accused of having been the originator of the scheme and President Mitterrand's principal adviser, Jean-Louis Bianco, was claimed to have participated actively in its planning.[8]

Once, however, the French press had digested the Tricot report and demonstrated its obvious inadequacies, it lapsed into a brief period of relative calm, punctuated by a few revelations about the details of the Auckland caper and the occasional special feature on the DGSE, on past French scandals, and on the "Turenges" in their New Zealand prison cells awaiting their trial for murder. So long as this lull continued, the French government could perhaps breathe a bit more easily. True, there were some problems. The New Zealand government continued its vociferous attacks, demanding official apologies and reparations, and even going so far as to having the New Zealand Labour Party propose that the French Socialists be expelled from the Socialist International. And DGSE officials, unhappy about their two colleagues being in a foreign jail and fearful that the government would take the easy way out and let them shoulder the entire blame, were clearly playing a game of their own that included providing a steady flow of damaging leaks to the press. Still, Charles Hernu had dodged the bullet and could continue to proclaim his innocence, while the prime minister and the president could begin to hope that the worst was over. Although hardly anyone really took the official version of the story seriously, in the absence of any more hard evidence no heads would have to roll and the scandal might just fade away. By 16 September, Mitterrand had regained enough of his composure to be able to write an aggressive letter to David Lange, complaining that France's reputation was being unjustly defamed and declaring that "it would be good if the accumulated complaints and the unfounded accusations of which France is the object were to be avoided."[9]

The very next day, however, the scandal was back on page one and the government found itself facing its most serious challenge yet. In an unprecedented four-column-wide front-page story, Le Monde put its unmatched reputation behind the accusation that a hitherto unmentioned "third team" of French DGSE frogmen had planted the mines on the Rainbow Warrior, using explosives brought from France by the crew of the Ouvéa and acting with the logistical assistance of the "Turenges."[10] The sabotage, according to the paper's very highly placed sources, had been authorized explicitly and planned by Charles Hernu, Admiral Lacoste, General Saulnier, and General Jeannou Lacaze, chief of staff of the French armed forces. The president, however, had not, according to Le Monde, been involved nor informed.

This revelation, backed up three days later by the weekly magazine L'Express and amplified by the rest of the press and the opposition parties, sent massive shock waves through the French political system. For about two weeks, the government appeared to be on the ropes. In the eyes of Prime Minister Fabius and a number of his allies in the cabinet, the only way to save the government and the president was to sacrifice Hernu, who would have to admit his role in the affair and resign. Neither Hernu nor the president agreed at this point, however, and the Le Monde bombshell was apparently followed by several days of vicious internal struggles before Fabius could get his way. With Mitterrand's encouragement, Hernu persisted in protesting his total innocence, in categorically denying the existence of any "third team," and in accusing the press of organizing a "campaign of rumors and insinuations" against the French armed forces.[11] Following a Cabinet meeting on Wednesday, 18 September, at which Mitterrand announced to his subordinates and to the public his intention to find out exactly what had happened ("I want to know!"), Hernu called a press conference and admitted for the first time having authorized a "surveillance" mission by the Turenges and the Ouvéa. He insisted, however, that nothing more than surveillance had been involved. The sabotage, he suggested, had been carried out by mysterious "malicious" forces on whom he was "trying to shed light." Those who persisted in accusing French intelligence and the country's defense establishment were endangering the national interest. "I am speaking to all of you," Hernu warned the assembled journalists; "let no one fall into the trap of undermining our nuclear deterrent."[12]

However, in the face of overwhelming and mounting evidence of both a government-sponsored sabotage and a vast cover-up effort, and given the determination of the prime minister, President Mitterrand could not hold on to his minister of defense. When Admiral Lacoste refused to reply in writing to a series of pointed questions put to him by Fabius concerning the attack, the latter demanded (for the fourth time), and this time secured from the president the dismissal of Hernu, whose resignation, along with that of DGSE Director Lacoste, was announced on the afternoon of Friday, 20 September. The government was not yet out of the woods, however. For the press and the opposition had already begun to train their guns on Fabius and even on the president himself. A true "regime crisis" seemed possible at this point. For *L'Express*, what was involved was a "major crisis," which could only be stopped by putting the blame on "one of the key figures" of the government.[13]

Very soon, however, Fabius had managed to bring the fire under control, although he himself got singed in the operation. One short week after proclaiming the existence of a "crisis at the top." *L'Express* found itself complaining about the "silence" that had broken out in the political arena and was forced to admit that the "affair seem[ed] locked away."[14] In two dramatic television appearances, one late on the evening of Sunday, 22 September and the other three days later, Fabius had presented to the French people a version of the affair that made more sense than before, fixing the blame on Hernu and Lacoste and not mentioning the president. Fabius's speeches did not in themselves put an end to the controversy, but by the following Monday the scandal had begun to recede from the front pages and very soon thereafter it had become yesterday's news. So rapidly did the French lose interest in this issue that when, two weeks later, Greenpeace's substitute flagship developed a suspicious power failure just as it was about to confront the French navy off Mururoa, the rest of the French press and the opposition failed to pay much attention to a story in the *Canard enchaîné* blaming the DGSE.[15]

The only aspect of the affair that appeared to concern the French press and public opinion any longer was the fate of the "Turenges," Alain Mafart and Dominique Prieur. At their trial on 4 November, the two DGSE agents pleaded guilty to charges reduced from "murder" to "manslaughter" and were sentenced to ten years in prison, a verdict which elicited a wave of indignant protests from French political figures and the media. Mafart and Prieur ultimately got off with a much lighter punishment. After lengthy negotiations, the governments of France and New Zealand reached an agreement, announced on 7 July 1986, whereby the two prisoners were transferred to a French military base in the South Pacific, where they were supposed to remain confined for three years. In return, New Zealand received $7 million in compensation, an official apology from the new prime minister, Jacques Chirac, plus (unofficially) a commitment that France would withdraw its veto against the upcoming renewal of New Zealand's trade agreement with the European Economic Community.[16]

The final episode of the affair came late in the summer of 1986. In July, both *Le Monde* and *Le Figaro*, reflecting on the scandal after the conclusion of the deal with New Zealand and around the anniversary of the sabotage, raised the ultimate question of "who had known what." Both articles pointed suspicious fingers at the president but without causing much of a stir.[17] Then, at the end of August, *L'Express* ran a cover story with the title, "Greenpeace: Mitterrand Knew." The article by Jacques Derogy and Jean-Marie Pontaut and their book that came out very shortly thereafter presented a carefully documented version of the events that argued quite convincingly that Mitterrand as well as Saulnier, Hernu, and Lacoste, had been involved in the sabotage from the start. Despite the explosive character of this revelation, the article and the book failed to produce more than a brief flurry of journalistic interest. Like photographer Fernando Pereira, the "Greenpeace affair" was dead and buried. Less than two years later, Mitterrand could insist, during a major television interview, that "Greenpeace" was "not a scandal" without having his comment generate any outraged replies in the following days' press.

To the comparative political scientist, the Greenpeace affair is an intellectual goldmine. If we look carefully at the way the scandal unfolded, we can unearth a number of intriguing puzzles. And in seeking to make sense of these, we will discover some important and distinctive features of French political institutions, processes, and culture. The rest of this essay will attempt to examine the Greenpeace scandal in this manner. First, I shall point out four aspects of the affair that appear worthy of comparative analysis. Then I shall attempt to make sense out of each of these puzzles in turn. The explanations I shall offer will often focus, inevitably, on specific features of this case as well as on the personalities and backgrounds of the principal actors. Whenever possible, however, I shall try to emphasize the contribution of factors that may be regarded as constitutive features of modern French political life and which are, as such, worthy of attention by students of comparative politics.

The first surprising feature of the events just described is the fact that they took place at all. At first sight, it appears incredible that a country like France should have devoted such enormous resources and used such dubious methods in order to counteract the efforts of such a small group of peaceful ecologists. Why, to quote one bemused commentator, did otherwise so sensible a political elite allow itself to be "frightened by a handful of defenders-of-whales in the South Pacific?"[18] Perhaps even more puzzling is the fact that the attack was planned and carried out under the auspices of a government led by the French Socialist Party, one of the most ideologically orthodox European members of the Socialist International, and a party whose undertakings since coming to power in the spring of 1981 had included not only a radical program of industrial nationalizations and social welfare reforms but also a vociferous advocacy of human rights both at home and abroad. Why, we must ask, did the French Socialist government feel that it ought to sabotage the vessel of a widely respected ecology organization?

The second puzzle is the cover-up. Once the "Turenges" had been apprehended, the French government found itself confronting a difficult choice. It could deny France's involvement in the matter in the hope that the truth would not emerge and that the two agents would not be convicted for anything more serious than carrying false passports. If it chose this strategy, however, it would be compelled by the niceties of international legal conventions to cooperate with Interpol and the New Zealand police and thus face the risk that some very embarrassing facts might be uncovered. The alternative was to admit, at least to the New Zealand authorities, that France was indeed responsible, to compensate the victim's family, and to begin private negotiations with Auckland for the release of the agents who could be said, according to the familiar phrase, to have merely been "obeying orders." That President Mitterrand and

Defense Minister Hernu, knowing what they knew, chose the first option is something that requires explanation. So, too, does their optimism that they could orchestrate an effective cover-up both in France and in New Zealand that would prevent the public from learning at least some of the truth. We also need to explain their belief that, even should the true story come out, they could avoid paying any exorbitant political price for their part in it. French leaders were certainly aware of what had happened to Richard Nixon when his carefully woven cover-up had come unraveled: why did they believe themselves immune from such a fate?

A third set of questions concerns the behavior during the affair of some of the principal participants. The behavior of President François Mitterrand is very difficult to understand. He appears to have sent his principal associates off in two opposing directions at one and the same time: Hernu and Saulnier were urged to pursue the cover-up, while Fabius and Joxe were encouraged to undertake a thorough and public investigation. In addition, long after it had become clear that the only safe way out of the crisis was to make Hernu shoulder the blame, Mitterrand refused to let go of his Defense Minister. How can we make sense out of this apparently contradictory and potentially self-destructive set of choices?

The actions of the prime minister appear no less confusing and confused. In the early moments of the affair, he condemned the attack in highly moralistic terms and promised that the culprits, should they be French, would be severely punished. Yet, when appointing an independent investigator to examine the affair, he chose a figure whose experience in the world of intelligence and defense and whose known commitment to the French state and to its *raison d'état* made it highly likely that he would conceal any seriously compromising evidence or at least that he would be widely suspected of having done so. After Tricot's report failed to end the crisis, Fabius—despite mounting evidence that the attack and the cover-up had involved some of his closest political associates and that his own aides had signed the forms authorizing the funds for the mission—continued to press for a rigorous investigation and for the punishment of those found to be responsible.

The behavior of the opposition parties also appears puzzling. Given the political points that could have been scored using the progressive revelations of the press, it is surprising to see how reluctant the main opposition parties, the RPR and the UDF, were to pick up the Greenpeace ball and run with it.[19] With a critical legislative election only half a year away, one might have expected the parties of the Right to seize upon the affair gleefully and to exploit to the full its potential for embarrassing the government and for casting doubt on the capacity of the Left to protect the national interest. In fact, the opposition parties were remarkably cautious in their approach to the scandal. As various journalists pointed out at the time, the principal leaders of all the major opposition parties and factions ("the tenors") were either silent or very moderate in their attacks, leaving the dirty work to minor figures. Calls for the resignation of the prime minister or even of the defense minister were quite rare until late into the affair, and criticisms of the president were few and far between. Very little pressure was exerted on the government to establish a parliamentary commission of inquiry: indeed, as soon as the prime minister himself proposed to create one, most of the opposition spokesmen decided it would be a bad idea and declined to sit on it.[20] Even the normally outrageous leader of the extreme right-wing Front National, Jean-Marie Le Pen, had very little to say about the scandal. Of the principal parties, only the increasingly marginal Communists attacked the government all-out. Moreover, during the parliamentary election campaign only a few months later, very little mention was made of the affair by any party.

A fourth puzzle, perhaps the most interesting of all, concerns the relatively limited dimensions assumed by the scandal. Given the seriousness of the acts that were committed and of the cover-up that ensued, it is (at least to this observer) astonishing how small a space the affair managed to occupy in the political life and the public consciousness of the French. Stories about Greenpeace occupied the front pages of the principal French newspapers consistently for only quite a short period—from the second week in August through the first week in October. Though Prime Minister Fabius's two television appearances on 22 and 25 September manifestly failed to satisfy the press or the opposition, or even to impress his own political allies, and even though the version of the story that he presented was obviously incomplete and problematical, within a week he had somehow managed to save his government and the president from a serious political crisis and to get the scandal off the public mind. How was such a remarkable turnabout possible?[21]

Even at the height of the scandal, moreover, French public opinion does not seem to have taken the affair very seriously. A poll published on 3 September indicated that only 30 percent of those interviewed claimed to have been following the story with a "strong or a fairly strong interest," while 62 percent admitted to a "very weak or a fairly weak interest." A remarkable 40 percent had "no opinion" on the question of who had committed the sabotage.[22] The French public seemed surprisingly unperturbed by use of the power of the French state to violate the rights of foreign citizens and the laws of a friendly nation or by the gross flouting of democratic procedural norms involved in the cover-up.

If the impact of the scandal is measured, furthermore, in terms of its consequences for the individuals involved and for the course of French politics, that impact also appears astonishingly limited. Very few careers were destroyed by the scandal. Admiral Lacoste lost his job at the head of the DGSE but soon found himself awarded a new position by the conservative government elected in March 1986. General Saulnier was quickly promoted to the top position in the French armed forces. Even Charles Hernu, who lost his cabinet post, found himself elevated to the status of a national hero, who was triumphantly re-elected to the National Assembly the following March and was even temporarily transformed in the eyes of his fellow Socialist politicians into a potential candidate for the presidential elections in 1988. Despite the revelations by Derogy and Pontaut, President Mitterrand escaped unscathed from what had looked as if it might become the worst crisis of his long and colorful career. Nor were any of the various military and civilian officials who had lied to Bernard Tricot as part of what was obviously a systematic and coordinated cover-up ever accused of any crime, fired, demoted, or even officially reprimanded in any way.[23] The only victims of the scandal, aside from the murdered photographer, were five military officers who were charged with leaking state secrets to the press; they were not convicted, but their careers were not likely to benefit from their adventure in whistle-blowing. Laurent Fabius, despite having played what appears to be either no role at all or a relatively small one at most in creating the problem, and an important role in having disposed of it, saw his popularity drop in the polls and his rapid rise from Mitterrand's protégé to prime minister to future presidential candidate temporarily slowed, though not at all permanently arrested.

At the level not of persons but of political forces, too, the scandal appears to have left few traces. Its impact on the elections of March 1986 seems to have been minimal. Above all, the predictions by various politicians and pundits during the height of the scandal that Mitterrand's involvement would reinforce the chances for a political crisis in March 1986 by making impossible any power-sharing arrangement between him and a conservative legislature and cabinet proved to be unwarranted.[24] The extremely limited impact of the scandal on French public opinion, on the fortunes of the major participants, and on the balance of political influence in the country at large invites us, I think, to undertake an effort of comparative political explanation, as do the three other puzzles that I have set out.

The first enigma we must resolve, then, is why the French government under the leadership of Socialist François Mitterrand felt it necessary, feasible, and politically justifiable to undertake such a dubious mission against the *Rainbow Warrior*. The hostility of French governments of the Right toward Greenpeace makes a certain amount of sense. For them, the highly publicized escapades of Greenpeace around Mururoa were not just an embarrassment; they were a profound threat. Greenpeace was not just a group of misguided if well-intentioned ecologists according to them; French conservatives were convinced that the organization was riddled with Soviet agents and that its efforts were designed to further the interests of France's enemies.[25]

By undermining French nuclear testing in the South Pacific, Greenpeace was not simply embarrassing France, it was attacking one of the central pillars of French defense policy and geopolitical strategy as they had been developed by General de Gaulle beginning in the early 1960s and pursued by each of his successors through 1981. The overriding foreign policy objective of de Gaulle and his conservative successors was to restore to France some of the prestige and some of the influence within the international system that it had possessed prior to its defeat by the Germans in 1940 and prior to the subsequent domination of the world by the two superpowers. Crucial to this effort was the development of a French nuclear deterrent (achieved between 1960 and 1964) and its liberation from any dependence on the United States or the Atlantic alliance (accomplished when de Gaulle withdrew France from the military wing of the North Atlantic Treaty Organization in 1966). With its own nuclear deterrent, completely independent of the United States and NATO, France could hope to play a role in world politics that its limited size and resources would not otherwise permit. Without the *force de frappe,* France was little more than a secondary power with a proud history, an impressive culture, and unrealistic ambitions.[26]

French activities at Mururoa were seen as an absolutely crucial component of this grand design. In order to keep its nuclear deterrent militarily credible, French strategists insisted on the need for constant modernization and testing. And the only place that such testing could be carried out without massive domestic political costs was in France's possessions in the South Pacific. Unlike the United States or the Soviet Union, France was a comparatively small and densely populated country lacking large, isolated, uninhabited spaces that could be used for experimental nuclear explosions. The Sahara Desert areas of France's North African colonies had been ideal test sites, but by the early 1960s France had found itself compelled to grant Tunisia, Morocco, and finally Algeria their independence and had lost its access to these regions.

That the conservative governments of Georges Pompidou or Valéry Giscard d'Estaing had regarded Greenpeace as a dangerous enemy is thus not all that hard to understand. That they had seen fit to undertake a variety of overt and covert actions against the organization over the years is also not that surprising, given the low priority assigned by these governments to civil liberties and to the norms of democratic process in both domestic and international affairs. Thus, since 1972, when Greenpeace began its efforts to obstruct French nuclear tests at Mururoa Atoll, the French military had repeatedly seized Greenpeace vessels and arrested their crews as they attempted to enter French territorial waters. Greenpeace vessels had also been victims of serious acts of sabotage—a fire, lost propellers, jammed engines, mysterious epidemics among the crew—for which the French were always the prime suspects, although no French agent was ever caught in the act.[27]

What is more difficult to understand is that the Socialist government of François Mitterrand would continue this pattern of behavior. The key to the puzzle is the quite recent conversion of the parties of the French Left from opponents of nuclear weapons into their ardent advocates. Traditionally, the Socialists and the Communists had been voluble critics of France's independent nuclear force. Indeed, the Common Program of Government that the two parties signed in 1972 as the centerpiece of their new electoral alliance—the Union of the Left—had specifically pledged that a government of the Left would eliminate the *force de frappe* and rely entirely on conventional weapons.

In 1977, however, as they prepared themselves for what was widely (but mistakenly) expected to be a major electoral victory the following March, first the Communist Party and then the Socialists did abrupt turnabouts and declared their support for France's nuclear defense. These sudden conversions were the results of complex processes with multiple causes.[28] Clearly, one important factor was a realistic, if not cynical, judgment by the leaders of both parties concerning the conditions for effective government by the Left in a country affiliated to the western bloc in a bipolar international system. One way to increase the freedom of maneuver of a future Left government was to sacrifice some of its autonomy in foreign policy in order to maximize the scope for radical economic and social reforms on the domestic front. By watering down those aspects of their foreign and defense policies that most alarmed American policymakers and French military circles, the Left might hope to reduce obstructionism where its domestic reform plans were concerned. Whatever the explanation for the shift, from this point on, France was unique among Western European nations not only in possessing the only truly autonomous national nuclear force but also in having the only major left-wing parties that were pro-nuclear.

Thus, when the Left finally did come to power in the spring of 1981, it did so as aggressive supporters of nuclear weapons, of French testing in the South Pacific, and of the right of France to prevent outsiders from interfering in such crucial activities. Although some deputies and activists within the Socialist Party in particular remained at best lukewarm in their support of the general national consensus on matters of defense, the leaders of the new government, and especially the president himself and his defense minister, Charles Hernu, had few doubts about this policy.[29] Indeed, their support for French nuclear testing and their willingness to use force if necessary to defend what President Mitterrand referred to as "France's rights in the Pacific" were perhaps even stronger than would have been the case with a government of the Right.[30] As the Socialists prepared to assume control of the government in the spring of 1981, they were still understandably nervous about the extent to which they could count on the cooperation, or at least the acquiescence, of important sectors of the state apparatus, and in particular of the police, the army, and the intelligence services. During almost twenty-five years of conservative hegemony, these agencies had become bastions of the Right, often indeed of the extreme Right, whose hostility to the Socialists could—in the highly charged ideological atmosphere of French political life—cause serious problems. In this atmosphere of mistrust, Mitterrand and his associates appear to have felt the need to reassure the army and the police of their loyalty to the basic contours of existing French foreign and defense policy. The appointment as defense minister of Charles Hernu, the most pro-nuclear and pro-military of Socialist leaders, was widely seen as a careful gesture by the Socialists in the direction of the armed forces.[31] And when, as appears to have happened in early 1985, the commander of the army's Directorate of Nuclear Test Centers in the South Pacific, Admiral Fages, began pushing for some dramatic action against Greenpeace's upcoming campaign at Mururoa, Hernu and Mitterrand were eager to cooperate fully, although their conservative predecessors appear, on several occasions, to have rejected such proposals in favor of more conventional tactics.[32] Indeed, it appears that Hernu had surprised even his military associates by his insistence on a full-scale attack against the *Rainbow Warrior* and his refusal to take no as an answer from a reluctant DGSE leadership.[33] In the extremely polarized atmosphere of the French political arena, then, the Socialists—recent converts to the dogmas of nuclear deterrence and testing—were willing to put their military credibility and the substance of their domestic reform program ahead of their commitment to the procedural norms of liberal democracy.

Just as surprising as the Socialists' sponsorship of the sabotage was the way in which the attack was carried out. Why did Hernu and Saulnier choose to attack the *Rainbow Warrior* rather than simply continuing the standard French practice of seizing the Greenpeace vessels as they entered French waters off Mururoa? Similarly, once they had opted for "neutralizing" the *Rainbow Warrior,* why did they order a bombing with all the risks that entailed rather than the more subtle forms of sabotage that French intelligence agents had previously used? The answer to the first question is apparently to be found partly in the (totally misguided) fears of French naval experts that the *Rainbow Warrior* was too heavy for French tugs to handle and in their apprehension that France would be made to look ridiculous in the eyes of world opinion if it could not stop the invading vessel.[34] Such a failure would be especially unfortunate because French leaders, both military and civilian, expected the Greenpeace flotilla to include a number of nationalist protesters from disputed French possessions in the area, especially from New Caledonia where a strong independence movement had recently emerged. Another important factor was electoral. Socialist leaders must have been reluctant to engage in highly publicized naval maneuvers against unarmed ecologists just seven months before decisive, and potentially very close, legislative elections. Not only might many of their own traditional supporters not be likely to appreciate such a spectacle, but it might outrage the 2 to 3 percent of the electorate who supported the various ecology parties and who might severely damage the Socialists' chances if they abstained or voted for the Right on the second of the two ballots in France's complicated electoral system.

The decision to sink the *Rainbow Warrior* rather than merely to disable it is more difficult to explain. Several versions of the affair report that the form taken by the sabotage resulted from the insistence of Defense Minister Hernu that the ship not be simply temporarily disabled but put permanently out of commission. What appears to have been at work here was a profound animus that Hernu and other Socialist policymakers felt toward the Greenpeace organization. Like much of the French political elite and much of French public opinion, Hernu was not only outraged that a handful of whale-lovers could threaten France's entire nuclear program and undermine her image in the South Pacific and in the international press. He was also convinced that to be able to do so, Greenpeace must be secretly benefiting from the assistance of governments hostile to French interests, and in particular the Soviets.[35] This suspicion resulted at least partly, in my opinion, from an interesting feature of French political culture—the absence of large, effective voluntary organizations able to mobilize considerable resources and large numbers of supporters. French voluntary organizations—unions, business associations, consumers' groups and the like—have always been very weak by comparison with those in most other advanced industrial societies. Nor had this peculiarity of French society lost much of its salience in recent years. Whereas elsewhere in Western Europe the years since 1968 had seen substantial expansion of the memberships and activities of organized interests (and especially of unions and other policy-oriented protest associations, such as peace groups and ecology associations), in France such expansion had been quite limited. Indeed, the spectacular growth of the French Socialist Party during the seventies may have been an important obstacle to the expansion of interest groups: in the highly conflictual political atmosphere of post-Gaullist France, the new Socialist Party appears to have provided an alternate and more attractive vehicle through which socially mobilized individuals and groups could express their convictions and realize their ambitions. This continued weakness of interest groups in France made it difficult for the country's elites, even the Socialists, many of whom were union members, to make sense out of Greenpeace. Given their knowledge of France's small and poor interest groups, they found it inconceivable that any organization could raise the large amounts of money Greenpeace appeared to command and find so many dedicated activists without the clandestine help of malevolent governments.

That the Mitterrand government decided to undertake the sabotage can thus be seen to make a certain amount of sense in the light of the history of the Left's foreign and defense policies, its delicate relationship with the army and the intelligence services, its understanding of the conditions necessary for effective domestic reform, the electoral constraints it was facing, and its perception of the Greenpeace organization.

The second puzzle that we must deal with concerns the cover-up undertaken by French officials from the president and the defense minister down through the ranks of the military and the intelligence services. Why, to begin with, did Mitterrand and Hernu choose to conceal what they had done rather than to admit their involvement, to invoke the higher interests of French national security, and thus to save the imprisoned "Turenges," who would then appear as government officials simply carrying out orders?[36] The answer to this question must, at this point, remain somewhat speculative. One thing that appears likely is that Mitterrand found himself torn between his own quite cynical belief in *raison d'état* and his political commitment and that of his party to the humanitarian ideals of socialism and internationalism. Mitterrand had, it seems, approved the mission on being assured by Lacoste and Saulnier that nobody would be killed and that no connection with France could be established. He now confronted precisely the situation he had been assured would not occur and decided that his role in the decision could not be acknowledged, especially with an election just around the corner.[37] It has also been suggested that Mitterrand and his advisers suspected, for the first few weeks at least, that they had been betrayed by right-wing members of the secret services, who had deliberately botched the attack in order to embarrass the government. The operation was studded with remarkable blunders—badly forged passports, a dinghy purchased in London by a man speaking almost no English and then abandoned near the scene of the crime, French-made oxygen bottles similarly left on the spot, the decision by the "Turenges" to return their rented car before leaving New Zealand, and a host of others. The Socialist leaders, knowing the right-wing affinities of much of the DGSE and the army, and knowing the resentments aroused within the secret services by the reorganizations and personnel changes introduced at the beginning of the socialist administration, thus could think it possible that they were confronting a "sabotage of the sabotage." In this case, confessing their involvement without waiting to see just what other traps had been laid for them might prove politically disastrous. This fear of a right-wing plot, along with a suspicion that the "Turenges" had been betrayed to the New Zealand police by the British secret services (surely, the police of such a tiny country could not have outsmarted the French secret service on their own!) provides a plausible explanation of why Mitterrand chose the apparently contradictory strategy of ordering an investigation while simultaneously orchestrating a cover-up: he truly wanted to know why the project had been so badly botched.

The possibility that perfectly rational, experienced, and highly intelligent political leaders like François Mitterrand and Pierre Joxe, his minister of the interior, considered a "sabotage of the sabotage" to be a plausible scenario suggests something quite important about contemporary French politics: the Left/Right cleavages that have defined the structure of French politics from the time of the Revolution remain very powerful, despite several generations of rapid and intense social, economic, and institutional change and despite the acceptance by the Left of many of the fundamentals of the Right's approach to foreign, and even to domestic, policy.

Mitterrand's choice of a strategy of cover-up also fits very nicely into what we know of his personality and political style. Mitterrand's nickname in political circles is "the Florentine," suggesting his fondness for secrecy, his mastery of complicated backroom political maneuvering, his love of intrigue and political risk.[38] The president is also a consummate political cynic whose long career in both the Fourth and the Fifth Republics and whose involvement in an impressive list of scandals, plots, and intrigues could serve to convince him that, like all those earlier scandals, this one, too, would pass without producing excessive damage, at least to him.[39]

Beyond these various motivations for deciding on a strategy of concealment, we ought also to consider why top French officials from President Mitterrand on down felt confident that they could succeed in this approach. Their optimism was probably reinforced by an understanding of certain features of French political life in the Fifth Republic. The French press, Mitterrand would know, was not particularly adept at investigative journalism. A few publications did have some capacity in this field—*Le Canard enchaîné*, which had always specialized in exposing scandals and spreading rumors, *Le Monde*, which had begun under the presidency of Giscard to add some investigative reporting to its tradition of sophisticated news analysis and commentaries, the weekly *L'Express*, and the widely read and highly iconoclastic daily, *Libération*. As a result, however, of the intensely partisan and ideological character of political and intellectual life in France during the long years of conservative dominance from 1958 to 1981, all of these publications except *L'Express* had become firmly aligned with the Left and would not be eager to embarrass the government, particularly during the run-up to critical elections. Mitterrand would also not have to worry much about radio and television news. Although the Left had considerably relaxed the day-to-day control over the electronic media that had been exercised by previous governments and had established a more or less autonomous council, the Haute Autorité de l'Audiovisuel, to supervise the networks, television news was still much less independent of the government than it was in most other western democracies, and the principal radio stations were still heavily dependent on the state.[40]

Mitterrand could also assume that, unlike Richard Nixon, who had been undone by a powerful, inquisitive and hostile Congress, he had little to fear from the direction of parliament. The constitution of the Fifth Republic (of which he had always been extremely critical when in opposition but to which he had adapted very easily once in office) gave the National Assembly and the Senate very few means for controlling, or even examining, the activities of the executive. Ever since 1958 when General de Gaulle had introduced a new constitution that vastly enlarged the power of the executive branch and drastically reduced the resources and autonomy of the National Assembly, the French legislature had been among the weakest in the western world in terms both of its formal powers and of its actual political role, a situation that the Socialist incumbency had done very little to change.[41] This unusual legislative impotence prevails in all areas of government activity but particularly in foreign and defense policy where power is concentrated overwhelmingly in the hands of the president. Besides, Mitterrand's supporters enjoyed a very comfortable majority in the National Assembly and could be counted on to head off any serious challenges. This was especially so because, despite its recent resurgence, the Socialist Party was, like all French parties, a comparatively weak structure with a small membership, limited resources, and few solid internal structures. Like the major parties of the Right, it was less an independent political force than a machine for the creation and support of presidential candidates and presidents.

Nor would Mitterrand be likely to run up against any French counterpart to John Sirica or Archibald Cox, the judge and the special prosecutor who had helped unseat Richard Nixon. Despite the recently increased activity of the

Constitutional Council in examining the constitutionality of legislative acts and executive decrees, the French judicial and legal system lacks the institutional resources, the cultural predisposition, and, above all, the independence from the government, to serve as an effective defender of the public's "right to know" the secrets of the executive branch. The judiciary in France is less a distinct "branch" of government as it is in the United States than a tool in the hands of the executive, which controls it via the minister of justice as it does the police through the minister of the interior.[42] In case of any trouble from this direction, or from the parliament or the press, the president would, moreover, be able to use his broad and unchallengeable discretion to invoke military secrecy *(le secret-défence)* to prevent access to damaging information.

Finally, Mitterrand would not expect to encounter much resistance from his own staff or from that of the prime minister or the other ministers. In contrast to the situation in Britain and the countries of the Commonwealth where elected leaders find themselves surrounded by permanent staffs of politically neutral civil servants whose primary loyalty is supposed to be to the state and to the public interest rather than to the current governing party, elected officials in France come to office with their own large entourages of advisers, who combine technical competence (as certified by diplomas from the top technical and administrative schools such as the Ecole Nationale d'Administration or Polytechnique) with strong personal and partisan loyalty. What makes this possible is the institution of *détachement* whereby a member of one of the upper divisions of the civil service (the *grands corps de l'état*) can go on long-term leave to work in politics or in the private sector without losing his or her status or seniority. Under these conditions, questions of democratic process might easily take a back seat to issues of political expediency, especially when the latter could be dressed up in the garb of "national security."

More surprising, however, than the fact that Mitterrand initially chose a strategy of denial was that he persisted in this approach long after its credibility had been destroyed by the unprecedented diligence of the press as well as by the work of the New Zealand police. Although it would have been difficult for Mitterrand to change his story and admit his own role in the sabotage, the president did have one way of trying to end the crisis being produced by the overwhelming evidence of high-level French complicity. He could (as his prime minister and his minister of the interior seemed repeatedly to have urged) sacrifice Defense Minister Hernu, who could serve as a perfect scapegoat or, to use the suggestive French image, a "fuse," taking the heat of the scandal while stopping the fire from reaching the president and the government as a whole. Why did Mitterrand resist until the very last moment taking this obvious and inevitable step? A number of factors appear to have come into play here. One was quite specific to this case, but two others point to significant, general features of the French political system.

Charles Hernu was not just one minister among many; he was one of François Mitterrand's oldest political associates as well as his friend. Throwing him to the wolves was, therefore, not so easy. Secondly, at a less personal level, Hernu was much too important a figure in Mitterrand's complex political plans to be jettisoned unless no alternative were available. What made Mitterrand's plans so complicated was the peculiar nature of the political institutions created by the 1958 constitution.

The Fifth Republic features two distinct sets of elections at the national level: legislative elections every five years to fill the National Assembly (the more important of the two legislative bodies) and presidential elections held once every seven years. As in the United States, the president is elected independently of the legislature and is not responsible to it in the sense that he does not need to maintain a working majority in it in order to retain his position. Unlike the American system, however, the French Fifth Republic contains a second executive figure, the prime minister, who along with the other ministers who compose the government, is appointed by the president but is responsible to the National Assembly. Since the president is elected for a seven-year term and the National Assembly for only five, it is entirely possible for a president of one political persuasion to find himself confronting a legislature of the other. Given the highly polarized nature of French party politics, such an outcome could produce a serious constitutional crisis, especially since the constitution is not very clear on the precise balance of power between the president and prime minister nor on the mechanisms for resolving serious conflicts between them. During the first twenty-eight years of the Fifth Republic, such a troubling situation had never arisen. From 1958 through 1981, the Right had controlled both the presidency and the legislature, and in 1981 Mitterrand dissolved the National Assembly immediately upon winning the presidency and the parties of the Left swept the subsequent legislative elections. The elections of March 1986 would, however, almost certainly force the institutions of the Fifth Republic to face up to this their most serious flaw. It appeared almost inevitable that the parties of the Right would win a majority of the seats. Elected in 1981, President Mitterrand would still have two years of his term remaining. The constitutional experts, the journalistic pundits, and the politicians themselves were seriously divided about what would happen next. Faced with a hostile legislative majority, what could Mitterrand do? Would he resign straight away? Would he immediately dissolve the new assembly, call a new election, and then resign if the new results were no more favorable? Would he try to ignore the popular verdict and retain a friendly prime minister and government, thus incurring the risk of a major constitutional confrontation? Or would he accept the outcome of the vote and agree to appoint a prime minister from among the leaders of the Right, perhaps making a deal preserving a few important cabinet posts for moderate Socialists? The latter scenario, popularly labeled "cohabitation" (Left and Right would be "living together" without any intention of ever getting married) was regarded by some experts and some important politicians (former Prime Minister Raymond Barre, for example) as inappropriate and unworkable. Others (including the leader of the RPR, Jacques Chirac, who was the most likely choice as prime minister in such circumstances) saw it as both desirable and viable, at least in the short run.

Should Mitterrand be willing to stay on and "cohabit" with a government of the Right (he, not surprisingly, refused to reveal his plans), the viability of the resulting "household" was, as of the summer and fall of 1985, widely seen to depend on whether or not the president and the new government would be able to agree on foreign and defense policy and whether the "defense and intelligence communities" would accept such a sharing of power. And it was widely believed that an important key to this cooperation and this acceptance was Charles Hernu, in whom both the Right and the military had a certain amount of confidence and who, either as minister of defense in a new government of national unity or as a presidential adviser on military matters, could serve as a guarantor of the viability of "cohabitation." Thus the persistence in the army and in conservative political circles of strong distrust toward the Socialists and President Mitterrand combined with the peculiarities of the 1958 constitution to make Hernu difficult to abandon.

The third factor that explains the maintenance of the cover-up approach for such a long time has to do with a feature of the operation of the executive branch under the Fifth Republic. In most western parliamentary democracies, some version of British "cabinet government" is the rule: all members of the cabinet are entitled to participate in discussions of all major government decisions, regardless of which departments and which ministers are especially concerned with a specific policy; and all, along with the prime minister, are considered "jointly responsible" for those decisions. The French cabinet does not seem to operate as this kind of forum for collective decision making, but rather as a sounding board for the president and as a rubber stamp for decisions already reached by him either alone or in concert with the prime minister and individual ministers. This is particularly true in matters of foreign policy, where, according to a careful observer, the cabinet has rarely undertaken serious discussions of important decisions.[43] As a result, the ministers rarely have input into decisions outside their specific areas of competence. This pattern seems to have held true in the Greenpeace affair, with the result that those members of the Fabius government who might have been expected to condemn both the bombing and the cover-up could not use the cabinet as a channel for generating debate about the appropriate response to take to the unfolding scandal.

The decision to cover up the scandal and other aspects of President Mitterrand's behavior do make a certain amount of sense if we begin by assuming that he knew all along that some sort of attack would take place, and if, furthermore, we take into consideration not only his personality and political style but also a number of fundamental characteristics of the French political system. Let us now turn to some of the other major actors in this perplexing drama and see if we can make sense out of their actions during the crisis.

One of the most puzzling performances in the entire drama was enacted by the prime minister, Laurent Fabius. There are two ways to make sense out of his actions. The first requires us to make a rather cynical judgment about him—that he knew about the plan either from the very start or at least very soon after the "Turenges" were arrested and that his repeated demonstrations of moral indignation and investigatory zeal were pure theater, designed to protect himself and the president while putting pressure on Hernu to shoulder the blame and resign. A second way to construe Fabius's behavior, and one that makes slightly more sense in my view, requires us to accept his claim that he knew little or nothing in advance about the attack, that he actually disapproved of the methods used, that both Hernu and Mitterrand lied to him after the attack, that at first he accepted their claims not to have been involved, that he, too, took seriously the possibility of a right-wing "sabotage of the sabotage," and that he only gradually became aware that he had been lied to not only by Hernu, whom he did not particularly respect anyway, but by his political mentor and sponsor, François Mitterrand, as well.

To those unfamiliar with the French system of government, the idea that the prime minister could have been unaware of the existence of such an important and risky project might be hard to accept. Familiarity with the constitution of the Fifth Republic and with the way in which it has been implemented since 1958 makes Fabius's protestations of ignorance considerably more credible. As we have seen, the 1958 constitution created a peculiar two-headed executive. A president and a prime minister were to share a vast array of greatly expanded executive powers, but the precise modalities of their interaction and the relative influence of each were not very clearly specified. The overwhelming personal influence of General de Gaulle, the careful self-effacement of his first two prime ministers, and the establishment in 1962 of a new procedure for electing the president by direct universal suffrage (instead of indirectly by a select group of politicians) all combined to aggrandize the role of the presidency beyond even the quite exalted position granted to it in the constitution and to reduce the prime minister's office to a very secondary rank. Nowhere was this development more pronounced than in the areas of foreign policy and defense. Despite the fact that the constitution assigned to the prime minister important functions in these matters, General de Gaulle made foreign and defense policy into a presidential prerogative through an exercise of constitutional imperialism in which his own prime ministers acquiesced, and which his three successors in the office of the presidency did nothing to reverse.[44] Not the least guilty in this respect was François Mitterrand. During his years as a leader of the opposition, he had been highly critical of this concentration of power in the hands of the president (he called the Fifth Republic a "permanent coup d'état"). As president, however, he continued to treat foreign policy as his private sphere and to exclude his prime ministers from any effective participation in its formulation. Discussing the issue of control over the *force de frappe,* Mitterrand declared in November 1983, "The lynch-pin of the French strategy of deterrence is the Head of State, it is I. . . ." And in July 1985, looking forward to a possible period of power-sharing with the Right, he declared that for the prime minister to attempt to take over the making of foreign policy would be a veritable "coup d'état."[45] Under the Socialists, then, the prime minister continued to play a marginal role in matters of foreign policy and defense. This was even truer of Laurent Fabius than of his predecessor, Pierre Mauroy. Whereas Mauroy had both his own political power base independent of that of the president and a certain interest in intelligence and foreign policy matters, Fabius owed his career largely to the patronage and protection of Mitterrand and he lacked much experience outside the area of domestic policy. It is thus entirely possible that Fabius knew nothing of the plan to sink the *Rainbow Warrior,* despite the fact that one of his aides had mechanically affixed his signature to the request for special funds that had been used to finance the operation. Whereas Mauroy insisted on having each special operation described to his aides before they would approve the funding, Fabius apparently issued orders that no questions were to be asked: he cherished his carefully cultivated image as a staunch defender of human rights and did not wish to be implicated in such morally dubious clandestine activities.[46]

Peculiar behavior was not, moreover, the exclusive preserve of the government: the moderation and caution manifested by the parties of the opposition is also quite puzzling. The government managed to get itself into a great deal of trouble with very little help from the parties of the opposition. Explanations for this exemplary behavior are not all that hard to find. All the parties of the Right found themselves in a very awkward position in this affair. By refusing to admit the role of France in the sabotage, Mitterrand and Hernu were presenting themselves as defenders of the "honor" of the military and of the intelligence services against the attacks of foreign nations, the press, and anti-nuclear activists. Now, the army and the secret services were traditionally the appanage of the Right and the extreme Right, not only in terms of ideology and symbolism but also in terms of personnel. The opposition, thus, could not make much political capital out of the scandal without appearing to abandon its own values as well as its friends among the generals, admirals, spies, and secret agents who were most directly implicated in the affair. Similarly, by denying the responsibility of the DGSE but still vigorously asserting France's right to use any means it chose in order to defend what President Mitterrand called "the rights of France in the South Pacific," the government was staking out the nationalistic high ground that the opposition would have liked to monopolize, thus leaving the RPR and the UDF with very little room for maneuver. Former President Valéry Giscard d'Estaing hastened to invoke the old patriotic saw, "My country, right or wrong," while former Minister Christian Bonnet, now a UDF senator, expressed quite baldly the nationalist sentiments that dominated the thinking of French conservatives and helped immobilize them in the Greenpeace affair: "Everybody [he told Le Monde] who has a respect for the State ought to eschew any partisan spirit. The duty of all governments is to keep up the elements that France needs to remain a nuclear power."[47] The government's choice of the widely respected Gaullist dignitary, Bernard Tricot, to investigate the affair also helped back the conservative parties into a corner: they, and especially the Gaullist RPR, could not openly criticize Tricot's whitewash without appearing to repudiate one of their own historical figures. Even once the press had begun to embarrass the government by revealing the role of the DGSE, the opposition remained disarmed. Because it shared the government's views on France's defense posture, on the desirability of nuclear testing in the South Pacific, and on the threat posed by Greenpeace, and because the previous conservative administrations were widely known to have used French intelligence agents for similar operations, the opposition was left with very little to criticize except the botched execution of the mission and the consequences of the fiasco for France's international prestige. Thus, an unidentified RPR "dignitary" admitted to journalists that "what we are denouncing, really, is that the operation was a failure."[48] For the right-wing press, the "real scandal" was "the inability of the Socialist government . . . to protect our special agents when they are put on trial by foreigners," and the most serious result of the affair was that France's intelligence agencies had been destabilized and the authority of the French state "trampled under foot."[49]

Perhaps the most important notion that the main opposition parties shared with the government and that induced them to proceed cautiously in this affair was the idea of "raison d'état." Even more so than the socialists, and despite their recent and loudly touted discovery of the virtues of "liberalism," French conservatives have great respect for the authority of the state (which they always spell with a capital letter). Even Jean Lecanuet of the UDF, one of the most vociferous critics of the government's actions, asserted that it was "necessary for a country like France to have secret services and to use them; when the secret services are caught out, it is the job of the political authorities to protect them."[50] Indeed, it would be hard to find a balder assertion by a western political leader of the primacy of *raison d'état* over democratic norms than a statement by a recent Gaullist minister of the interior. Defending his refusal to discuss his own role in another scandal, that of the Carrefour du développement, Charles Pasqua declared: "Democracy stops where the interest of the State begins."[51] Believing so firmly in the "reason" of the French state, the leaders of the French Right were reluctant to delve into the intricacies of the Greenpeace affair. Rejecting Fabius's proposal for the establishment of a parliamentary commission, Lecanuet insisted that "the legislature should not stick its nose everywhere. . . . A secret that is examined, even after the fact, is no longer a secret."[52] At a moment when the ineptitude of its secret agents and the theatrics of the Greenpeace people had made France appear ridiculous in the eyes of the world, the ardent nationalists of the various opposition parties were inclined to rally more or less silently around the flag.

Even if the leaders of the opposition had been better placed to attack the government on Greenpeace, most of them would still probably have proceeded very cautiously, given the prevailing electoral and constitutional situation. In the first place, nobody seems to have had much desire to provoke an immediate political crisis and early legislative elections. It was taken for granted by all informed political actors that March 1986 would bring a conservative victory. There must have seemed little point in forcing matters by pushing the government to resign just in order to chase the Socialists from power a few months ahead of schedule.[53]

In addition, the prospect of the constitutional difficulties likely to emerge from these parliamentary elections seems to have inclined most of the leaders of the Right to be cautious concerning attacks on the president. Two of the principal leaders of the Right, Jacques Chirac and Valéry Giscard d'Estaing, found themselves in a rather uncomfortable situation: opinion polls consistently suggested that they would each finish far behind Raymond Barre should a crisis bring about Mitterrand's resignation and an early presidential election. As a consequence, they were very nervous about the possibility that the scandal could undermine Mitterrand's legitimacy or even force him out of office. They had to hope that "cohabitation" would work, at least long enough to increase their own popularity ratings and cut into Barre's. They and their supporters were therefore careful to focus their criticisms on the defense minister and on the prime minister while sparing the president.[54] Barre, as the overwhelming leader in every opinion poll for the previous two years, could afford to be less circumspect. Although he himself remained silent on the Greenpeace affair, his spokesmen were occasionally willing to try to undermine President Mitterrand by blaming him directly for the scandal. Thus in the wake of the "third team" revelations, various important supporters of Raymond Barre either demanded the resignation of Mitterrand or declared that "cohabitation" was no longer viable. Jean Lecanuet, for example, declared the president to be "clearly non-cohabitable" and another prominent UDF leader, Jean-Claude Gaudin, stated that "one cannot cohabit with people who set up duplicity as *raison d'état*."[55] Even Barre and his lieutenants, however, were cautious in their handling of the president's role in the scandal. Barre was eager to take over a presidency with its full powers and prestige intact: he was not eager, as one observer cleverly put it, to saw off any of the legs of a throne in which he himself hoped to sit one day.

The final puzzle to be examined is the surprisingly limited scope assumed by the scandal both in terms of its duration and in terms of its ultimate impact on French political institutions and processes. The Greenpeace affair is far from the first major political scandal in modern French history to have titillated French political elites and public opinion for a brief period and then faded away, leaving very few permanent scars. During the period since 1958, one scandal after another has erupted, threatened to undermine the reputations of major political figures or the legitimacy of key institutions, and then disappeared from sight. A list of such scandals would include the Ben Barka affair of 1965 (members of the French secret services kidnapped the leader of the Moroccan opposition, who was then killed); the Markovic affair of 1968 (the bodyguard of actor Alain Delon, a friend of Prime Minister Pompidou and his wife, was assassinated and allegations were made concerning the personal life of Mrs. Pompidou); the *Canard enchaîné* affair of 1973 (officials of the secret services were caught installing microphones in the new offices of the Parisian satirical newspaper but no trials or convictions ensued); the Bokassa diamond scandal in 1979–80 (President Giscard d'Estaing accepted numerous gifts of diamonds from a brutal African dictator, lied repeatedly about the matter, and instituted administrative penalties and legal proceedings against *Le Monde* for investigating the story); the "sniffer airplanes" affair, revealed in 1982 (large sums of public money were found to have been invested under Giscard d'Estaing in companies controlled by his political friends in a scientifically implausible scheme to develop airplanes supposedly capable of detecting oil and mineral deposits from the air); and three suspicious murders or suicides involving prominent conservative politicians or cabinet ministers—the duc de Broglie in 1976, Joseph Fontanet in 1978, and Robert Boulin in 1980.[56] With the partial exception of Giscard's diamonds, none of these scandals had more than a brief currency or presented more than a minor threat to the stability of the government or the legitimacy of its leaders. It seems clear, then, that in examining the reasons for the limited scope and impact of the Greenpeace scandal we shall be confronting not an isolated phenomenon but some profound regularities of French political life.

The first factor to take into account is that the only major institution that undertook to push the Greenpeace scandal towards its limits was the press and, indeed, only a very small fragment of that—a few daily papers and a few weekly magazines, none of which could marshall the combination of financial resources and investigatory skills that had enabled the big American newspapers to undermine Richard Nixon. The French press received very little support in its efforts from institutions and organizations that in other countries have helped expose important scandals. For the reasons we have discussed, neither the French electronic media, nor the opposition parties, nor the parliament, nor the judiciary had the motivation or the resources to pick up the leads developed by the investigative journalists of *Le Monde* or *L'Express* and help keep the Greenpeace scandal alive. Without such help even the most talented of journalists can run out of steam and out of leads. And by mid-October 1985, the few journalists who were still working on the story had run up against the limits of what mere journalism—lacking the subpoena powers and the sanctions of courts or parliamentary panels—could continue to uncover in an affair where only a very small number of highly placed elected and appointed officials actually knew the remaining secrets.

Nor did the Greenpeace organization possess large and well-organized cohorts of supporters in France who could have exerted pressure on the political system, reinforcing the efforts of the press and increasing the incentive of the politicians to get to the bottom of what had happened. The French ecology movement has always remained small compared to its counterparts elsewhere in Europe. Of the 1,200,000 members claimed by Greenpeace worldwide in 1985, only about seven thousand were French, compared to seventy-five thousand in Britain, eighty thousand in the Netherlands, and two hundred thousand in West Germany. The small French branch of Greenpeace had, moreover, just been even further weakened by a set of internal battles and a schism that had occurred several months before the attack.[57] In addition, as Tony Chafer has pointed out, French ecologists have paid surprisingly little attention to nuclear weapons, concentrating their efforts on industrial pollution and nuclear energy production.[58] The peace movement, similarly, has been extremely weak in France compared to the massive movements that have emerged in Great Britain, West Germany, the Netherlands, and even North America since the late 1970s. A variety of factors have been suggested to explain this weakness: these include the ability of French governments since de Gaulle to capture (by creating a French nuclear force and a powerful nationalist ideology) the anti-American and anti-bloc sentiment that has fed the peace movement elsewhere; the discrediting of the French peace movement in the eyes of many potential sympathizers by the prominent role within it played by the French Communist Party, whose support for the Soviet Union and for the *force de frappe* makes its pacifist credentials rather suspect; the pronounced weakness in France of social movements and voluntary organizations of all kinds; and the distinctive pattern of recent French political history, that is, the domination of French public life during the 1970s by the long struggle of the Left to take shape and to break the generation-long hegemony of the Right and the fact that the victory of the Socialists in 1981 satisfied some of the same urges for social change that in other countries have served to generate support for the peace movement.[59] Regardless of the exact weight we might wish to assign to each of these factors or to others, it is undeniable that the disarmament and the ecology movements have been much weaker in France than elsewhere, and that as a result, the international Greenpeace organization lacked a large group of sympathizers who would have been outraged by the sabotage and able to do something about it.

Nor did French political opinion, either at the elite or the popular levels, provide a fertile ground for the full development of such a scandal. To begin with, the possibilities for moral indignation were severely restricted by the existence of a broad consensus of both elite and popular opinion on the basic foreign policy issues raised by the affair—the necessity for and the desirability of an independent French nuclear force; the "right" of France to maintain post-colonial territories in the Third World and to use them for nuclear tests not regarded as appropriate for metropolitan France; the prevalence in the outside world of a widely distributed hostility toward France and its efforts to play an appropriately grand role in world affairs; the suspicions of the political inten-tions and financial resources of Greenpeace; and the right of France, like any other state operating in the fundamentally amoral context of international power politics, to use any means necessary to defend its territories, its military resources, and its fundamental foreign policy interests.[60] This broad consensus on a highly nationalistic and strongly "realist" approach to foreign policy made it difficult for French politicians, journalists, and citizens to feel much sympathy for a suspicious group of meddling ecologists and a Portuguese photographer excessively zealous about saving his equipment.

Directly related to the existence of this consensus on defense and foreign policy but deriving also from the extraordinary hegemony of the executive in these matters is the marked indifference of French parliamentary and public opinion to questions of international affairs. In the words of one observer, the National Assembly "does not get excited about foreign policy": only 2.5 percent of the questions addressed to the government during question period in 1983, a quite typical year, concerned international matters. The French public dis-plays a unique lack of interest in and knowledge about the kinds of foreign policy issues that have caused massive concern elsewhere in Europe. The proportion of French respondents having "no opinion" or "no response" to questions concerning such matters as nuclear war, disarmament, and the American "Strategic Defense Initiative" is consistently the highest in Europe.[61]

Another feature of French political culture that may be said to have allowed the government to get away, at least partly, with its cover-up was the remarkable absence of any widespread moral indignation either among French elites or within the citizenry at large concerning the violations of democratic norms and processes involved in this case. Criticism of the sabotage and the subsequent cover-up lacked the intense moral dimension displayed, for example, by the American elite and by public reactions to the transgressions of Presidents Nixon and Reagan. The French at all levels—the political elite, the press, and public opinion—seem to have been for the most part remarkably unconcerned by the moral and legal dimensions of the affair—the bombing of an unarmed vessel in the waters of a friendly country; the killing of an unarmed civilian; the increasingly obvious, systematic lying by almost every French official involved. Very few of the politicians, journalists, and academics who commented on the affair in the media emphasized moral or legal issues. In the press, only the left-wing Catholic weekly, *Témoignage chrétien*, and on occasion the pro-Socialist *Nouvel Observateur* condemned the government's actions on ethical rather than political or tactical grounds. The editorialists of the Catholic daily, *La Croix*, for example, accepted the sabotage as an unavoidable piece of "State law-breaking" and distinguished the Greenpeace cover-up from the one generated in the Watergate affair on the grounds that the Americans had perpetrated a "sordid lie" on behalf of party political interests while French leaders had engaged in a much less reprehensible "patriotic dissimulation" on behalf of national se-curity.[62] Similarly, the prominent conservative political scientist and commen-tator Alain Duhamel wrote in *Le Quotidien de Paris* that had it not been for an "unfortunate but totally accidental" death, the affair "would not have deserved one-tenth of the current ballyhoo and hubbub. A few sighs, a few sickly smiles would have been more than enough."[63] What *did* cause French politicians and commentators to get their moral dander up was, first, that the French police had been ordered to help their New Zealand counterparts in identifying the "Turenges" and investigating their activities and, secondly that two brave French agents were being allowed to languish in foreign jails.[64]

The predominant tone of French elite and popular response to this scandal was not the moral indignation of Americans in the face of Watergate or of the British confronting the Profumo or Parkinson affairs but rather a remarkable cynicism. Just before the publication of the Tricot report, 70 percent of those questioned felt that the report would conceal at least part of the truth. Some three weeks later, 67 percent of another sample felt that they would *never* learn the truth about the affair. Similarly, in the latter poll, 61 percent felt that the government was lying but only 28 percent and 24 percent respectively felt that either the prime minister or the president ought to resign. Such cynicism was not just an isolated phenomenon.[65] It had little to do, I would suggest, with any special properties of the affair itself but was, rather, typical of the French approach to politics and political ethics in general. Observers of France have often noted a widespread and profound cynicism among French citizens concerning politics and politicians. As one commentator put it, the French tend to assign politics to the "world of the ignoble" and are not, therefore, outraged or even surprised when their political leaders bend or break the law.[66] For the French public, as for the country's political elites, democratic politics is much more about the effective exercise of state power than about the assertion and protection of fundamental rights and procedural norms.

The coexistence of a widespread conviction of the guilt or complicity of major political leaders alongside a reluctance to demand their punishment may suggest, finally, something else about contemporary French political culture besides this striking cynicism. The reluctance of French politicians and the French public to push the evidence to its increasingly obvious conclusions reveals, I think, a profound trait of contemporary French political culture. Despite the success of the institutions of the Fifth Republic, despite the broad consensus of the constitution, despite the apparent calming down of France's traditional ideological battles, the French remain comparatively insecure about the stability of their political system. Having seen the Fourth Republic collapse in the wake of colonial warfare and military sedition and another nearly toppled by the student protests and workers' strikes of May 1968, the French are much less willing than the Americans to risk ousting their top leaders for ethical offenses. This reluctance, this "sense of national vulnerability," was of course intensified by the possibility of a major constitutional impasse that was widely expected to emerge from the March 1986 elections.

It is, I believe, to this political insecurity and its reflection at the elite level that we must look if we are to understand why the crisis generated by the scandal and brought to a head by the *Le Monde* revelations of 17 September dissipated so quickly once Hernu and Lacoste had been dismissed. It was, I submit, clear to the press and to the leaders of the opposition that any further efforts to expose the truth would likely lead to the Elysée Palace and the president. As one of the president's closest advisers put it, "Whoever wants to go any further, will have to aim very high, strike very hard, and, above all, advance without any covering fire."[67] Very few people with the power to do so seemed eager to take the next, fateful steps. The vast powers wielded by the president of the Fifth Republic meant that provoking his resignation or even seriously undermining his legitimacy was not something to be undertaken lightly so long as the regime itself was not regarded as absolutely secure. Needless to say, the prospect of a major constitutional crisis in March 1986 did not increase people's willingness to take risks with the stability of the regime.

In politics, then, as in medicine, pathology can teach us many interesting things about normal anatomy and biology: our examination of the Greenpeace affair has, I submit, helped us direct some useful light on important features of French political culture, institutions, and processes. Our analysis of this scandal not only helps us gain a better grasp of prominent features of French politics. It also enables us to confront one of the most interesting arguments in the recent literature on France: the notion of a "decline of French exceptionalism." Scholars and commentators have recently begun to argue that French politics has started to lose many of the traits that once made it so distinctive. This shift is attributed to a variety of mutually reinforcing causes—rapid economic and sociological development, European integration, the influence of American cultural and political patterns, generational and demographic shifts, to list only some of the most frequently mentioned factors. Evidence of this transformation is said to be found in a number of recent developments including the drastic decline of the Communist Party as an electoral, organizational, and cultural force; the emergence of effective judicial review of legislative and executive practice via the growing role of the Constitutional Council; the successful transfer of power for the first time in a generation from the Right to the Left in 1981 and then back again, partially, in 1986; the development, partly as a result of the political experiences of the last six years, of a growing convergence in the thinking of Left and Right in France on a wide array of important issues; the emergence of a broad wave of political, journalistic (and supposedly popular) "liberalism," that is, enthusiasm for private enterprise and initiative and hostility to state intervention; the recent French mania for things American, whether culinary, literary, linguistic or vestamentary; and a supposedly widespread disenchantment with political ideologies of all sorts accompanied by a desire by people in all parties to approach political questions in a more empirical manner.[68]

While some of these claims seem persuasive, an examination of the Greenpeace scandal reinforces my predisposition to be rather skeptical about the overall argument. This analysis has revealed that France in the mid-1980s is still very much what Philip Williams portrayed it as during the 1950s and 1960s, a "classic land of the political scandal," a country, that is, where scandals emerge quite frequently but where those implicated suffer very few serious or lasting consequences.[69] It has demonstrated, as would detailed examination of the other scandals that have emerged in the past few years (the Carrefour du développement affair, the Chaumet bankruptcy, or the revelation of secret sales of arms to Iran with the full knowledge of President Mitterrand and other high Socialist officials) that France under Mitterrand has remained highly prone to scandals and largely immune from their consequences. Moreover, this is true in large part because of the stubborn persistence of a number of key features of the French state, of French society, and of French political culture.

To recapitulate, we have seen that the structure of the French state remains highly conducive to the abuse of political power. Authority is highly concentrated in the hands of the president, especially in matters of foreign policy, defense, and intelligence. No other state institution possesses enough effective, independent power to enable it to counterbalance this overmighty executive: in France's highly unitary state, local and regional institutions remain notoriously weak, even after the Socialists' decentralization measures; the legislature is hamstrung by its lack of procedural autonomy, legislative initiative, oversight capacity, and effective committee organization; the judiciary and the police remain tightly controlled by the executive; the top staffs of presidents, prime ministers, and ministers consist largely not of permanent, neutral civil servants but of rotating teams of political loyalists. And the susceptibility of the Fifth Republic's institutions to serious structural crisis ("cohabitation") appears to discourage a serious "throw the rascals out" approach to political scandals either by the opposition parties or by the voters.

French society, moreover, provides very few strong obstacles to abuses of power by the state: political parties are weak and highly dependent on their top leaders; pressure groups are notoriously small and politically dependent, and "public interest" groups are especially feeble; the communications media have traditionally lacked independence from the state as well as the capacity or willingness to undertake serious investigative reporting. And French political culture continues to provide an environment highly conducive to the exaltation of *raison d'état* and quite unfavorable to the vigorous advocacy of democratic procedures and norms. Despite the decline of the Communist Party and the growing moderation of Socialist elites, French political competition continues to pivot around sharp and deeply felt ideological cleavages. This sort of conflict appears to encourage government secrecy while making the Left in particular hesitant to buck the military or the intelligence services. At the same time, elites and citizens of all political stripes increasingly share a powerful nationalism, a cynical vision of the primacy of power and efficacy over democratic values and processes in international and domestic politics, and a nervousness concerning the stability of France's domestic institutions and its international stature.

Ironically, even where evidence of political change and convergence is strongest, such innovation often seems to have acted not to reduce the country's susceptibility to scandals but actually to increase it. What I have in mind is the phenomenon of *alternance*. The long-delayed accession of the Left to a share of power in the Fifth Republic and the resulting transformation of a Right-dominated regime into one with a reasonable prospect of regular alternations of competing partisan coalitions has, I think, been a major reason for the fact that so many scandals have erupted over the past decade. As party competition has intensified and Left and Right have begun to move in and out of power, each side has developed not only stronger incentives but also greater capacity (through access to official documents while in office and to well-placed civil servants while in opposition) to unearth scandals in their opponents' conduct of government and to exploit these revelations for partisan ends. It might be thought that this increasing partisan exploitation of scandal might at least after a while begin to raise the price of scandals for the perpetrators and thus contribute to a reduction over the long haul of the tendency of ruling politicians to use their power without regard for democratic norms. However, the way in which this *alternance* has occurred seems to militate against such a development.

One of the crucial shifts that made *alternance* possible was, as we have seen, the Left's abandonment of its opposition to the essentials of Gaullist foreign and defense policy. As the unfolding of the Greenpeace scandal makes eminently clear, with both the government and the opposition in fundamental agreement on the essentials of a highly chauvinistic and "realist" vision of French national interest, the likelihood that the French government will attempt to ride roughshod over democratic norms both at home and abroad in the name of national security and the "rights" of the state in the international system has increased substantially. At the same time, the likely costs of such actions have declined: the foreign policy consensus is now so broad that government actions of the Greenpeace variety are even less likely than before to run into substantial criticism either among political elites or at the level of the media and public opinion.

In addition, the accession of the Left to power has increased the scope for executive abuse of power because of the way in which Mitterrand and his associates chose to operate the political power they acquired. During the Socialists' long years in opposition they and the Communists represented the only sources of organized criticism of the antidemocratic features of the Fifth Republic's institutions. As the Left came closer to power, however, the Socialists in particular began to mute considerably their criticism of the constitution and once they were in power, Mitterrand and his associates appeared quite happy to use the enormous powers of the presidency in much the same way that their predecessors had. By taking over the institutions of the Fifth Republic and operating them essentially unchanged, Mitterrand and the Socialists have given new legitimacy to features of the French political system that have consistently played an important role in facilitating the abuse of political power and lowering its costs.

The emergence of a more balanced party system in France appears to have helped increase the frequency of scandals (both by making political elites more inclined to ignore democratic norms and by making it more likely that their actions will be uncovered and exploited for partisan purposes), but without making it any more likely that the perpetrators will suffer any serious or lasting consequences for their actions.

The persistence, therefore, of many important features of French political institutions and culture and the "perverse effects" of some recent changes in policy and ideology combine, I submit, to ensure that those of us who find political scandals such a rich source of edification and amusement are not likely to lack for French material in the years to come.

NOTES

The author would like to thank Dominique Moïsi for his help; Stanley Hoffmann, Georges Marion, Edwy Plenel, and Gérard Le Gall for their advice; and the Laboratoire de sociólogie du changement des institutions of the Centre national de la recherche scientifique in Paris for providing the resources and the atmosphere that made the writing of this essay possible.

1. English-language journalists have produced a number of "instant books" on the affair, including John Dyson, *Sink the Rainbow! An Enquiry into the 'Greenpeace Affair'* (London: Victor Gollancz, 1986); The Sunday Times "Insight" Team, *Rainbow Warrior: the French Attempt to Sink Greenpeace* (London: Arrow Books, 1986); and Richard Shears and Isobelle Gidley, *The Rainbow Warrior Affair* (London: Counterpoint/Unwin Paperbacks, 1986). The best treatment in French is Jacques Derogy and Jean-Maire Pontaut,

Enquête sur trois secrets d'Etat (Paris: Robert Laffont, 1986) on which I have relied extensively in this essay.

2. The initials stand for Direction générale de la sécurité extérieure (Central Office for External Security). Domestic surveillance is carried out by the DST, the Direction de la sécurité du territoire (the Central Office for Internal Security).

3. Conclusive evidence of the president's complicity has not been found. The most serious study of the affair, *Enquête sur trois secrets d'Etat*, by Jacques Derogy and Jean-Marie Pontaut, makes, however, an extremely convincing case against him and their version has not been challenged by anyone, including Mitterrand himself.

4. The texts of the letters can be found in Derogy and Pontaut, *Enquêt*, pp. 195–96.

5. The full text of the report was reprinted in *Libération* of 27 August 1985 and the interviews reproduced in *Le Monde*, 28 August 1985, as well as in Derogy and Pontaut, *Enquête*, p. 211.

6. The reactions of the international press are summarized in *Libération*, 28 August 1985 while that of the French press can be found in *Le Monde*, 27 August, 28 August, and especially the article entitled "Contradictions" of 29 August 1985; *Le Figaro*, 28 August 1985 ("Vingt raisons de croire à la piste française" "Twenty Reasons to Believe in the French Connection"); and *Libération*, 29 August 1985, "Douze questions sur le Rapport: Tricot répond" (Twelve Questions on the Report: Tricot Replies).

7. The full text of the Prime Minister's 26 August 1985 statement can be found in *Le Figaro*, 27 August 1985.

8. The principal articles appeared in *VSD*, 14 August 1985; *Le Monde*, 12 August, 14 August, 15 August, and especially 17 August; *Libération*, 14 August and 19 August; and *L'Express*, 23 August. Good summaries of the various press revelations can be found in *Libération*, 27 August, and *Le Matin*, 15 August.

9. Cited in Derogy and Pontaut, *Enquête*, p. 213.

10. Bertrand Le Gendre and Edwy Plenel, "Le *Rainbow Warrior* aurait été coulé par une troisième équipe de militaires français," *Le Monde*, 18 September 1985. Note that since *Le Monde* appears in the afternoon and is delivered to subscribers by mail the following morning, it always carries the date of the following day.

11. Communiqué issued on the evening of Tuesday 17 March 1985, reported in *Libération*, 18 March 1985. A similar defense of the army against "the campaign of calumnies being conducted against French military officials" was to be repeated by Hernu in a press conference the next day (*Libération*, 19 March 1985 and *Le Monde*, 20 March 1985).

12. *Le Monde*, 20 September 1985.

13. *L'Express*, 27 September 1985.

14. *L'Express*, 4 October 1985.

15. *Le Canard enchaîné*, 16 October 1985.

16. See *Le Monde*, 8 July 1986. In October of the following year, an international arbitration tribunal awarded the Greenpeace organization a settlement of £5,000,000 (*Manchester Guardian Weekly*, 11 October 1987).

17. Edwy Plenel and Bertrand Le Gendre, "Qui a menti?' (Who Lied?), *Le Monde*, 9 July 1987, and Jean Bothorel in *Le Figaro*, 23 July 1986.

18. Serge July, *Les Années Mitterrand: Histoire baroque d'une normalisation inachevée* (Paris: Grasset, 1986), p. 231.

19. The RPR, the Rassemblement pour la République (Coalition for the Republic), is the Gaullist party that claims the direct succession to the ideas and accomplishments of the general. Its principal leader is the current prime minister, Jacques Chirac. The UDF, the Union pour la démocratie française (Union for French democracy) is a coalition of three parties. Its principal leaders are former President Valéry Giscard d'Estaing and former Prime Minister Raymond Barre.

20. See the analysis in *Libération*, 24 September 1985.

21. Comments on Fabius's performances can be found in *Libération*, 24 and 27 September 1985, and in *L'Express*, 4 October 1985. See also the article entitled "Personne ne

croit Fabius" ("Nobody believes Fabius") in *Le Quotidien de Paris* of 27 September and the very cautious piece by Edwy Plenel in *Le Monde* of 27 September entitled "Deux silences" ("Two Silences"). It was Mr. Plenel who, in a personal interview, drew my attention to the importance of this article.

22. The poll was conducted jointly by the polling organization SOFRES and the radio network "Europe 1" and was reported in *Le Matin*, 3 September 1985.

23. I owe this insight to a conversation with journalist Georges Marion currently of *Le Monde* and previously of *Le Canard enchaîné*.

24. Such predictions could be heard not only from the followers of Raymond Barre— who dominated the popularity polls among potential conservative presidential candidates and who, therefore, stood to gain the most from the failure of Mitterrand and the Right to reach a *modus vivendi*—but also from observers with no such personal interest, such as journalist Jean-François Kahn who in the 26 September 1985 issue of the weekly *L'Evénement du jeudi* declared that the possibility of *cohabitation* between Left and Right had, "barring a spectacular recovery," been ruled out by Greenpeace.

25. See, for example, the comments of Alexandre de Marenches (former director of French Intelligence) in Christine Ockrent and Alexandre de Marenches, *Dans le secret des princes* (Paris: Stock, 1986), p. 298.

26. On the importance of rank and prestige in French foreign policy, see Alfred Grosser, *Affaires extérieures: La Politique de la France, 1944–1984* (Paris: Flammarion, 1984), p. 11. On the role of nuclear weapons in French strategy, see Stanley Hoffmann, *Essais sur la France: Declin ou Renouveau?* (Paris: Seuil, 1974), pp. 334–38, and Wilfrid Kohl, *French Nuclear Diplomacy* (Princeton: Princeton University Press, 1971).

27. See *L'Express*, 23 August 1985.

28. See Michel Dobry, "Le jeu du consensus," *Pouvoirs* 38 (1986): 47–67, especially 48–56; David Hanley, "The Parties and the Nuclear Consensus," in Jolyon Howorth and Patricia Chilton, *Defense and Dissent in Contemporary France* (New York: St. Martin's Press, 1984), pp. 75–94; and Jolyon Howorth, "Defense and the Mitterrand Government," ibid., pp. 94–134.

29. Hernu stated his position very clearly in an interview with *Le Monde*, 11 June 1981, while Mitterrand reasserted his commitment to the *force de frappe* many times during the election campaign, for example in a declaration of 22 April 1981, cited in *Le Monde* of 8 May 1981.

30. The quotation is from the president's speech during a visit to the Mururoa Atoll cited in *Le Figaro*, 8 July 1986.

31. For a provocative analysis of the "deal" worked out between the Socialists and the army and for Hernu's pivotal role in this deal, see Dobry, "Le jeu du consensus," pp. 54–55.

32. Pierre Messmer, defense minister under Pompidou in the late 1960s, claims to have rejected such proposals (see *Le Monde*, 8 October 1985) and Bernard Stasi, who was minister of overseas possessions in the early 1970s claimed to have done the same in 1973 (*Le Monde*, 22 August 1985).

33. Derogy and Pontaut, *Enquête*, pp. 272–73.

34. Ibid., p. 272.

35. He shared this suspicion with President Mitterrand, with the hierarchy of the DGSE and with a considerable proportion of French public opinion. Ibid., pp. 192, 269.

36. According to commentator Jean-François Kahn (in *L'Evénement du Jeudi*, 26 September 1985) 80 percent of the public would have rallied behind the president if he had taken this tack.

37. See July, *Les Années Mitterrand*, p. 234.

38. Ibid., pp. 18–19, 23–24, 27–32, 231–32.

39. Mitterrand's calm cynicism in the early stages of the crisis is admirably conveyed by Derogy and Pontaut, *Enquête*, pp. 192–93 and 162.

40. See Raymond Kuhn, "France and the New Media," *West European Politics* 8, 2 (April 1985): 50–66 as well as the symposium in *Intervention* 15 (March 1986): 44–73.

41. On the weakness of the legislature in the Fifth Republic, see the special issue of *Pouvoirs* 34, (1985) "L'Assemblée."

42. See, for example, the provocative comparison of the French and American judicial systems in Laurent Cohen-Tanugi, *Le Droit sans l'etat: Sur la démocratie en France et en Amérique* (Paris: Presse universitaires de France, 1986).

43. Cohen, *La Monarchie nucléaire*, pp. 19–20.

44. Foreign and defense policy came to be regarded as part of the president's "reserved domain," a term generally attributed to de Gaulle but which was, Professor Stanley Hoffmann informs me, never actually used by him but was rather coined by Jacques Chaban-Delmas, minister in various of the general's governments and prime minister under Pompidou.

45. Quoted in Cohen, *La Monarchie nucléaire*, pp. 15, 20.

46. Derogy and Pontaut, *Enquête*, pp. 208–9.

47. *Le Monde*, 21 August 1985.

48. *Libération*, 20 August 1985.

49. The first quotation is from Pierre Pujo, "Le vrai Scandale," *Aspects de la France*, 29 August 1985; the second is from Xavier Marchetti in *Le Figaro*, 6 November 1985.

50. Cited in *Le Monde*, 21 August 1985.

51. Cited ibid., 28 February 1987.

52. Cited in *La Croix*, 29 August 1985.

53. I wish to thank Mr. Gérard Le Gall for bringing this point to my attention.

54. See for example, Robert Pasqua's article in the RPR's newsletter, *La Lettre de la Nation*, of 5 November 1985 in which he asserts that "the real culprit in my eyes . . . is the Prime Minister."

55. See *Libération*, 19 September 1985.

56. On the scandals in the early years of the Fifth Republic, see Philip Williams, *Wars, Plots and Scandals in Post-war France* (Cambridge: Cambridge University Press, 1970). The Giscard period is discussed in Jacques Derogy and Jean-Maire Pontaut, *Enquête sur les "Affaires" d'un septennat* (Paris: Robert Laffont, 1981).

57. Sunday Times Insight Team, *Rainbow Warrior*, pp. 120–21.

58. Tony Chafer, "Ecologists and the Bomb," in Howorth and Chilton, *Defense and Dissent*, pp. 217–27.

59. For attempts to explain the weakness of the peace movement in France, see Dominique Moïsi,"Les Limites du consensus," in Pierre Lellouche, ed., *Pacifisme et dissuasion* (Paris: Institut français des Relations internationales, 1983), pp. 253–67; Nicole Gnesotto, "La France, fille aînée de l'Alliance," ibid., pp. 267–85; Jolyon Howorth and Patricia Chilton, "Introduction: Defence, Dissent and French Political Culture," in Howorth and Chilton, *Defense and Dissent*, pp. 1–26, esp. pp. 14–20; Christian Mellon, "Peace Organisations in France Today," ibid., pp. 202–26, esp. pp. 202–5; E. P. Thompson, "Postface: France and the European Peace Movement," ibid., pp. 247–52.

60. In a BVA–*Paris-Match* poll taken on 20–21 September 1985 and reported in *Liberation* on 26 September 1985, 66 percent of those interviewed agreed that Greenpeace was receiving "the active support of certain foreign powers," while only 38 percent were opposed to the continuation of French nuclear testing in the South Pacific. Similarly, as late as 3 September 1985, only 29 percent of a SOFRES–Europe 1 sample (*Le Matin*, 3 September 1985) believed that the French secret services had been responsible, but 22 percent blamed "the secret service of a foreign power." In the same poll, 54 percent approved the president's statement that the navy should use force if necessary to protect the nuclear tests.

61. See the four-country survey reported in *Libération*, 16 February 1987 in which French respondents had the highest proportion of "no opinion" on all seven questions and by substantial margins in most cases. The same pattern appears in the international surveys presented by Gregory Flynn, "Opinions publiques et mouvements pacifistes," in Lellouche, *Pacifisme et dissuasion*, pp. 223–38.

62. The first quotation is from Bernard Leconte in *La Croix*, 12 September 1985, while the second is from Etienne Borne in the issue of 5 October of the same newspaper.

63. *Le quotidien de Paris*, 23 August 1985.

64. The extent of this patriotic fervor can be gauged from the fact that, shortly after taking over from Charles Hernu as minister of defense, Paul Quilès took the extraordinary step of telephoning the prisoners on live television during one of the network news programs. More recently, Prime Minister Jacques Chirac paid a special and highly publicized visit to the "Turenges" at the French military base in Hoa where they are still confined.

65. The first poll was done by the Harris agency and reported in *Libération* on 30 August 1985. The second poll was by BVA and reported in *Paris-Match*, 4 September 1985.

66. Alfred Grosser, "La Ve République et la société française," *Pouvoirs* 4 (1982): 143.

67. Cited in *L'Express*, 4 October 1985.

68. See, for example, Diana Pinto, "The Left, Intellectuals and Culture," in Stanley Hoffmann, George Ross, and Sylvia Malzacker (eds.) *The Mitterrand Experiment* (Oxford: Polity Press, 1987), pp. 217–28 and the symposium "Y a-t-il encore des idées de gauche?" in *Le Débat* 42 (November-December 1986). See also the article by Olivier Duhamel, "Ce Qui Divise les Français," in *Le nouvel observateur*, 7 March 1986.

69. Williams, *Wars, Plots and Scandals*, p. 3.

5 • Italy: A Web of Scandals in a Flawed Democracy

JUDITH CHUBB
MAURIZIO VANNICELLI

"There is no distinctly American criminal
class—except Congress."
—Mark Twain

Introduction

On the evening of 3 September 1982, General Carlo Alberto Dalla Chiesa and his wife were gunned down in their car on one of the central streets of Palermo, the capital of Sicily and Italy's sixth largest city. General Dalla Chiesa was but the most eminent in a progression of brutal mafia assassinations of high-ranking police officers, magistrates, and politicians in Palermo that began in the late 1970s.[1] Nationally acclaimed as the man who had led the successful struggle against the network of terror created by the Red Brigades in the 1970s, Dalla Chiesa had been sent to Sicily in May 1982 as prefect of Palermo. His task—to mount an all-out offensive against the mafia. The general's death marked the end of the first serious attempt by the post–World War II Italian state to combat the mafia. Although the profound shock generated by Dalla Chiesa's murder in political circles and in public opinion more generally led to the rapid enactment of major new legislation (the La Torre–Rognoni Law)[2] against the mafia and to the conferral upon his successor of broad special powers that had been denied to the general, the political will to implement fully these new legislative and administrative powers has inexorably subsided since

1982. Today only a handful of dedicated and courageous police officers and magistrates continue the struggle that General Dalla Chiesa began.

On 18 June 1982, Roberto Calvi, who had for over a decade played a leading and controversial role in Italy's financial world, was found hanging under Blackfriars Bridge in London. The victim of a most unsuicidal suicide, Calvi was a banker who by any standards qualified as unusual. Quite unusual, in fact, was his career, which within a few years had catapulted him from the lowly position of bank clerk to uncontested control over Italy's largest private bank, the Banco Ambrosiano. His political contacts and financial allies were also quite uncommon. A master at the game of founding mailbox companies and holdings in fiscal havens around the world, Calvi had created a financial empire that successfully circumvented international banking regulations, cutting across national boundaries and ideological lines. (The Nicaraguan branch of the Ambrosiano was, for instance, the only private bank that the Sandinistas allowed to continue its operations after the fall of the Somoza regime, supposedly to reward Calvi for the financial assistance he had given them during the Nicaraguan revolution). As the main channel through which the Vatican's bank, the Istituto Opere Religiose (I.O.R.), and its head, Monsignor Paul Marcinkus, invested their capital abroad, Calvi had become known in the financial world as "God's Banker." Finally, the collapse of Calvi's financial empire in the early 1980s also had historic proportions; according to reliable estimates the bankruptcy exceeded one billion dollars.[3]

Calvi's onetime mentor and partner in the shadiest meanderings of the international financial world, Michele Sindona, also succumbed to a rather unsuicidal suicide.[4] On 20 March 1986, two days after an Italian court had condemned him to a life sentence for having ordered the assassination of the lawyer appointed by the Ministry of the Treasury to investigate his banking empire, Sindona was found poisoned in his prison cell. Like Calvi, Sindona too had reached a position of prominence in Italy's financial system. In the period from the mid-1960s until his bankruptcy in 1974, his network of banks and holding campanies had played a decisive part in the country's financial life. As the trusted banker of the Vatican (a role in which he would subsequently be replaced by Calvi), as the financier (both overtly and covertly) of Italy's major political parties, as the conduit through which much of the drug-related earnings of the mafia on both sides of the Atlantic were recycled, and as the sole owner of the twenty-fifth largest American banking institution, the Franklin Bank, Sindona had acquired unprecedented financial and political power. At the peak of his influence, Sindona was lionized by the international press and the Italian political establishment alike, with *Time Magazine* characterizing him in one of its cover stories as Italy's most successful man since Mussolini, and then–Prime Minister Andreotti toasting him as the savior of the lira.[5] But, as Italian taxpayers and the thousands of individuals who had deposited their savings in his Italian and American banks were to discover, his financial empire was a castle built on sand.

Scandals Italian Style

What do these three episodes have in common? At the most obvious level they epitomize the corruption and political violence that increasingly pervade the struggle for power, both economic and political, in Italy.[6] Over the past decade, the growing paralysis of Italy's formal democratic institutions has provided a fertile terrain for the growth of various types of informal or "occult" power, penetrating and competing with legitimate centers of power. The three episodes sketched above are but the tips of a massive iceberg of interlocking scandals whose ramifications penetrate to the highest levels of Italy's political, economic, and financial establishments.

The Dalla Chiesa, Calvi, and Sindona affairs, however, are not just the three most notorious manifestations of an underlying climate of corruption and violence in Italy. Direct and disturbing linkages connect these three cases. In the mid-1970s, the Sicilian mafia gained a dominant position in the international drug trade, passing from purely intermediary activities to the direct production of heroin. This represented a qualitative leap from earlier mafia activities, requiring more solid and far-reaching financial connections than the local power base of the mafia could provide. Unscrupulous bankers like Roberto Calvi and Michele Sindona became the conduits through which the mafia acquired financial capital and in turn recycled the enormous illicit profits from the drug trade into high-level national and international financial circuits.[7] An episode from Sindona's decade-long battle against the Italian legal system illustrates his connection with organized crime. In 1979, Sindona was allegedly "kidnapped" in New York by a "Revolutionary Proletarian Group for a Better Justice." He was later discovered to have been living in disguise in Palermo under the protection of a powerful mafia boss, who, through his connections with the American mafia, had helped Sindona stage his own kidnapping.[8]

The greatly enhanced economic power of the mafia that came from the drug trade in turn translated into political clout, further strengthening the already close ties between the mafia and certain sectors of the Italian political elite. By the early 1980s, the political and economic influence of the mafia extended so far beyond the traditional confines of Sicily that Eugenio Scalfari, editor of the prestigious daily *La Repubblica*, could write, "What is at stake is no longer . . . only the destiny of a region suffocated by a malignant and parasitical plant. What is at stake is the very existence of the democratic state—in Palermo, as in Rome and Milan."[9]

The Dalla Chiesa, Calvi, and Sindona cases clearly suggest that, while Italian scandals in their superficial manifestations share some basic characteristics with those that occur in other liberal democracies, their contents, implications, and long-term repercussions are peculiar to Italy. With virtually no exceptions, the many scandals that have taken place in Italy in the postwar period have never been isolated cases, episodic pathological aberrations from an otherwise healthy political and economic system, *accidents de parcours* in the life of a democratic system.[10] Quite the contrary, because of their nature and their protagonists, Italian scandals tend to be interconnected. Very often, in fact, the same individuals reappear in different scandals. Furthermore, the implications of Italian scandals are inevitably political, because virtually every scandal, even the least political on the surface, emanates from or overflows into the political system. Lastly, and perhaps most perplexingly, the majority of Italian scandals seem to leave few, if any, traces. In most instances, as soon as the immediate uproar caused by a scandal has subsided, a business-as-usual attitude gains the upper hand. Despite their magnitude, the Calvi and Sindona financial scandals have not been deemed important enough by the country's political establishment to induce the Italian parliament to introduce reforms that would more effectively regulate the banking system, especially the areas of currency exchange and holding companies—a reform that would, among other things, comply with directives issued by the Commission of the European Community. Similarly, although the escalation of political killings by the mafia has led to the introduction of tough new legislative measures that in theory at least should facilitate the struggle against organized crime, the heart of the mafia's power, its capacity to penetrate into legitimate centers of economic, financial, and political power, remains largely untouched.[11]

In a nutshell, irrespective of their specific nature and manifestations, Italian scandals are the byproduct of structural problems that are deeply rooted in the country's political, institutional, and social fabric. In this sense, they reflect the inner workings of the broader political and economic system, and since they almost always involve state institutions, their connotations are inevitably and distinctly political.[12] It is no exaggeration to say that most Italian scandals are "state scandals" or, as an analyst aptly put it, in Italy a scandalous affair is usually "the *affaire* of the affairs of the state."[13] The uninterrupted and seemingly ever more entangled web of scandals that has punctuated Italy's postwar history can thus be viewed as a mirror—albeit a darkened and distorted one—of the country's political evolution.

Confronted with the spider-like quality of Italian scandals, the methodological alternatives available to the analyst are restricted. To focus the analysis on one case would provide an incomplete picture of the nature of Italy's scandals. Only by looking at the whole tapestry of scandals that break out with alarming regularity in the country is it possible to understand and assess their roots and characteristics on the one hand and their relationship to the Italian political system on the other. The analyst must become an archeologist, digging both horizontally and vertically through the multiple layers of Italy's history of scandals, attempting to bring into the open the connections among scandals that have occurred in different historical periods as well as those that unfold within the same period. While this approach might make the thrust of the analysis and the focus of the narrative less precise, it allows for greater interpretational scope. In particular, it sets the stage for an analytical approach that focuses on the multidimensional roots of scandals and on the responses to them, or lack thereof, on the part of state institutions. In addition, by adopting this approach, scandals can be treated as an integral component of the country's broader political and institutional system, symbiotically intertwined with its inner workings and dynamics, with ramifications that extend into the very heart of the state. Lastly, and most importantly, applied to the Italian case, such an approach permits the analyst to draw generalizations about the nature of the country's democratic system, especially with regard to the role of political parties, the issue of the legitimacy and effectiveness of state institutions, and the problem that is central to politics: the management (or mismanagement) of power.

The well-publicized affair of the P–2 (Propaganda 2) Masonic Lodge, which first burst into the open in the spring of 1981, is probably the most telling example of the interconnected, highly political, and structurally rooted nature of Italian scandals. In many ways, it represents the "end sum" of the many scandals of Italy's postwar history as well as the end station of the country's political voyage since the early 1960s. The last two decades have been a most turbulent period indeed, punctuated by the rampant labor and student militancy of the late 1960s (the so-called "hot autumn"), by right-wing (the infamous "strategy of tension") and left-wing terrorism (epitomized by the Red Brigades and the killing of Aldo Moro) of the 1970s, by the challenge posed by the Eurocommunist phase of the Italian Communist Party (which culminated in the PCI's indirect participation in a government of "national solidarity" in the period from 1976 to 1979), and by the loss of the prime ministership in 1981 on the part of the Christian Democratic Party, which had monopolized it throughout the postwar period.

Symptomatically, it was the investigation into the Sindona affair, which—as we have seen—was in turn linked to the Calvi case and the mafia, which catapulted the P–2 Lodge onto the front pages of the national and international press. On 17 March 1981, officers of the special branch of the Italian police in charge of fiscal and financial issues raided the residence of Licio Gelli, the "venerable master" of the P–2 Masonic Lodge, in Tuscany. The documents uncovered by the police sparked the most traumatic political scandal in Italy's postwar period. While many documents were found that demonstrated the remarkable extent to which Gelli's secret organization had penetrated the nerve centers of the country's political and, in part, financial institutions, one document was particularly explosive: a list of the highly selected (and inevitably very powerful) members of the lodge. The list of 962 members included two cabinet ministers, over fifty generals and admirals (including virtually all the present and former heads of the various branches of the country's intelligence agencies), a score of prominent industrialists, bankers, diplomats, high-ranking police officers, and high-level civil servants. In addition, the list revealed that twenty-four journalists (some of them editors of the country's most prestigious newspapers) had been members of the P–2 or were in the process of being inducted into the lodge. Finally, thirty-eight members of parliament were listed as "members in good standing," drawn from all the political forces represented in the country's parliament, with the exception of the Communist Party and the minuscule Radical Party.

The reconstruction of the internal structure of the P–2 as conducted by the magistrates was even more revealing. While Gelli operated as the unchallenged and untouchable catalyst around which the entire secret network of the organization revolved, the lodge was divided into eighteen groups according to an organizational model reminiscent of military structures.[14] Each group represented, in fact, a sector of the country's political, economic, and institutional life, and each was headed by those members of the P–2 who were particularly prominent and powerful in that given sector. (It is, for instance, no coincidence that Calvi was the leading representative of the "financial-banking" group of the P–2, and that Sindona too was a member of the lodge.) Clearly, the lodge had all the makings of a "state within the state," or perhaps of an alternative state, which, regardless of its actual long-term purposes, was able to influence through its organizational network some of the country's most vital political, economic, and institutional sectors.[15] No other organization, secret or otherwise, has been able to acquire so much overt and covert power in postwar Italy. Able to capitalize on tentacles that linked bankers skillful at illegal financial dealings, virtually the entire high echelon of the country's secret services, the conspirators behind the right-wing "strategy of tension," and the world of organized crime, Gelli and the P–2 had become—or were on the verge of becoming—the center of the system of "occult powers" that constitutes the dark underside of Italian democracy.

While the broader implications and significance of the P–2 scandal will be discussed in a later section of this essay, a few comments should be offered here. To begin with, the country's political establishment was deeply involved in the P–2 scandal, and the significance of this involvement went well beyond the fact that thirty-eight members of parliament officially belonged to the Masonic Lodge. It is unlikely, in fact, that an organization such as the P–2 could have existed and prospered without the connivance, if not the support, of state leaders and institutions. Interestingly, for two months after the discovery of the P–2 documents the government, then headed by Arnaldo Forlani, a leading member of the Christian Democratic Party, resorted to Nixonian tactics in order to stall and prevent the publication of the membership list, invoking considerations of national security and state interests. Only the resolve of the magistrates who had ordered the search of Gelli's residence eventually led to the publication of the list; in order to do so, they had to circumvent the government by sending the documents to the parliamentary commission in charge of investigating the Sindona case.

Secondly, the P–2 affair underscores the high level of corruptibility of Italian political and economic life. Only in this way is it possible to explain the acquisition of enormous political power on the part of Gelli, the owner of a mattress factory who, by masterfully using a mix of coercion, blackmail, and bribes, was able to become, in his own words, a puppetmaster, influencing the behavior of some of the country's leading politicians, businessmen, and state officials. The explanations put forth by some of the P–2 members for their decision to join a secret society—something expressly forbidden by article 18 of the Italian constitution—are quite revealing; above all, they point both to the receptiveness of the Italian political system to corrupt practices and to the effectiveness of Gelli's strategy, one that was almost Machiavellian in its genial simplicity. The typical member of the P–2, say an ambitious military man, would join the lodge not because of some philosophical adherence to Masonic principles; rather, he would seek membership because, as promised by Gelli, the extensive network of contacts and political influence spawned by the P–2 would allow him to advance his career more rapidly, often eliminating political obstacles and opposition. In a country as politicized as Italy, where an individual's success in most careers, including those in the business world, is often a measure of one's political contacts and party affiliation, there is no doubt that the merchandise sold by Gelli was a most desirable commodity. As admitted by Amintore Fanfani, a veteran leader of the Christian Democratic Party who as general secretary of the DC had received a substantial "loan" from Sindona, in his testimony before the parliamentary commission entrusted with the task of investigating the P–2 phenomenon, "the strength of Gelli was born out of the weakness of [his followers]"[16]—the weakness and, one might add, the ambition of assorted power-seekers. The end result was a positive-sum game: the increased power and influence of a P–2 member inevitably resulted, after being filtered and appropriately calibrated by Gelli, in the increased (real or potential) power and influence of other P–2 members, which in turn strengthened the hold of the organization created by the "puppetmaster" over the country's economic and political system. This is why, contrary to most interpretations, we tend to regard the P–2 phenomenon not as a conspiratorial attempt to subvert, or perhaps even to replace the state, but rather as a conspiracy among certain political and economic leaders whose purpose was to undermine the normal functioning and *raison d'être* of the democratic system in order to further their individual and collective interests.

Lastly, as the P–2 affair once again demonstrated, in Italy perpetrators of scandals are rarely punished. Certainly forewarned by his well-placed affiliates, Gelli was able to flee the country before the police search of his residence and to seek refuge in South America, where he could count on the protection of right-wing political and military leaders. It took Italian authorities over ten years after the collapse of his financial empire in 1984 to obtain Sindona's extradition from the United States, and then only on the understanding that he would be tried exclusively for his role in the assassination of the man in charge of investigating his financial irregularities. Calvi himself had been able to leave Italy undisturbed on the way to his tragic and mysterious end in London, even though he had already been sentenced for violations of currency regulations.[17]

Even when the perpetrators of scandals are punished, a strange pattern seems to be at work: the political protectors of individuals engaging in acts of financial and economic piracy are almost never brought to trial. A clear correlation exists between the power of an individual politician (or the power of his political party), and the degree to which he is able to survive unscathed his involvement in a given scandal. When, at the time of the Lockheed scandal, a former minister, Mario Tanassi, was eventually sentenced to serve a prison term, this was largely due to the fact that his political fortunes had been declining even before the outbreak of the scandal and that he had the misfortune of belonging to a minor political party; he was, in short, expendable. More powerful politicians, who had also been the beneficiaries of Lockheed bribes, continued in their careers undisturbed.[18]

The never-ending case of Giulio Andreotti, who has been in and out of the government for over three decades, serving five times as prime minister, is perhaps the most telling example of the capacity of powerful Italian politicians to remain unaffected by scandals in which they have been directly or indirectly involved. In comparison to Andreotti's turbulent political career, Nixon's "seven plus one crises" fade in importance. There has virtually been no scandal or affair in Italy's postwar history in which Andreotti has had no role; at the very least, even if he was not directly implicated, he happened to be in charge of the ministry in whose area of responsibility a given scandal occurred. Clearly, as suggested by a major critic of Andreotti, he should at least have been impeached for repeated dereliction of duty.[19] His efforts when he was prime minister to help Sindona overcome his legal and financial difficulties, as well as his many contacts with Gelli and the protection he has accorded over the years to other prominent members of the P–2 lodge, have led many observers to conclude that Andreotti might have been the grey eminence behind the Masonic Lodge, manipulating the self-proclaimed "puppetmaster" Gelli. That Andreotti has been able over the years to muster enough political support in parliament to survive twenty-five attempts at impeachment, and the fact that on the occasion of the last such attempt he was rescued by the votes of the bulk of Communist parliamentarians, attest to his immense political power.

In summary, it might be an overstatement to argue that the P–2 affair and the other scandals we have mentioned above are the inevitable consequences of an imperfect political and economic system. Yet, it is certainly true that some of the structural imperfections and dysfunctions of the Italian democratic system have produced a "cultural atmosphere" that is conducive to the proliferation of scandals on the one hand and to their partial or complete cover-up on the other. To be sure, not even the most perfect democratic political system is immune to scandals. When scandals, however, become the rule, and not the exception, in a political system, and when such a system is consistently unable or unwilling to extirpate the roots of the merry-go-round of scandals which afflict its existence, only one conclusion is possible: the practices and realities of that political system have failed to live up to the ideals upon which it is predicated.

Scandals and the Italian Political System

A vast array of historical, political, institutional, and cultural factors coalesce to make Italy, by comparison with other Western parliamentary democracies, a flawed democracy. Of course, no political system, be it a liberal democracy or different variations on socialism, is perfect. To limit ourselves to the western experiment in democracy, its history amply demonstrates how difficult it is to translate ideological prescriptions into a political system that faithfully embodies them. The jump from theory to practice is neither simple nor smooth; and, above all, it is a never-ending process that constantly requires institutional adjustments, well-timed theoretical redefinitions, and salutary acts of social engineering. The ideal of ideological purity is indeed a seemingly unreachable goal, always eluding the grasp of the practitioners of politics. The practice of politics will in fact always fall short of the theory that presumably inspires it, resulting in political systems that are "mixed" in that they contain elements from different ideological traditions and orientations.

Instead of focusing on the long-term goal of attaining a democratic system (which presupposes that the gap between ideal and reality can be closed), the analyst is better served by stressing the process by which ideal and reality interact. In this way, the principles of an ideological ideal are to be viewed more as signposts of a complex process than as the end station of the voyage of democracy. A few of these signposts should be mentioned, however, since they are shared by all democratic systems, irrespective of the degree to which they have successfully translated the democratic ideal into reality. Above all, pluralism can be singled out as the centerpiece of a democratic system. In practical terms, pluralism should mean more than the possibility for the population to articulate its political preferences, either through the ballot or other means of political expression; rather, it should provide institutional mechanisms, primarily in a party system, which permit the representation of different political views and interests. Relatedly, in order to be effective, pluralism requires that the management and distribution of governmental power reflect, possibly in a proportional fashion, electoral results. This implies the existence of mechanisms that allow for the alternation of power among competing political groups, and thereby the possibility of holding the government accountable to the electorate. Lastly, a truly effective democratic system must possess institutionalized channels for registering popular support for (or, more importantly, discontent with) state policies, bureaucratic institutions that are responsive to the needs and aspirations of the population, and a legal system that is both efficient and unencumbered by political influences. If operative, such a system would fulfill another requirement of the democratic ideal: it would assure the legitimacy of state institutions, defined as an attitude of trust among the citizenry with regard to the capacity and willingness of state institutions to represent the interests and preferences of the population.

As Italy emerged out of the destruction of the second World War, leaving behind two decades of Fascist rule, the democratic ideal was adopted as the frame of reference for the newborn republic. Consisting of representatives of all the political parties that had been active in the Resistance against fascism and the Nazi occupation, the Constituent Assembly drafted a constitution that both in its spirit and its letter, was almost celebratory in its adherence to the democratic ideal. Yet the introduction of a democratic constitution and of democratic political practices could not effect a *tabula rasa*, a new beginning that could sweep away with one bold stroke a legacy of distorted experiments in democracy. And, unlike the optimistic prediction by Benedetto Croce, Italy's most prominent modern philosopher, fascism turned out not to be an "historical parenthesis" that would cease to have any effect on the country's political life as soon as democratic principles and institutions were introduced. Although they were painted over with democratic colors, some of the features of the fascist era continued to be operative after 1945, particularly in the institutional realm. That the failure to eradicate the heritage of the past might have served the interests of political forces that rose to power after 1947 is of secondary importance here. More important is that old and new problems merged, creating a political milieu that contributed to making Italian democracy imperfect or, to be more blunt, flawed.

Overall, the institutional structures of the Italian political system are basically similar to those of other western parliamentary democracies. It is rather in the functioning of the institutions of parliamentary democracy and above all in the nature and role of the political parties that the unique features of the Italian political system become evident.[20]

First and foremost, in contrast to the democratic ideal, Italian democracy is one in which there has been no alternation of power in the forty years since the establishment of the republic in 1946. The dominant party, the Christian Democratic Party (DC), has held power uninterruptedly throughout the postwar period, while the major party of opposition, the Communist Party (PCI), has been excluded from governmental participation except for a brief period of broad coalitions of national solidarity in the immediate postwar years (1945–47) and for the 1976–79 period, when the PCI "participated from without"—to use the Byzantine formula coined by Italian politicians—in coalition governments led by the Christian Democrat Andreotti.[21] Hence, a fundamental principle of democratic government, the accountability of the governing party or coalition effected by means of the possibility of electoral defeat and alternation of power, has been absent in Italy, where the major party of opposition has until very recently not been considered a legitimate contender for power.

By comparison to other Western democracies, Italy is often represented as an extreme example of political instability. In the forty-one years since the end of World War II, there have been forty-five governments, the average life of a government being a mere ten months. Behind this facade of instability, however, Italy can be seen paradoxically as the most stable of Western democracies. As noted above, a single party has dominated Italian politics throughout the postwar period; although the identity of the DC's coalition partners has changed over the years, the Christian Democratic Party has constituted the keystone of every government since 1947. Stability is also evident in the composition of the country's political elite. Over a period of forty years, top ministerial positions have been monopolized by a small group of Christian Democratic leaders, remarkably unaffected by political or generational change. The times and the DC's political partners may change, but the same faces continually reappear in a kind of musical chairs of ministerial realignments. Of the top 1,331 governmental positions (ministers and undersecretaries) distributed between 1946 and 1976, two-thirds were held by 152 politicians, and 480 by only thirty-one politicians.[22] One observer has likened the Italian government to a repertory company, in which a small group of actors continually rotates among the leading roles.[23] And it is no exaggeration to add that this company often resembles those of *commedia dell'arte* fame.

This long-term stability of party rule and of political leadership is in turn reinforced by an equally remarkable pattern of electoral stability. Despite the tremendous social and economic changes over the past four decades that have transformed Italy from a predominantly agricultural country into a modern urban and industrial society, the political preferences of the Italian electorate have remained surprisingly stable. Elections in Italy have often been presented as an ideological plebiscite, a "choice of civilizations" between two mutually exclusive camps, the Catholics and the Marxists. To be sure, since the mid-1970s, the increasing modernization and secularization of Italian society have begun to undermine traditional subcultural, ideological, and patronage-based appeals, leading to increasing electoral mobility. In the words of Italian political scientists Arturo Parisi and Gianfranco Pasquino, the subcultural "vote of belonging" and the clientelistic "vote of exchange" are being replaced by a more modern "vote of opinion." [24] At the same time as the votes for the specific parties are becoming more volatile, however, the general alignment of the electorate among political "areas"—left, center, and right—has remained surprisingly stable. Even in the 1983 parliamentary elections in which the Christian Democratic Party suffered major losses for the first time since 1946, what took place was not any significant shift of votes among the left, center, and right blocs, but rather a reshuffling of votes among the parties within each ideological bloc. The relative balance of forces between the Communists and their allies on the left and the parties of the governing Center-Left coalition remained virtually unchanged.

How can these unique characteristics of Italian democracy be explained? The answer lies above all in the weakness of formal institutions and the concentration of real power in the hands of the political parties, creating what the Italians call *partitocrazia,* or rule by party. While political parties play a central role in any western democracy, ordinarily governments, once in place, have a certain autonomy from the party organizations that sustain them. In Italy, on the contrary, real power lies not with the prime minister but rather with the secretaries of the parties constituting the governing coalition. During some periods, like the years between 1976 and 1979, when the Communist Party sustained the parliamentary majority without formal participation in the government, this practice of policymaking not by government ministers but rather by consultation and bargaining among the leaders of the major parties was extended even to the "opposition."[25]

The dominant position of the parties arises, among other factors, from the failure of elections to play any meaningful role in the creation of governments, the selection of the country's top leadership, or the formulation of policy choices. The fragmentation of the party system (over ten parties currently hold seats in parliament) and an electoral system of proportional representation that allows parties with only one percent of the vote to gain parliamentary representation have prevented any one party from gaining a clear majority,[26] although the DC has remained the party of relative majority with 32 to 40 percent of the vote. (See Table 5. 1.) The lack of a clear parliamentary majority necessitates the formation of coalition governments and it shifts the choice of government from the electorate to negotiations among potential coalition partners after the vote. Because of their strategic importance for the creation of a parliamentary majority, small parties can gain disproportionate leverage at the governmental level, as evidenced by the granting of the prime ministership in 1981 to Giovanni Spadolini, leader of the tiny Republican Party (which got 3 percent of the vote) and in 1983 to the Socialist Bettino Craxi, whose party held 11 percent of the vote.

The political weight of the minor parties is further magnified by the exclusion from power of the Communist Party, which has throughout the postwar period represented approximately one-third of the electorate. As a result, the political base for the formation of coalition governments has been narrowed, the alternation of power between majority and opposition has been precluded, and any accountability of the governing parties for their actions or policies has thus been rendered highly problematic. Despite the erosion of ideological barriers in the 1970s and 1980s, and despite the DC's unenviable record of inefficiency, corruption, and scandal, the DC remains an eternal party of government and the PCI an eternal party of opposition.

The key to understanding Italy's "flawed democracy" thus lies in the nature of the political parties and the party system. Two definitions coined by Italian political scientists—"polarized pluralism" and "imperfect bipartyism"—point to those characteristics that distinguish the Italian party system from those of other western democracies.[27] In the first place, the Italian party system is highly fragmented. Over ten parties are represented at the national level, while local and special-interest lists (e.g., the Lega Veneta, the Partito Sardo d'Azione, lists representing the interests of pensioners, and of untenured university professors and researchers) proliferate in regional and local elections. These parties reflect the deep ideological, social, and regional cleavages that continue to divide Italy. Parties range from the Communists, Socialists, and small "new-left" groups on the Left to the Christian Democrats and the small "lay" parties (Republicans, Social Democrats, and Liberals) in the Center to the neo-Fascist Movimento Sociale Italiano (MSI) on the Right. Although the divisions among many of these parties reflect the impact of historical issues long since past (e.g., Italian unification, the Russian revolution, church-state relations), the electoral system, combined with the logic of organizational self-preservation, has prevented amalgamation and indeed has at times promoted schismatic divisions, since it guarantees even tiny parties parliamentary representation.

At the same time, the political system is polarized around two political ideological, and social poles—the Catholics and the Marxists. Beginning in 1948, the Christian Democrats and the Communists emerged as the two dominant parties, sharing two-thirds to three-fourths of the vote between them.

Table 5.1

Election Results: Chamber of Deputies (in percentages; number of seats in parentheses)

Party[a]	1948	1953	1958	1963	1968	1972	1976	1979	1983
DC	48.5 (305)	40.1 (263)	42.4 (273)	38.3 (260)	39.1 (266)	38.8 (267)	38.7 (262)	38.3 (262)	32.9 (225)
PCI	31 (183)[b]	22.6 (143)	22.7 (140)	25.3 (166)	26.9 (177)	27.2 (179)	34.4 (228)	30.4 (201)	29.9 (198)
PSI		12.8 (75)	14.2 (84)	13.8 (87)	14.5 (91)[b]	9.6 (61)	9.6 (57)	9.8 (62)	11.4 (73)
PSDI	7.1 (33)	4.5 (19)	4.5 (22)	6.1 (33)		5.1 (29)	3.4 (15)	3.8 (20)	4.1 (23)
PRI	2.5 (9)	1.6 (5)	1.4 (6)	1.4 (6)	2 (9)	2.9 (14)	3.1 (14)	3 (16)	5.1 (29)
PLI	3.8 (19)	3 (13)	3.5 (17)	7 (39)	5.8 (31)	3.9 (21)	1.3 (5)	1.9 (9)	2.9 (16)
PR	—	—	—	—	—	—	1.1 (4)	3.5 (18)	2.2 (11)
DP	—	—	—	—	—	—	1.5 (6)	0.8 (—)	1.5 (7)
PdUP	—	—	—	—	—	—		1.4 (6)	—[c]
MSI	2 (6)	5.8 (29)	4.8 (24)	5.1 (27)	4.4 (24)	8.7 (56)	6.1 (35)	5.3 (30)	6.8 (42)
Monarchists	2.8 (14)	6.9 (40)	4.8 (25)	1.7 (8)	1.3 (6)	—	—	—	—
Others[d]	2.5 (5)	2.7 (3)	1.7 (5)	1.3 (4)	6.0 (26)	4.0 (4)	0.8 (4)	2.7 (6)	3.2 (6)

Source: Istituto Centrale di Statistica (ISTAT).

[a] DC (Democrazia cristiana), PCI (Partito comunista italiano), PSI (Partito socialista italiano), PSDI (Partito socialista democratico italiano), PRI (Partito repubblicano italiano), PLI (Partito liberale italiano), PR (Partito radicale), DP (Democrazia proletaria), PdUP (Partito di unità proletaria per il comunismo), MSI (Movimento sociale italiano).

[b] Parties presented joint election lists.

[c] Ran on PCI lists.

[d] Includes South Tyrol People's party (SVP), Sardinian Action party (PSA), Valdôtaine Union (UV), and Socialist Party of Proletarian Unity (PSIUP). SVP generally accounts for 3 seats; PSIUP won 23 seats in 1968.

These two parties are in turn linked to organized subcultures that came into being with the creation of mass political movements at the end of the nineteenth century, thereby extending their reach far beyond the limited confines of electoral politics. This polarization is the basis of Italy's "imperfect bipartyism." The deep subcultural roots and opposing ideological appeals of Italy's two major parties, the DC and the PCI, throughout most of the postwar period have "frozen" the Italian electorate into two counterposed ideological blocs.

Strangely enough, despite these deep ideological divisions, in the day-to-day functioning of Italy's political institutions substantial cooperation occurs across ideological barriers. Indicative of this cooperation is the fact that 75 percent of Italian legislation is enacted in committees rather than on the floor of parliament, and of these laws 90 percent are approved unanimously.[28] Such cooperation between the majority and the opposition has a long tradition. As a parliamentary strategy, *trasformismo*—the cooptation of the opposition into broad and amorphous parliamentary majorities—was initiated in 1876 by Prime Minister Agostino De Pretis, who induced opposition deputies to shift their votes to the government majority in exchange for personal benefits and, above all, for access to state patronage. *Trasformismo* soon became the keystone upon which governments were formed and sustained.[29] As a result, parliament was transformed into a kind of bazaar, characterized not by political debate but by perpetual bargaining among government ministers, deputies, and their respective clienteles. One hundred years later, despite the Fascist interlude and the rise of "anti-system" opposition parties, parliamentary politics in Italy continues to a large extent to function according to the logic of *trasformismo*. Throughout the postwar period, Italian politics has been characterized by the attempt to construct ever broader parliamentary coalitions cutting across ideological lines. In the 1950s, the Monarchist Right was almost entirely absorbed into the Christian Democratic Party. In the 1960s, the famous "opening to the left" split the opposition by bringing the Socialist Party (PSI) into the government coalition; although the new Center-Left formula was based on promises of far-reaching reforms, the practice of Center-Left governments soon degenerated into precisely the same type of personalistic and patronage-based politics that the Socialists had condemned when they were in the opposition. In the years 1976 through 1979, this process was carried one step further with the formation of governments of national solidarity, in which the Communist Party first abstained and then formally supported the DC-led government majority, without however directly participating in the government itself. Although the PCI returned to its traditional role of opposition in 1979, important sectors of both the PCI and the DC continue to seek a government formula based on collaboration rather than confrontation between the country's two major parties.

Because of the fragmentation of the Italian party system and the ideological differentiation among the parties, Italian governments tend to be congenitally weak, reduced to immobility by guerrilla warfare among the erstwhile allies. Although the DC's coalition partners share with it positions ranging from the center-right to the center-left of the political spectrum, they are deeply divided by distinct histories, philosophies of government, and constituencies. Consequently, there is rarely any policy consensus, and governments are patched together more on the basis of the distribution of levers of power and patronage than on the basis of any coherent policy program. Not surprisingly, such coalitions hold together only so long as no important policy choices need to be made or until temporarily submerged power struggles among the governing parties, their internal factions, or individual leaders burst into the open and propel the government once again to the verge of crisis.[30] Given the exclusion of the PCI from the "governmental area," government crises usually result not in any major shifts in the majority coalition, but rather in a reshuffling of ministerial positions and patronage levers among the leaders and factions of the governing parties. The formation of each new government is an act of delicate political engineering. The result is a process of constant bargaining, involving overt and covert trade-offs and mutually constraining compromises among coalition partners. This is clearly a fertile ground for the proliferation of scandals.

Partitocrazia goes beyond the domination of parliament and the executive by the political parties to embrace a broad cross-section of the economic, social, and cultural life of the country. Virtually no section of Italian life is free from party interference. The boards of directors of a far-reaching network of public and semipublic agencies—including banks, state-owned industries, hospitals, social security and health insurance programs, radio and television—are subject to government (i.e., party) nomination. Thus, the Italian state and Italian society have been "colonized" by the political parties, creating a vast spoils system in which levers of power are strictly apportioned according to the electoral weight of the various parties, including since the mid 1970s even the Communists. This system of *sottogoverno* [31] constitutes a reservoir of partisan power and patronage without equal in any other western democracy. The basis for the creation of such a system of power has been the tremendous expansion of state intervention in the postwar period, the progressive interpenetration of the governing parties, especially the DC, with the state administration, and the consequent privatization of state power for political ends. In Italy, power has come to signify above all access to patronage, and patronage further reinforces entrenched power—for individual politicians and factions as much, or more so, than for any particular party.

A major constraint on party power, however, arises from internal factionalism. Only the Communist Party is free from formally organized factions, the role of which is particularly pronounced within the Christian Democratic Party and was within the Socialist Party prior to its closing of ranks behind the present party secretary and Prime Minister Bettino Craxi. Internal power struggles impede the formulation of coherent party programs and are primary factors behind government crises. Party factions, while formally justified in ideological or programmatic terms, in reality are rooted more in personal power struggles than in differences of ideology or policy. Each faction is a kind of political fiefdom, often with its own funding, its own headquarters and publications, and its own links to specific interest groups. Party and faction, rather than professional qualifications, are the determining factors in the distribution of ministerial portfolios and other positions of power. In fact, in order to accommodate factional demands, the Italian cabinet is the largest in any Western democracy.

Another constraint on party power is the vast bureaucracy that forms the foundation of the Italian system of *sottogoverno*. The government administration continues to be fashioned after the Napoleonic model, rigidly centralized and hierarchical, with lengthy and highly formalistic procedures and lines of command. There is so little delegation of authority within the bureaucracy that some ministers must personally sign as many as two hundred documents per day. Only with the creation of regional governments in 1970 was any of the power of the central administration delegated to lower territorial levels.[32] Even so, over a decade after the enactment of the reform, bureaucratic obstructionism at the center continues to hinder the effective transfer of important portions of those powers now reserved to the regions.

Control of the bureaucracy is of key political importance in Italy not only because of the extent of direct or indirect state control, but also because recruitment to the civil service has constituted one of the prime levers of patronage upon which political careers are built. As a result, an already slow-moving, cumbersome, and inefficient bureaucratic structure is further weighed down by a class of civil servants whose primary qualification is political loyalty rather than technical skills.

Within this vast bureaucratic machine there is remarkably little communication or coordination even among departments within the same ministry or agency (ente), let alone among different sectors of the state administration. Each ministry constitutes a kind of sealed compartment, a power unto itself. The consequences come clear in the extreme difficulty of implementing any policy or program that cuts across narrow sectoral lines.

The dysfunctions of the Italian bureaucracy—excessive red tape, lengthy delays in obtaining even the most simple public document, lack of communication and coordination—provide a fertile terrain for political maneuvering of both the licit and the illicit variety. Individual politicians have constructed political fortunes through their privileged access to key sectors of the bureaucracy and their ability to use their political connections to produce results that might otherwise require months or even years. But the importance of personal intervention in the workings of Italy's Byzantine bureaucracy is not limited to greasing the wheels of an otherwise slow-moving and irresponsive administrative machine. In fact, the protagonists of some of the most notorious scandals of the past decade—e.g., Licio Gelli and Francesco Pazienza—owed their meteoric careers precisely to their talents as intermediaries.[33] Their power lay in their ability to cut across political and institutional boundaries and to link formal institutions with outside centers of power in the pursuit of somewhat less-than-legitimate interests. They thus performed a function that although it has no constitutional or legal basis, is absolutely critical for the functioning of a highly fragmented political, economic, and administrative system like that of Italy—to provide channels for the flow of information, for personal contacts, and for the coordination of policy across otherwise almost insuperable institutional and political barriers.

Therefore, financial scandals like those associated with Michele Sindona and Roberto Calvi, as well as broader phenomena like the mafia and the P-2, should not be viewed as criminal activities distinct from and directed against the legitimate institutions of Italian democracy, but rather as an integral part of the existing system of power. Italy's "flawed" model of parliamentary democracy—the degeneration of the party system into sterile bickering over positions of power and patronage increasingly divorced from the real problems of the country, and the consequent paralysis of formal institutions—has created a void of effective decision-making power into which so-called "occult powers" have stepped. In addition, the colonization of the state and broad sectors of society by the political parties, and the resulting logic of *lottizzazione*[34] and patronage as the heart of political struggle, have resulted in a blurring of the lines between public and private and in a pervasive conception of the state as above all a vehicle for personal and factional interests.

Given the extent of the "primacy of politics" and the ways in which the political system penetrates into all aspects of Italian life, it is not surprising that the extensive state intervention in the economy (approximately 40 percent of the country's economy is directly or indirectly controlled by the state) should provide ample opportunities for corrupt practices.[35] Even though in no advanced industrial state is it any longer possible to draw a clear distinction between the economic and the political dimensions of life, in Italy the blurring of traditional lines between these two dimensions has become a major source of corruption. What is critical in the Italian case is not the massive size of the state's direct or indirect intervention in the economy, but the manner in which state presence in the economic system is managed and perhaps more importantly the fact that it is often a stake in the struggle for power and the bargaining among political parties. Inevitably, appointments of heads of state-owned enterprises reflect the distribution of power that exists among the parties of the governmental majority at any given point in time, and the policies pursued by these state managers are often based on calculations of political gain rather than on considerations of economic rationality.[36]

The P–2 affair—and, in this context, the financial whirlwind set in motion by Sindona and Calvi must be viewed as part of the broader P–2 phenomenon—illustrates the extent to which the state's economic choices, the interests of political groupings, and the workings of the "occult powers" merge, creating opportunities for corrupt activities. As the catalyst of a secret organization with ramifications in the country's political, economic, and institutional sectors, Gelli was obviously in a position to exercise decisive influence. The ENI–Petromin scandal is a telling demonstration of this. In June 1979, ENI, a state-owned oil company and one of the world's largest enterprises outside the United States, concluded an agreement with Petromin, Saudi Arabia's oil company, for the delivery of large quantities of oil to Italy over a period of five years. As revealed by documents found in Gelli's residence, part of the agreement was the stipulation for a kickback of over two hundred million dollars, the bulk of which was to go to ENI itself and to the political parties, especially the PSI.[37] Not surprisingly, virtually all the individuals implicated in the scandal—executives of ENI, several political leaders, high-ranking officials of state-owned banks, and fiscal authorities—were prominent members of the P–2, with Gelli acting as the *trait d'union* among them. Equally revealing of the pervasiveness and interconnectedness of the system of power established by Gelli is the fact that in the period from 1978 to 1980 ENI's foreign-based branches had lent a total of $160 million to holding companies owned by Calvi's bank, the Ambrosiano, a rather strange activity indeed for a state-owned enterprise whose stated purpose is to procure oil deliveries to Italy and, if possible, to reduce the country's heavy dependence on foreign sources of energy.

Clearly, where the purpose of the state is seen as primarily the enhancement of positions of personal, factional, and party power, the distinction between legitimate and illegitimate forms of political power and influence fades away. As a result, mafia bosses who control blocks of votes essential to the political careers of parliamentary deputies and government ministers receive major public works contracts, and in some cases they are directly elected to local administrations in certain areas of the south. Licio Gelli's P–2 lodge became a major scandal precisely because its members included an impressive cross-section of the country's political and economic elite. Before the crashes of their respective banks, the two largest private banks in Italy, Michele Sindona and Roberto Calvi financed the entire spectrum of political parties, as well as important national and local newspapers, in addition to their less wholesome role in setting up channels for the recycling of the mafia's enormous profits from the drug trade. In neither its legitimate nor its illegitimate forms would the power exercised by these individuals or groups be conceivable without high-level political connections and protection.[38]

It is therefore inevitable that legitimacy, as the cornerstone of an effective democratic system, should have a most tormented existence in Italy. This is not to suggest that the Italian political system is illegitimate in the strict sense of the word. As argued by some apologists of the country's political system, the source of most of the country's problems might be an "excess of democracy," exemplified by the multitude of political parties represented in parliament. It is fair to contend, however, that legitimacy cannot be measured by counting the number of elections (which, as is well known, are quite frequent in Italy) or the number of political parties present in parliament. Nor can it be argued that a country's political system is legitimate because it is able to absorb, somehow, periodic outbursts of popular discontent. In a democratic system, the issue of legitimacy is fundamentally intangible, for it rests, as Tocqueville suggested over a century ago, on "moods"—the trust that the population feels toward the state and its institutions, the belief that the political class is bent on promoting public rather than private interests, and the conviction that the rules followed by the political establishment reflect the general will of the citizenry.

In a pathbreaking study on political culture published over two decades ago, Gabriel Almond and Sidney Verba concluded that Italian political culture was marked by a high level of "alienation."[39] Their assessment is still valid today. Recent trends in the country's political life indicate that the overall level of alienation has, if anything, increased in the last decade. Recent patterns of electoral behavior support this argument. Although Italy continues to have one of the highest rates of electoral participation in the West, abstention is becoming a widespread phenomenon.[40] Some observers have argued that this rise in abstention rates indicates that Italy is finally moving toward levels of voter turnout more typical of western democracies. In the Italian context, however, it seems more likely that such a decline in electoral participation reflects above all a growing disillusionment with a blocked party system that is seen as increasingly unresponsive to the needs of a rapidly changing society. Likewise, the never-ending spectacle of scandals whose protagonists usually remain unpunished certainly reinforces the popular belief that politicians are corrupt, oblivious to the general interest, and unreceptive to the needs and aspirations of the people.[41]

This reinforces in the "collective conscience" of the nation the perception that scandals constitute the norm of public behavior rather than a pathology or deviation to be isolated and condemned. In Italian politics there rarely emerges a "purifier" who reasserts the norms of proper conduct and reinforces the legitimacy of the democratic process by punishing offenders. In Italy, on the contrary, in most cases the major offenders continue unperturbed in the exercise of power, their reputations not only untarnished but often reinforced by their aura of "untouchability." Far from serving a ritualistic function of catharsis and relegitimation, as is the case in some of the liberal democracies examined in this volume, scandals in Italy form part of a *delegitimizing* spiral in which the credibility of democratic norms and procedural guarantees is ever further undermined and the gap between the citizen and political institutions grows ever wider.

Although one can only speculate about their actual importance as contributors to the mounting political apathy of the Italian population, two other factors must be mentioned here. The first concerns the evolution of the Communist Party, which has clearly lost much of its traditional capacity to aggregate protest from below and to act as the spokesman for those voters who derive few benefits from the system of political and economic power established by the DC in the postwar period and reinforced in more recent years by various Center-Left government coalitions. As the PCI has moved to eliminate or downplay many of the ideological and organizational features that made it a party "different from the others," the traditional image of the PCI as an agent of change has become blurred. Likewise, the experience of the PCI in the 1976–79 period, when the party supported the government without being able to affect economic and social policies, led many voters to perceive the Communists as a component—albeit *sui generis* and somewhat reluctant—of the political establishment. Finally, although in recent years PCI leaders have placed much emphasis on the so-called "moral question," meaning the proliferation of corrupt practices in the country's political and financial-economic systems, the fact that some local Communist administrators too have been involved in scandals has eroded the party's credibility as the only "clean" political force in Italy.[42]

Second, in recent years the Italian trade union movement has witnessed a sharp decline of what has traditionally been one of its unique characteristics: the capacity to articulate and to represent demands from below. While it might have been unreasonable to expect the unions to maintain the power they had acquired in the late 1960s and early 1970s (the "hot autumn" period), when they often acted as if they were a political party or a fourth estate in the country's political landscape, the weakening of their overall political power has been substantial. Their influence on the country's economic and social choices has become irrelevant; disaffection among the rank and file is rampant; and, after years of incremental expansion, union membership has been declining.[43]

In sum, the failure of the Italian political establishment to translate into practice the principles enshrined in the country's constitution has produced a political system that encourages corrupt activities by unscrupulous individuals and groups. Growing apathy and cynicism on the part of the citizenry with regard to state institutions and the political elite have generated a cultural climate in which the evasion of civic responsibilities (e.g., the paying of taxes) and the use of public power in the pursuit of private gain have come to be widely accepted as normal, and therefore unreproachable. While the democratic ideal remains the generally accepted frame of reference, the realities of Italy's political, social, and economic life have if anything widened the traditional gap between the "real" Italy and the "legal" Italy, a gap that greatly contributes to the proliferation of scandals.

Living with Scandals

Italy is a country in which corrupt practices can be carried out with impunity, or at least one in which the perpetrators of scandals are usually able to enjoy a kind of diplomatic immunity that protects them against punishment. The response to scandals is usually a "nonresponse." How can this incapacity of the Italian political and judicial systems to respond effectively to scandals be explained?

The answer lies, as we have seen, with *partitocrazia*, the domination of the Italian state and of broad sectors of Italian society by the political parties. To begin with, *partitocrazia* is a most expensive system. Italian elections are fought in pursuit of gains that, though generally minuscule, can alter the internal distribution of power among government partners, which can in turn translate into disproportionately large political and economic gains for those parties that are able to expand their presence in the government by "winning" an election. This forces the parties to embark upon expensive electoral campaigns, which have been occurring with growing frequency. In addition, with the exception of the tiny Radical Party, all Italian parties have over the years become bulky organizations, increasingly assuming mastodontic bureaucratic proportions. The phenomenon of internal factionalism that, with the exception of the Communists and the Radicals, afflicts all the political parties further contributes to the exponential growth of their bureaucratic apparatuses and their corresponding financial needs.

Despite the passage of laws on the financing of political parties in the mid-1970s, which had precisely the purpose of mitigating the problem of parties seeking illicit sources of financing, funds continue to be a scarce commodity. This is one way in which unscrupulous bankers such as Calvi and Sindona became of critical importance to political leaders. Able to rely on labyrinthine networks of banks and holding companies, many of them situated in various fiscal havens around the world, Calvi and Sindona had no difficulty in providing funds to Italy's major parties, often in the form of long-term and easily renewable loans. It goes without saying that the party system's financial dependence on Calvi and Sindona was not without its political costs. The benefits that they derived from their financial support of the parties went well beyond political influence per se. Much more important to Calvi and Sindona was the political protection that in view of the illegal nature of most of their financial activities, guaranteed the continued existence of their financial empires. Moreover, because the bulk of their contributions to the parties occurred through illegal channels, the bankers were able to acquire a weapon of potentially formidable importance should the system of protection they had acquired break down: blackmail. This is precisely the weapon that Sindona skillfully wielded throughout his decade-long struggle against those Italian magistrates who were determined to get him extradited from the United States, and it constitutes a plausible explanation for his untimely death.

The issue of party-controlled media, particularly newspapers, is closely linked to the problem of the parties' financing. In Italy, the importance of party newspapers goes beyond immediate electoral purposes. Perhaps more important is the fact that they serve as a forum through which different political leaders convey messages to allies and foes, test the waters for new coalitions, suggest new policies, and often transmit only thinly veiled threats to those members of the power elite who challenge the status quo. Since each party has its own official newspaper, plus a score of magazines and assorted journals, including those sponsored by internal party factions, the result is an intricate maze of party-controlled publications.

Once again, only resort to outside sources of financing allows the political parties to keep their newspapers in operation, since huge deficits are what all these publications have in common. Interestingly, not even Communist newspapers have been able to escape collusion with unscrupulous bankers. The example of the PCI-controlled *Paese Sera* is most telling. At the peak of Calvi's financial power in the second half of the 1970s, this newspaper was able to avoid bankruptcy thanks to repeated loans from Calvi's Banco Ambrosiano. Considering Calvi's close relations with the Center-Left government and his affiliation with the P–2, this was a most unique transaction, one which helps explain the recalcitrance that characterized the response of the Communist press to the legal vicissitudes of Calvi and, in part, of Gelli.

With regard to both the press and other media, the interests of the power elite and of Italy's major economic groups seem to converge. They both need and therefore seek control over the country's media.[44] The constant changes in the ownership of *Il Corriere della Sera,* Italy's largest and most prestigious newspaper, perfectly illustrate this situation. In the last decade, control over this newspaper has shifted from one economic group to another, each representing a different political orientation and a different set of economic interests. Each change in ownership has corresponded to a change in the newspaper's political preferences, which shifted from support for the temporary alliance between the DC and the PCI in 1976–79 to anti-Communism and advocacy of a lay prime ministership in the early 1980s. For a brief period, Gelli and the P–2 were able to control *Il Corriere della Sera* as a result of Calvi's acquisition of a majority share of its publishing company, which inevitably resulted in extensive and favorable interviews with Gelli and, at the time of his legal troubles, in a concerted attempt to present a clean image of Calvi.[45]

Just as the absence of an independent press in Italy has until recently impeded the public exposure of many scandals, so party colonization of the banking system and of the judicial branch of the government has obstructed effective investigation and prosecution of those scandals that do become public. Despite its international reputation as Italy's most efficient and independent state agency, even the Bank of Italy is less politically autonomous than it might appear to be on the surface. This is amply demonstrated by the vicissitudes experienced by the bank as a result of its attempts to investigate Sindona's illegal dealings. Using a combination of threats, political pressure, and occasional coercion, the political protectors of Sindona were able for years to stall the bank's effort to untie the complex knot of Sindona's financial empire.[46]

The situation in the judicial system is even more serious. The Italian constitution of 1948 strove to create an independent judicial branch immune from politics by making access to the judiciary dependent upon a rigorous public examination, appointing magistrates for life, and holding them responsible only to the Superior Judicial Council. However, as in other spheres, the judiciary has become mired in precisely the political and ideological conflicts that the framers of the constitution had hoped to avoid. By the late 1960s, the judiciary was polarized into competing political and generational factions reflecting the ideological cleavages within the country as a whole over fundamental issues regarding the interpretation of the law and the proper role of judges. The division of the judiciary into political factions was in turn carried over into the Superior Judicial Council, thereby subverting its autonomy, an autonomy that was already undermined by the nomination of one-third of its members by parliament (i.e., the political parties). Under such conditions, political pressures cannot help but influence the administration of justice.[47]

The problems of the Italian legal system, however, go beyond its politicization. Like the rest of the state administration, it is highly bureaucratized. In addition, the courts, chronically underfunded, lack adequate and qualified administrative staff and modern data storage and processing systems.[48] As a result, the administration of justice is extraordinarily slow. There is a huge backlog of cases, and the average case requires seven to ten years to work its way through the three main jurisdictional levels. The situation is further complicated by the jungle of legal codes that judges confront. The present civil and criminal codes were drawn up during the Fascist era, and the principles of the republican constitution were simply superimposed upon them. The result is a confusing and at times contradictory body of law and substantial scope for judicial discretion. In the words of Luigi Barzini, "a tropical tangle of statutes, norms, regulations, customs, some hundreds of years old, some voted last week by Parliament and signed this morning by the President, could paralyze every activity in the land . . . if they were suddenly applied."[49]

Confronted with criminal organizations like the mafia, which are intimately connected with the political elite and able to draw upon massive financial resources, it is inevitable that the Italian legal system should most frequently be the loser in the battle against criminality and corruption. Until recently, the conclusion of almost every mafia trial was a ritual "acquittal because of insufficient evidence"—a verdict that attested to the power and political connections of mafia bosses and at the same time further magnified the aura of fear, respect, and prestige that surrounded them.

In the case of scandals that directly involve members of the political elite, the cases rarely even reach the courts. In order for the courts to proceed against a member of parliament, parliamentary authorization is required—an authorization that is almost never granted. Instead, scandals tend to be investigated by special parliamentary commissions, a procedure hardly conducive to the public exposure of political complicity.[50] Given the influence that the political parties exert over the judicial branch, it is relatively easy in those few cases which do come before the courts for powerful political leaders to silence independent-minded judges. This is what happened for instance in 1983–84 when a courageous judge, Carlo Palermo, attempted to investigate the financial benefits that had accrued to the political parties, notably the PSI, from the sale of arms abroad by Italian firms, many of them connected with state-owned enterprises. In a perplexing distortion of his institutional powers, the Socialist Prime Minister Bettino Craxi publicly denounced this judge, which eventually resulted in the latter being forced to abandon his investigation and to accept his relocation to Sicily, where he barely survived an assassination attempt by the mafia.[51]

In a system where formal democratic institutions have been subordinated to the logic of personal and partisan political struggle, scandals serve the function of keeping in operation a network of power revolving around a relatively small power elite that is self-contained and refractory to change. Part and parcel of the interconnected web of Italian scandals, members of the ruling elite and their allies from the financial-economic world, above all shady bankers and politicized state managers, have established a network of mutual protection that is in many instances above the law. The economic and political benefits that result from scandals are commodities that an individual or a faction acquires for the purpose of preserving and possibly enhancing the amount of power at their disposal. But in order to be able to acquire such a commodity without fear of political or legal punishment, they need the connivance or tacit support of the other individuals, factions, and parties that comprise the power elite. What the latter receive in return is usually an increased share of the political pie, often in the form of cabinet posts or greater access to the centers of power of the state-controlled sector of the national economy, usually through the appointment of a group's political protégés to the directorships of state-owned enterprises and banks. Hence, the gains that the beneficiaries of a scandal accrue translate into gains for all participants in the existing system of power, which paradoxically helps maintain the country's political and economic status quo. Only when the nature of a given scandal precludes the distribution of trade-offs or the rivalry among the members of the power elite is too intense does this system of collective complicity break down.[52]

Even individual members of the political-economic establishment who might not have been personally engaged in corrupt practices have reason to fear the exposure of scandals; because they are part of a complex and interlocking web of trade-offs and compromises, the exposure of scandals potentially threatens the overall structure on which the system of power is based. Once again, the P–2 affair is most revealing. The hearings conducted by the parliamentary commission in charge of investigating Gelli's activities witnessed the sad spectacle of the country's major political leaders, including the general secretary of the PCI, claiming that they had no knowledge of Gelli's organization or, if they were compelled to admit some knowledge, that they had no reason to suspect the magnitude of the P–2 network[53]—a most perplexing series of admissions in view of the fact that Gelli had at the apex of his influence granted extensive interviews to *Il Corriere della Sera* in which he discussed in much detail the extent and depth of his network of influence.

A Future Full of Scandals?

The preceding pages have painted a pessimistic picture of the capacity of Italian society and the Italian political system to eradicate the system of "occult powers"—of which the mafia and the P–2 are emblematic—which have penetrated deeply into legitimate political, economic, and financial spheres of the society. Yet, in the midst of a grave degeneration of democratic legality over the past decade, a few signs of hope have begun to appear. First, a "new" type of press has emerged, independent of the political parties and of major economic and financial groups, which has played an important role in exposing scandals and in sensitizing public opinion to the threat to democratic institutions that phenomena like the mafia and the P–2 represent. At the forefront of this independent press are the daily newspaper *La Repubblica* and weekly newsmagazines like *L'Espresso* and *Panorama*. Second, and relatedly, public opinion has become more receptive to the so-called "moral question." Until the death of General Dalla Chiesa in 1982, diffuse public cynicism and alienation had not been translated into political action directed against those individuals or parties most closely associated with the scandals. The assassination of General Dalla Chiesa marked a turning point. Under the pressure of an aroused public opinion, parliament enacted tough legislation directed against the economic base of mafia power (the La Torre–Rognoni law), and in the 1983 parliamentary elections, the Christian Democratic Party suffered serious losses for the first time in the postwar period. This shift in public opinion and the new measures adopted by parliament after Dalla Chiesa's death in turn made possible the third and most important new development in the struggle against criminality and corruption. A small group of committed magistrates (the so-called *pretori d'assalto*), armed with new investigatory powers have successfully reconstructed the activities of the "new mafia" of the 1970s and 1980s on the basis of which unprecedented judicial proceedings ("maxi-trials") have been initiated against hundreds of defendants in Palermo and Naples.[54] Although the final verdicts in these trials have yet to be delivered, the very fact of a visible and large-scale public commitment to the struggle against corruption and organized crime is of central importance in eroding a cultural climate that has tended at least tacitly to condone such activities.

Thus, repressive measures like the La Torre–Rognoni law and the "maxi-trials" in Palermo and Naples represent important landmarks in the battle against corruption insofar as they have begun to erode the myth of invincibility that has for so long surrounded the perpetrators of such phenomena. But just as the roots of systems of "occult power" like the mafia and the P–2 are ultimately social, economic, and political, so must any solution go beyond purely repressive measures if it is to be effective. The heart of the problem—and the heart of any solution—remains the linkage between various forms of corruption and the political system. More than the enactment of special laws (like those of the 1970s against terrorism), what is necessary is the political will to apply existing laws and to rally the full weight of the state in support of those police officers and magistrates exposed in the front lines of the struggle.

It is the absence of that unanimous and unambiguous political will that is the most striking difference between the battle against the mafia, for example, and the successful campaign against the Red Brigades in the late 1970s and early 1980s. This difference was clearly perceived by General Dalla Chiesa, who led the successful campaign against terrorism before being sent to Palermo to head the struggle against the mafia. In the campaign against terrorism, Dalla Chiesa had felt secure in the full support of the state apparatus, the political parties, and public opinion. On the contrary, he lamented, in the struggle against the mafia he felt himself increasingly confronted with indifference, if not hostility, on the part of precisely those political and institutional leaders whose function it should be to defend law and order and democratic institutions.[55]

The mafia, the P–2, and the Calvi and Sindona cases are in the last analysis a logical extension as well as the ultimate degeneration of a pervasive culture of clientelism, favoritism, and the appropriation of public resources for private gain that permeates the Italian political system and large sectors of Italian society. In the 1870s, Leopoldo Franchetti and Sidney Sonnino observed that the mafia, which we take here as a symbol of the broader climate of corruption, flourished where the concept of the rule of law was subordinate to the bonds of personal obligation and the affirmation of personal might.[56] A century later, General Dalla Chiesa launched the same accusation in even more brutal terms: "So long as a party card continues to count for more than the state, we will never win the battle."[57] What has changed since 1875 is that what was to a large extent a regional problem (albeit even then with national ramifications) has now infested the entire political system, by means of precisely those political developments—the construction of a far-reaching system of DC power and the expansion of the welfare state—which from a different perspective have been identified with the creation of a modern democratic state in Italy.

The key to defeating the mafia and the corrupt practices in the country's political and economic system thus lies in a profound transformation of the relationship between the Italian state and its citizens, and of the prevailing political culture that accepts scandals as the norm rather than as the exception. What is urgently needed is to restore the credibilty of democratic institutions, seriously undermined by clientelism, corruption, and the dysfunctions of an elephantine bureaucracy, where even the most basic public services are available only through the intercession of a powerful protector. This means guaranteeing the legality and transparency of public life, providing public services with efficiency and impartiality, and instituting mechanisms of inspection and control aimed at limiting the vast discretionality that currently exists, thereby reducing the margins for favoritism, clientelistic maneuvers, and corruption.

Such reforms require first and foremost, however, a profound transformation of the political parties themselves and of the methods by which they attempt to attain and to maintain power. Lamentably, the paradox of this solution lies in the fact that the initiative for any reform of public institutions and any moralization of public life must come from precisely those political actors who are among the prime causes of the degeneration. As the Liberal Deputy Napoleone Colajanni warned at the turn of the century,

> To combat and destroy the kingdom of the mafia, it is necessary, it is indispensable, that the Italian government cease to be the *king of the mafia!* But the government has acquired too great a taste for the exercise of this dishonest and illicit authority; it is too practiced and hardened in its misdeeds. Have we come to a point where we can no longer hope for the cessation of the function without the destruction of the organism?[58]

NOTES

1. For an excellent collection of essays that covers both the circumstances leading to the assassination of Dalla Chiesa as well as his activities as the prefect of Palermo, see Corrado Stajano et al., *Morte di un generale* (Milan: Mondadori, 1982). For a more personal account, and one that deals explicitly with the political responsibilities behind the general's death, see the book by his son, Nando Dalla Chiesa, *Delitto imperfetto* (Milan: Mondadori, 1984).

2. An important provision of this law is the elimination of bank secrecy for accounts owned by individuals suspected of engaging in criminal activities. This has allowed magistrates to investigate more thoroughly corrupt activities and to strike at the economic heart of criminal organizations like the mafia.

3. For a detailed appraisal of the Calvi affair, see Rupert Cornwell, *God's Banker: An Account of the Life and Death of Roberto Calvi* (London: Victor Gollancz, 1983). A British journalist who has covered Italian affairs for almost a decade, Cornwell successfully debunks the contention that Calvi committed suicide. However, while he suggests a number of different explanations for the mystery surrounding Calvi's death, he avoids adopting any specific interpretation.

Though more speculative and less rigorous than Cornwell's book, the controversial work by David A. Yallop, *In God's Name* (New York: Bantam Books, 1985), offers interesting insights into the Vatican's financial investments and the I.O.R.'s connection with Sindona and Calvi. The same can be said about the book by Gordon Thomas and Max Morgan Witts, *Pontiff* (New York: Doubleday, 1984).

4. Not surprisingly, the number of books on Sindona is quite substantial and is bound to increase exponentially as a result of his mysterious death. As far as the analysis contained in this essay is concerned, we have relied primarily on the text of the sentence issued by the Italian court that found him guilty of having ordered the assassination of Giorgio Ambrosoli, *Gli atti d'accusa dei giudici di Milano*, with a preface by Maurizio De Luca (Rome: Editori Riuniti, 1986).

5. In an insightful article that assesses the dynamics of the Sindona-Andreotti relationship, Massimo Riva has argued that the purpose of Andreotti's praises of Sindona was to convey the message to the banker that both the Vatican and the DC would covertly support him in his legal struggle against Italian judges (*La Repubblica*, 26 September 1984). For Andreotti's explanation of his role in the Sindona affair, see his article in *Il Tempo*, 7 October 1984. Whatever his motives for helping Sindona, in the summer of 1978 Andreotti, who was then prime minister, officially asked one of his most loyal political allies, Gaetano Stammati (then a minister and a member of the P–2), to intercede on behalf of the banker by applying pressure on the Bank of Italy. See *Gli atti d'accusa dei giudici di Milano*, p. 21 ff.

6. In an appendix to his book on the P–2 phenomenon, Massimo Teodori offers a detailed description of approximately thirty "mysterious deaths" of secret service officers, members of organized crime, journalists, and neo-Fascist terrorists—deaths that are directly or indirectly linked to the activities of Gelli's Masonic Lodge. It is therefore difficult to disagree with his conclusion that the P–2 was *also* a phenomenon that produced a "culture" centered around the physical elimination of opponents and friends who had become unreliable; see Massimo Teodori, *P2: la controstoria* (Milan: SugarCo, 1981), pp. 237–47. A member of the Radical Party who served on the parliamentary commission in charge of investigating the P–2 phenomenon, Teodori's book can be regarded as a sort of minority report through which the author expresses his dissent with the conclusions reached by the commission.

7. According to Pino Arlacchi, the mafia's overall earnings are approximately 700–800 billion lire (approximately $400–$500 million) per year. Pino Arlacchi, *La mafia imprenditrice* (Bologna: Il Mulino, 1983), p. 232.

8. It remains somewhat of a mystery what Sindona actually did while hiding in Palermo. It has been speculated that his "kidnapping" had a twofold objective. First, he wanted to convince the New York judges who were trying him for the bankruptcy of the Franklin Bank that his financial difficulties were due to a conspiracy orchestrated by the Italian Left. Second, by returning to Italy Sindona was able to intensify his efforts to coerce his onetime political protectors to help him, to intimidate his political foes more successfully, and to establish closer contacts with Gelli and the P–2. See *Gli atti d'accusa dei giudici di Milano*, pp. 57–123.

9. *La Repubblica*, 6 October 1982.

10. A useful compendium of the major scandals that have occurred in Italy in the postwar period is a booklet published by *L'Espresso* in conjunction with the magazine's issue of 24 March 1985, "30 Anni di scandali, 1955/85."

11. In late 1984 two members of the hitherto untouchable "third level" of mafia power were arrested. Vito Ciancimino, a former Christian Democratic mayor of Palermo, and Antonino and Ignazio Salvo, proprietors of the largest economic empire in Sicily and themselves a major force within the Christian Democratic Party, had been cited at length in the 1972 and 1976 reports of the parliamentary commission investigating the mafia, but a decade elapsed before they were called to answer for their activities. Although the arrests of Ciancimino and the Salvos marked a major landmark in the struggle against

the mafia, many observers feel that they served as scapegoats to forestall action against more highly placed political figures. For example, Salvo Lima, head of the Andreotti faction of the DC in Sicily and a member of the European Parliament, was mentioned 149 times by the parliamentary anti-mafia commissions, but continues his political career untroubled by either party or judicial sanctions. For a more in-depth account of the power system of the DC in Palermo, see Judith Chubb, *Patronage, Power and Politics in Southern Italy* (New York: Cambridge University Press, 1982).

12. For a thorough review of the various political-economic scandals that have occurred in Italian history since the country's reunification in 1870, see Sergio Turone, *Corrotti e corruttori dall'Unità d'Italia alla P2* (Rome: Laterza, 1984). The linkage between the political system and most of the major scandals that have taken place in the post--World War II period is analyzed in full by Giorgio Galli, *L'Italia sotterranea. Storia, politica e scandali* (Rome: Laterza, 1983).

13. Massimo Teodori, *P2: la controstoria*, p. 12.

14. Gelli first joined the freemasonry in the mid-1960s. Within less than a decade, he was able to emerge as the "venerable master" of the P–2, making it virtually independent of the organizational framework of Italy's freemasonry. Until then, the membership of the P–2 had largely consisted of military officers, many of them working for the country's secret services. After 1975, Gelli launched an intense recruitment drive among politicians, journalists, and members of the business community. For accounts of Gelli's life and rise to power within the P–2, see Gianfranco Piazzesi, *Gelli* (Milan: Garzanti, 1982), and Pino Buongiorno and Maurizio De Luca, eds., *L'Italia della P2* (Milan: Mondadori, 1981).

15. For different interpretations of the P2 phenomenon by leading Italian politicians, see the summary of their depositions before the parliamentary commission in charge of investigating Gelli's organization, as reported by Massimo Teodori, *P2: la controstoria*, pp. 34–46.

16. Quoted ibid., p. 40.

17. The parliamentary commission investigating the P–2 case ascertained that, although Calvi actually left the country with the aid of individuals linked to organized crime, a high-ranking magistrate who was a member of the P–2 had returned to Calvi his passport in exchange for a substantial sum of money deposited in a secret Swiss bank account. Rupert Cornwell, *God's Banker: An Account of the Life and Death of Roberto Calvi*, p. 123 ff.

18. Giovanni Leone, then president of the Italian Republic, was forced to resign in the midst of the Lockheed scandal on suspicion of having received kickbacks. But, as persuasively argued by Camilla Cederna, the Lockheed scandal was only the last straw in a long series of affairs and indiscretions that characterized Leone's presidency and led to his resignation. Camilla Cederna, *Giovanni Leone: La carriera di un presidente* (Milan: Feltrinelli, 1978).

19. Massimo Teodori, *P2: la controstoria*, pp. 221–34. For Teodori, Andreotti is the Italian politician who embodies most "effectively" the degeneration of the country's political system.

20. A more thorough discussion of Italian political institutions can be found in Frederic Spotts and Theodore Wieser, *Italy: A Difficult Democracy* (Cambridge: Cambridge University Press, 1986).

21. In practical terms, this formula meant that the Communist Party supported or at least did not oppose government-sponsored legislation in parliament, without however having either official participation in the government or a direct say in implementing policy. In return for its support, the PCI was consulted by the DC and its government partners during the process of policy formulation.

22. Mauro Calise and Renato Mannheimer, *Governanti in Italia: un trentennio repubblicano 1946–1976* (Bologna: Il Mulino, 1982).

23. John Chancellor, NBC News, 15 August 1986.

24. Arturo Parisi and Gianfranco Pasquino, "Changes in Italian Electoral Behavior: The Relationship Between Parties and Voters," in *Italy in Transition: Conflict and Consensus,* ed. Peter Lange and Sidney Tarrow (London: Frank Cass, 1980), pp. 6–30.

25. The growing tendency by the government to resort, in recent years, to decrees and emergency legislation as means for implementing its policies is a further indication of the weak and subordinate role of Italian parliament.

26. Only in the first postwar parliamentary elections in 1948 did the Christian Democrats win a clear majority of the seats in parliament.

27. Giorgio Galli, *Dal bipartitismo imperfetto alla possibile alternativa* (Bologna: Il Mulino, 1975); Giovanni Sartori, *Parties and Party Systems: A Framework for Analysis* (Cambridge: Cambridge University Press, 1976).

28. A thorough analysis of this phenomenon can be found in Franco Cazzola, *Governo e opposizione nel parlamento italiano* (Milan: Giuffrè, 1974).

29. The establishment of *trasformismo* as the decisive unwritten rule of Italian political life coincided with the outbreak of the first scandals in Italy following the country's unification in 1870. As pointed out by Sergio Turone, the content, manifestations, and implications of the scandals that occurred in the last two decades of the nineteenth century closely resemble those of the scandals that have taken place in recent years. *Corrotti e corruttori,* esp. p. 25 ff.

30. A recent governmental crisis aptly illustrates this. In June 1986 the alliance between the Christian Democrats and the Socialists broke down largely because De Mita, the general secretary of the DC, argued that the time had come for the DC to regain the prime ministership, while Craxi stressed the legitimacy of his claim to continue to serve as prime minister. What made the struggle between De Mita and Craxi a particularly distasteful spectacle was that their respective claims rested neither on changes in the electoral power of the two parties nor on concrete political grounds; rather, it was a blunt expression of the intense power struggle between two parties that are allegedly government partners. For an appraisal of the Craxi prime ministership, see John H. Harper, *Bettino Craxi and the Second Center-Left Experiment,* Occasional Paper, No. 52 (Bologna: The Johns Hopkins University, Bologna Center, April 1986).

31. *Sottogoverno* (literally "subgovernment") refers to the myriad of government agencies and other publicly controlled bodies (including state industries), the directors of which are subject to political appointment.

32. The creation of regional governments was mandated by the 1948 constitution but, due to resistance by the Christian Democratic Party, which feared that regional governments would be dominated by the Left, the constitutional provisions were not implemented for twenty years.

33. Neither Pazienza's career nor his role is atypical in Italy's peculiar political-economic world. Acting as what the French euphemistically call a *brasseur d'affaires* and capitalizing in full on his friendship with the head of Italy's secret services and with the then–general secretary of the DC, Flaminio Piccoli, Pazienza was able in the early 1980s to develop an impressive network of contacts with the political and financial world. As a result, he played a critical role in some of the major scandals and controversial events of the early 1980s, from the Calvi case to the secret services' involvement in right-wing terrorism and the P–2. It has been speculated that Pazienza also had a major part in setting in motion the so-called "Billygate," which greatly damaged Jimmy Carter's chances for reelection in 1980. See Rupert Cornwell, *God's Banker: An Account of the Life and Death of Roberto Calvi.*

34. Although it resembles the spoils system typical of most political systems, *lottizzazione* is more a pervasive and institutionalized system of clientelism and patronage. In its essence, it implies that the parties that traditionally comprise the government coalition divide up among themselves the spoils that derive from the state participation in the economy and the political parties' penetration of the state administration. Directorships of state-controlled banks (approximately 60 percent of the country's banking system) are, for instance, distributed among members of the five parties of the government coalition

in such a way as to reflect the importance of each party in the coalition. For a compelling analysis of the origins of the process through which the Christian Democrats and their political allies have "colonized" the Italian state, see Ruggero Orfei, *L'occupazione del potere* (Milan: Longanesi, 1976), esp. p. 80 ff.

35. For a thorough discussion of the Italian state's intervention in the economic system, see Gisele Podbielski, *Italy: Development and Crisis in the Post-War Economy* (Oxford: Clarendon Press, 1975).

36. In a famous book published in the early 1970s, Eugenio Scalfari and Giuseppe Turani argued that the peculiar ways in which state intervention has occurred in Italy has produced a new class of "politicized managers" who act as the representatives of political factions and parties in the economy. Eugenia Calfari and Giuseppe Turani, *Razza padrona* (Milan: Feltrinelli, 1974).

37. Massimo Teodori, *P2: la controstoria,* p. 171 ff.

38. An excellent analysis of the connection between members of the political parties, occult powers, and organized crime is the book by Sergio Turone, *Partiti e mafia dalla P2 alla droga* (Bari: Laterza, 1985).

39. Gabriel Almond and Sidney Verba, *The Civic Culture: Political Attitudes and Democracy in Five Nations* (Boston: Little, Brown and Company, 1965), pp. 308–10. See also the essay by Joseph LaPalombara, "Italy: Fragmentation, Isolation, Alienation," in Lucien W. Pye and Sidney Verba, eds., *Political Culture and Political Development* (Princeton: Princeton University Press, 1965).

40. Electoral participation in national elections has gone down from 93.1 percent in 1972 to 89.0 percent in 1983. If one includes blank or spoiled ballots, considered a form of protest vote in Italy, the 1983 abstention rate rises from 11 percent to 16 percent.

41. For a discussion of this point, see Giorgio Galli, *L'Italia sotterranea,* p. 291 ff.

42. For a detailed analysis of the effects of its "participation" in the government in the 1976–79 period on the PCI's strategy and position in Italian society, see James Roscoe, *On the Threshold of Government: The Italian Communist Party, 1976–81* (New York: St. Martin's Press, 1983).

43. The evolution of the Italian trade union movement is discussed by Peter Lange and Maurizio Vanicelli, "Strategy Under Stress: The Italian Union Movement and the Italian Crisis in Developmental Perspective," in P. Lange, G. Ross, and M. Vannicelli, *Unions, Change and Crisis: French and Italian Union Strategy and the Political Economy, 1945–1980* (London: Allen & Unwin, 1982), pp. 95–189.

44. The case of RAI, Italy's state-owned radio and television network, is most revealing. Reflecting a deliberate exercise in *lottizzazione* (see footnote 34), the directorships of the three TV channels controlled by RAI have been distributed among representatives of the major political parties. As a result, Channel 1 has a clearly Christian Democratic bias, Channel 2 is usually aligned with the Socialists, while Channel 3—which broadcasts regionally—is more oriented towards the minor government parties as well as the PCI.

45. For an account of the penetration of Italian newspapers by the political parties and their economic allies, see Giampaolo Pansa, *Comprati e venduti* (Milan: Feltrinelli, 1979). Obviously, in no Western democracy, not to speak of Eastern European countries, is the media refractory to the influence of political and economic groups. In no other major Western democracy, however, are the leading national and local newspapers so much under the control of the economic and political power elite, to the extent that major industrial corporations as well as state companies own major newspapers. For instance, Turin's *La Stampa* belongs to the Agnelli family, Fiat's major shareholders. In the early 1960s the late Enrico Mattei, the powerful chief executive of the state-owned oil company, founded a new newspaper, Milan's *Il Giorno*, with the express purpose of supporting the emerging Center-Left alliance between the Christian Democrats and the Socialists. Similarly, Montedison, a state-owned multinational corporation, which is Italy's largest industrial enterprise, has in recent years purchased and supported a number of regional and local newspapers.

46. In March 1979 Mario Sarcinelli, then a much-respected director of the Bank of

Italy, was arrested on charges of adminstrative irregularities. It was eventually demonstrated that the charges were politically motivated. Symptomatically, the judge who had ordered Sarcinelli's arrest was a close political ally of Andreotti and Sindona. Rupert Cornwell speculates that the arrest reflected the desire of certain political and economic groups to "teach a lesson" to Sarcinelli and through him to the Bank of Italy and to punish them for their independent roles in the Sindona and Calvi investigations. Rupert Cornwell, *God's Banker,* p. 82 ff.

47. For a more detailed analysis of the Italian judicial system, see Frederic Spotts and Theodore Wieser, *Italy: A Difficult Democracy,* pp. 150–79.

48. For instance, only 0.76 percent of the 1984 state budget (as opposed to 1.82 percent in 1974) went to the administration of justice, and this figure included wages and the operating costs of prisons. Sergio Turone, *Partiti e mafia dalla P2 alla droga,* p. 31.

49. Quoted in Frederic Spotts and Theodore Wieser, *Italy: A Difficult Democracy,* p. 156.

50. Italy's major postwar scandals (the mafia, Sindona, the P–2) have all resulted in the creation of special parliamentary commissions, which have carried out lengthy investigations and issued voluminous reports. Despite substantial evidence in these reports as to the involvement of high-ranking politicians, parliament has been careful to avoid the attribution of political responsibility or to recommend judicial action.

51. With Italy ranking fifth or sixth among the world's major weapons suppliers, the arms traffic is a very lucrative business that has long attracted the attention of the political parties. As Falco Accame, a former Socialist deputy and the PSI expert on security issues, admitted in his testimony to Judge Palermo in 1973, all parties of the government coalition benefit from the massive legal and illegal traffic of weapons that either originates in Italy or goes through the peninsula. *Il Messaggero,* 27 October 1983.

52. Symptomatically, the above mentioned ENI–Petronim affair became public because the internal power struggle between two competing factions of the PSI, one revolving around Bettino Craxi and the other led by his "left-wing" opponent Claudio Signorile, had escalated to such heights as to make this type of "exchange" impossible.

53. Massimo Teodori, *P2: La Controstoria,* pp. 34–46.

54. For the reconstruction of the mafia's activities and internal structure conducted by the judges of Palermo, see Corrado Stajano, ed., *Mafia. L'atto di accusa dei giudici di Palermo* (Rome: Editori Riuniti, 1986).

55. For a detailed account of the evolution of the general's views on the mafia-politics equation during his one hundred days in Palermo, see Nando Dalla Chiesa, *Delitto imperfetto.*

56. Leopoldo Franchetti and Sidney Sonnino, *Inchiesta in Sicilia,* vol. 2, "Condizzioni politiche e amministrative della Sicilia," (Florence: Vallecchi, 1974), p. 36.

57. Dalla Chiesa, *Delitto imperfetto,* p. 50.

58. Napoleone Colajanni, *Nel regno della mafia* (Palermo: Renzo Mazzone, 1971; reprint of the 1900 original edition), p. 110.

From *Spiegel* to Flick:
6 • The Maturation of the
West German *Parteienstaat*

ALINE KUNTZ

Introduction: The *Spiegel* and Flick Scandals

On 26 October 1962, officials from the West German Federal Prosecutors Office, the Federal Criminal Office, and the local police raided the Hamburg headquarters of the German weekly *Der Spiegel*. The magazine's archives were immediately impounded and three staff members were arrested. *Spiegel* publisher Rudolf Augstein could not be located that evening, but news of his impending arrest prompted Augstein to turn himself in to the authorities the following day. Associate *Spiegel* editor Conrad Ahlers and his wife were vacationing in Spain at the time. Awoken at 3:00 A.M. by local police, Ahlers was escorted to Malaga and incarcerated until 28 October, when a Lufthansa flight brought him back to face arrest in Frankfurt. In the ensuing days and weeks, the scene was repeated elsewhere and the arrest list grew to include not only *Der Spiegel*'s employees, but members of the Defense Ministry and the German Intelligence Service as well. According to the Federal Prosecutors Office, Augstein, Ahlers, and others were suspected of publishing "state secrets" that "endangered the security of the Federal Republic and the safety and freedom of the German people".[1]

The original object of the controversy was a feature article by Ahlers on NATO defense strategy, which had appeared in *Der Spiegel*'s 10 October 1962 issue. Heavily critical of Defense Minister Franz Josef Strauss and of the Bundeswehr's (West German Army) "inadequate" conventional military capabilities, Ahlers had concluded that the army was only "conditionally prepared to defend" in the event of a Soviet attack. This position collided directly with Strauss's own policy and called into question the defense minister's leadership capacity. For the flamboyant and authoritarian Franz Josef Strauss, such criticism was tantamount to treason.[2] Indeed, the defense minister was so outraged that he circumvented West German laws to effect Ahlers's arrest.

Reaction to the raids was swift and unequivocal. Students, journalists, and the Federal Republic's intellectual elite staged protests against the government's heavy-handed action and decried the continued restraints placed on *Der Spiegel's* publication. Foreign opinion drew disconcerting parallels with the methods of the Third Reich. To the informed public, allegations of treason could not justify the abridgement of press freedom the government had committed by muzzling *Der Spiegel's* editors. For example, a group of writers, artists and publicists protested:

> The German journalist Rudolf Augstein, publisher of *Der Spiegel*, has been arrested in connection with an alleged betrayal of so-called military secrets and under charge of having revealed them to the public. An act of state arbitrariness against *Der Spiegel* accompanied this arrest. The undersigned express their respect for Herr Rudolf Augstein and are solidly with him.[3]

In a later suit before the Federal Constitutional Court, *Der Spiegel* effectively demonstrated that Ahlers's article had revealed nothing that could not be culled from any decent library. Well before the official verdict, however, the "treason" charges against the magazine took a back seat to the government's handling of the affair. Since Strauss had long been a favored *Der Spiegel* target, it was difficult to dismiss the impression that the government's response was politically motivated.[4] Ahlers's arrest in Spain was of special concern, for the Federal Republic had no extradition treaty with Spain covering political crimes.

The mysteries of the case unfolded during a series of parliamentary sessions in November 1962. These were among the most acrimonious the Bundestag had witnessed, and strained the governing Christian Democratic Union (CDU)/ Christian Social Union (CSU)/ Free Democratic Party (FDP) coalition to the breaking point.[5] Strauss finally admitted that it was at his ministry's request that the Spanish authorities had arrested Ahlers,[6] a serious breach of procedure that forced the defense minister's resignation. Chancellor Adenauer, who had remained strangely silent in the first week of the debacle, exacerbated the dispute by publicly labeling Augstein a traitor.[7] The chancellor's recklessness cost him dearly; the FDP withdrew from the cabinet and would return only with the stipulation that Adenauer retire before the next national elections (in 1963).

The *Spiegel* affair remains one of the most carefully scrutinized events in the Federal Republic's history. The secretive midnight raids, the sharp public reaction, and partisan investigations left little doubt that this was a full-blown political crisis. Any democracy would have been hard pressed to ignore the implications of such events. What made *Spiegel* a milestone at the time, however, was the proximity of these events to Germany's authoritarian past. Nearly every press account, whether foreign or domestic, evoked disturbing memories of the Third Reich and thereby challenged the performance of the Bonn system. The judgments rendered were as disparate as the issues the scandal raised, but observers agreed that the affair had seriously damaged public confidence in an era when democratic legitimacy was already fragile.

A succinct account of the Flick scandal is more difficult. The affair bears the name of what was formerly West Germany's largest family-owned company, but the Flick concern was only the focal point of a much wider tangle involving tax evasion and political corruption.[8] The *Süddeutsche Zeitung* estimated that throughout the 1970s Flick had made over twelve million dollars in payments to an astoundingly lengthy list of public officials. As the paper editorialized in 1984, "The entire Federal Republic has become an impenetrable network of political appointees and (has) grown almost helpless to move."[9]

The affair's beginnings were inauspicious. In 1975, the Flick holding company sold three-quarters of its substantial interest in Daimler-Benz and reinvested the proceeds. Yet the company faced a huge tax bill unless its new investments could be classified as "furthering the overall health of the West Germany economy."[10] Flick was granted a tax exemption on precisely these grounds in 1976, but the suspicion of tax fraud persisted, and officials began examining the records more closely.

Unfortunately for Flick, its chief operating officer Eberhard von Brauchitsch had a penchant for meticulous documentation. According to later indictments, the company's books revealed payments to countless politicians, ostensibly in return for preferential treatment.[11]

At first the tax waiver for the Daimler-Benz sale occupied center stage of the controversy. Economics Minister Otto von Lambsdorff (FDP), whose name appeared conspicuously amid Flick's numerous entries, was suspected of having received $50,000 for his role in pushing the tax exemption. Lambsdorff's predecessor, Hans Friedrichs (FDP), was similarly charged. The drawn-out investigative process, however, eventually widened into a story of pervasive corruption affecting virtually all of the Federal Republic's major politicians and spanning more than a decade. Lambsdorff resigned his ministry upon indictment, and Bundestag Speaker Rainer Barzel (CDU) left his post after admitting that Flick had paid him half-a-million dollars.[12]

In early 1987, Lambsdorff, Friedrichs, and Brauchitsch were convicted of tax evasion but cleared of the more serious charges of corruption and bribery. These verdicts were of course only a partial conclusion to the scandal, but they expose nonetheless one of the principal ambiguities of the Flick affair. All of the major political figures who admitted having accepted corporate money denied that the payments implied either political favors or individual gain. The funds were channeled into party coffers through tax-free "donations" to dummy charities, the latter established to circumvent West Germany's restrictive party finance laws.[13] Because under-the-table contributions had been tolerated for so long, a blanket judgment of illegality would have convicted almost the entire governing class. Not surprisingly, the Federal Republic's main parties scrambled to prevent such an outcome.[14]

The complexities of the Flick case apparently did not make good copy. *Der Spiegel* led the press in pursuing the affair, but the magazine constantly found itself on the defensive, blamed by several politicians for "creating a falsely cynical impression" of West German politics.[15] The Bundestag investigations, which began in 1981, failed to hold the public's attention unless the witnesses were especially prominent. Neither the events nor their coverage carried the same sense of heightened drama that had accompanied the *Spiegel* affair. Moreover, the scandal's effects on the electoral picture were difficult to assess: the FDP, whose leaders had been among the chief defendants, rebounded in the 1987 elections, to nearly everyone's surprise.

One might be tempted to argue that these two cases actually have very little in common. Apart from the different substantive issues each raised, more than twenty years separate *Spiegel* from Flick. Surely a mature democratic system will react less nervously to crisis than one in its infancy? In part this is an accurate portrayal, for the Flick scandal never sent protesters into the streets. Indeed, in 1984 the authors of an extensive account of the affair openly chastised the public for its complacency. Flagrant manipulations of the law apparently moved the citizenry "about as much as the daily weather report".[16] While this may be too strong a condemnation, the "politics as usual" response to the Flick scandal did contrast sharply with the dramatic demonstrations that accompanied the *Spiegel* affair.

This essay, however, is only tangentially concerned with the magnitude of the public's response. All scandals are to some extent time-bound; what shocks in one era produces barely a ripple in another. Particularly in the Federal Republic, where the political culture has clearly undergone a basic transformation, a simple comparison of how the two scandals were received yields few new revelations. The value of examining both affairs lies instead in the political mechanisms each exposes. Though these are historically specific, they contain a common core: the stories of *Spiegel* and Flick are intimately intertwined with the power of political parties in West Germany.

Accordingly, the analysis that follows first outlines the origins of the West German *Parteienstaat*—a term used to connote a fusion of party and state evident almost since the Federal Republic's inception. As the chief "bearers" of the postwar order, West German parties carry heavy responsibilities in times of normalcy; their role is all the more problematic when they are (as they were in both scandals) enmeshed in controversy. Set against this crucial backdrop, the *Spiegel* and Flick scandals offer not only unique glimpses into the workings of the Bonn variant of party democracy, but they illuminate as well the costs of such a system. Paradoxically, the belated maturation of West German parties has meant an increasing distance from the society they are charged with representing.

The Origins of Party Hegemony

When the war in Europe finally ended in 1945, most Germans were too preoccupied with day-to-day survival to give much thought to their political future. And the climate was scarcely favorable for a hard look back at the past. Indeed, the question uppermost in most foreigners' minds—why Auschwitz?— was of little relevance to the average German citizen. Scholars could speculate endlessly on the German Problem, but to the masses 1945 was *Stunde Null* (hour zero): the collapse of every reference point that had heretofore guided German political life.

Yet the western allies had rather definite ideas about both the significance of Germany's past and the shape of her political future. For the Americans especially, democracy was impossible without thoroughgoing moral reeducation. Because Weimar's carefully crafted political regime had failed so miserably, constitutional reform alone seemed an inadequate basis for viable popular government. Only by first rooting out and extinguishing the vestiges of Nazism could the Germans overcome their rampant authoritarianism. Denazification was thus the first step toward political rebirth. After a decent interval, and under strict Allied supervision, the economy that had powered the Nazi war machine would be allowed to revive as well. But here again American priorities would dominate. Germany's enormous cartels would be dismantled and replaced with small-scale competitive firms.[17]

Such plans were by no means matters of consensus. Among the western powers, the French remained most fearful of a German resurgence and most suspicious of any design for the country's economic recovery. The British, on the other hand, were less worried about the prospect of a centralized German economy, but they viewed the denazification effort with skepticism. American preferences came to dominate largely because of the emergent rivalry with the Soviet Union. As the cold war deepened, "the conservative fear of communism gradually replaced the liberal fear of fascism,"[18] and the western powers put aside their differences and set about restoring political and economic life in the areas they controlled. This task meant compromising the denazification program and quickening the pace of economic recovery. In practical terms, it meant collaboration with existing German elites.

These were not the same groups that had monopolized the German state since the late nineteenth century. For all its horrors, the Third Reich had unwittingly swept away one longstanding obstacle to German democracy—the semifeudal military caste. The Junker vision of duty, hierarchy, and state worship had persisted into the Weimar years, ultimately undermining the republic from within.[19] But at war's end the Junker estates were no more; what the Nazi *Gleichschaltung* had not destroyed,[20] the Allies had buried with the division of Prussia.

Despite the occupation's restrictions and mass political indifference, 1945–46 witnessed the tentative birth of a new governing class. As local and regional government was hastily reconstituted in the the face of the Soviet threat, political activities, most with ties to the Weimar era, organized to contest elections in the western zones. Their initial efforts were loosely coordinated, and subject to Allied veto, but the political parties granted licenses during this crucial formative period were favorably situated to determine the Federal Republic's future. Well before the first national elections (in 1949), political parties had penetrated the committees, councils, and administrative structures that became the foundation for central institutions.[21] They authored, as well, a constitution uniquely sensitive to the power of political parties.

Of the major players, Social Democracy held the strongest claim to historic continuity. Unlike its counterparts, the SPD possessed an existent organizational base and a leadership untainted by collusion with the Nazis. Such advantages dovetailed with the spirit of the times, as progressive politics held an appeal for those who connected conservatism with the Depression, the Third Reich, and the subsequent catastrophes of recent memory. The SPD's early programs conformed to classic principles of reform socialism; democracy meant drastic revision of the capitalist order. During the 1950s, however, when the Left seemed consigned to permanent opposition, the party shed the trappings of Marxism in pursuit of a wider constituency.[22]

The groups that merged to form the Free Democratic Party (FDP) were less cohesive. Germany's liberal tradition had long been plagued with weakness and factionalism, and its nationalist wing stood accused of collaboration with the far Right. In an attempt to avoid similar schisms, the FDP issued early electoral platforms that were decidedly vague. What then set the liberals apart was a comparatively strong commitment to free market capitalism and a pervasive secular outlook, each of which suggested different coalition possibilities.[23] Though overshadowed from the beginning by the main representatives of Left and Right, the FDP came to play a pivotal role in the party system. Because neither the Social Democrats nor the Christian Democrats could command sufficient votes to govern alone, both courted FDP support.

German conservatism also faced formidable obstacles after World War II. Conservatives had never been able to bridge the social, religious, and regional cleavages that had kept them divided into rival parties and factions. Their lack of unity (which mirrored equally obstinate divisions among the German middle class) was widely seen as a contributing factor to the fall of Weimar. Many conservative leaders, moreover, had demonstrated only limited loyalty to the republican system and had been either unwilling or unable to save it from the Nazi challenge.

The postwar conservative restoration thus intentionally struck out on a different path. Its primary theme was reconciliation—both social and religious. For the first time, Protestants and Catholics were to find a common political home under a multiclass movement that downplayed traditional conservative tenets. The Christian Democratic Union (CDU) and its Bavarian affiliate, the Christian Social Union (CSU), advocated a mix of pragmatic, moderate policies conceived as a bourgeois counterweight to socialism.[24] Although Christian Democracy's early programs were progressive and even anticapitalist, the CDU/CSU (Union) rather quickly evolved into an essentially conservative force with key support among businessmen, farmers, and small independent proprietors.

That these three political tendencies should have come to dominate the nascent party system of the Federal Republic was surprising in itself. Though all could trace their ideological roots far back in German history, as political participants all had been marginalized. In none of the German state's former epochs had parties been the locus of governance. Under Bismarck, the nobles and industrialists who ruled the Reich tenaciously averted popular pressures channeled through parties. The Reichstag[25] could never become a truly representative institution, because the regime either coopted or repressed its political party challengers. Decision making instead was the province of the executive, the bureaucracy, and economic elites. After World War I, mass politics arrived with a vengeance; Weimar was notorious for the vast array of parties it produced. Yet the republic's instability was testimony to the weak, fragmented nature of these associations. Narrowly based and ideologically rigid, Weimar's parties proved incapable of maintaining order, and hence they were crippled by executive decrees and finally overrun by the extreme Right.

Mindful of such impotence, leaders from all the major postwar parties strove to elevate their organizations to an unassailable position. At a minimum, this required formal guarantees that would protect parties from executive encroachment. But the constitution (the Basic Law) actually went farther; its specific grants of power rendered parties the equivalent of other state organs. Later legislation, notably the Party Law of 1967, added public financing to the benefits of "paraconstitutional status".[26]

Political parties are of course prominent features in every advanced democracy. In the Federal Republic, however, the constitutional protection afforded them had distinct ramifications. Despite the language of the Basic Law, which charged parties with "forming the will of the people" and thus appeared to stress a representative function, subsequent legal interpretation underscored the parties' role as instruments of governance.[27] And the parties themselves behaved from the outset more as "bearers of the state" than as recipients of electoral mandates. Here the contrast with Weimar is again instructive. Though the Weimar Republic managed to establish party democracy, in other words, parties became the key vehicles for mass ideologies, a party state was unattainable. The state remained in large measure the possession of the old authoritarian elite.

Evolution of the *Parteienstaat*

Given the tragedies of the German past, it was quite natural for early postwar observers to cast the emergent *Parteienstaat* in a favorable light. As party officials (or those responsible to them) gradually captured parliament, bureaucracy, the media and other institutions, their preeminence was generally deemed a belated victory for popular government. After all, Bonn's new power brokers, unlike their forebears, were wedded to the democratic order. That partisan affiliation entailed privilege disturbed virtually no one; independence had always before signified a contempt for participatory values.

The full import of the parties' rehabilitation became evident only toward the end of the Christian Democratic era, when the opposition SPD began to speak regularly of the "CDU–state." The term, coined in the 1950s, had a dual meaning. It referred both to the surprising electoral success of Konrad Adenauer and the Union and to the related politicization of national institutions. While the Social Democrats had reason to question a system that barred them from power, their criticisms went to the heart of the Bonn republic's mode of operation. In penetrating the state, parties had assumed the state's chief function—the creation and maintenance of order. Inevitably, this meant a diminution of their role as societal representatives.

What once applied exclusively to the conservative parties became a universal indictment in the 1960s. The SPD's cooperation with the Christian Democrats in the Grand Coalition years (1966–69) first illustrated the drawbacks of stable party government. With the small FDP alone in organized opposition, and with the state organization monopolized by both major parties, social dissent was forced to circumvent the parties entirely. Significantly, the most prominent alternative movement of the times labeled itself the extraparliamentary opposition, a thinly veiled testimony to the growing irrelevance of Bonn's chief "popular" institution.[28] Nor did the Social/Liberal epoch reverse these trends. On the contrary, the Left proved every bit as skillful as the Right in preserving party hegemony. Admittedly, the Social Democrats were often more sensitive to demands for greater democratization, and they even initiated reforms designed further to open the political system, but they too were caught in the state's embrace.

More than twenty years ago, German sociologist Ralf Dahrendorf couched the *Parteienstaat* in the familiar parlance of the German Problem. Although few would today accept in unmodified form the gloomy verdict of *Society and Democracy in Germany,* the work remains illuminating for what it suggests about the parties' abdication of their representative responsibilities.[29] According to Dahrendorf, the advent of party governance brought about a less-than-total break with an ignominious past. Rather, "the destructive process has not yet led to the construction of a political class that gives expression to the competing diversity of social forces and is capable of supporting a liberal democracy".[30] Those who viewed the Federal Republic through the lens of German history and found its moderate style and catch-all parties a welcome advance over previous experience had completely missed the point. Pragmatism and party collusion epitomized abiding fear rather than true political maturity. Dahrendorf spoke of government by a "cartel of anxiety"—a leadership so dogged by visions of imminent social chaos that it artificially imposed orderly, consensual solutions.

If recent scholarship has amended Dahrendorf's once-dominant notion that Germans secretly hanker after an authoritarian past, the seminal function of West German parties is still widely recognized. And one need not affix such a sinister interpretation to the *Parteienstaat* to notice that the trajectory of party political power in the Federal Republic has moved increasingly away from society. It is in this respect that Bonn's parties appear to be heirs to older traditions. Far from bringing the state down from its lofty position and making it more accessible to the masses, parties have guarded their insulation from societal pressures.

Scandals and Parties

Because the *Spiegel* and Flick scandals stand at opposite poles in the evolution of party rule, the ways in which the parties were drawn into the controversy differed markedly. In the *Spiegel* case, the concept of an organized opposition had not yet lost its meaning, because the state was then penetrated primarily by the Right. Though the spd's drive to national power was clearly under way by the early 1960s, the Social Democrats within limits continued to comport themselves as the regime's official critics. Conversely, the Christian Democrats, whose leaders were key figures in the affair, reacted as if the state itself were under siege. The parliamentary sessions were notable for their sharp partisan conflict—a signal, as the Flick case illustrates, that the identification between state and party was incomplete.

By the time Flick had been transformed from a routine tax investigation into a saga of political corruption, none of the Federal Republic's established parties were accustomed to functioning as the "classic" opposition. That task fell instead to the Greens and to certain segments of the press. Clearly, the substance of the affair lent itself less easily to partisanship than did the *Spiegel* affair, because at various points leaders from all three major parties were implicated.[31] But in as much as the allegations hit the liberals and conservatives hardest, the spd might have pursued the matter more vigorously. The answer to the Social Democrats' reticence lies in the solidification of the *Parteienstaat*.

Spiegel and the Loyal Opposition

The *Spiegel* affair raised issues that reached beyond the party-political dimension, including the status of basic civil liberties and the boundaries of the press in an open society. Additionally, as noted, the infancy of the Federal Republic automatically rendered the scandal a test case for the entire system. Of this the principal protagonists were acutely aware; the Adenauer government was unduly sensitive to criticism, and the spd constantly worried that its loyalty was in doubt. Yet such tendencies stemmed at least in part from the early relationship between the parties and the state. Adenauer (and the party organized to elect him) strongly identified with the Federal Republic's first policy achievements: economic recovery and boom, international respectability, and a smooth integration into the western alliance network. Since these measures were inextricably bound up with the Union's self-image—indeed, they substituted for a coherent *Weltanschauung*[32]—any challenges to the prevailing agenda were taken as challenges to the state.[33]

The SPD's situation was more complex. The optimism of the immediate postwar years when national power seemed within the party's grasp soon proved illusive. The Social Democrats suffered some spectacular defeats through the 1950s, and had only recently staged a comeback.[34] Their political posture was therefore in a state of flux, reflecting the search for a strategy that would yield electoral results without compromising important principles. Owing to a longer history and richer ideological heritage, however, the Social Democrats possessed a collective identity separate from the state. Once the government had failed to contain the scandal, the party reverted to its familiar stance as the state's watchdog.

Whether Ahlers's article would have aroused the wrath of a defense minister other than Franz Josef Strauss remains a contentious point. The ambitious young leader of the Christian Democratic movement in Bavaria had already carved out a reputation for stubborn singlemindedness. And his autocratic bent alarmed critics like *Der Spiegel's* editors, who feared Strauss had set his sights on the chancellorship. Prior to the 10 October issue, the magazine had run a series of features implying that the defense minister posed a "danger to democracy,"[35] a charge to which Strauss responded with a libel suit. Given the mutual acrimony, it was almost inevitable that Strauss would employ whatever power he possessed to take *Der Spiegel* down a peg. But there was also more at stake here than Strauss's personal vendetta. Ahlers's analysis was in effect a critique of the Union's defense policies, precisely the area in which the Christian Democrats had vested both their legitimacy and that of the state. Adenauer's ill-fated fulminations on the floor of the Bundestag underscored just how broadly the Union construed treason. In simply opposing CDU/CSU priorities, *Der Spiegel* had "endangered the nation."[36]

The seriousness of the allegations initially placed the SPD in a quandary. Despite the party's pronounced sympathy for Augstein and for *Der Spiegel's* editorial views, the Social Democrats felt themselves vulnerable on defense matters. Having suffered under similar charges in the past, SPD leaders were not about to rush into a hasty affirmation of *Der Spiegel's* integrity at the risk of again being labeled disloyal. Indeed, had the Union promptly disclosed the extent of its involvement in the affair, or at least given the impression of proceeding impartially, the scandal might have never pitted the opposition against the government.[37]

Absent a plausible clarification of the facts, and with *Der Spiegel's* archives still impounded, the Social Democrats somewhat reluctantly began their parliamentary assault. Among the many unanswered questions, Strauss's role was the most nagging. Specifically, the opposition sought to determine whether the defense minister had led the crusade against *Der Spiegel,* and particularly whether Strauss or one of his underlings had effected Ahlers's arrest in Spain. If these accusations could be proven, the law had undoubtedly been violated.

Investigations of treason fell within the competence of so-called "nonpolitical" authorities, presumably the Federal Prosecutor's Office, and should not have involved the defense ministry directly.

Strauss's replies stopped short of full candor, for the defense minister was adept at evading the central issues.[38] Nonetheless, continual Social Democratic prodding cast suspicion on Strauss's former denials of involvement. As one account of the scandal euphemistically surmised, Strauss's public statements "seriously abused the truth."[39] Evidence in the government's official report brought forth additional revelations. Acting on his own initiative, Strauss had telephoned Spain on the night of 26 October 1962 with the request for Ahlers's arrest. Moreover, the defense minister had ignored the legal impediments that forbade his intervention.

Although Strauss bore the brunt of the criticism hurled at the Christian Democrats in the wake of the affair, he did not so much instigate the Union's troubles as embody them. Unable to separate a transitory set of policy preferences from the permanence of the state, Adenauer's CDU/CSU had grown markedly intolerant of opposing views. That *Der Spiegel* provoked a response far out of proportion to its "crime" owed something to the magazine's iconoclastic style, but this was hardly an isolated case. As the SPD could well attest, challenging the Union on national security policy was a perilous endeavor.[40]

Despite some rather formidable obstacles, the SPD's posture throughout the scandal closely resembled that of parties elsewhere that are determined to check government power. Using the formal parliamentary means of Question Hour,[41] the Social Democrats forced admissions from key officials that ultimately substantiated the charges of governmental impropriety. Whether narrow partisan considerations or genuine outrage prompted this strategy is really beside the point. More relevant for our purposes is what it represented in terms of the party-state relationship. Only a party still tied to its social constituency could lend any meaning to the role of organized opposition. This the SPD did in the Spiegel case, albeit not without equivocation.

Still, the limits to Social Democracy's opposition were equally telling. The outwardly acrimonious tone of the Bundestag sessions in fact concealed an underlying moderation of the Left's approach. Ever careful to isolate "proper" matters for debate from the larger, more fundamental issues of the scandal, the Social Democrats retreated from a comprehensive critique of the system. While not surprising to those whose memories reach back no farther than the Schmidt era, when compared with Social Democratic recalcitrance in the early 1950s, such restraint was striking. It would become a hallmark of both Left and Right with the Flick case.

Flick and the Venality of Office

If the *Spiegel* affair seemed an episode destined for historic prominence, the Flick case, in contrast, seemed eminently forgettable. There were no midnight raids by the authorities. Instead, the evidence that finally impelled a government investigation was found to be painstakingly documented in the Flick company's account books. There was no single public official on whom to pin major responsibility for wrongdoing. *Spiegel* (temporarily) thwarted the ambitions of Franz Josef Strauss. But Flick implicated, among others, Helmut Kohl,

Rainer Barzel, Eberhard von Brauchitsch, and Otto von Lambsdorff.[42] Indeed, the Green party's leadership alone escaped suspicion. Nor was there an identifiable "closure" to the affair. *Spiegel* ran its course relatively quickly; by late 1962 the principal blame had been assigned and the offenders "punished." The Flick case, however, earned the dubious distinction of becoming the longest-running crisis in the Federal Republic's experience.[43]

"Crisis" is actually something of a misnomer in this case. For many observers, the Flick case constituted little more than a mundane saga of political corruption, the sort of affliction to which all governments are susceptible. The names of public officials who succumb to the lure of monetary advantage rarely remain on the front pages. And outright bribery is notoriously difficult to prove. Yet the universality of the transgressions belies a uniquely German twist. By the beginning of the 1980s, the relentless advance of the *Parteienstaat* had buried the classical opposition. Consequently, the task of defending society's interests rested with those outside the locus of power.

Two examples aptly illustrate the point. The first involved an attempted revision of the party finance laws in 1981. With the Federal Prosecutor's Office eagerly poring over Flick's explicit records, the three established parties maneuvered to insert an amnesty clause in a proposed new law that would have removed the legal penalties for previous under-the-table corporate donations to parties.[44] Only after loud protestations from the press and the Greens did the Social Democrats withdraw their support. At best the appearance of elite collusion was ill-timed. Secondly, the polite tenor of the Bundestag investigations was punctuated, significantly, by the attacks of an "antiparty party." When Green Deputy Jürgen Reents charged in 1984 that Chancellor Kohl's way to power had been bought with Flick money, he unwittingly provided the scandal's confrontational apex. Termed a "monstrous" affront, the allegation touched still-sensitive memories of the powerful corporations responsible for bankrolling the Nazis, and thus brought momentary pandemonium to the chamber. Normalcy was restored by having Reents expelled.[45]

The temptation to stifle dissent was strong. Though the political parties most enmeshed in the scandal, the FDP and CDU, worried at times that the affair would undermine public confidence, in general their leaders treated the Flick inquiry as a minor aggravation. Since the legal proceedings neither toppled the Kohl government nor resulted in bribery convictions for the principals, perhaps such complacency was warranted. But however common the venality of office, its repercussions are scarcely favorable for the governed. The spectacle of the Federal Republic's major parties scrambling to avoid accountability seemed to confirm what dissenters like the Greens had long argued. West Germany's coming of age had imprisoned parties in the state. As such, they operate in an arena ever farther removed from the clash of social values and interests.

That the Flick scandal should ultimately have returned to the classic German dilemma of the state emphatically does not imply a reemergence of the German Problem. In an epoch when governance has grown increasingly complex, demanding more technical skill than virtue, the masses are everywhere peripheral to the decisions that affect them. Yet the *Süddeutsche Zeitung's* 1984 reflections on the affair nonetheless captured the seminal issue. The lack of an entry in the Flick company's ledger reading "for the benefit of the Federal

Republic"[46] manifested the difficulty of defining the general welfare in a system so thoroughly overlaid with party-political power. Where party and state became synonymous, the opposition is easily marginalized.

NOTES

1. Ronald Bunn, *German Politics and the Spiegel Affair. A Case Study of the Bonn System* (Baton Rouge: Louisiana State University Press, 1966); Alfred Grosser and Jürgen Seifert, eds., *Die Spiegel Affäre*, 2 vols. (Olten: Walter Verlag, 1966); John Gimbel, "The Spiegel Affair in Perspective," *Midwest Journal of Political Science*, no. 9, 3 (August 1965): 282–97; David Schoenbaum, *The Spiegel Affair* (Garden City: Doubleday, 1968). The summary here is drawn primarily from Bunn.

2. Franz Josef Strauss was the leader of the Christian Social Union (CSU) and minister-president of Bavaria until his death in October 1988. The CSU has had a parliamentary alliance with the Christian Democratic Union (CDU) since the first Bundestag elections in 1949, but the CSU is a separate, autonomous party with its own leadership, party congresses, and electoral platforms. Strauss's career dates back to the earliest years of the Federal Republic. In addition to his current posts, he has been federal defense minister (prior to his resignation after the *Spiegel* affair), finance minister (during the Grand Coalition, 1966–69), and the Christian democratic chancellor candidate (1980).

3. From *Die Welt*, 31 October 1962, quoted in Bunn, *German Politics*, pp. 61–62. Most of the signatories were prominent artists, writers, and publicists. Comparably worded telegrams were sent by the academic community as well.

4. The *Spiegel* affair surfaced just as a Bundestag investigating committee was probing Strauss's involvement in the so-called Fibag Affair. Strauss was alleged to have improperly intervened to obtain housing contracts for a German company on recommendation from a personal acquaintance. Most accounts of the *Spiegel* affair argue that the SPD changed its strategy as a result of the slow investigative process in the first scandal and chose instead to employ the Question Hour. *Der Spiegel's* coverage of Fibag was more extensive than that of other parts of the West German press.

5. The Federal Republic's major parties are designated as follows: Christian Democratic Union (CDU); Christian Social Union (CSU); Free Democratic Party (FDP, also commonly referred to as Liberals); Social Democratic Party (SPD).

6. Strauss's admissions were incremental and contradicted his earlier denials of involvement. At issue was whether a "political" ministry (Defense) had usurped authority belonging principally to the Federal Prosecutor's Office. In his first public statements on the affair, Strauss tried to maintain that Defense had only "assisted" the investigation. The government's later official report on the scandal revealed that Strauss had actually telephoned Spain himself requesting Ahlers's arrest. Grosser and Seifert, *Die Spiegel Affäre*.

7. Adenauer's remarks were made on the floor of the Bundestag on 7 November 1962. Bunn, *German Politics*, pp. 129–30, quotes from the Bundestag records as follows: " . . . (Adenauer) "Treason has been committed—(prolonged protests from the SPD)—by a man who had in his hands a power, a journalistic power. . ." Adenauer was later taken to task by FDP leaders for having publicly prejudged a pending legal case.

8. Indeed, the affair is too narrowly focused on Flick. Other large German firms, among them AEG, Kaufhof, and Henkel were accused of similar political payoffs. The investigations began, however, as inquiries into possible tax evasion.

9. *Süddeutsche Zeitung*, 20 October 1984.

10. According to existing West German tax laws, exemptions could be granted on these grounds at the recommendation of the Economics and Finance Ministries.

11. The entries typically read *"wegen* (on account of)————." See especially Hans Werner Kilz and Joachim Preuss, *Flick. Die Gekaufte Republik* (Reinbek bei Hamburg:

Rowohlt, 1983). Eberhard von Brauchitsch, Flick's chief executive at the time the alleged bribes were dispersed, was also president-elect of the Federation of German Industry. The latter is the most powerful employer organization in the Federal Republic. Brauchitsch resigned the post when the federal prosecutor's investigation reached its height. In early 1987, Brauchitsch was convicted of tax evasion, but the charges of bribery and corruption were dropped.

12. The accusations made against Barzel were actually much more serious. Barzel, who had been Helmut Kohl's principal rival for CDU leadership in the early 1970s, was suspected of having taken Flick money to, in effect, step down in favor of Kohl. Barzel vehemently denied the charges. *New York Times*, 23 October 1984. Hans Friedrichs was head of the large Dresdner Bank at the time of his indictment.

13. The laws in effect at the time limited donations to DM 20,000 unless the donor's identity was made public. Charities were not subject to the same restrictions. *Economist*, 6 March 1982.

14. Kilz and Preuss, *Flick*. See also the concluding section of this essay.

15. Not surprisingly, the charges came mainly from Franz Josef Strauss. *Economist*, 3 November 1984. *Der Spiegel* and the *Süddeutsche Zeitung* also published much of the evidence being employed by the Bundestag subcommittee. The latter consisted primarily of Flick's account books.

16. Kilz and Preuss, *Flick*, p. 314.

17. The Americans dominated among the western occupying powers, and hence, American preferences tended to influence most heavily the initial restoration of political life. The German economy's industrial concentration was distinctly at odds with the American ideals of free market capitalism, and the latter was, in the American mind, intimately linked to democracy.

18. V. R. Berghan, *Modern Germany* (Cambridge and New York: Cambridge University Press, 1982), p. 187.

19. The Junkers were a group of noble landowners whose power base was primarily in Prussia. Their large estates were operated on a semifeudal basis well after industrial capitalism hit Germany with full force in the late nineteenth century. The classic work on Germany's late industrialization and the political consequences of continued Junker power is Alexander Gerschenkron, *Bread and Democracy in Germany* (New York: H. Fertig, 1966).

20. Literally, "coordination." The term refers to the Nazi practice of penetrating existing institutions and social structures, including the Junker elite. See especially Barrington Moore, Jr., *Social Origins of Dictatorship and Democracy* (Boston: Beacon Press, 1966); Ralf Dahrendorf, *Society and Democracy in Germany* (Garden City: Anchor Books, 1967).

21. The West German state was created, almost literally, from the ground up. Local government was first allowed to revive because democratic traditions were stronger here. Gordon Smith, *Democracy in West Germany*, 2d ed. (New York: Holmes & Meier, 1982).

22. The SPD's Godesberg Program of 1959 is widely recognized as inaugurating an officially "centrist" position. While the German SPD had had reformist tendencies since its beginnings in the nineteenth century, scholars argued that the party's official reformism was largely a response to the CDU/CSU's electoral success. See especially Otto Kirchheimer, "The Vanishing Opposition," in *Political Opposition in Western Democracies*, ed. Robert Dahl (New Haven: Yale University Press, 1966).

23. When the FDP leadership has stressed economic issues, the CDU/CSU has been the most likely coalition partner. When civil rights and liberties, or the "politics of internal reform" have dominated, the FDP gravitated toward the Social Democrats.

24. Geoffrey Pridham, *Christian Democracy in Western Germany* (New York: St. Martin's Press, 1977), especially part one. The depiction of the Union as a pragmatic and largely nonideological alliance should not be applied to the CSU. The latter has always adopted a more markedly conservative posture.

25. The Reichstag is the term for the German parliament from unification (1871) to

the end of World War I. Though it was popularly elected in part, votes were weighted so as to exclude any threats to the social coalition that supported Bismarck and the state.

26. Political parties are normally considered representatives of society, and hence they are generally not mentioned in constitutions. In West Germany, this is but one manifestation of a unique fusion of public and private power. See especially Peter Katzenstein, *Policy and Politics in West Germany: The Growth of a Semi-Sovereign State* (Philadelphia: Temple University Press, 1987).

27. Article 21 of the Basic Law explicitly mentions parties as participants in "forming the will of the people." The Federal Constitutional Court has ruled since that parties are *Staatsorgane*—literally, organs of the state. See Gordon Smith, *Democracy in West Germany*, p. 67. See also Kenneth Dyson, *Party, State and Bureaucracy in West Germany* (Beverly Hills: Sage Publications, 1977) and Herbert Döring and Gordon Smith, eds., *Party Government and Political Culture in Western Germany* (New York: Macmillan, 1982).

28. The Extraparliamentary Opposition (APO) was most active during the late 1960s. It was a loose coalition of New Left groups and the student movement, which some analysts view as the antecedent to the Green Party.

29. Dahrendorf, *Society and Democracy*.

30. Ibid., p. 220.

31. This was principally because the tax exemption for Flick's Daimler-Benz sale and related aspects of the scandal occurred with the Social Democratic/Liberal coalition in power. The principal defendants in the legal proceedings and key witnesses in the Bundestag inquiry, however, were either FDP or CDU members. Among these, Otto von Lambsdorff (FDP) and Rainer Barzel (CDU) were the most prominent.

32. Christian Democracy tended to espouse certain themes, but given the Union's heterogenous social base, these themes did not (and probably could not) comprise a coherent world view.

33. Pridham, *Christian Democracy*.

34. The worst setback was the 1957 election, in which the Christian Democrats received an absolute majority of the vote. The landslide was attributed principally to Adenauer's personal popularity and to the success of West Germany's economic recovery in the 1950s.

35. Bunn, *German Politics*, pp. 13–29.

36. See note 1 above.

37. The SPD's overall opposition strategy was then in the midst of a transition. The principled, programmatic opposition of the early 1950s had already given way to a milder, issue-specific form.

38. Indeed, the government's subsequent report—issued only with SPD prodding—revealed contradictions in Strauss's various statements. Grosser and Seifert, *Die Spiegel Affäre*.

39. Bunn, *German Politics*, p. 172.

40. The SPD, throughout the 1950s especially, was dogged by charges of weak support for German interests. The party's first leader, Kurt Schumacher, attempted to steer the SPD along more "nationalist" lines, for the electorate seemed to fear that an SPD government would not safeguard German integrity.

41. Question Hour provided a more direct means for confronting the government than, for example, a Bundestag investigating committee. The latter would have been controlled by the coalition, a problem the SPD had encountered in the Fibag inquiry. Given the SPD's overall strategy, the use of Question Hour can also be seen as an attempt to bring the issues into a more "public" forum.

42. Helmut Kohl (CDU), West German chancellor; Rainer Barzel (CDU), speaker of the Bundestag and former rival of Kohl for the position of Union chancellor candidate; Eberhard von Brauchitsch, Flick Company chief operating officer, former president of Federation of Germany Industry (BDI); Otto von Lambsdorff, economics minister. Lambsdorff was a significant casualty for the FDP. A popular leader, he had been instrumental in leading the FDP away from the Social Democrats and into the coalition

with the CDU/CSU that commenced in 1982. The courts' verdict of tax fraud does not preclude Lambsdorff from seeking another ministerial post in the future.

43. The alleged violations ostensibly began in the early 1970s, the Bundestag investigations commenced in 1981, and the courts handed down the verdicts on Lambsdorff, Friedrichs, and von Brauchitsch in early 1987.

44. *Economist*, 6 March 1982. The proposed amendment would have granted amnesty to those who paid the back taxes formerly sheltered in "dummy charities." The party finance laws were subsequently revised to allow greater corporate and individual donations. Because, for purposes of this essay, the legal issues are secondary to the political implications of the scandal, the former have not been addressed in detail here.

45. *New York Times*, 23 October 1984.

46. *Süddeutsche Zeitung*, 20 October 1984.

7. Austria: The Withering of Consociational Democracy?

ANTON PELINKA

The Scandal

At the height of Austria's postwar reconstruction period and coinciding with the country's independence in 1955, a decision was reached that year to erect a major medical complex in Vienna. Befitting the *Zeitgeist* in which a blind faith in megaprojects was an accurate reflection of the general reliance on growth and technology as the best agents for economic progress and social justice, this hospital was to be far and away Austria's biggest. Aiming to attain "international dimensions" and "European standards," all of which were measured in terms of quantitative size and technological prowess at the time, the planners envisioned a hospital with the following specifications: It was to employ nine hundred doctors, nineteen hundred nurses, and seven hundred technical assistants. There were to be two thousand beds in addition to facilities for seven thousand ambulatory patients. Lastly, the complex was to include teaching facilities for well over one thousand students.

Tellingly for the Austria just emerging from the rubble of World War II and the subsequent ten-year occupation by the four Allied powers, the decision to build this hospital, the Allgemeines Krankenhaus (AKH), derived from a completely bipartisan arrangement between the country's two large parties and coalition partners, the conservative Austrian People's Party (Österreichische Volkspartei—ÖVP) and the social democratic Austrian Socialist Party (Sozialistische Partei Österreichs—SPÖ). In addition to being the result of an informal agreement between these two actors that made all important decisions in the country subject to bipartisan approval, there were some structural conditions involving both parties in the AKH project. Since the hospital was to be built in Vienna and serve as one of the city's municipal institutions, that city's

166

governing party, i.e., the SPÖ, viewed the project as being in its purview. Having been conceived as a teaching hospital as well, the project thus entered the domain of the country's university establishment, thereby involving the federal government, which, until 1970, also meant the Austrian People's Party. Hence, from its very beginning, the project remained under the dual competence and responsibility of Austria's two largest political parties.[1]

Construction proceeded at a slow pace. Between 1955 and 1972 parts of the hospital's infrastructure were finished, such as accommodations for the nurses and parking garages. A number of ancillary clinics were also completed, notably one for pediatrics and another for neuropsychiatry. However, it was not until 1972 that construction on the main complex was begun in earnest.

Three years later and in part responding to the growing number of critical voices that demanded some explanation for the constant and crippling delays of the operation, an overall planning agency was founded precisely to increase efficiency and streamline all activities. Named "Allgemeines Krankenhaus Wien, Planungs- und Errichtungs-Aktien-Gesellschaft" (AKPE), one half of this agency was owned by the City of Vienna and the other half belonged to the federal government. Adolf Winter, a member of the Socialist Party and a high-level civil servant employed by the City of Vienna, became AKPE's director and chief executive officer. Even prior to the creation of this new agency, Winter had already been responsible for the AKH project. As such, he had major executive powers and superb contacts in the public domain of the federal and municipal governments as well as in the world of private contractors and large firms. Winter's party affiliation and contacts in government, furnished by the Socialist Party on both the federal and the municipal levels as of 1970, complemented his excellent relations with some of Austria's leading industrial firms, all of whom continued to foster their traditionally close ties to the country's leading conservative force, the ÖVP. Winter founded several "mailbox firms" with Liechtenstein addresses in 1972, none of which, of course, existed in reality. By the mid-1970s, large sums of money were deposited to the bank accounts of these firms by companies whom Winter had promised a major role in the construction of the AKH's main complex. This was the first step in a string of abuses in which party affiliations, public positions, and business contacts were systematically employed by key actors for the enhancement of their private gain at the direct expense of the public good.

The questionable entanglements continued in the course of the 1970s. In 1976, Winter added another firm to the management of the AKH project. Called Ökodata, it had been founded in 1975 by Franz Bauer, a leading executive of Consultatio, a management consulting and accounting firm largely owned by Hannes Androsch, then minister of finance in the country's socialist government, vice chancellor as of 1976, and unquestionably the SPÖ's "number two" man and clear heir apparent to Bruno Kreisky at that time.[2] In short order Ökodata proceeded to receive a few million Austrian schillings from the project without having rendered it any commensurate services in return. Other firms and persons who in some fashion maintained connections with Ökodata or more directly with Winter's original AKPE also obtained payments for little, if any, services rendered to the project.

Two types of criticism began to arise by 1977 and their eventual merging led to the full exposure of the scandal three years later. On the one hand, in full accordance with the Zeitgeist, a number of people began to question the rationale of this megaproject whose huge dimensions they viewed not only as a waste of resources and as completely ill-conceived in relation to its surrounding environment, but also as detrimental to optimal health care.[3] In addition to this fundamental critique of the AKH project's very essence, discontent regarding the huge expenditures became more pronounced. Cost overruns did indeed reach astronomical dimensions. Whereas the project was slated to cost one billion schillings in 1962, Finance Minister Androsch mentioned fifteen billion schillings in 1975, only to inform parliament five years later that expenditures for the project would exceed thirty-seven billion schillings when all was said and done.

It was not until that year (1980) that the Austrian public became fully informed about all dimensions of the AKH affair. The Viennese journalist Alfred Worm, employed by Austria's leading newsweekly *Profil,* published a cover story in the magazine headlined "18 millions to Liechtenstein." In his investigative article, Worm launched a head-on attack on the various financial manipulations surrounding the maze of companies involved in the AKH project. Above all, he exposed Adolf Winter for having received huge sums of money in the form of kickbacks from companies that were purportedly contributing to the hospital's completion. Much of Worm's evidence derived from an off-the-record interview he conducted with Winter that was secretly taped by Worm.

The article in *Profil* caused a snowball effect in Austrian public life. A scandal of major proportions unsettled the idyllic arrangements and top-level corporatist "deals" so characteristic of the Austrian model of politics. A special parliamentary committee was appointed to investigate the scandal, the courts became involved, and key public figures were arrested and subsequently convicted. In addition to Winter and others directly involved in the AKH project, a number of prominent Austrian industrialists and politicians saw their reputations severely damaged in the wake of this scandal. Thus, for example, Fritz Mayer, chief executive officer of ITT-Austria until 1976 and president of the Association of Austrian Industrialists (Vereinigung österreichischer Industrieller—VÖI) in 1980 was arrested in August of that year for having made illegal payments on behalf of ITT to several of Winter's phantom firms in Liechtenstein. Mayer, who eventually was found guilty, had to resign his key positions at ITT as well as at the VÖI, which is one of Austria's two key employers' associations and as such a completely legal and major contributor to the coffers of Austria's two bourgeois parties, the already mentioned ÖVP and the much smaller, though still substantial, right-wing Freedom Party (Freiheitliche Partei Oesterreichs—FPÖ). Hannes Androsch had to resign as finance minister and vice chancellor in 1981 as a consequence of being the main owner of Consultatio and for having had close personal ties to people in the front lines of the AKH project and its ancillary associations. Although a number of legal investigations regarding Androsch's financial dealings have yet to be concluded at the time of this writing (early 1987), the former finance minister has never been formally charged with any wrongdoing. Indeed, he still continues as chief executive officer of Austria's largest bank, the Creditanstalt Bankverein.

The political implications of the AKH scandal center on the entanglement of individual culpability, political planning, and party interests. On the face of it, Adolf Winter seemed little more than your "average" white-collar criminal. However, the scandal involved not only the prestigious Austrian branches of leading multinational corporations such as Siemens and ITT, but it also implicated key members of the country's political establishment, among whom Mayer and Androsch were only the most exposed. Above all, the scandal shed much unexpected light on the close entanglements existing between the country's industrial complex and the financing of the two major political parties. It made it amply clear that the parties' financial affairs remained virtually uncontrolled by the public as well as by the government in Austria. Furthermore, it also became clear that Austria's political culture did not exact a sharp enough differentiation between personal and political interests. The realms of the public and the private remained uncomfortably blurred. Lastly, the akh scandal demonstrated clearly the structural problems of an Austrian polity virtually monopolized by a "party state." Regarding the latter point, the scandal emphasized the following typical features of Austria's political arrangements:

(1) More than perhaps any other liberal democracy, the Republic of Austria is a party state. Twice in its history, in 1918 and 1945, it was the political parties who founded the republic and determined the content and tone of the constitution. The parties are older than the state, which they thus see as their creation and property.

(2) In their role as founders of the state and framers of the constitution, the parties have systematically expanded their "gate-keeping" functions over time. As a consequence of having occupied this position, which controls access to most key positions in Austrian society, the parties in Austria have exercised a much greater influence on the country's public sphere and its political system than has been the case in other liberal democracies. Parties have enjoyed a much greater presence in Austrian politics and society than in any other liberal democratic system.

(3) Thanks to processes of stabilization and normalization that have shaped the Austrian political system in the decades after 1945, the political parties have lost much of their original ideological character. One of the consequences of this "secularization process" has been the increase of various pragmatic "machinations" and the quest for nonideological "deals," which not only have led to a deideologization of the parties but also to a concomitant proliferation and legitimation of individualized careerism. Often linked to schemes of personal enrichment, the loss of ideology has upon occasion also led to an increase in the temptation toward criminal deeds.

Andrei S. Markovits and Mark Silverstein, in their introduction to this volume, describe the process of political scandal as an "abuse of the liberal tradition," which "inevitably culminates in a celebration of the values of that tradition." The Austrian case seems to give emphasis to a slightly different linkage: the lack of a liberal tradition has to be seen as one of the preconditions of the Austrian "party state." The akh scandal was responsible for creating an atmosphere favorable to the strengthening of the values of liberal tradition. The scandal itself was important in that it made up for the lack of that tradition.

The Rules of the Game

It was the Federal Constitutional Act of 1920 that originally provided Austria with a consistently structured parliamentary system.[4] Amended by the Constitutional Act of 1929, the parliamentary character of the Austrian political system—denoted by the merger of government and the parliamentary major-

TABLE 6.1

AUSTRIAN CONSTITUTIONAL RULES OF THE GAME

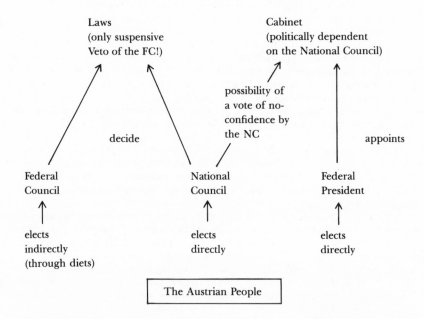

ity—also featured a federal president who is directly elected by the people and whose key tasks include the formal appointment as well as dismissal of the federal chancellor (i.e., the head of government) and of the individual members of the federal government (i.e., the cabinet). These constitutional arrangements were also assumed by the Second Republic. This Austrian mixture of parliamentary and presidential democracy was somewhat akin to the political system of the Weimar Republic, just as it has many parallels to the Fifth Republic of contemporary France. Typical for these hybrid institutional arrangements is the inherent possibility of a stalemate between the chief executive (i.e., the federal president) and the parliamentary majority (i.e., the majority in the National Council) both of whom derive their legitimacy from direct election by the people. Contrary to genuine presidential democracies such as the United States, the Austrian arrangement could potentially cause a paralysis in governmental activities because the cabinet needs the confidence of the federal president as well as the political support of the National Council. While the federal president can dismiss the cabinet (the government) at any time, so can a majority of the National Council by means of a vote of no confidence. The same censure procedures can be brought to bear upon individual members of the cabinet as well, thus enforcing their resignation from executive office.

Thus far, however, the possibility of this kind of institutional paralysis has never occurred in the history of the second Austrian republic. By tradition and convention, the federal president exercises restraint of his constitutional powers, especially in regard to his relations with the federal government, whose formation he has yet to contest against the majority of the parliament's National Council. Thus, as in other parliamentary democracies, in Austria it has not been the head of state (the federal president) but rather a parliamentary majority of the National Council that ultimately decides the composition of the cabinet and, concomitantly, the party allegiance of the head of government (the federal chancellor). The president confines himself to a role of legitimation and approval by entrusting the largest party's nominee for chancellor with the formation of a cabinet and subsequently accepting the cabinet as the federal government of the land.

Thus, for all intents and purposes, the formal arrangements of Austrian politics bear the markings of a parliamentary system in which there exists a linkage of power between parliament and government, as well as the *de facto* domination of the government over parliament, both of which constitute rather common characteristics of modern parliamentary democracies. This linkage of power, institutionally anchored in the cabinet's political responsibility vis-à-vis parliament (the feasibility of a vote of no confidence being a good illustration of this arrangement) does not lead to a dependence of the cabinet on parliament, rather to the inverse situation, mediated by the requirement of a parliamentary majority based on one single party or a coalition of parties.

Parliamentarism in Austria

Parliamentarism arrived late in Austria.[5] Until 1918 the Austrian parliament remained relatively powerless, laboring in the shadow of a semiabsolutist emperor and a cabinet responsible only to him. The emperor's and his cabinet's right to make unimpeded use of emergency rule emasculated parliament to the point of its virtual dispensability. The 1918 proclamation of the republic turned the underdeveloped parliamentarism of the monarchy into a genuine one. The introduction of the parliamentary system placed the center of political gravity in the federal cabinet, even though a traditional separation of powers was still retained in the terminology of constitutional discourse. Following the establishment of this parliamentary system, the Austrian parliament developed into the institutional locus where party-empowered and party-loyal representatives of the people bring to bear decisions reached elsewhere in the political process.

The structures of parliamentarism in the Second Austrian Republic have the following major institutional characteristics:[6]

(1) An "uneven" two-chamber system: in addition to the directly elected National Council there also exists the second chamber, the so-called Federal Council, whose members hold their seats "indirectly" by virtue of having been appointed by the provincial diets. The Federal Council's competence lags far behind that exercised by the National Council.

(2) Equilibrium of power between plenary bodies and parliamentary committees: The Austrian parliament, especially its National Council, derives much of its legitimacy from having been consciously constituted as a locus of opinion and debate as well as an institution of legislative formulation and implementation (*Rede-und Arbeitsparlament*).

(3) Institutionalized compromise: by means of the establishment of the so-called presidial conference, most of the procedures in the National Council as

well as the parliamentary behavior of the parties represented in the legislature have *in fact* occurred consensually.

(4) Party discipline: by compelling all legislators to follow strict party lines in their parliamentary behavior, there can be no doubt that Austrian parliamentarism has assumed a party-dominated characteristic, rendering the state into a "party state" *(Parteienstaat)* for all practical purposes.

(5) Proportional representation: this electoral system, already decreed by the Federal Constitutional Act of 1920 and further improved in 1971, strengthens the parties' already substantial domination over the individual representatives, making the latter structurally subservient to the parties as organizations empowered as such to conduct all parliamentary affairs and in effect to govern the country.

Although federalism constitutes the formal framework of Austria's governmental system—as reflected in the country's bicameral legislature—there can be no doubt of the center's structural predominance over the periphery. While the Austrian parliamentary system does include regional representation of its individual states as embodied in the Federal Council, this chamber's competence and purview—already rather circumscribed on paper—remains even further limited in reality. The National Council's primacy in relation to the Federal Council becomes evident in the following areas:

(1) The cabinet is only accountable to the National Council and not to the Federal Council. Only majorities in the former, never the latter, bear any influence on the formation of the cabinet, thus on the government of the country.

(2) The Federal Council can only delay, never alter or annul, legislation passed by the National Council. With the help of a simple majority vote, the National Council can override any opposition it may encounter in the Federal Council.

(3) As a matter of course, all legislation is first discussed in the National Council before it reaches the Federal Council, thus rendering the debates in the latter chamber somewhat redundant and as a consequence less important.

(4) Like the National Council, the Federal Council is organized along party lines. Thus, unlike regional representations in some other parliamentary democracies, the Austrian Federal Council embodies party rather than regional interests.

(5) In terms of public recognition and general appreciation, the National Council has consistently far outdistanced the Federal Council. Befitting this image, the parties have often resorted to using the latter as a training ground and "farm system" for their potential players in the country's "major league," as represented by the National Council.

(6) Almost never does the Federal Council make use of its rights—such as, for example, that of initiating legislation—because, as a consequence of the unshakable control exerted by the political parties, these matters have over the years typically become the unquestioned prerogatives of the National Council.

Both councils comprise plenaries as well as committees. Committees in both chambers correspond to the existence of ministries—each ministry has its corresponding parliamentary committee in the National as well as the Federal Council. Plenaries and committees in the National Council meet with greater frequency and require greater intensity of work than their counterparts in the Federal Council. Plenary meetings are usually the preferred stage for con-

Table 6.2
VOTING BEHAVIOR IN THE AUSTRIAN NATIONAL COUNCIL SESSION,
1979–1983

	UNANIMOUSLY	MAJORITY			TOTAL
		SPÖ	SPÖ + ÖVP	SPÖ + FPÖ	
Legislative Acts	351 = 75.3%	68 = 14.6%	29 = 6.2%	18 = 3.9%	466
International Agreements	199 = 97.0%	2 = 1.0%	2 = 1.0%	2 = 1.0%	205
Reports of the Federal Cabinet	97 = 74.6%	18 = 13.8%	2 = 1.5%	13 = 10.0%	130
Overruling the Federal Council's Veto	–	8 = 72.2%	–	3 = 27.3%	11

Source: Data by the Austrian Parliament

frontations between the leading figures of the government and those of the opposition in the National Council. In the committees and subcommittees, one can definitely discern a greater inclusion of additional party representatives, often featuring the work of backbenchers.[7]

Even after 1966—following the end of the first Grand Coalition between the Socialist and the People's parties and the subsequent establishment of single-party governments and small coalitions, until the beginning of 1987 when once again a Grand Coalition began to govern Austria—an overwhelming consensual atmosphere was the norm in the daily workings of the National Council. It is no secret that during Grand Coalitions the "Big Two" agree beforehand on each of their parliamentary measures in the National Council. That this collusion seems largely independent of the actual governmental arrangement ruling the country is best borne out by the fact that similar *a priori* agreements were the rule even between 1966 and 1987. Most laws are passed unanimously by the Austrian National Council, regardless of the party or parties comprising a particular government.

One of the reasons for this remarkable consensus rests with the already mentioned presidial conference. This institution of the National Council comprises its three presidents (speakers) and the floor leaders of the parties represented in parliament (i.e., three until 1987, and four since then). The conference fulfills two crucial parliamentary tasks: It is in charge of seeing to a smooth and orderly implementation of all plenary debates; moreover, it is entrusted with resolving all disputes concerning parliamentary procedures. In addition, the presidial conference serves as a permanent clearing-house for an array of arrangements and contacts among the parliamentary parties.

Undoubtedly, however, it is the parliamentary representations of the parties (i.e., the *Fraktionen*) that constitute the most important institution of the Austrian parliamentary establishment.[8] Organized in so called "clubs," the parliamentary representations of the parties remain the actual decisionmakers concerning all parliamentary matters.

It is, in the last analysis these bodies that decide the composition of the presidial conference, since it is they who determine the identities of the three speakers as well as those of their own floor leaders, respectively.

It is these parliamentary bodies that dictate events in the plenum by controlling a number of key procedural functions, such as, for example, the submission of speakers' lists, which determine not only who will speak on what topic but also in what order.

All parliamentary committees are directly dependent on the parliamentary parties, since all appointments to committee membership remain the sole responsibility of the *Fraktionen*.

The parliamentary parties determine all plenary decisions because as a matter of course these bodies agree on jointly acceptable proceedings before each plenary debate.

The parliamentary parties define the public's image of parliament and parliamentary democracy, which, as a consequence of the rigidly enforced and deeply internalized party discipline *(Fraktionszwang)*, is inevitably experienced as a mere reflection of party-dominated confrontations.

Party discipline, virtually never violated in Austria, is further strengthened by the elaborate proportional representation system that governs Austrian elections. Members of the National Council are elected according to a combined system of proportional representation and party lists.

Through this combined system of proportional representation and party lists, the electoral system enhances the representatives' already substantial dependence on their parties in and out of parliament. By having all committee work be completely under the parties' control, the system discriminates against the participation of independent representatives to the extent of their virtual exclusion from the parliamentary process. While the latter can speak in plenary sessions, they are barred from any meaningful parliamentary participation, making independence from a party on the parliamentary floor tantamount to political death. This mechanism provides the parties with an iron-fisted control over potential dissidents and challengers to the party line.

Professional politicians, sociologically rather divergent from their electoral supporters whom they purport to represent, constitute the vast majority of representatives in the National Council.[9] Typically parliamentary representatives are disproportionately more male than their voters; only about 10 percent of the National Council's members have been women over the years. Parliamentarians, nearly 50 percent of whom were university graduates by the mid-1980s, are much better educated than the general Austrian electorate. Members of parliament are older than the young voters, but younger than the very old voters. Representatives under forty and over sixty-five are rarities indeed. With 60 percent of parliamentarians belonging to the civil service, this sector of Austrian society is definitely overrepresented in the country's highest circles of power and decision making.

Austria's parliamentarians are more polarized on religion than the voters. Explicitly agnostic, perhaps even more expressly anti-Catholic, members of parliament on the one hand, and particularly devout and active Catholics on the other are overrepresented in both chambers. Compared to the Austrian electorate as a whole, the disproportionately large proportions of active anticlerical politicians and their opponents, politicized Catholics, among the country's parliamentarians hail from the historical legacy that has pitted these two "camps" against each other during much of the twentieth century.

Much of the legislative process in the National Council is anticipated—perhaps even preempted—by powerful institutions that are ancillary to parliament. Most legislation involves the state bureaucracy and the government in addition to the party headquarters and key interest groups before parliament proper.[10] Since about 90 percent of Austrian laws emanate from government bills, all of which deeply engage the state bureaucracy in one form or another, the importance of this structure in the country's policy formulation process hardly needs any further elaboration. Moreover, by subjecting government bills to a review process in which the country's leading interest groups and the representatives of the provincial governments are the automatic reviewers, it is obvious that all major political positions on any issue of importance are not only well-known before they reach the floor of parliament but are often already completely reconciled.

The weighty importance of the pre-parliamentary sector or sphere reflects the very strong position of certain interest groups and their close entanglement with the parties in the Austrian political system. Austria's famous social partnership, representing a specific and concrete manifestation of neocorporatism in that country, operates by means of the active involvement in this pre-parliamentary sector of interest groups belonging to capital and labor. It is largely due to the fundamental understanding reached by all contestants in this pre-parliamentary sector that such a high degree of unanimity has become commonplace in the Austrian legislative process.

While little has changed in this highly ritualized and well-institutionalized game in which the dominant players have seldom if ever been challenged, some recent developments have occurred at the margin that might be the harbingers of a slight loosening of this well-entrenched system of conflict management. We mean in particular the more frequent occurrence of referendums as mechanisms for legislative change and initiative, a sign that a substantial part of the Austrian population has been eager over the last fifteen years to use channels of political articulation that lie explicitly outside the conventional purview of the parties and key interest groups. Referendums are legislative initiatives that require the necessary signatures of at least ten thousand voters or the support of a certain number of parliamentary representatives. They can be used to bring a very specific issue before the Austrian public. Provided that the measure then gets an additional one hundred thousand signatures—around 2 percent of the eligible voters—the National Council becomes constitutionally obliged to treat the matter as being comparable to a bill and to vote on its fate, whether to reject it or make it the law of the land.[11]

The history of referendums in Austria shows that they are far more likely to succeed when they are not used by the opposition as instruments to embarrass the government, as was the case in 1982 when the conservative People's Party instigated a referendum against the governing Socialists opposing the construction of a United Nations conference center in Vienna and also in 1976 when the same party—in collaboration with the Catholic Church—supported a referendum opposing the legalization of abortion. While these referendums were initially successful in that they mobilized a large number of Austrians on behalf of their respective causes, their aims were never attained because of their

TABLE 6.3
PARLIAMENTARY LEGISLATURE

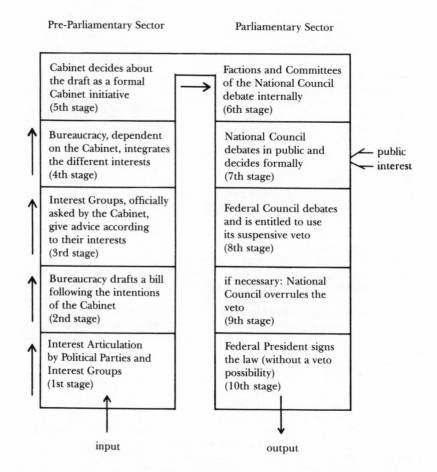

Pre-Parliamentary Sector   Parliamentary Sector

Cabinet decides about the draft as a formal Cabinet initiative (5th stage) → Factions and Committees of the National Council debate internally (6th stage)

Bureaucracy, dependent on the Cabinet, integrates the different interests (4th stage) | National Council debates in public and decides formally (7th stage) ← public ← interest

Interest Groups, officially asked by the Cabinet, give advice according to their interests (3rd stage) | Federal Council debates and is entitled to use its suspensive veto (8th stage)

Bureaucracy drafts a bill following the intentions of the Cabinet (2nd stage) | if necessary: National Council overrules the veto (9th stage)

Interest Articulation by Political Parties and Interest Groups (1st stage) | Federal President signs the law (without a veto possibility) (10th stage)

input   output

defeat at the hands of the Socialists' parliamentary majority in the National Council. Conversely, referendums that enjoy broad support among an eclectic group of Austrian citizens and that are not clearly identified with the positions of any political party—such as the referendum of 1969 opposing the thirteenth school year—are typically rewarded with complete success and ultimately become the law of the land. In cases of this kind, it is noticeable that far fewer signatures supporting the referendum's initial stages are needed than are needed in the more partisan versions.

The most powerful populist instrument provided by the Austrian constitution is the plebiscite. However, in the history of the Second Republic this measure only occurred once when in 1978 a bare majority of 51 percent of the

Austrian electorate voted against the start-up of an already completed nuclear power station in Zwentendorf near Vienna. The rare occurrence of plebiscites as compared to referendums derives from a peculiar constitutional limitation that states that plebiscites in Austria can only be conducted as a result of legal decrees issued by the National Council. A simple parliamentary majority suffices in the case of issues concerning regular laws. In matters related to constitutional subjects, one-third of the delegates either to the National or the Federal Council is needed to initiate a plebiscite. In the event of any changes in the constitution proper, the Austrian constitution then stipulates that a plebiscite be conducted.

On the state (provincial) and local level, plebiscitarian forms of democracy are much more common than in the federal arena. It is in this context that debates concerning constitutional reforms have been quite passionate in Austria, since many people would favor that conditions presently confined to the less important realms of provincial and local politics be applied on the national level as well. After all, this measure of direct democracy—clearly conceived as an alternative to the more prevalent form of indirect democracy embodied in the parliamentary process—still depends on the very structure it was originally designed to circumvent.

Two trends, favoring interparty competition, can be seen as having been responsible for the political impact the AKH scandal had: the revaluation of the opposition in parliament after 1966, when for the next two decades the administration was challenged by an opposition party that was interested in changing roles with the governing party; the increase of plebiscitarian democracy as a permanent incentive for dramatizing political conflicts, especially for and by the mass media. The political environment, more and more sensitive to open and unlimited competition, and more and more "westernized" in the sense of being a competitive democracy, became mature enough to produce a liberal reaction to a big-scale scandal. The political environment of an extremely stabilized consociational democracy, so typical of Austria in the first decades after 1945, would have been much less receptive to public critique. This flexibility can be seen as a criterion for competitive, liberal systems.

Government, Civil Service and the Judiciary in Austria

The constitution bestows powers upon the Austrian president that are quite similar to those held by the president of the Fifth Republic in France. The underlying constitutional reality, however, makes the Austrian president more like the British monarch.[12] Still, the very fact that the Austrian president assumes office by virtue of a direct popular vote distinguishes this position from comparable ones in Europe's other parliamentary democracies. Even though the Austrian president refrains from intervening in the country's daily governance by the mechanisms of a parliamentary system, the direct election of the president through regularized and recurring popular elections makes this arrangement of Austrian democracy rather special.

Austrian presidents are elected for six-year terms. They can only serve two terms in office. The career profiles of all Austrian presidents clearly show either that they have never belonged to the top brass of either of the two dominant parties or that they were former party leaders who were "rewarded" with the role of president before their complete retirement from public life.

TABLE 6.4

FEDERAL CHANCELLORS AND COMPOSITION OF CABINETS IN THE 2ND
REPUBLIC

CHANCELLOR	DATES	PARTIES REPRESENTED IN THE CABINET	PARTIES IN OPPOSITION
Karl Renner (SPOe)[1]	1945	SPOe, OeVP, KPOe	–
Leopold Figl (OeVP)	1945–1953	OeVP, SPOe, KPOe[2]	KPOe,[2] VDU[3]
Julius Raab (OeVP)	1953–1961	OeVP, SPOe	FPOe,[4] KPOe[5]
Alfons Gorbach (OeVP)	1961–1964	OeVP, SPOe	FPOe
Josef Klaus (OeVP)	1964–1970	OeVP, SPOe[6]	SPOe,[6] FPOe
Bruno Kreisky (SPOe)	1970–1983	SPOe	OeVP, FPOe[7]
Fred Sinowatz (SPOe)	1983–1986	SPOe, FPOe	OeVP
Franz Vranitzky (SPOe)	1986–	SPOe, FPOe,[9] OeVP[8]	PeVP,[8] FPOe,[9] Greens[10]

[1] Provisional Cabinet before the first General Elections; Renner was not called Federal, but State Chancellor.

[2] Communist Party of Austria—it stayed in the Cabinet till 1947, then it went over to the opposition.

[3] Independent Party, predecessor of the FPOe, in parliament since 1949.

[4] Till 1956 VDU.

[5] Lost its last members of parliament in 1959.

[6] After the elections of 1966, which resulted in an overall majority of the OeVP in the National Council, the SPOe went over to the opposition.

[7] 1970/71, when Kreisky didn't have an overall majority of Socialists in the National Council, the FPOe backed the SPOe minority cabinet informally.

[8] After the November 1986 elections, the OeVP and the SPOe started to bargain for a new Grand Coalition, which was to start in 1987 with Vranitzky as Chancellor and Mock, the OeVP leader as Vice-Chancellor.

[9] In fall 1986, Vranitzky cancelled the coalition with the FPOe and the FPOe is going to oppose the new Grand Coalition.

[10] In parliament since 1986.

Under no circumstances has the Austrian presidency been the ultimate career aim of any of the politically active leaders in either of the "Big Two."[13]

Their aim has always been the attainment of the office of the federal chancellor. Constitutional reality, which emphasizes the primacy of parliament, has traditionally made the federal chancellor, the head of government, the most important political actor in Austria. The chancellor's position as *primus inter pares* hails from his position as the leader of the country's majority party. With only a few exceptions lasting brief periods, all federal chancellors of the Second Republic have also been leaders of their parties. The exceptions have typically occurred in transition periods, such as the one at the time of this writing, when the federal chancellor (Franz Vranitzky) and the leader of the largest party, the SPÖ (Fred Sinowatz), are not the same person.[14]

The chancellor's power rests totally on his role as the party leader. It is his intraparty position that determines the boundaries of his influence. It is for this reason that each coalition government substantially curtails the chancellor's otherwise considerable power and influence. During the period of the first Grand Coalition (from 1945 to 1966), the chancellors, always furnished by the People's Party, never even tried to extend their rule to the ministries that belonged in the purview of their coalition partners. The vice chancellors, all belonging to the Socialist Party, were *de facto* "chancellors" within their own sphere of government by virtue of the primacy of party domination in the Austrian parliamentary system. The same principle prevailed during the SPÖ's "small" coalition with the Freedom Party between 1983 and 1987, and it has once again been resumed on a grand scale with the renewed establishment of the Grand Coalition between SPÖ and ÖVP as of January 1987. It is only on the condition of one party's uncontested majority as was the case between 1966 and 1983, that the federal chancellor enjoys virtually unbridled power to act as he sees fit. Supported by a cabinet whose members he has chosen and backed by a parliamentary majority of his party where discipline virtually never crumbles, the chancellor is then well placed to realize the creation and implementation of his legislative program in an unencumbered manner. Under these conditions, it would not be inappropriate to liken the Austrian chancellor to the British prime minister.

The government, nominally appointed by the federal president following the federal chancellor's suggestions, exists by virtue of majoritarian conditions in the National Council. In addition to the chancellor and the vice chancellor, the government also comprises all federal ministers (secretaries) heading the various ministries and their deputies, the junior ministers or assistant secretaries. Although each of the federal ministers is only responsible to her/his portfolio, reality dictates dependence on the chancellor. The junior ministers, always fewer in number than their senior counterparts, are there to assist the senior ministers, especially in the large ministries. In periods of coalition government, junior ministers are typically the other party's watchdog in a department controlled by a senior minister belonging to the rival party. The appointment of certain kinds of junior ministers can also serve to convey a particular intraparty message, such as, for example, when Chancellor Bruno Kreisky tried to further the cause of women inside his own Socialist Party by appointing four women as junior ministers in 1980.

The vice chancellor between 1966 and 1968 and then continuously since 1970 has been responsible for a ministerial portfolio in addition to his job as vice chancellor. The federal chancellor and the vice chancellor and all senior as well as junior ministers collectively form the Council of Ministers. This body reaches all its decisions (for example, the formulation of government bills) on a unanimous basis, junior ministers not being allowed to vote. This tradition of unanimity in the Council of Ministers always strengthens the junior partner in a coalition government, because the otherwise applicable principle of majority rule does not pertain to the government's decision-making process. The presence of a veto on the part of every coalition partner facilitates mutual control but also contributes to the possibility of blockages among the parties at the peak level of decision making. This mechanism creates something of a built-in opposition inside coalition governments themselves, whereby a governing party controls its other governing partner(s) in its quasi-official role as the opposition.[15] Opposition and government are thus merged into one.

The ministers enjoy complete freedom of staffing in their ministries, as does the chancellor with respect to the chancellery. Although the Austrian constitution calls for a professional civil service that should in theory be completely independent of partisan considerations in its staffing, reality has witnessed a strong influence of the parties over the civil servants appointed to the various ministries. It is fascinating to see the longevity of the patterns established during the Grand Coalition that existed between 1945 and 1966 because they still endure to this day. In the ministries controlled by the SPÖ during that period, this party continues to win handily in the regularly held staff elections for representatives on the works councils. The same pattern holds true for all the ministries under the ÖVP's control, where, despite this party's disappearance from the federal government between 1970 and 1987 and the Socialists' concomitant hegemony, the People's Party has uninterruptedly maintained a clear edge over its rivals.

In addition to the just-mentioned close link to the political parties, the thorough politicization of the civil service is evident on a number of other accounts. By virtue of the prominent position accorded to the pre-parliamentary procedures in the legislative process, civil servants enjoy an unofficial but all the more important role in the formulation of laws. Moreover, civil servants form the most significant pool for the recruitment of politicians in Austria. The civil service, formally entrusted with the mere administration and execution of the laws, has a far greater influence than that on the average Austrian's daily routine. It should not be forgotten that it remains up to the individual civil servant to concretize the country's political decisions among ordinary citizens. As such, the civil service in Austria continues to assume the major role of a political "transmission belt" between the government of the country on the one hand and its citizenry on the other.[16]

According to the principles of a constitutionally anchored liberal democracy, the country's judiciary is supposed to be independent of the administrative-executive structures as well as of the legislature. In all matters of regular jurisdiction, up to the self-recruitment of judges, a constitutionally mandated autonomy strengthens the independence of this branch. This autonomy also means that in the concrete application of the laws by the courts, certain built-in attitudes and a particular political culture are continuously being reproduced, subject to little challenge from the outside.

Besides the framework of regular jurisdiction, there also exists the so-called Administrative Court, which is in charge of adjudicating the country's public law. Lastly, the Constitutional Court's task is to serve as Austria's interpreter and arbiter in all matters pertaining to the constitution and constitutional law. Whereas justices of the former are recruited from within the system, their counterparts on the Constitutional Court are political appointees from the outside. This difference has occasionally led to divergent decisions, as was the case in the "Habsburg conflict" of 1963 when the Administrative Court ruled in Otto Habsburg's favor pertaining to his reentry into Austria and the Constitutional Court opposed it.[17]

The justices of the Constitutional Court—its president, vice president and twelve members—are appointed by the federal president pursuant to nominations by the cabinet, the Federal Council, or the National Council. These nominations are *de facto* binding on the president. As a consequence of this arrangement, it is conceivable that the justices could all represent one political orientation, in the case where one party frequently exercised its options of appointment during a particularly lengthy period of its majoritarian advantage in parliament. An informal agreement between the "Big Two" has prevented this from occurring in reality. This agreement stipulates that a political equilibrium be maintained at all times among the justices of the Constitutional Court. Thus, for example, whenever a justice reaches the mandatory retirement age of seventy, the agreement sees to it that he/she will always be replaced by someone belonging to the same political party that nominated the retiring incumbent.

The political proportionality of the Constitutional Court is therefore rather evident.[18] Each member can clearly be identified as belonging to or at least sympathizing with either the spö or the övp. This of course in no way implies that the justices are party officials or in any way unqualified for their high office and calling. It just means that the Constitutional Court exhibits a special sensitivity in its jurisdiction to the political constellations in Austria.

Institutions, Parties, Interest Groups and the Media as Factors in the akh Scandal

The akh scandal proved the presence of a wide gap separating the constitution of the Second Austrian Republic from political reality. The scandal demonstrated beyond much doubt that the constitution—the result of a compromise reached by the two dominant political parties in 1920—continues to be viewed by its creators as their rightful property. Nevertheless, the scandal also showed unmistakably that this hitherto unshakable "party state" was suffering a certain erosion of legitimacy and control vis-à-vis Austrian society.

The constitution of the republic sanctions a parliamentarian democracy. Constitutionally sanctioned political conflict should occur between the governing parliamentary majority and the parliamentary minority constituting the opposition. Thus, according to this model, it should have been the task of the parliamentary opposition to discover, expose, and analyze the scandal. But it was not the parliamentary opposition—at that time comprising the People's Party and the Freedom Party—which engaged in any of these activities. These two parties only began to focus their attention on the scandal after the media had already publicized it widely in Austria and even abroad.

The reason for this secondary role of the opposition rests with the specific nature of the Austrian "party state." Some key activities, performed by the state in other political systems, have become the exclusive domain of the two dominant parties in Austrian public life. This was most certainly the case during the Grand Coalition between 1945 and 1966, precisely the period in which all fundamental decisions concerning the construction of the hospital were reached. But even after the collapse of the Grand Coalition, the parliamentary opposition in Austria continued to be included in the exercise of state power, albeit often in a more indirect fashion than the majority party. This, however, in no way diminished its political influence, which it maintained uninterruptedly on the following two levels:

(1) The principle of federalism in Austria guarantees that neither of the two

major parties is ever likely to remain completely excluded from governmental power, even if it happens to be in opposition on the national level. Since six out of the nine federal provinces have traditionally been governed by the ÖVP, with the remaining three being sure bets for the Socialist Party, neither of the "Big Two" has hitherto been completely turned out of state power, as would have been the case with regularity in a centralized, unitary system.

(2) Austria's much-vaunted social partnership has been characterized by close cooperation between employers and labor.[19] This very particular form of neocorporatism has also implied an indirect collaboration between the two dominant parties in a number of para-public and para-political realms. Labor, represented by the Austrian Trade Union Federation and the Chambers of Labor, has been dominated by the Socialist Party. The employers—represented by the already mentioned VÖI, as well as the Chambers of Commerce and Agriculture—have consistently remained very close to the People's Party. The fact that the institution of social partnership has continued to work regardless of the two parties' respective strengths in parliament and their roles in government serves as *prima facie* evidence that a constant and close cooperation between these two parties outside of parliament has characterized Austrian social and economic arrangements since 1945.

It is in this manner that all opposition by one of the two dominant parties remains curtailed and never develops into a full-fledged challenge to the governing party. In the case of the AKH scandal, this muted virtually nonexistent opposition was once again replicated by virtue of the close links between the People's Party and the country's leading industrial firms. Although the ÖVP as the opposition party at the time should have been keen on exposing and embarrassing the Socialist-dominated government to the fullest possible extent, it refrained from doing so because it, too, felt a part of the government by virtue of its very elaborate connections to the VÖI, which counted all the firms embroiled in the scandal as its members.

The SPÖ, as the governing party at the time, was also deeply involved in the scandal. Not only were the Socialists governing all by themselves on the national level between 1970 and 1983, but they had been the sole and uninterrupted rulers of "red" Vienna since the beginning of the Second Republic in 1945. Their structural culpability as a consequence of these two positions of power and domination was further enhanced by the personal involvement of some leading members of the SPÖ in the scandal, notably Hannes Androsch. While he was never convicted by a court of law, few experts had any doubt of this man's complicity in the affair at a time when he was minister of finance and vice chancellor as well.

The fact that both parties were entangled in the scandal impeded the development of any serious institutional conflict in the Austrian polity. The government and parliament remained "beyond reproach." By establishing a special investigative committee, parliament conveyed a measure of flexibility that was appreciated by a public completely caught up with the scandal by that time.

The parties, too, reacted rather flexibly to the scandal once it had become public. The whole AKH project had been subjected to rigorous criticism inside the SPÖ even before the scope of the scandal was fully known. In addition, the party wasted little time in demoting Hannes Androsch and others implicated in the affair. The ÖVP, as the leading opposition party, tried to take advantage of the critical atmosphere dominating public discourse in Austria at the time, without, however, endangering the all-important stability of the real governing mechanisms described in this chapter. The People's Party's flexible response to the scandal manifested itself more on the personal than on the structural level, as exemplified by its placing Alfred Worm, the discoverer of the scandal, on its list for the Vienna provincial elections of 1983. Worm was actually elected as an independent on the ÖVP's list and became a prominent member in the ranks of that party's Viennese representation, specializing as a troubleshooter on matters of institutional control. The right-wing FPÖ also directed its flexible response to the scandal by making important shifts in and new appointments of key personnel. Thus, for example, the judge adjudicating many of the legal proceedings that occurred in the wake of the AKH scandal, a woman named Helene Partik-Pable, was made one of this small party's most prominent parliamentary members as a consequence of her much-publicized role in exposing the scandal's criminal dimensions.

The nature of these responses on the part of all three parties conveyed the extent to which they had developed into "catch-all" parties. Rather than seeking structural reforms, which could have been the other option of response, the parties concentrated on personalities. These measures could, of course, never challenge the hegemonic presence of the "party state." Nor were they meant to. These personalized forms of response to a major scandal demonstrated the existence of some underlying systemic problems; they were reminiscent of actions typically taken by American parties, rather than responses of the traditional class or ideological parties hitherto characteristic of Austrian political history.

The SPÖ, founded as a Marxist labor party in 1889, represented the prototypical European class party until the end of the First Republic in 1934.[20] The Christian Social Party, the ÖVP's direct predecessor, embodied the prototypical party of political Catholicism.[21] The two parties that assumed the FPÖ's roles during the First Republic and formed this party's precursors during this turbulent time of Austrian history—the Grossdeutsche Volkspartei and the Landbund—concentrated their political and programmatic activities on attaining Austria's *Anschluss* with the German Reich.[22]

The existence of the Austrian parties as class and *Weltanschauung* (ideological) parties reached its peak in 1934. The authoritarian *Ständestaat,* a clerical and fascist political system, replaced the party-dominated and competitive liberal democracy of the First Republic with the dictatorship of the Christian Socialists in this new regime. Following the *Anschluss* of March 1938, the National Socialists assumed power, supported by the previous sympathizers of the Landbund and the Grossdeutsche Volkspartei. Together, they repressed the Social Democrats and the Christian Socials.

The Second Republic was proclaimed in 1945. SPÖ and ÖVP picked up the threads of their past. The experience with Austro-Fascist dictatorship, the tyranny of National Socialism, and the end of the Second World War all contributed to a gradual change in the Austrian parties. With Austrian society undergoing parallel changes (industrialization, urbanization, etc.) of equal magnitude, the parties saw themselves compelled to keep up with these economic and social changes in order to maintain their chances with the voters. This process led to a concentration of the party system in which the two dominant parties became increasingly similar to each other, shedding the major differences of their respective pasts. In a certain way it could be argued that Austria's parties became "Americanized" without ever reflecting this process openly and frankly.[23]

The parties' reactions to the AKH scandal highlights the main features of their post-1945 gradual conversion. Both their involvement in the scandal and their responses to it attest to recent changes. It would be safe to assume that neither a Marxist class party nor a party steeped in political Catholicism would have allowed for comparable political corruption to develop in a virtually unimpeded fashion. Marxism as well as political Catholicism are—theoretically—more immune toward market incentives. Conversely, neither of these parties would have reacted so promptly in terms of personnel decisions.

The changes affecting the parties had their parallels in the world of the media. The role played by some newsmagazines and a handful of journalists has come to resemble American-style "investigative journalism." Like the court system, the media too have proved to be an important independent institution. It is safe to say that the scandal never would have been discovered, let alone publicly discussed, had it not been for journalists such as Alfred Worm. The role that the media played in the AKH scandal has to be viewed in the context of the peculiarities of the Austrian press. Austrian newspapers are highly dependent upon their patrons, who typically hail from the world of the political parties or of key interest groups, such as business associations like the VÖI. The weekly *Profil* is also at least indirectly dependent on the VÖI.[24] The fact that the media could nevertheless develop an effective independent kind of "investigative journalism," constituting a decisive factor in the unveiling of the scandal, showed the media's maturation whereby it had gradually emancipated itself from the country's traditional power elites.

The Ramifications of the AKH Scandal

The AKH scandal did not cause the collapse of the Austrian political system. It led neither to any changes being made in the country's constitutional system nor to any alterations being made in the rules of the political game. The scandal also did not lead to the formation of new institutions. Rather, its consequences were most palpable in an indirect way. The AKH scandal was not the creator but a kind of catalyst of essential atmospheric changes in the Austrian political system and in the country's political culture.

First and foremost, the AKH scandal contributed to an accelerated opening of political consciousness and consequently to substantial changes in political behavior. The AKH scandal rocked the foundations of the party-state that had consolidated itself over the years as the comfortable bailiwick of Austria's two largest parties and of the country's traditional elites. While not the first and only cause of this process of erosion in Austria's political establishment, the AKH scandal most certainly represented a major accelerator of this process.

In addition to these changes in political consciousness, culture, and behavior, the scandal led to a deconcentration of the power wielded by the two main political parties. The Austrian party system was until 1975 the most highly concentrated multiparty system anywhere among liberal democracies. This was all the more remarkable because the country's elections were governed by one of the purest systems of proportional representation anywhere in Europe, a system favoring the emergence and persistence of small parties. Until the

TABLE 6.5
DEGREE OF CONCENTRATION OF THE PARTY SYSTEM

GENERAL ELECTIONS	PERCENTAGE OF VOTES FOR SPOE AND OEVP TOGETHER	PERCENTAGE OF VOTES FOR VDU OR FPOE	PERCENTAGE OF VOTES FOR FOURTH PARTIES
1949	82.7	11.7	5.6[1]
1953	83.4	11.0	5.6[1]
1956	88.9	6.5	4.6[1]
1959	89.0	7.7	3.3[1]
1962	89.4	7.1	3.5[1]
1966	91.0	5.4	3.6[2]
1970	93.0	5.5	1.5
1971	93.1	5.5	1.4
1975	93.4	5.4	1.2
1979	92.9	6.1	1.0
1983	90.9	5.0	4.1[3]
1986	84.4	9.7	5.9[4]

[1] Mainly KPOe (Communist Party of Austria—1949: 5.1; 1953: 5.3; 1956: 4.4; 1959: 3.3; 1962: 3.3).

[2] Mainly DFP (Democratic Progressive Party, a Socialist splinter group, which didn't get a seat in the National Council—3.3).

[3] Mainly the two not yet united Green-Alternative groups VGOe (more centrist) and ALOe (more leftist), together 3.5.

[4] Mainly the now united Greens (4.8).

middle of the 1970s, the Austrian party system's degree of concentration—as measured by the percentage of votes attained by the two big parties—had increased steadily. As of 1979, this process has been consistently reversed and the AKH scandal played an important accelerating role in this.[25]

In 1979 it was still the FPÖ, the smallest among the country's traditional parties, which benefited from the beginnings of this deconcentration process. By 1983, however, it was the parties of the Green-Alternative spectrum that had gained the most from this relatively recent development. Three years later, in the parliamentary elections of November 1986, it was the FPÖ as well as the Green-Alternatives who garnered substantial electoral increases at the direct expense of the Big Two.

Austria's traditional two-and-a-half party system, hailing from the nineteenth century, was forced open by the success of the Greens in 1986. Neither the Austrian Communist Party (Kommunistische Partei Österreichs—KPÖ) nor any other party could penetrate the political space occupied by the "camps" of the existing parties until 1986. The meteoric rise of the Greens to become the fourth parliamentary party in Austria is the result of a secularization process that has engulfed the traditional party system for quite some time. The most noticeable manifestations of this process have been the established parties' increasing difficulty in rallying voters to their cause by appealing to traditional loyalties and identities.

The social background of this secularization is the lessening significance of the cleavages that have informed the political reality of the parties in the past. "Class" as the paramount division for the Socialist Party, "religion" for the People's Party, and "German national consciousness" for the FPÖ have all increasingly lost their importance for the voters in a postindustrial society. It has been especially the younger, better educated, and urban voters who over the last few years have begun to desert the traditional parties, swelling the ranks of the Greens.[26]

Functioning as a catalyst, the AKH scandal accelerated these tendencies. It became evident that the parties' behavior did not conform to their own principles and that their daily activities had little in common with the traditional loyalties that formed their *raison d'être* in the first place. Concretely, it would not be wrong to argue that the SPÖ's political practice hardly exhibits the features commonly associated with those of a workers' party. Nor is today's ÖVP even remotely a Catholic party in any meaningful sense of that term. In fact both parties have proved to be quite alike. They have developed into comprehensive, Americanized catch-all parties.

This gradual change in Austria's political system and culture was marked not only by the formation of a new parliamentary party. Even before the emergence of the Greens as Austria's fourth party, new issues that had remained unarticulated by the traditional parties had become quite important. The new topic of ecology and the environment emerged rather forcefully alongside and rivaling such traditional issues as wages, prices, and jobs under the cluster of "class" issues; and education, family, marriage, and abortion in the cluster of "religious" issues.

The "new middle class," comprising younger, better educated, and urban voters, began to express its changed values by increasingly focusing on environmental questions, especially in the context of energy policy. Already in 1978, even before the AKH scandal became public, these postmaterialist tendencies led to the first plebiscite in Austrian history. In a political event unique to the entire industrial world, Austrians decided by a small margin not to permit the operation of a nuclear power plant that had already been completed.[27] This act remains all the more remarkable since the facilities in the village of Zwentendorf near Vienna would have been Austria's first and only nuclear power plant. The plebiscite has thus kept Austria free of nuclear energy to this day.

Another expression of this value change informing Austrian politics can be gauged by the fact that an increasing number of Austrians associate the traditional parties with corruption. The AKH scandal, together with some lesser political and economic "mishaps," has lent additional credence to the already prevalent view that "the politicians" and "the parties" have not been mainly concerned with the welfare of the republic but rather with their own welfare.

This new distancing on the part of the population vis-à-vis the political parties has led to an Austrian paradox. Austria continues to remain the country with the highest degree of party concentration in the sense that almost one-third of the electorate belongs to parties by formal membership. (This density not only exceeds any comparable figure in any other liberal democracy but is higher than in virtually every one-party state, including that of the Soviet Union.) This political clientelism, resulting both from the long tradition of the party-state and the parties' gate-keeper functions limiting and channeling political participation, has suffered little in the wake of this secularization process. The growing mobility of the voters has not (at least not yet) caused any perceptible erosion of this clientelism. On the one hand, Austrians are increasingly ready to criticize fundamentally their country's traditional politics and established parties, yet on the other hand, they still show great reluctance to abandon the political clientelism that has so fundamentally shaped their political reality for the better part of this century.

The AKH scandal helped to launch and accelerate a process of emancipation of the citizens from the state. Twice—in 1918 and 1945—the parties founded republics in Austria and devised their respective constitutions. After 1945, the parties—so to speak as "parents" of the republic—stabilized a society whose contradictory structures led to the demise of democracy in 1934 and to the loss of Austria's independence in 1938. This stabilization was in good part built on the foundations of a new Austrian patriotism, which, as a direct antithesis to the *Anschluss* and to the notion of Austria being a part of the "German nation," actively fostered the reality of an Austrian nation.[28] An essential ingredient in this stabilization process was Austria's voluntary declaration of permanent neutrality in the international arena, proclaimed in 1955.[29] Helped by the state treaty of 1955, to which all four victorious powers of World War II contributed as signatories, Austria entered the family of "normal" Western liberal democracies, comfortably exhibiting some small pecularities, such as its pledge for permanent neutrality, for example, and its "special relationship" with its past, symbolized by Kurt Waldheim's election in 1986.

This stabilization, quite akin to a growing-up process, means that the "parents" of the republic have gradually become superfluous in their dominant role as guardians. This was self-elimination by success. Yesterday's parents had become mediocre, which in turn meant that they were increasingly susceptible to corruption. The political parties had given Austria a fairly normal, relatively effective liberal democracy in which citizens began to feel comfortable and at home.

It is for this reason that Austria's political parties lost their previous role of "substitute nation" in which each party more or less managed its own political subsystem independently. The parties had attained society's integration, which led directly to the demise of their original specialness. They transferred loyalty onto the republic, the nation, and the political system as a whole.

The AKH scandal was an exemplary illustration of this process: A minister of finance and vice chairman of the SPÖ under suspicion of tax evasion; a president of the VÖI found guilty of corruption; and parties with their finances out of control. These parties, exhibiting such political cultures, simply could not muster the traditional loyalties exacted by their predecessors barely a few years before. As the scandal clearly manifested, the Austrian *Parteienstaat* had lost some of its most profound legitimation.

The AKH scandal as a catalyst helped establish a comprehensive *conscience collective*, as Markovits and Silverstein put it in their introduction. Political culture in Austria was characterized by the coexistence of different *consciences collectives*, according to party frontiers and the "camp mentality" the parties were able to create for decades. Now the dawn of a country-wide *conscience collective* beyond the party-state and crossing party lines is coming. The scandal played an important role in the beginnings of this new political culture.

In Hans Christian Andersen's tale of the emperor's new clothes, the main aspect is not the nakedness of the emperor. Rather, the significance of the story

188 · ANTON PELINKA

lies in the fact that someone—and not by chance a child, symbol of a new generation—recognizes this nakedness and proclaims it for the whole world to hear. The AKH scandal contributed substantially to direct the voters' attention to the already considerable nakedness of the traditional institutions of Austrian political life.

(Translated by Andrei S. Markovits)

NOTES

1. For the history of the whole scandal, see generally Alfred Worm, *Der Skandal. AKH: Story, Analyse, Dokumente, Europas größter Krankenhausbau* (Vienna: Orac, 1981).
2. About Hannes Androsch, see Melanie A. Sully, *Continuity and Change in Austrian Socialism: The Eternal Quest for the Third Way* (New York: Columbia University Press, 1982), pp. 220–22, 232–34.
3. Worm, *Der Skandal*, pp. 61 and 68.
4. For the Austrian Constitution, see generally Ludwig K. Adamovich, Bernd-Christian Funk, *Österreichisches Verfassungsrecht. Verfassungsrechtslehre unter Berücksichtigung von Staatslehre and Politikwissenschaft*, 2d ed. (Vienna: Springer, 1984).
5. Helmut Widder, *Parlamentarische Strukturen im politischen System. Zu Grundlagen and Grundfragen des österreichischen Regierungssystems* (Berlin [West]: Duncker und Humblot, 1979), pp. 178–92. Rainer Nick and Anton Pelinka, *Parlamentarismus in Österreich*, (Vienna: Jugend und Volk, 1984).
6. Peter Gerlich, *Parlamentarische Kontrolle im politischen System. Die Verwaltungsfunktionen des Nationalrates in Recht und Wirklichkeit* (Vienna: Springer, 1973). Siegbert Morscher, *Die parlamentarische Interpellation* (Berlin [West]: Duncker und Humblot, 1973).
7. Anton Pelinka and Manfried Welan, *Demokratie und Verfassung in Österreich* (Wien: Europaverlag, 1971), pp. 108–26.
8. Heinz Fischer, "Die parlamentarischen Fraktionen," in *Das politische System Österreichs*, ed. Heinz Fischer, 3rd ed. (Vienna: Europaverlag, 1982).
9. Herbert Matis and Dieter Stiefel, *Der österreichische Abgeordnete. Der österreichische Nationalrat 1919–1979* (Vienna: University for Economics).
10. See, for instance, the case study by Karl F. Atzmüller, *Die Kodifikation des kollektiven Arbeitsrechts* (Vienna: Braumüller, 1985).
11. Adamovich and Funk, *Österreichisches Verfassungsrecht*, p. 181f.
12. Klaus Berchthold, *Der Bundespräsident* (Vienna: Springer, 1969).
13. Manfried Welan, *Das österreichische Staatsoberhaupt* (Vienna: Verlag für Geschichte und Politik, 1986).
14. Manfried Welan and Heinrich Neisser, *Der Bundeskanzler im österreichischen Verfassungsgefüge* (Vienna: Hollinek, 1971). Friedrich Weissensteiner and Erika Weinzierl, eds., *Die österreichischen Bundeskanzler. Leben und Werk* (Vienna: Österreichischer Bundesverlag, 1983).
15. Manfried Welan, "Vom Proporz zum Konkurrenzmodell: Wandlungen der Opposition in Österreich," in *Parlamentarische Opposition. Ein internationaler Vergleich*, ed. Heinrich Oberreuter (Hamburg: Hoffmann und Campe, 1975).
16. Eva Kreisky, "Zur Genesis der politischen und sozialen Funktion der Bürokratie," and Heinrich Neisser, "Die Rolle der Bürokratie," both in Fischer, *Das politische System*, pp. 181–232, 233–70.
17. Margareta Mommsen-Reindl, *Die österreichische Proporzdemokratie und der Fall Habsburg* (Vienna: Böhlau, 1976).
18. Manfried Welan, "Der Verfassungsgerichtshof—eine Nebenregierung?" in Fischer, *Das politische System*, pp. 271–316.
19. Anton Pelinka, *Modellfall Österreich. Möglichkeiten und Grenzen der Sozialpartnerschaft*

(Vienna: Braumüller, 1981). Bernd Marin, *Die Paritätische Kommission. Aufgeklärter Technokorporatismus in Österreich* (Vienna: Internationale Publikationengesellschaft, 1982). Peter Gerlich, Edgar Grande, and Wolfgang C. Müller, eds., *Sozialpartnerschaft in der Krise. Leistungen und Grenzen des Neokorporatismus in Österreich* (Vienna: Böhlau, 1985).

20. Fritz Kaufmann, *Sozialdemokratie in Österreich. Idee und Geschichte einer Partei. Von 1889 bis zur Gegenwart* (Vienna: Amalthea, 1978). Anson Rabinbach, *The Crisis of Austrian Socialism: From Red Vienna to Civil War. 1927–1934* (Chicago: University of Chicago Press, 1983). Anson Rabinbach, ed., *The Austrian Socialist Experiment: Social Democracy and Austromarxism, 1918–1934* (Boulder, Colo.: Westview Press, 1985). Melanie Sully, *Continuity and Change*.

21. Reinhold Knoll, *Zur Tradition der christlichsozialen Partei. Ihre Früh- und Entwicklungsgeschichte bis zu den Reichsratswahlen 1907* (Wien: Böhlau, 1973). Ludwig Reichhold, *Geschichte der ÖVP* (Graz: Styria, 1975). John W. Boyer, *Political Radicalism in Late Imperial Vienna: Origins of the Christian Social Movement 1848–1897* (Chicago: University of Chicago Press, 1981).

22. Max E. Riedelsperger, *The Lingering Shadow of Nazism: The Austrian Independent Party Movement Since 1945* (New York: Columbia University Press, 1978). Viktor Reimann, *Die Dritte Kraft in Österreich* (Vienna: Molden, 1980). Bruce F. Pauley, *Hitler and the Forgotten Nazis: A History of Austrian National Socialism* (Chapel Hill, N.C.: University of North Carolina Press, 1981).

23. Peter Gerlich and Wolfgang C. Müller, eds., *Zwischen Koalition und Konkurrenz. Österreichs Parteien seit 1945* (Vienna: Braumüller, 1983). Fritz Plasser and Peter A. Ulram, *Unbehagen im Parteienstaat. Jugend und Politik in Österreich* (Vienna: Böhlau, 1982). Anton Kofler, *Parteiengesellschaft im Umbruch. Partizipationsprobleme von Großparteien* (Vienna: Böhlau, 1985).

24. Hans Heinz Fabris: "Das österreichische Mediensystem," in Fischer, *Das politische System*, pp. 501–35.

25. Anton Pelinka and Fritz Plasser, eds., *Das österreichische Parteiensystem* (Vienna: Böhlau, 1988).

26. See especially Plasser and Ulram, *Unbehagen*, and some articles in Pelinka and Plasser, *Parteiensystem*, especially Herbert Dachs, *Bürgerlisten und grün-alternative Parteien in Österreich*, pp. 181–208.

27. Anton Pelinka, "The Nuclear Power Referendum in Austria," *Electoral Studies*, 2, no. 3 (December 1983): 253–61.

28. Felix Kreissler, *Der Österreicher und seine Nation. Ein Lernprozeß mit Hindernissen* (Vienna: Böhlau, 1984).

29. Thomas O. Schlesinger, *Austrian Neutrality in Postwar Europe: The Domestic Roots of a Foreign Policy* (Vienna: Braumüller, 1972).

•
THE NON-EUROPEAN EXPERIENCE

While the two countries considered in this final section are vastly different in their historical, political, cultural, and social traditions, they are among a handful of functioning liberal democracies that exist outside of Europe and North America. The great difficulties in establishing liberal democratic rule are highlighted in the experiences of Japan and Israel. Despite the inherent problems of liberal democracy, which are in fact accentuated in these two cases, the resolution of these scandals ultimately reaffirms the commitment that these societies have made to the virtues of liberal democracy.

The Lockheed Scandal and
8 • the High Costs of
Politics in Japan

TERRY MACDOUGALL

Prime ministers and high officials have been on the take for years; Mr. Tanaka stands accused of doing it more aggressively than most, and if convicted might blow the whistle on just about everyone of importance in Japanese business and politics. . . . The politico-economic system of Japan is inherently corrupt. The combination of capitalists, power brokers and government leaders known as 'Japan, Inc.,' which produced an eye-popping rate of growth and catapulted a defeated island nation into the front rank of economic superpowers, cannot by its nature be anything but corrupt.

—William Safire

The cries of corruption are often misunderstood by foreigners. . . . Political corruption is not widespread in Japan, as compared with many countries and is probably much less than in local government in the United States. There is little vote buying in Japan. . . . The national bureaucracy has been entirely untainted by scandal, though politicians and local bureaucrats are sometimes suspected, not of stealing public funds, but of receiving bribes for political favors. In the case of politicians, such payments are probably taken not so much for personal gain as for campaign purposes.

The chief problem in Japan, as elsewhere, is the vagueness of the line between legal and illegal political contributions. The lavish entertainment of politicians and bureaucrats by businessmen well provided with expense accounts can have an unsavory odor, as can also the Japanese propensity for giving gifts, even though these are merely customary. More serious is the fact that almost all politicians receive and expend vastly greater funds for elections than they are allowed to by law.

—Edwin Reischauer

On 4 February 1976, during hearings of the Subcommittee on Multinational Corporations of the United States Senate Committee on Foreign Relations, it

193

was revealed that Lockheed Aircraft, an American corporation, made illegal payments in Japan, the Netherlands, Italy, Turkey, and elsewhere as part of a worldwide campaign to boost the sale of its planes in a desperate effort to avert bankruptcy.[1] The Lockheed revelations were a by-product of the Watergate scandal, which had inspired an explosion of righteous indignation in the United States over all forms of nonaccountable power, including corporate corruption. The Subcommittee on Multinational Corporations originated in 1972, when Frank Church, Democratic senator from Idaho, established it following disclosures of ITT's interventions in Chile. With the goal of investigating the extent of influence or involvement of large corporations in foreign policy formulation, the Church committee extended its reach from ITT to the oil giants, Gulf, Exxon, and Mobil, opening public hearings on May 1975. Operating concurrently with the Watergate investigations, the Church committee momentarily stole the limelight with revelations of huge, systematic bribes being paid by the oil companies to officials of foreign countries. Emboldened by its success, the subcommittee expanded its investigations further to include the aircraft industry, beginning with Northrop and then Lockheed. Watergate had shown how domestic corruption could weaken democratic government. The Church committee was determined to show how the corruption of American businesses abroad could subvert the western alliance and weaken the United States' international standing. The assumption of some American businessmen that foreign contracts could be won only through the generous use of bribes is a particularly dangerous one when dealing with liberal democracies, such as Japan or Italy, where, as noted in the introduction to this volume, the same distinction is made as in the United States between the public and private realms. Also, when people who are taken as representatives, whether public or private, of a country, particularly a hegemonic one like the United States, ignore the rule of law of a foreign country or of the international system, the credibility of the country's political system and its trustworthiness as an alliance partner are weakened.

The Subcommittee on Multinational Corporations struck it rich with the Lockheed investigation. No sooner was it opened than dramatic revelations of bribery by the officials of the company of national leaders of some of America's closest allies created a sensation. The Securities and Exchange Commission (SEC) and the Senate Banking Committee, led by William Proxmire, a long-time critic of Lockheed, also entered into the fray. The upshot of these investigations in the United States was the passage in 1977 of the Foreign Corrupt Practices Act, which was designed to establish a code of ethical behavior for American enterprises abroad and to inhibit their influence over American foreign policy.

Abroad, the scandal climaxed differently in the various countries involved, from a whitewash in Spain and a cover-up in Turkey to a thorough investigation and resignation by Prince Bernard in the Netherlands. In Italy and Japan, the scandals led to major trials and "Lockheed elections," in which the ruling parties suffered unprecedented losses. In Italy, "the Lockheed affair served both to reinforce the widespread notion that corruption is endemic in Italian public life and to disprove the equally widely held assumption that it has lost all power to shock."[2] (See the chapter in this volume by Judith Chubb and Maurizio Vannicelli for a detailed analysis of Italian politics in this regard.) The scandal also had a great impact in Japan. The saga of Lockheed continues in

Japan to this day, as former Prime Minister Kakuei Tanaka appeals his conviction for accepting bribes for the use of the authority of his office to influence the purchase of Lockheed planes by All Nippon Airways (ANA). The scandal and its aftermath reveal as much about the successes of postwar Japanese democracy as they do about the country's alleged "structural corruption." Successes and failures, however, have one common denominator in Japan: the high costs of politics. Ironically, the quest for political power in the Japanese liberal democracy has elevated the need for political funds to the point where the political system is highly vulnerable to corruption and scandal.

The Unfolding of the Scandal: From Exposure to Conviction

During the hearings of 4 February 1976 of the Subcommittee on Multinational Corporations, documents obtained by the SEC from Lockheed were revealed that indicated that over ten million dollars were paid by the company to Yoshio Kodama, a right-wing "fixer" with strong ties to the conservative political establishment in Japan, and to the Marubeni Corporation, Japan's third largest general trading company, which had served as Lockheed's agent since 1959.[3] Two days later, Lockheed Vice President A. Carl Kotchian testified before the same committee that some two million dollars were passed through Marubeni to a high Japanese government official and that Kenji Osano, one of Japan's largest hotel investors and a close associate of former Prime Minister Kakuei Tanaka, had also been used as an intermediary in the company's efforts to sell Lockheed's L–1001 TriStar airbuses to ANA, Japan's premier domestic airline. These revelations were dramatized by the display of a cryptic receipt found in the Lockheed files. It read:

August 9, 1973
I received One Hundred Peanuts.
(signed) Hiroshi Ito

The American investigation triggered an uproar in the Japanese National Diet (parliament) and the press, which had a field day with the "peanuts" receipt. In the House of Representatives Budget Committee, the chief forum for scrutiny of governmental policy, the four major opposition parties pursued the question of Lockheed's payments to Japanese politicians to influence ANA's purchase of the TriStar in place of McDonnell-Douglas's DC–10s, on which ANA had already taken an option. Appearing before the committee, Prime Minister Takeo Miki vowed to get at the truth: "I will make it a point of honor for Japan to investigate the Lockheed contribution and to clarify the issue for our people."

Among the leaders of the ruling Liberal Democratic Party (Japan's conservatives), Miki undoubtedly was the most likely to follow through on such a promise. Less than two years before, despite the relatively small size of his faction among LDP parliamentarians, Miki had been selected as party president and as prime minister on the strength of his image as "Mr. Clean." The LDP had needed a fresh and honest look after Prime Minister Tanaka was forced to resign following public revelations of irregularities in his personal finances and of his use of insider information to enrich himself and his business supporters. Subsequently, Prime Minister Miki had pushed through the National Diet, over the protests of many within his own party, revisions of the Public Office Election Law and the Political Funds Control Law to check the escalating costs of elections, widely viewed in Japan as the principal cause of political corruption and scandal.

Concern over the Lockheed incident was further heightened when the highly respected Deputy Director General of the Self-Defense Agency, Takuya Kubo, revealed that in October 1972 the policy of domestic production of the PXL as the next generation antisubmarine warfare plane had been reversed by then–Prime Minister Tanaka, along with his Deputy Chief Cabinet Secretary Masaharu Gotoda and the chief of the Budget Bureau of the Finance Ministry. Instead, the Lockheed P3C Orion was designated for this purpose.

The Budget Committee quickly opened its own hearings on these matters, receiving sworn testimony from witnesses for the first time in eleven years, and subjecting them to possible charges of perjury should they later be found to have given false testimony. Osano testified on 16 February 1976; but Kodama refused to appear, pleading illness. Tokuji Wakasa, president of ANA, and Hiro Hiyama, president of Marubeni, also testified, along with three other Marubeni officials, including Hiroshi Ito, whose name appeared on the "peanuts" receipt. Blanket denials of wrongdoing and lack of candor by these witnesses made it clear that American materials related to the Lockheed incident would be necessary to pursue the investigation. A joint session of the lower and upper houses of the National Diet unanimously approved a resolution addressed to the U.S. government and to the U.S. Senate requesting access to their materials. The request was further backed by a private letter from Prime Minister Miki to President Gerald Ford seeking his cooperation. It was widely felt that the United States, as the architect of postwar Japanese liberal democratic institutions as well as the source of the illegal funds, had an obligation to respond positively.

The same day, acting independently, Japan's law enforcement agencies moved decisively into action. The Tokyo District Public Prosecutor's Office, the Metropolitan Police Headquarters, and the Tokyo office of the National Tax Bureau launched an unprecedented joint investigation, searching twenty-seven locations including the headquarters of Marubeni and Yoshio Kodama's home. While the National Diet began a second stage of receiving sworn testimony and awaited an American response, the Public Prosecutor's Office carried out a criminal investigation of Kodama, which resulted in his indictment on 13 March 1976 for tax evasion relating to commissions received from Lockheed totalling approximately Y1,895,000,000 ($6,274,000). About the same time as this indictment, President Ford agreed to supply relevant materials from the Lockheed investigation on the condition that they be used only in the official investigation and courts and that they not be released wholesale to the public.

Prime Minister Miki agreed to this condition, reinforcing opposition party suspicions of a cover-up that had already led to an opposition boycott of Diet deliberations. Miki's more potent adversaries (and those most anxious to close the books on the incident), however, were within his own party. By early May, Etsusaburo Shiina, the deputy LDP president who had been chief architect of Miki's selection as premier, conferred with the leaders of the party's three largest factions, former Prime Minister Tanaka, Finance Minister Masayoshi Ohira, and Deputy Prime Minister Takeo Fukuda. They all agreed that Miki's administration must end as soon as possible. Thus began a seven-month effort to unload Miki and to put a lid on the escalating revelations. Miki, however, took advantage of the momentum of the exposures, constant mass media attention, and an aroused public outrage to maintain himself in power and to pursue the investigation. By the time Miki resigned, after the LDP had suffered significant losses in the December 1976 elections to the House of Representatives, the investigations (including from mid-May those of the newly established Special Investigative Committees on the Lockheed Problems in both houses of the National Diet) and related criminal proceedings had reached the point of no return.

Well before this, however, the LDP faced a new and totally unexpected crisis within the party. On 13 June 1976, seven of its parliamentarians, including Yohei Kono, Takeo Nishioka, and Seiichi Tagawa, all well-known to the public, left the LDP in protest over its corruption and lack of candor. On 25 June 1976 they formed the New Liberal Club, thereby becoming the first genuine threat to LDP hegemony among Japanese conservatives since the party's formation in 1955.

Meanwhile, Japan's law enforcement agencies accelerated their investigations. The Public Prosecutor's Office used materials received from the American authorities in April as well as from its domestic searches to pinpoint violations of the law. The Tokyo District Court, through the Japanese Embassy in Washington, submitted a request to the U.S. Justice Department to permit Lockheed Vice President Kotchian and two others to testify in Japan under a grant of immunity from prosecution. This was followed on 22 June 1976 with the first arrests by the Public Prosecutor's Office and the Tokyo Metropolitan Police of Toshiharu Okubo of Marubeni, Yuji Sawa of ANA, and two others and, within the next two weeks, of Hiroshi Ito and the former president of Marubeni, Hiro Hiyama, and President Tokuji Wakasa of ANA. All were indicated on suspicion of violating the Foreign Exchange Control Law in connection with receiving under-the-table money for which receipts denoted in "units," "pieces," and "peanuts" were presented.

The climax of arrests, however, came on 27 July 1976, when in a carefully planned move of which only the highest levels of the Public Prosecutor's Office, the Chief of the Prosecution Bureau of the Justice Ministry and one of his subordinates, and Justice Minister Osamu Inaba were aware, two members of the Special Investigation Department of the Tokyo Public Prosecutor's Office appeared at 6:30 A.M. at the front door of former Prime Minister Tanaka's residence to take him into custody. In a maneuver befitting his long political experience as well as his credentials as a Doctor of Law and one of the ruling party's leading experts on constitutional matters, Justice Minister Inaba had delayed informing Prime Minister Miki of the impending arrest until moments before Tanaka appeared before the Public Prosecutor, thereby preempting some of the inevitable political criticism within the LDP that Miki had sacrificed Tanaka. Hence Prime Minister Miki scarcely had a chance (even if he had chosen to do so) to order Inaba to employ the executive authority of the justice minister to protect Tanaka, a procedure by means of which several top conservative officials in earlier scandals had avoided arrest. Tanaka spent the next few weeks in jail. On 16 August 1976 he was indicted for violation of the Foreign Exchange Control Law and for receiving bribes of Y500 million ($2.1 million). The next day, bail was set at Y200 million and he was released.

In all, the Japanese government indicted sixteen people—politicians, Marubeni and ANA officials. Osano and Kodama—on charges including bribery, violation of the Foreign Exchange and Foreign Trade Control Law and the Tax Law, and perjury. Illegal funds had been passed along four "routes," Marubeni, Kodama, Osano, and ANA, the first three of which were apparently intended to elicit political support for an ANA decision favorable to Lockheed. Additional politicians were implicated by testimony supplied by Kotchian, but it was impossible to indict these "gray officials" under Japanese law, which in a bribery trial requires proof that the defendant actually received the money, that he knew it was a bribe, and that he was in a position of authority to influence official business of the government.[4] Except for Kodama, whose trial was suspended because of illness (and who died on 17 January 1984), all those indicted were found guilty. Former Prime Minister Tanaka was convicted on 12 October 1983 and sentenced to four years in prison and a fine of Y500 million, equal to the amount of the bribe he had received. Appeals by Tanaka and several of the others have thus far all been dismissed. In what undoubtedly will be a vain gesture, Tanaka is now making his final appeal, to the Supreme Court.

The Rules of the Game in Japanese Politics

The Lockheed scandal dominated the headlines of the Japanese press in 1976 and it still makes front-page news whenever new court proceedings, verdicts, and appeals take place. The scope of the scandal, involving a former premier, the country's third largest general trading company, and its major domestic airline, one of Japan's most notorious right-wing fixers, and an array of other politicians and businessmen is grounds enough for its prominence in the history and folklore of political corruption and scandal in Japan. But what does the scandal tell us about Japanese politics more generally? Is the Lockheed scandal at all typical of Japanese-style political corruption or instructive as to Japanese political processes and culture, or is it exceptional in character as well as scope? Just how prevalent is political corruption in Japan? Is all such corruption scandlous?

William Safire, as quoted at the beginning of this chapter, refers to the collusive behavior of Japanese politicians, businessmen, and bureaucrats as "inherently corrupt." Japanese critics of their own political system in a somewhat similar way refer to this close interaction of elites as "structural corruption."[5] As I shall elaborate below, there are indeed a number of structural features of the Japanese political system, especially its strong public bureaucracy, a single dominant political party, and constant pressure by private interests for the intermediation of politicians with government agencies on their behalf, which tend to hide much of the policymaking process from public view and to obscure the distinction made in all liberal democracies between the public and private realms. Unquestionably, this lack of transparency and the interpenetration of private and public interests in the policymaking process provide numerous occasions for possible corruption and scandal. These structural features of the Japanese system, however, are not, *ipso facto*, proof of the existence of corruption and scandal. Virtually all liberal democracies suffer defects in the "transparency" of their policy processes, which is why the issue of the public's "right to know" has become so prominent in many of them, including Japan. Similarly, the distinction between the public and private realms is not always clear; and there are almost always competing claimants for defining what constitutes the public interest.

The key to understanding Japanese politics and the issues of corruption and scandal in Japan rests precisely in this interaction between a strong, relatively centralized state and politicians who in the conduct of democratic politics have become critical intermediaries (brokers) for important private interests in society. The state in modern Japan has always been strong, but politicians have not always been perceived to be legitimate or effective intermediaries between state and society. One consequence of their increasingly effective brokerage has been the wrestling away from the state bureaucracy of its predominance in defining the public interest. Although no one would argue that the Japanese state is weak in shaping perceptions of the public interest, there is significant disagreement as to whether its "autonomy" is circumscribed by a kind of limited "corporatism," representing major interests outside of labor, or by a more fragmented "pluralistic" system of competing interests. In either case, one of the central characteristics of Japanese politics is the high degree of tolerance it has for the ambiguities between the private and public realms and the impressive extent to which it has managed this interaction with a minimum of scandal.

The question remains, of course, whether political corruption is far more prevalent than the occasional scandals that surface and elicit public outrage. In other words, is scandal but the tip of the iceberg and "structural corruption" its submerged base, which, if known in greater detail, would also be scandalous? That is not a question that can be answered adequately here, because the necessary evidence is not apparent. What can be addressed, however, is the question of how the Japanese political system manages the ambiguities in the interpenetration of the public and private realms and at what point collusive elite interaction, removed from public scrutiny, is perceived as a threat to legitimate government.

Political corruption and scandal, of course, is by definition bad. Yet there is no agreed-upon definition of what constitutes corruption. General definitions such that "corruption occurs whenever a person, in exchange for some private advantage, acts other than as his duty requires,"[6] do not take us very far, because by such tests almost all politicians in liberal democracies are corrupt and could easily be involved in political scandal. The problem is further complicated in a society like Japan's where gift-giving is customary and lavish expense accounts are a part of everyday business.

Lines are drawn in every country, however, between what is legitimate behavior and what is considered corrupt. There is a kind of "common sense," the normative foundations of political society, which, when breached, makes certain activities appear to threaten legitimate government. It is at that point that certain modes of behavior, perhaps viewed as "business as usual" by some and as "corrupt" by others, become scandalous to virtually all concerned. The periodic outbreak of political scandals in liberal democracies involving the encroachment of private interests upon the public domain indicates that such political systems are premised upon a widely shared understanding, norm, or "common sense" notion concerning the separation of these two realms. The scandal, as elaborated in the Introduction of this volume, is in effect the playing out on the public stage of political society's reaffirmation of its normative foundations by its investigation, trial, and condemnation of blatant violations of the separation of the public and private domains.

In the Japanese case, "influence buying" by private interests and "influence peddling" by politicians with bureaucrats on behalf of private interests is at the heart of so-called "structural corruption," but there appears to be a certain "common sense" that distinguishes much of this behavior from that which actually threatens legitimate government. In effect, I shall argue that as distasteful and (sometimes) as dysfunctional as such behavior might be, it has achieved a certain legitimacy within the Japanese system that distinguishes it from scandal. The key distinguishing factor seems to be one of content rather than form, "by whom was it done, for whom, and with what consequences for Japanese society?"

Our starting point for clarifying these matters first must be to outline the predominant patterns of behavior in the Japanese political system and their constitutional and consensual underpinnings. In doing this, I shall emphasize four aspects of the postwar Japanese political economy that have made "influence peddling" so prominent a part of the nation's politics. They are (1) the strong bureaucratic state with highly centralized finances and numerous levers of influence and control over the economy,[7] (2) competitive democratic politics in which candidate-centered and constituency-oriented political machines substitute for poorly articulated party structures, (3) rule by a predominant party creating stable patterns of relations among elite political actors, and (4) a constantly expanding economy providing growing resources for state and society.

THE STRONG STATE

The Meiji Restoration in 1868 marked the turning point between a semifragmented country governed by samurai and the modern, unified Japanese state. The first principle of modern Japanese political thought, so clearly articulated by the Meiji leadership, was that Japan must be a single strong and unified state. Fragmentation, such as existed in the mid–nineteenth century, would lead only to further encroachments on Japanese sovereignty by the technologically superior and militarily aggressive western nations.

Creating that strong state meant the establishment of a centralized administrative apparatus capable of reaching, controlling and mobilizing the people as a whole, and the development of the people's allegiance to the state. To do this the Meiji leaders revived some traditional institutions (e.g., the centralized and professional bureaucracy), borrowed some structures from the West (from Prussian and French administrative structures and constitutional forms), incorporated consensual modes of political activity that appeared to strengthen western states (such as representative institutions), and recreated their own tradition (the emperor system) in a manner that would unify society and give coherence to the Japanese state. This effort and its experimentations took two decades, culminating in the Meiji Constitution of 1889, which remained in effect and without revision until after World War II.

Despite its western form, the modern Japanese state bore many similarities to the classical Confucian state. An emperor, served by advisers presumed to be both good and wise, presided over a centralized bureaucracy recruited on the basis of talent sifted through a competitive examination system. Moreover, it represented not just temporal authority but also moral virtue. Those moral principles of harmony, hierarchy, obedience, and filial piety were embodied most concretely in the Imperial Rescript on Education, promulgated in 1890 and thereafter until 1945 established as the foundation of the Japanese educational system. In effect, the Meiji leaders had embraced the view that there is no fundamental distinction between the moral order, or natural law, and the actual social order. They interpreted this to mean that the state, developed in accordance with the character of humanity, was not subject to human control but rather controlled its subjects.[8]

From the start, the modern state in Japan was not only strong; it was also active. The foreign threat and Japan's technological backwardness were understood clearly by the Meiji leaders, most of whom had come from samurai backgrounds. Hence they set out to create a "rich country and strong army" (*fukoku kyohei*). Again, a great deal of experimentation occurred. Conscription was instituted, the military command restructured, and enormous resources plowed into military modernization. The success of military modernization could be seen in Japan's victories over China (in 1895) and Russia (in 1905) and its emergence as a major imperialist country. An industrial economy could not be so readily created, but after an initial period of direct government ownership of new factories, the government settled on a pattern of supportive activities for private entrepreneurs that seemed to work tolerably well until the economic crises of the 1920s. That the government would be actively involved in some way in the economy was a foregone conclusion in a country undergoing a process of defensive modernization on the basis of a limited resource base.

Leaders of Japan in the Meiji period from 1868 to 1912 and thereafter as well realized that the forces they had set loose through their reforms in education, industry, and politics could lead to social turmoil. They were particularly concerned that this not deteriorate into the type of class conflict they saw in Europe. Hence the strong, developmental state of prewar Japan also became one preoccupied with social control, expressed in a wide array of restrictive legislation.

Prewar Japan also had a long history of party politics and elections dating from the 1870s. As will be noted in more detail, the political parties came into their own after World War I and organized the government (cabinet) from then until 1932. But in a constitutional system based on imperial, not popular, sovereignty, the parties never established a legitimate claim to dominant control of the cabinet and to the running of the Japanese state. Various elite groups functioned at the pinnacles of state power. Civil bureaucrats, military officers, and aristocratic advisers to the emperor all competed with party politicians in defining the "imperial will" by which the Japanese state would function. Each had a constitutional basis for its voice in governmental decision making; but which voice would be most persuasive at any given point of time was determined more by the problems facing the nation than by established procedures for coordinating the plural power centers. The paramount political issue of prewar Japan always remained one of how to coordinate the country's system of plural elites.

Domestic and international economic crises from the late 1920s into the 1930s and foreign policy and security crises in the 1930s and 1940s served to strengthen state control precisely at the time when the voice of party politicians was weakened relative to those of the military and of reform-minded bureaucrats. New institutions of bureaucratic planning and control developed as Japan pulled itself out of recession into a period of sustained growth in heavy and chemical industries in the 1930s and faced foreign policy and security crises from the late 1930s until the end of World War II. These developments were to facilitate the transfer of the prewar legacy of a strong, activist state into the postwar years.

The Allied occupation (from 1945 to 1952) reconstructed and in some measure weakened the Japanese state. It disbanded the military and, according to Article 9 of the 1947 Constitution, imposed severe limitations on rearmament. The constitution prescribed a separation of local administrations from national bureaucratic control and established the direct popular election of prefectural governors and city, town, and village mayors as well as local assembly members, thereby providing additional incentives for political responsiveness to local constituencies. Changes in the laws governing the educational and police systems also provided for a more decentralized administration of those functions, although these changes were largely reversed by the mid-1950s. Similarly, legislative bodies at all levels of government were significantly strengthened vis-à-vis the executive. And the constitution designated the reformed National Diet, now with both houses elected by universal suffrage, as the highest decision-making organ of government. The cabinet, led by a prime minister selected by and from the Diet and comprised primarily of parliamentarians, was made responsible to the Diet. Although the institution of the emperor was retained, he was reduced to a symbol of the state and the unity of the people, while the various aristocratic organs of government that had advised him in the prewar years were abolished.

Whereas the Meiji constitutional system had been based on the concept of imperial sovereignty, the postwar Japanese state found its theoretical underpinnings in the concept of popular sovereignty. Popular sovereignty was implemented by extending the scope of the people's control of their representatives by means of direct elections and by the constitution's absolute guarantee of their basic rights. Members of both houses of the National Diet and local chief executives (governors and mayors) as well as local assembly members were now directly elected. An independent court system, endowed with the power of judicial review, was to serve as a watchdog of civil liberties.

This remaking of the Japanese political system established the basis for a far more open and competitive politics than had existed heretofore in Japan, but it did not erase the legacy of the strong and activist Japanese state. One of the principal reasons for this was that the occupation itself, being indirect in character rather than operating as a military government, had to function through the institutions of the Japanese state. Reform and reconstruction implemented in this way reinforced the activist thrust of the national ministries and agencies. It also gave national bureaucrats innumerable opportunities to shape many details of the operation of the reformed institutions. Hence, for example, at the insistence of high-level bureaucrats, the national ministries retained significant authority to delegate work to local governmental bodies and to guide them in their performance.[9] Similarly, no genuine decentralization of public financing took place, leaving national authorities in charge of allocating huge funds to local governments and to private enterprises.

Furthermore, with the elimination of military and aristocratic institutions and the purging from public life of many political and business leaders, only the bureaucracy, among those elite groups that had governed prewar Japan, survived the occupation reforms relatively unscathed. Indeed, the exigencies of recovery dictated that Japan would have a highly regulated economy, thereby putting a variety of policy tools in the hands of national economic bureaucrats: licensing business operations and construction, control over the use of foreign exchange, granting of permission to local authorities to issue bonds and to private enterprises to engage in various activities, allocation of credit through government financial institutions, and significant influence over private lenders, among others.

The centrality of the bureaucracy in policymaking pretty much assured that to get things done in Japan one had to work with the ministries and agencies of the national government. Neither the political parties nor National Diet committees had significant independent policymaking machinery during the first two postwar decades; and their ability to generate policy initiatives has only gradually increased since then, mainly in the case of the ruling LDP. As will be elaborated, relatively little policy originates in public view within the Diet. Instead, it originates in the more secretive confines of the bureaucracy and in its interaction with politicians and clientele groups in society. Hence, access to the bureaucracy, and to the many resources it controls directly or indirectly is a *sine qua non* for getting things done in Japanese politics. One critical measure of political leadership in Japan is the ability of a politician to gain the cooperation of the bureaucracy.[10]

DEMOCRATIC POLITICS

Political parties and local elections in Japan date from the 1870s. The first election to the House of Representatives of the Imperial Diet was held in 1890, under the Meiji Constitution. From the start, political parties won a majority of the seats and attempted to use their numbers (and their ability to block appropriations) to win policy and procedural concessions from the Meiji oligarchs. The latter, men like Hirobumi Ito, Aritomo Yamagata, and Masayoshi Masukata controlled the government through their dominance of the cabinet, through their direct access to the emperor, and through their networks of protégés and associates in the military, civil bureaucracy, and aristocratic institutions. By the early twentieth century, compromise and mutual cooptation between the oligarchs and the party politicians had opened a place for the latter in "transcendental" cabinets—that is, cabinets responsible only to the emperor and not to the Imperial Diet. Finally, in the 1920s oligarchic rule was displaced by party government. Between 1924 and 1932 the prime minister was always the leader of the majority party in the House of Representatives. By then the parties had developed their own networks of connections to local influentials who mobilized the electoral constituencies, to business interests that funded their operations, and to the bureaucracy with whom they lobbied for "pork-barrel" benefits.

This period of party ascendancy, often referred to as "Taisho democracy," after the reign name of the emperor who had come to the throne in 1912, was one of considerable liberalization for the Japanese state. Universal manhood suffrage, for example, was enacted in 1925. Although it was accompanied by the restrictive Peace Preservation Law to control the activities of various social and socialist movements, new parties of the political Left did get their start at this time. Reforms of the administrative structure loosened some hierarchical controls over local governmental bodies. And a variety of social legislation was either passed or seriously debated in the Imperial Diet. Taisho democracy, however, stumbled on the shoals of intractable agrarian problems at home and economic, political, and security problems abroad. The parties seemed incapable of resolving these crises and were also severely criticized for their close ties to big business interests while the plight of the countryside and of small businesses went unheeded. After 1932, when the last party premier was assassinated, the parties progressively lost influence to other elite elements. Moreover, they never challenged the constitutional system that denied them a claim, as elected representatives of the people, to a special legitimacy for organizing the government.

Postwar reforms changed the rules of the game. The National Diet became the highest decision-making organ of government. Even if legislation did not originate there, it had to be passed and thereby legitimated by the Diet. And it was the Diet that selected the prime minister, whose cabinet could be held accountable through a vote of no confidence (three of which have passed in the postwar years), which would necessitate resignation of the prime minister and cabinet or new elections. Control of the Diet has meant that political parties have become the ultimate legitimators of governmental action. Party politicians have been thrust into the center of politics and policymaking. State bureaucrats, as powerful as they may be, cannot rule without them. Indeed, one of the important dynamics of postwar Japanese politics has been the gradual shift of policy leadership toward the politicians. Disciplined party voting in the style of European parliaments rather than the American Congress, however, means that Japanese politicians must pursue their policy agendas first within their own parties and in consultations with bureaucrats rather than in the Diet.

Free and competitive elections also meant that politicians became vulnerable to the demands of their constituents and financial backers. The same is true, of course, in any liberal democracy, but the degree of constituency orientation among Japanese politicians is unusually high. Perhaps only American congressmen come close. Vulnerability to constituency demands in the Japanese case, particularly among politicians from the largest parties, is exacerbated because of the absence of significant social cleavages in the Japanese polity, by the character of the electoral system, the poor articulation of political parties at the local level, and the high cost of electioneering. These factors give Japanese politics a strongly personalistic, localistic, and pragmatic cast.

The Japanese people are not divided by ethnic, linguistic, religious, or regional differences that frequently lead voters in most western democracies to favor one party or one candidate over another. Persons employed in certain types of occupations do tend to prefer one party rather than another, but this tendency is weakening and class identity plays little role in Japanese politics. (Approximately 90 percent of the adult population see themselves as middle class.) Although differences among the parties on ideology, foreign policy, and constitutional issues persist, these are far less pronounced than in the past and appear less salient than ever. It is no wonder that among the liberal democracies, party identification is weakest in Japan, forcing the individual politician to do more on his own. Japanese politics at the mass level where politicians mobilize votes and see to the needs of their constituents more closely resembles American politics in its focus on the individual politician than those of Europe, where party structures are better developed at the grass-roots level. But Japanese politics throws an even larger burden upon the individual politician than politics does in the United States. The incredibly high cost of political campaigning and the blatant illegality of many campaign practices discourages voters from working actively in elections, thereby impelling Japanese political candidates to develop their personal support associations, known as *Koenkai*, which are manned by political pros, while providing services to mass constituencies much in the manner of traditional American urban machine politics.

This tendency is reinforced by the character of the electoral system. In elections for Japan's powerful House of Representatives, voters cast their ballots for a single candidate in a multi-member district. Any party that seeks to win more than a single seat will find its candidates competing against each other as well as against those of other parties. Hence, the individual politician is thrown back upon his own resources. This is all the more the case because the two parties most likely to run multiple candidates, the Liberal Democrats and the Japan Socialists, have few local party organizations.

Liberal Democratic candidates have come to deal with this situation by building *koenkai*, individual candidate support associations.[11] *Koenkai* are constituency-wide organizations designed to mobilize the vote at election time. Local politicians and leaders of local social organizations (merchant, neighborhood, welfare, and crime prevention associations, for example) normally serve as middle- and lower-level lieutenants in the *koenkai*. Anyone may become a member and participate in a wide range of activities from political study groups to outings. These activities justify the classification of *koenkai* as social organizations rather than political associations, which by law are not supposed to operate outside designated campaign periods. The *koenkai* involve enormous financial costs and also become a significant channel of interest articulation by constituents to individual politicians. Conservative candidates have found *koenkai* to be an effective mechanism for mobilizing the vote and for keeping themselves attuned to the mood of the people at the grass-roots level.

Socialist candidates too must either spend large sums of money, which they generally do not have, building *koenkai*, or they must become dependent upon labor unions for managing and financing their campaigns. In either case, they are pulled in the direction of pragmatic interest articulation much in the way of their conservative rivals; but they must make even more compromises of principle, because they, as the perpetual "outs," do not have as good an access to the bureaucracy or influence over legislation as their conservative counterparts.

Managing a *koenkai* and competing against members of one's own party as well as the opposition contributes to the very high cost of politics in Japan. A host of other factors also adds to this cost. For now suffice it to say that raising those funds, which for Japanese Liberal Democrats exceed those of American congressional or even senatorial candidates, leaves politicians as vulnerable to the demands of special interests as politicians in any other country who have to nurture contacts with large private donors.

It is this combination of a high degree of vulnerability to the demands of constituents and other private interests on the one hand, and the centrality of the bureaucracy in policymaking and implementation on the other, that accounts for the prevalence of the intermediary (brokerage) role of Japanese politicians.[12] As brokers, they have to be concerned with delivering to their local and interest group constituents favorable government action in legislation, regulatory behavior, and the allocation of credit, public works, subsidies, and other scarce or limited resources. Opening channels of access, or reinforcing those that exist, between constituents and bureaucrats is one important part of their job. Inducing bureaucrats to go along with their own priorities, determined most often by the need for reelection, is another.

ONE-PARTY DOMINANCE

The ruling Liberal Democratic Party was formed in 1955 out of the merger of existing conservative parties, the major ones of which traced their roots to the prewar years. This first-ever unification of Japanese conservatives occurred in part to counter a resurgent Socialist Party. In the first postwar decade, Japan had a relatively fluid multiparty system. The Socialists were a part of two coalition governments in 1947–48 and even when they were out of power they were frequently capable of gaining concessions by maneuvering among the divided conservatives. Shutting the Socialists out of this position of influence and out of cabinet posts was an important objective of the conservative union. Big businesses also pressed for conservative unity as a way of minimizing and rationalizing the demands of politicians for political funds and as a means of avoiding embarrassing exposures of political corruption, points to which I shall return.

The Liberal Democrats have dominated Japanese politics ever since. The Socialist resurgence petered out by the end of the 1950s; and the 1960s saw a fragmentation of the opposition. A small, politically moderate group broke off to form the Democratic Socialist Party in 1960. The Communists also gained significant ground at the expense of the Japan Socialists in the 1960s and early 1970s. Meanwhile, a new party, *Komeito* (Clean Government Party), was formed in 1964 on the basis of an urban socio-religious movement known as *Sokagakkai* (Value Creation Society), which appealed to those who had been relatively unrepresented and left out of Japan's headlong rush into affluence. Along with the Democratic Socialists, Komeito came to occupy the middle ground of Japanese politics. This fragmentation of the opposition contributed substantially to the LDP's ability to hold on to the reins of power.

Although conservatives united in the LDP to exclude the Socialists, that unification did not dampen their internal struggles for leadership of the party and government. These struggles took the form of a highly articulated factionalism. Japanese party politics has been rent with factionalism from the prewar years. The primary mode of alternation in power in the prewar heyday of the parties (from 1924 to 1932), for example, was by the defection of a Diet faction of the ruling party to the opposition, resulting in the formation of a cabinet by the newly enlarged party, which would then dissolve the House of Representatives and conduct (and win) new elections. Those factions were characterized by diffuse personal relations and obligations between leaders and followers. Early postwar conservative parties and factions had a similar character; but gradually, after the 1955 unification, the factions shed some of the personalistic aspects of the leader-follower bonds and became more functional career advancement mechanisms. One major continuity, however, was the role of the faction and particularly its leader in raising political funds for its members.

LDP factions differ from "factions" or "political tendencies" in British political parties by their focus on career development rather than policymaking.

Among contemporary European parties, the Italian Christian Democrats exhibit a factionalism somewhat like that of the LDP; but even that is not as highly structured as it is in the Japanese case. LDP factionalism is essentially a phenomenon of the party's Diet membership. Factional leaders maneuver to get would-be followers the party's formal endorsement at election time. Once elected, the new LDP parliamentarians will almost always remain a member of the same faction, at least until there is some change in factional heads that might precipitate a split in the faction. Regular factional meetings become an important means by which new LDP parliamentarians learn the ropes of national politics and they serve as an effective channel of communication between the party's leadership and its numerous backbenchers. The faction member can expect to receive considerable financial help from the faction and assistance in making the proper connections so that he too can generate political contributions. With every reelection, the faction member achieves greater seniority in the faction and can expect to be rewarded with parliamentary, party, and, eventually, cabinet posts. It is the function of the faction head and his chief lieutenants, longtime LDP parliamentarians who may aspire to factional leadership or major posts themselves, to bargain with the leadership of other factions for a significant share of the available posts.

The whole LDP factional system comes to a head in the selection of the party president, who, because of the LDP's majority, will be chosen in a Diet vote as prime minister. The LDP party president has generally been selected either by a vote of the party's Diet membership or by consultation among factional heads, possibly with the participation of other long-time LDP leaders. The process involves a kind of "coalition formation" within the party. The "winning coalition" gets not just the presidency but also a disproportionate share of other available posts. The remaining factions are not shut out of the distribution of posts, since that could precipitate their defection from the party or at least constant and bitter criticism of the party's leadership. As will become apparent in the discussion of Tanaka, much of the dynamics of Japanese politics revolve around factional struggles.

Another critical aspect of the LDP, as the sole governing party, is its strong working relations with the bureaucracy and with a wide range of interest groups. LDP leaders, largely but not exclusively in their functions as cabinet members, set budget and policy priorities in consultation with high-ranking bureaucrats, who reflect both the professional judgment of their ministries and some degree of sensitivity to the exigencies of politics. Most actual policymaking, however, takes place at a lower level in more fragmented settings. The LDP's policymaking apparatus, the Policy Affairs Research Council (PARC), manned by the party's Diet members who are backed by a small professional staff, consults constantly with the relevant sections and departments of the government ministries. Interest groups, of course, maintain contact with both the relevant regulatory sections of national ministries and sympathetic LDP parliamentarians. Such "subgovernments" of bureaucrats, politicians, and interest groups are critical both for generating proposals that will eventually become LDP cabinet bills and in providing a route for influencing the administrative implementation of existing laws and programs. This highly fragmented interpenetration of public and private interests focused on the bureaucratic section underscores the centrality of working with the bureaucracy to get things done in Japanese politics. One of the most surprising and impressive aspects of Japanese politics, however, is that this system results in so few scandals. The professionalism of Japanese bureaucrats in defending their own views of the public interest and seeing to it that even the most "political" scheme has some salutory public benefit is important for managing the ambiguities of the system.

Bureaucratic professionalism persists despite the efforts of LDP leaders subtly to influence personnel matters by such means as "capturing" specific cabinet posts for themselves or their associates over long periods of time. Nevertheless, bureaucrats do not function in a political vacuum. They must accommodate politicians to some extent, since only the latter can legitimate policy. Moreover, politically ambitious bureaucrats will have to develop ties of mutual confidence with LDP leaders if they hope to enter conservative politics. Since its founding, the LDP has drawn roughly 25 percent of its Diet membership and most of its party presidents (Nobusuke Kishi, Hayato Ikeda, Eisaku Sato, Takeo Fukuda, and Masayoshi Ohira) from ex-bureaucrats. Needless to say, Japan's perpetual opposition parties enjoy far less extensive and cordial relations with professional bureaucrats than does the LDP.

Close ties between the conservative parties and big business interests, of course, date from the prewar years, and were even then a source of much popular criticism and even assassinations. These ties were critical for the revival and growth of the conservatives in the postwar years. Indeed, insofar as party politicians became the chief legitimators of governmental policy in the postwar period, the need of business groups for political connections only increased. In the chaotic situation at the end of the war, many fortunes were lost, while others (frequently of a rather shady sort) were made. Yoshio Kodama, the man who served as Lockheed's consultant in Japan from the late 1950s until 1976, was one of those who emerged from the chaos a very rich man. His rather substantial fortune was a crucial factor in getting one of the postwar conservative parties restarted and his own reputation as a fixer established.[13] The scrounging around by conservative (and some Socialist) politicians for such funds, however, was a fundamental cause of constant political corruption scandals. Hence, stabilization of political funding became a high priority for both politicians and businessmen and was a major factor in impelling the conservative merger in 1955.[14]

The year 1955 marked a turning point in Japanese economic and business development as well as in politics. By then the Japanese economy had recovered to prewar (1935–36) levels of production and was at the beginning of a period of rapid economic growth. It was also at that time that big business leaders recovered their confidence and coalesced into four major national associations, which emerged as critical links to the LDP and to government planners: Keidanren (Japan Federation of Economic Organizations), which represents large businesses; Nikkeiren (Japan Federation of Employers Organizations), representing big companies as employers; the Japan Chamber of Commerce, serving businesses of all sizes; and Keizai Doyukai (Japan Committee on Economic Development), a small group of policy-oriented business leaders. In addition, industrial federations (gyokai), of companies in individual industrial sectors, for example, the Iron and Steel Federation, were also consolidated by this time and had become important lobbies, sources of vital information for planning purposes, and political funders.

Intimate LDP-business ties developed apace from this time. A central funding agency, the Conference for Economic Reconstruction, was established to channel business contributions to political parties, overwhelmingly to the LDP. Both *gyokai* and individual corporations made contributions in this way as a form of generalized "investment" in the LDP without such contributions having a strong taint of special interest corruption. Although the peak associations as such did not contribute to the party, Keidanren eventually worked out a formula—known as the Hanamura-*wariate* (Hanamura quota), named after the organization's secretary general, who allegedly formulated it—assessing individual corporate sectors (steel, autos, and banking, for example) and allocating quotas for political contributions to them.

As investors in the LDP, Japanese big business seeks political stability, seen as a vital ingredient to predictability in business and as a precondition to economic growth; such investments reflect a strong commitment to capitalist (as opposed to socialist) expansion. Business' shared beliefs with the LDP, however, extend far beyond this commitment, encompassing important aspects of foreign policy (such as a close alliance with the United States) and domestic affairs. Relations of a personal sort also run deep. Many top leaders of the LDP and business community (as well as the bureaucracy) have studied at the nation's leading universities, especially Tokyo, Kyoto, Hitotsubashi, Waseda, and Keio. Old school ties, including prewar higher schools, are an important basis for lifelong personal associations in Japan, even among those who may have attended at different times. Individual politicians, especially but not exclusively conservatives, draw on these and other important connections made during their careers to form support networks involving interest group representatives, bureaucrats, and (sometimes) individual "brains" and behind-the-scenes "fixers." Elements of these networks help sustain individual politicians financially and the intraparty factions to which they belong. Such networks are also drawn upon by politicians to help sustain their brokerage deals, involving such things as concessionary government financing and various special administrative dispensations to private business.

Business groups, of course, have direct access to the bureaucracy; and the smooth flow of communications between government economic bureaucrats and the business community is one of the significant factors explaining the success of Japanese industrial policy. LDP leaders like Tanaka come into the picture not only as guardians of capitalist expansion in a generalized sense, but also as intermediaries, arranging specific deals that private interests would not otherwise have extracted from government offices. In such cases, the line between public and private and between legitimate and illegitimte interactions among politicians, businessmen, and bureaucrats becomes blurred and scandal is an ever-present danger. In other words, the so-called structural corruption in Japan derives from the central role of politicians as brokers in the country's "bureaucratic capitalism." What is most surprising about this system is not its prevalence, which is a natural outcome of a strong bureaucracy, a thriving private sector, and a single predominant party, but rather that it produces so little scandal, and almost none involving the bureaucracy directly.

There is another aspect of LDP single-party dominance that should not be overlooked—its historical transition from a narrowly based party supported largely by farmers, merchants, and small business operators to a genuine catchall party, appealing to wide segments of the Japanese people. In the late 1950s, the LDP received over two-thirds of its votes in national elections from these three large "traditional" segments of the Japanese labor force but had relatively shallow support among the blue-collar and white-collar workers in the rapidly expanding "modern" sector of the economy. The Japan Socialists were backed heavily by the latter but also appealed to broader segments of the electorate.[15]

In the early postwar years, the conservatives built a strong base of support in the traditional sectors of the economy. Land reform, initiated by the Allied occupation and facilitated by the cooperation of tenant unions, created a large class of farmer-owners. Conservative politicians moved quickly, in contrast to their prewar immobilism on the agrarian problem, to provide subsidies for land improvement, price supports, and protection from foreign imports. These moves were in concert with the high priority that government planners put on reviving the country's ability to feed itself after the devastation of the war and the loss of colonial sources of food. Conservative politicians also consolidated their support among merchants and small business operators by means of a wide range of benefits, including protectionism, price supports, tax breaks, and safeguards against encroachment on their domains by larger retailers or manufacturers.

Support from these traditional sectors, based on shared values and concrete benefits, however, would not have been enough to have kept the LDP in power in the years ahead, particularly given the precipitous decline of the agrarian sector. The party would have had to broaden its appeal. Rapid economic growth provided a reservoir of resources that it used for this purpose.

RAPID ECONOMIC GROWTH

The Japanese GNP grew approximately 10 percent a year in real terms between 1955 and the mid-1970s. Japan was transformed from a relatively poor country based on agriculture and light industry to an economic giant with the third largest GNP in the world, an enormous heavy and chemical industrial plant, and an affluent society. Government expenditures increased more than thirtyfold during these years. Expenditures on public works and various grants-in-aid to local governments, two areas of particular sensitivity to political intermediation, grew even more rapidly, accounting for a third of the national budget by the mid-1970s.[16] As the only party in power with ultimate responsibility for the governmental budget and for the direction of public policy more generally, the LDP naturally did everything it could to use the enlarged resources of the government to perpetuate itself in power, by rewarding its supporters and cultivating new ones. The necessity for an activist approach to extending its electoral base was all the more pressing because of the rapid erosion of its segments of the voters as a result of the changing social and economic structure of the country.

The LDP got down to business very quickly in the 1960s. Prime Minister Hayato Ikeda, a former top Ministry of Finance bureaucrat who had been brought into politics by Shigeru Yoshida in the early postwar years, put the political confrontations of the late 1950s with the Socialists behind him. His predecessor, Nobusuke Kishi, had confronted the Socialists on precisely those issues of foreign policy, defense, internal security, labor, and education on which the latter could mobilize broad opposition to the government. In contrast, Ikeda deemphasized these areas of conflict, announced a plan to double the national income, and sought consultation with the Socialists on the management of the Diet. Ikeda's LDP, in effect, was less ideological and more pragmatic in its emphasis on policies for which there existed a widespread consensus already in society.

The Socialists attempted to make a similar transition, somewhat like the West German Social Democrats had done in 1959 but using instead the idea of "structural reform," suggested by Italian Communist Party leader Palmiro Togliatti—in effect, trying to bring about the gradual achievement of a socialist society through parliamentary-based reforms.[17] The party, however, failed to make the transition. Its efforts got intertwined in leadership struggles that centered on factions that had become careerist as well as policy groupings. Moreover, the party was pulled to the left by its most powerful support group, Sohyo (The General Council of Trade Unions), the largest national federation of trade unions. Sohyo membership is strongly skewed toward the public sector unions (for example, local governmental employees and public school teachers), which have remained more militant than unions in the private sector in part because of their continuing struggle to regain the right to bargain collectively and strike. The Socialist Party became increasingly dependent upon labor for its financing, candidates, and campaigning, with a concomitant erosion of its support in other sectors. The emergence of a fragmented opposition helped sustain the LDP in power during this transitional period, while the party's leaders tried to cope politically with the country's rapid social and economic transformation.

One of the strategies of the LDP was to appeal to the "weak" regions of the country. Japan's industrial complex was heavily concentrated along the Pacific coast from Tokyo, through Nagoya, to the Osaka area on the Inland Sea. Government planners, including those who compiled Ikeda's Income Doubling Plan, sought to exploit the large markets and the concentration of existing infrastructure along the Pacific industrial belt to speed up the country's economic transformation. The LDP politicians from other regions of the country, however, were under strong pressure from their districts to spread the development more widely. From prewar times, one of the country's most difficult social problems has been large regional differences in living standards. In the early 1960s, the standard of living in most prefectures was still less than half what it was in the Tokyo area. Thus, LDP politicians could argue strongly and persuasively with government planners that something should be done to correct this discrepancy. The result of this intermediation by conservative politicians between the country's periphery and national planners was the New National Land Development Law of 1962 and several other regional development laws, including the New Industrial City Promotion Law of 1964. These laws channeled huge sums of money into designated areas on the periphery and created substantial incentives, often matched by local governments, to attract industry into those areas.

Local areas throughout the country also benefited from the greatly enhanced public works and local aid budgets, which were themselves often the product of political entrepreneurship. Many of these programs merely involved the proper filing by local authorities of requests for funding; but others were more complicated, involving the integration of these requests into comprehensive local development plans. These plans usually had to be discussed in detail with the Ministry of Construction and other government agencies whose jurisdiction might be involved. In addition to sending their mayors and other top officials to Tokyo to work with government bureaucrats on these matters, localities routinely called upon parliamentarians, especially Liberal Democrats, to emphasize the importance of their requests to the bureaucracy. Naturally these politicians claimed success whenever national government support was received, whether or not their influence had been a deciding factor. Local conservative politicians also made the best of the situation at election times by claiming a "direct pipeline to the center."[18] Reciprocal electoral support between conservative local and national politicians, therefore, constituted a kind of "virtuous circle" reinforced by this center-periphery financial linkage based upon local interest articulation and distribution politics.

Rapid economic growth enabled the LDP to cater to demands for public works and for regional development without upsetting national finances. Budgets were balanced until 1965, when the insatiable appetite for such programs finally pushed the budget into the red. But deficits did not reach serious proportions until over a decade later. In the meantime, a different challenge came from escalating demands for a higher "quality of life." By the late 1960s, the unrestricted and one-sided emphasis on industrial development had led to a serious deterioration of the living environment. Urban sprawl and rural depopulation had also become pressing problems. Moreover, the urbanization of the population and the growing proportion of nuclear families created a need for new social services that could no longer be met by the traditional buffers of the extended family.

The LDP was slow in addressing these new issues. As citizen protests of the deteriorating living environment grew, opposition parties at the local level (where they had fewer fundamental ideological and policy differences than in national politics) rallied around independent reformist candidates for mayoral and gubernatorial posts, who ran on platforms for the amelioration of urban, social, and environmental problems. As a result, the LDP lost control of many critical local chief executive positions, especially in the more urban areas. At one point in the early 1970s, over 40 percent of the population lived in cities or prefectures with a mayor or governor supported exclusively by the leftist (Communists and Japan Socialists) and/or centrist (Komeito and Democratic Socialist) parties.

While the LDP dragged its heels at the national level, local authorities instituted new pollution control mechanisms, health and welfare policies, and urban planning processes. Some of these measures required little funding, while others were extremely expensive (for example, free medical care for the aged and childhood allowances). Economic growth provided a margin sufficient to institute at least rudimentary local programs to ameliorate the most pressing problems. An increasingly skilled local civil service, which was now drawing salaries comparable to or in excess of those for national bureaucrats, provided capable management of an expanded policy role for local governments. With some justification, the Japanese press gave much of the credit for local innovation to the political opposition. Local conservatives, who toned down their claims of a direct pipeline to a seemingly unresponsive center, desperately sought a change in direction nationally.

That change came in the early 1970s. In December 1970, the LDP somewhat reluctantly presented fourteen new strong pollution control laws to the National Diet. The following year a national Environmental Agency was established. In the next two years, the Liberal Democrats turned to health and welfare issues. In addition to "nationalizing" programs initiated locally, such as free medical care to the elderly, the national government significantly enlarged the annuity (social security) system and instituted other welfare programs. 1974 is known in Japan as "the first year of social welfare" *(shakai fukushi gannen)*. These measures diffused what had been developing as a significant new policy cleavage on environmental and welfare issues between government and opposition in national as well as local politics. By coopting the environmental and welfare policies of the opposition parties, however, the LDP was able to undercut the basis for a Center-Left coalition against itself. Consequently, the centrist parties began to shift their policy cooperation and coalitional visions away from the Left and toward the LDP. The political Left lost both its partners and its policies, while the LDP laid a basis for extending its reach into sectors of society, including both blue-collar and white-collar urban workers, among whom it had not hitherto had much support. Only the political corruption scandals of the mid-1970s delayed the full realization of this change.

Kakuei Tanaka and Money Politics

Kakuei Tanaka is something of a folk hero in Japan. Not only did he survive a forced resignation from the country's premiership in 1974 and the Lockheed scandal two years later, but he actually increased his political influence in subsequent years. He was the kingmaker without whose help Prime Minister Nakasone might never have arrived at that office. The size of Tanaka's faction of LDP parliamentarians grew to unprecedented proportions in the years following the Lockheed scandal. Shortly after his conviction for bribery in 1983, he received his highest vote tally ever in the Third District of Niigata from where he hails. It was only after his stroke in 1985 that his political influence declined significantly. Despite this "folk hero" status, however, the ruling party and virtually all those associated with Japanese politics breathed a sigh of relief as Tanaka faded from the scene. The Japanese political system had at last "purified" itself of the shame of the Lockheed scandal and of a leader who had gone too far in exploiting the ambiguities of the system.

Tanaka's folk hero status derives not simply from his tremendous political power but also from his humble origins, political foresight, and atypical style. He is the "common man," whose dogged determination and extraordinary efforts won him a place of glory among Japan's more favored elites. Moreover, despite his acquisition of great personal wealth, he never lost touch with the common folk of his district. Symbolic of this special quality, upon his appointment as minister of posts and telecommunications he went on the airwaves and in his gravelly voice sang *naniwabushi* (Japanese folk songs).[19]

Examining the atypical person can sometimes put the typical person more into perspective, particularly if they have enough else in common to make the contrasts illuminating. That is the case with Tanaka and more typical LDP leaders like Ikeda, Sato, and Fukuda, all prime ministers who have been skilled intermediaries (brokers) and who at some points in their careers have been involved in political scandals, although perhaps none of the magnitude of Tanaka's.

ENTERING POLITICS AT A TIME OF TURMOIL AND RECONSTRUCTION

Tanaka's Niigata electoral district is a rural area on the "backside" (Japan Sea coast) of the country, which traditionally has supplied rice, electricity, manual workers, and elements of the underclass to the Pacific coast "face" of Japan.[20] The area is known as Japan's "Snow Country," the combination of cold moist air from Siberia and the warm currents of the Japan Sea resulting in accumulations of over fifteen feet of snow a year. Nobel Prize–winning novelist Yasunari Kawabata wrote his famed *Yukiguni* (Snow Country) while staying at an inn in Niigata. In Tanaka's early years, towns and villages in the region were often isolated for long periods of time, the roads (such as they were) being impassable. Women were often left alone at home; the men went off to the cities on seasonal jobs and the children were boarding in crude school dorms. Niigata was a hotbed of unrest among radical tenant unions during the 1930s; and in the early postwar years its towns and villages elected many Communist and Socialist mayors, a rarity in Japan.

After graduating from middle school in 1933, Tanaka worked as a day laborer in construction, got some further education in civil engineering in Tokyo, and was eventually drafted and sent in 1939 to Manchuria, which, although it was formerly a part of China, was at that time a puppet state of the Japanese Empire. He was discharged two years later, after a near-fatal bout with pneumonia. Returning to a menial construction job in Niigata, Tanaka struck it rich the next year when he married the daughter of a local construction company owner and inherited the company. Shortly before the end of the war, Tanaka's company was awarded a Y22,000,000 (ca. $11 million) contract to relocate a piston ring plant from Japan to Taejon, Korea. Repatriated to Japan when the war ended, Tanaka had ample funds to undertake his first (and only unsuccessful) bid for a seat in the House of Representatives in 1946. Running as a conservative but courting left-leaning farmers rather than the local conservative establishment, Tanaka promised his constituents roads, tunnels, schools, reclamation projects, and similar amenities. The following year, at age twenty-eight, he was elected as the youngest member of the Diet and began his long quest to deliver on his promises.

War and reconstruction had a profound impact on the cast and characters of the conservative political leadership. The Allied occupation's 1946 purge from political life of prewar politicians extended to almost 90 percent of the conservative members of the House of Representatives, including Ichiro Hatoyama, who was about to become prime minister. Shigeru Yoshida, a prewar diplomat who had been brought out of retirement by Prime Minister Higashikuni at the end of the war to serve as foreign minister, replaced Hatoyama as head of the Liberal Party and as premier. It was Yoshida who brought many high-ranking ex-bureaucrats into conservative politics and who also nurtured other upstarts like Tanaka. Members of the "Yoshida School" were to dominate LDP leadership after 1960.[21]

While the country as a whole was impoverished, certain individuals like Tanaka came out of the war with new-found wealth. By far one of the most important of these persons was none other than Yoshio Kodama, who was to become Lockheed's chief Japanese consultant for two decades. In the early 1930s Kodama had been deeply involved in extremist right-wing activities; one group he founded was even implicated in an assassination plot against the prime minister. Later in the decade he moved to China, where he served as a procurement agent for the Japanese Imperial Army and also trafficked in precious metals and other contraband. He picked up a navy contract after that to buy and otherwise expropriate rare metals in the Shanghai area.

Kodama returned to Japan at the end of the war a very rich man. Some of his wealth went to fund Yoshida's Liberal Party and to assist Hatoyama and Kishi, whom he had met during his 1946–48 imprisonment. Both Kishi (who had been minister of munitions during Hideki Tojo's wartime cabinet) and Kodama had been designated as Class-A war criminal suspects, but they were released without prosecution. Kishi entered conservative politics and Kodama went behind the scenes as a funder of conservative politicians and as an intermediary between legitimate politics and the world of gangsters and right-wing fringe groups.

Tanaka also got in trouble with the law. He was arrested in 1948 for receiving Y1 million (ca. $3,000) from Fukuoka mine owners to vote against a bill nationalizing the coal mines. During his brief stint in jail, Tanaka met Kishi, Kodama, and Osano, the latter two of whom were to become Lockheed's channels of contact with him. Tanaka was found guilty but had the verdict reversed upon appeal.

The Coal Mining Administration Incident in which Tanaka was involved was actually penny-ante stuff compared to the Showa Denko scandal of the same time.[22] Showa Denko, a fertilizer manufacturer that had been a major recipient of funds from the Reconstruction Finance Bank, which had been established to invest government funds in priority growth areas, attempted to obtain increased support by distributing thirty million yen ($90,000) worth of valuables and cash to politicians and bureaucrats with influence in government finance. Major arrests included Economic Stabilization Board Director General Takeo Kurusu (a Democrat), Bamboku Ono (a Democratic Liberal), Deputy Prime Minister Suehiro Nishio (a Socialist), and Finance Ministry Bureau of the Budget Chief Takeo Fukuda. Former Prime Minister Hitoshi Ashida was also arrested soon after his cabinet fell in ignominy. Unlike Tanaka, who had to carry out much of his first reelection campaign from jail, Fukuda (who was to become Tanaka's chief political rival in the years ahead) walked away a free man, after testifying that he had not realized the money he had received was a bribe.

Fukuda was not the only elite bureaucrat (or ex-bureaucrat turned politician) to get off so easily. Corruption scandals abounded during those years of political fluidity and social upheaval. Many of the future top LDP leaders were implicated in one or another scandal, including future prime ministers Tanaka, Fukuda, Ikeda, and Sato. The latter two, former high-ranking bureaucrats who had been brought into the Liberal Party by Yoshida, were implicated in the Shipbuilding Scandal of 1954. The shipbuilding and shipping industries had fallen into recession when the special procurement boom of the Korean War ended. The government had responded to the plight of this priority industrial sector by passing in 1953 the Law for the Subsidization of Interest and Insurance Against Losses in Oceangoing Shipbuilding. Industry leaders wanted more and prevailed upon the Transportation Ministry and the major conservative parties to strengthen the law, which they did. In the spring of the following year, however, it was revealed that the revision had been secured at a cost of approximately Y50 million (ca. $140,000) distributed to about thirty conservative politicians and a few bureaucrats.

The presidents of five major shipbuilding and shipping companies, several Diet members, and the chief of the Transportation Ministry Secretariat were arrested. Transportation Minister Mitsujiro Ishii, Liberal Party Secretary General Eisaku Sato, and Liberal Party Policy Affairs Research Council (PARC) Chairman Hayato Ikeda narrowly averted arrest. The Public Prosecutor's Office had decided to seek House of Representatives' approval before arresting Sato, who occupied the number two post in Prime Minister Yoshida's party. In the interim, Yoshida ordered Justice Minister Takeru Inukai (who was also a suspect) to invoke his executive authority *(shikiken)* over the Public Prosecutor's Office to block these arrests and to suspend prosecution. In 1976 Tanaka, of course, would expect the same of Prime Minister Miki and Justice Minister Inaba, and he was hurt and outraged at what he took to be their betrayal.

The Shipbuilding scandal spelled the end of Yoshida's long (1946–47 and from 1948 to 1954), distinguished, and often stormy tenure in office. Big business interests sought an end to Yoshida's administration and to costly rivalries among the conservative parties. As noted earlier, business's efforts to stabilize political funding and to avoid embarrassing scandals such as this one, in which major corporate leaders were arrested, were a significant factor in the union of conservative parties in 1955. Political scandals did not disappear in subsequent years, but rarely were high-ranking leaders of business, the LDP, or the bureaucracy implicated, until the mid-1970s with Tanaka's financial scandal and Lockheed. To many observers, this simply meant that political corruption had been pushed below the surface and become structural, a part of business as usual.

INTERMEDIATION BETWEEN THE PUBLIC BUREAUCRACY AND PRIVATE INTERESTS

One of the classic struggles within the LDP during its first decade was between former high-ranking bureaucrats who had entered politics laterally to fill top party posts and the so-called pure politicians. Kishi, Ikeda, Sato, and Ohira were among the former and Hatoyama, Miki, Bamboku Ono, and Ichiro Kono among the latter. The ex-bureaucrats predominated by the 1960s. Although Tanaka was as pure a politician as there was to be found, he had already cast his lot with the elite ex-bureaucrats in the 1950s, allying with them in political struggles and assisting in their political funding. They rewarded him for his loyalty: He became minister of posts and telecommunications (1957–60) under Kishi, minister of finance (1962–65) under Ikeda, and minister of international trade and industry (1971–72) under Sato. He also held the party's second most powerful post, secretary general, twice during Sato's long tenure in office. In 1970 he outmaneuvered Fukuda to become heir to most of Sato's powerful parliamentary faction. Tanaka and Ohira were also close friends and political allies for two decades.

As a young Diet member, Tanaka first made his mark in the areas of construction, transportation, and broadcasting. But it was as finance minister under Ikeda in the early 1960s that his exceptional skill in dealing with bureaucrats became evident. The Finance Ministry is generally considered to be the most powerful of Japanese government offices because of its legal responsibility for setting the national budget and, for this reason, it is said to attract the most talented of the country's senior civil service recruits. As the watchdogs of the fiscal integrity of the government, Finance Ministry officials have traditionally disdained constituency-oriented politics and tried to impress on new finance ministers, influential LDP politicians appointed by the prime minister to that post, the complexity and gravity of their charge. When Tanaka was appointed finance minister, however, it was he who took charge and impressed the career bureaucrats. This self-made man from the hinterland demonstrated a grasp of the details of finance and taxation that astounded the Tokyo University Law Faculty graduates who predominated in the ministry. He soon earned their respect and cooperation.

Tanaka was minister of finance during a propitious time, at the height of the Income Doubling Plan and the beginning of new regional development projects. Real annual growth rates at the time were in excess of 15 percent. As finance minister, Tanaka greatly sped up the pace of public works and initiated some major land reclamation projects. He also sold huge tracts of government land to private construction and manufacturing firms. (By one count more government land was sold in Tanaka's three years as finance minister than during the whole remainder of the period between 1957 and 1971).[23] Choice parcels of former governmental land in central Tokyo went to the three major Tokyo-based mass circulation newspapers and to several large business corporations.

Tanaka's service as LDP secretary general and minister of international trade and industry was no less illustrious. As secretary general, he ran two highly successful general election campaigns for the LDP. In doing this, he again showed a tremendous capacity for work in detail as well as for electoral strategies. While minister of international trade and industry, he negotiated an end to the U.S.–Japan textile dispute by getting Japanese textile producers to agree to export restrictions in exchange for large government payments. He also worked with MITI bureaucrats to develop his "Plan to Rebuild the Japanese Archipelago." This plan was largely aborted during his premiership because of rapid increases in land prices, inflation fueled by the oil crisis, and the scandal regarding his personal finances that cut short his tenure in office. Nevertheless, it was the basis of several major projects, such as the construction of a new science city in Tsukuba, bridge links between the islands of Honshu and Shikoku, and the tunnel connecting Hokkaido to Honshu. Moreover, Tanaka's political vision of redirecting the flow of rural emigration away from the crowded and politically diverse metropolitan centers to regional industrial cities with more traditional social networks and conservative political cultures has largely been realized. The result has been an industrialization of much of the Japanese countryside without a concomitant radicalization.

TANAKA'S CONSTITUENCIES: PORK BARREL AND POLITICAL FOLLOWERS

Tanaka's District

Among the greatest beneficiaries of Tanaka's intermediation with the bureaucracy were the people of the Third District of Niigata. The prefectural capital is now linked with Tokyo by a bullet train that makes the trip in less than two hours. Niigata is lined with superhighways; and the back-roads of Tanaka's district are paved and replete with an impressive array of tunnels. Kashiwazaki, the district's second largest city, is home to a major atomic power plant. The district's largest city, Nagaoka, was designated in the early 1980s as one of the country's nineteen new "technopolises," which are supposed to serve as new growth centers in Japan's transition to a society based on high technology. Moreover, in recent years, Niigata has ranked number one or number two in the country in public works expenditures per capita. In 1980, for example,

Niigata topped the per capita public works expenditure list with a rating of 255, while the national average stood at 100 and Tokyo attained less than forty.[24]

As in most liberal democracies, political longevity in Japan, particularly in the ruling party, usually is accompanied by increased political influence and opportunities for leadership at the elite level. As we have seen, building a strong base of individual support among the local electorates is essential for remaining in public office in Japan. Tanaka has been enormously successful in this regard, having been elected sixteen straight times for over forty years as a Diet member. Even in the five national elections after the Lockheed scandal broke, Tanaka not only won, but continued to be by far the highest vote-getter in his district. The key to Tanaka's success at this level has been his identification with the needs of his district and the development of a local support group, the *Etsuzankai*, as a conduit for addressing those needs.

The *Etsuzankai* is said to have a membership of approximately ninety-five thousand people in an electoral district of 560,000 voters.[25] It is subdivided not simply according to municipality but into 313 district units based upon old, preamalgamation, town and village lines. The modus operandi of the *Etsuzankai* was established during Tanaka's first reelection campaign, waged from his jail cell. To assure his reelection under those circumstances, Tanaka's associates worked intensely to broaden the geographic reach of Tanaka's electoral base beyond his home town and the city of Kashiwazaki to the even poorer rural areas of the district. The resounding success of this campaign led to a long-term electoral strategy of building support from the poorer areas to the richer ones, from the outer fringes of the towns to their centers, and from farmers to unskilled workers in commerce and industry to those in more established fields.

Tanaka's incorporation into the *Etsuzankai* of most of the district's road and construction companies, including their workers' unions, provided the critical nexus linking his electoral strategy to his brokerage role as a politician. Directing his efforts as a politician to the enlargement of government expenditures for public works and attracting them to Niigata, Tanaka provided growth opportunities for local construction and transportation companies and jobs for the numerous people who combined farming with work as day laborers or migrant workers. This expanding base of support soon drew into the *Etsuzankai* local politicians, including by 1983 twenty-six of the thirty-three city, town, and village mayors and thirteen of the twenty prefectural assembly members from Niigata's Third District. These people and others in municipal assemblies served the dual function of mobilizing voters at election time and serving as a "pipe" through which to distribute the vastly increased funds available to local authorities through transfers via the relatively centralized public finance system. So important has the *Etsuzankai* become in the prefecture that its local head is known as the "shadow governor."

The *Etsuzankai* is similar to (although more extensive than) most *koenkai* of LDP parliamentarians. Although theoretically "individual" in focus, *koenkai* are actually centerpieces in the "virtuous circles" of mutual support between local and national conservative politicians that enhance their ability to tap the public purse for concrete benefits to distribute, in an entirely legal manner, to their districts. Actually, *koenkai* in many cases have become virtual political machines. As such, they are frequently transferred intact to political successors. According to one estimate, approximately one-third of the LDP's lower house members "inherited" their *koenkai* from relatives or from those they had served loyally in the past.[26] Like all machines, it takes a lot of money to keep them well oiled. This is part of the high cost of politics in Japan, to which we shall return.

Tanaka's Followers

Factional leadership in the LDP derives from seniority, broad experience in government and party posts, fund-raising ability, and brokerage skills. Tanaka had demonstrated all of these by the time he took over most of the Sato faction in 1970. He became a master of LDP factional politics largely by legal and noncorrupt means. Over his many years in office he demonstrated an unusual grasp of the details of policy, increasing his clout with national bureaucrats, especially in the Ministries of Construction and Finance. He reinforced his influence in these ministries and in the Ministry of Posts and Telecommunications by capturing in the hands of his followers the cabinet portfolios for them during long periods of time in the 1960s and 1970s. Tanaka further cultivated elite bureaucrats by providing political support for many of their policy positions, expanding or creating new public corporations to which many of them would move after retiring from government at an early age, and recommending some of them for LDP candidacy to the National Diet. All of these networks, which illustrate the murky relationship between the public and private realms in Japanese politics, reinforced Tanaka's ability to serve as an effective intermediary for a wide range of business interests nationally as well as for local constituents and the bureaucracy. Consequently, Tanaka, as a person who could get things done, found business responsive to his pleas for support with contributions of political funds. These funds could be used in LDP factional politics to win a place of importance for himself and to nurture a following among LDP Diet members and candidates. His unusual grasp of electoral strategy and his willingness to expend considerable personal energy to advance the electoral chances and careers of would-be followers further reinforced his strength within the factional system.

The upshot of Tanaka's mastery of this system was his winning of the party presidency and premiership in 1972, despite Sato's desire to have his other long-time associate, Fukuda, succeed him. (The Tanaka-Fukuda rivalry grew so intense that it almost split the party in later years.) The size of Tanaka's faction dropped somewhat in the aftermath of the Lockheed scandal, but it resumed its upward climb in the 1980s to reach 142 (eighty-seven in the lower house and fifty-five in the upper house) in 1986. He worked assiduously applying all his talents to build his faction to a level unprecedented in the party. Despite the lingering taint of scandal surrounding Tanaka, his faction was able to attract many new recruits who saw in it the party's most talented electoral strategists, a disproportionate share of its policy leaders, and a collective ability to put the right people together to solve concrete policy problems. It was, in short, an exciting and rewarding place to serve a political apprenticeship.

It is a sad postscript to Tanaka's brilliant, if controversial, career that his foremost concern in building such a powerful political machine was self-preservation through the construction of political alliances that would protect him from parliamentary sanctions and an adverse court decision over Lockheed. Hence in 1978 he plowed enormous resources into Ohira's successful campaign to wrest the reins of party and government control away from Prime Minister Fukuda, Tanaka's long-time rival. After Ohira's death in office in 1980,

Tanaka threw the support of his faction behind Suzuki and then Nakasone, factional leaders who might not have reached the premiership without Tanaka's help. Tanaka, the Kingmaker, however, was unwilling to pass on control of his faction to its heir apparent, Noboru Takeshita, for fear that his personal influence would wane. Hence, he saw the faction slip gradually from his grasp after his 1985 stroke, until Takeshita seized control of most of it before becoming prime minister in 1987.

"Money Politics" and "Structural Corruption" in Japan

Money is the lifeblood of Japanese politics, and the amounts that flow in the veins of the body politic are enormous by any standard. Total political funds reported under the Political Funds Control Law in 1983, a year of major local and national elections, amounted to 147.2 billion yen (about $600 million at the then-current exchange rate or over $1 billion today).[27] This figure dropped to 116 billion yen in 1984, which saw no major elections, but it has increased significantly since then. The Communist Party reported the highest total, 21.7 billion yen. Among the other opposition parties, Komeito reported 10.2 billion yen income, the Japan Socialists 6.3 billion yen, the Democratic Socialists 1.7 billion yen, and the New Liberals .4 billion yen. The Liberal Democrats reported 13.2 billion yen, behind the Communists, but in fact far ahead of all the other parties combined. Their national fund-raising organization, the People's Political Association (Kokumin Seiji Kyokai), raised 9.3 billion yen, the five major factions 4.0 billion yen, and the ten top fundraisers among individual LDP politicians another 0.6 billion yen. Whereas the Communists and Komeito raised the vast majority of their funds from publications, reflecting their organizational strength, the Japan Socialists relied heavily on party dues and union contributions as well as on publications. Corporate contributions accounted for the bulk of reported LDP funds and were a significant component of those of the New Liberals and Democratic Socialists as well. The actual total of political funds is said to be several times that officially reported, since extralegal (if not illegal) means of making political contributions abound. It is likely that a few billion dollars in political funds are raised each year.

As elaborated earlier, the high cost of politics among conservative national politicians is rooted, at the mass level, in the lack of a well articulated LDP organization locally and in the multimember district electoral system, which forces members to compete with each other in mobilizing support among local conservative politicians and influentials. This is done largely, although not exclusively, through koenkai, such as Tanaka's Etsuzankai. The high cost of politics is reinforced by cultural norms of reciprocity, gift-giving, and the exchange of favors. Traditionally, local influentials have served as patrons for their communities, providing material benefits in return for loyalty and service. National as well as local politicians today are still expected to contribute gifts and money to community events from weddings, funerals, and festivals to the opening of new businesses and community construction projects. The koenkai, somewhat like American urban party machines in the days of Boss Tweed, serve as employment agencies, school placement offices, counseling centers, and social clubs, all costly institutions or services. National conservatives transfer huge amounts of political funds to local politicians and influentials who play pivotal roles in their koenkai and mobilize the vote. Supposedly, little of this money is pocketed by these intermediaries, whose real payoffs are said to come from public works projects and the demonstration of political clout at the center.

At the elite level, advancement within LDP factional politics is greatly facilitated by an ability to raise political funds and the skill to use them for securing a leadership role, developing a followership, and forging alliances. Traditionally, the factions have been a major conduit for political funds and for the introductions and assistance necessary to develop one's own ability to tap corporate contributors. Funds distributed by the factions to their members for electoral purposes are far larger than those received directly from the party. Factional funds are also important in the struggle for posts within the party and government, especially the party presidency and premiership.

Fund-raising from corporate sources is an integral part of what is known as "structural corruption" in Japan, the collusive behavior among political elites discussed earlier. The other major component, of course, is the intermediation by politicians with the bureaucracy on behalf of special interests. The relationship between political fundraising and "structural corruption," however, is not a simple one, because contributions vary considerably in the degree to which they have been "sanitized" by passage through public or at least transparent channels. This can be illustrated graphically in the following manner:

FIGURE 7.1

CHANNELS OF POLITICAL CONTRIBUTION

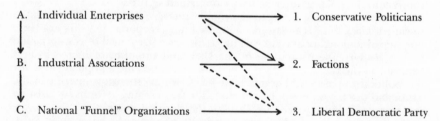

A. Individual Enterprises		1. Conservative Politicians
B. Industrial Associations		2. Factions
C. National "Funnel" Organizations		3. Liberal Democratic Party

The industrial associations (B) are the *gyokai*, such as the Iron and Steel Federation. The national funnel organizations (C) have evolved in three stages. The Conference for Economic Reconstruction was established in 1955 to channel big business contributions to the newly unified Liberal Democratic Party in a manner that would not be perceived as corrupt. It was replaced in 1961 by the National Political Association, which developed the Hanamura allocation system for assessing corporate contributions to the LDP. In the wake of Tanaka's financial scandal of 1974 and the revision of the Political Funds Control Law in 1975, the LDP renamed its funnel the People's Political Association, with the supposed goal of raising small contributions from a far larger number of sources. Among the theoretically possible channels of political contributions, channels A–3 and A–B–3 were widely used before the conservative merger in 1955 but they have been insignificant since then.

The major channels can be ordered in the following way to show, in decreasing probability, the likelihood of direct bribery: A–1 > A–B–1 > A–B–2 > A–B–C–3. A–B–C–3 is the most easily justified and least subject to charges of bribery. Funds channeled in this manner are for the maintenance of conservative rule and hence for the capitalist system. The national funnel organizations (C) were clearly established as a way to sanitize and legitimate the much criticized close relationship between big business and conservative politicians.

It should not be assumed, as many critics do, that specific pay-offs in the form of favorable legislation or administrative dispensations are the necessary *quid pro quo* for corporate contributions made through the other major channels. The bulk of corporate contributions are regularized contributions aimed at building access and influence over the long run. Still, the timing of some corporate contributions, relative to administrative or legislative decisions, lends itself to suspicions of influence-buying and influence-peddling. Even more serious because they are almost entirely removed from the possibility of public scrutiny, however, are the flows of "backstage money" along these broad channels of corporate political financing. Many of these practices, such as those that got Tanaka into trouble in 1974, are technically legal, but barely so. For example, companies can transfer stock to a politician below or at market value prior to an anticipated short-term gain.[28] Or they can sell real estate to a politician cheaply and buy it back at a higher price. Those that engage in such practices are known as "men who stay just on the inside edges of the law" *(ho suresure aruku hito).*[29] Other collusive activities of business and politicians include the practice of awarding government contracts to businesses that have worked out their bids and a division of the project in advance on the basis of information fed to them beforehand regarding government budgeting. Local enterprises expect to contribute a percentage of the cost of any government contract to the political intermediary who helped secure it.

Political fund-raising emerged as a significant issue in the late 1960s with the so-called "black mist" scandals involving backstage corporate pay-offs to a large number of national politicians.[30] The result was a great deal of consternation by LDP leaders, the dissolution of the Diet, and promises of more virtuous behavior in the future. "Political ethics" *(seiji rinri)* became a popular cause for the political opposition. The mass media, however, soon lost interest in the issue, and the LDP sidestepped demands for far-reaching reforms by insisting that they be tied to a general overhaul of the electoral system.

The issue of political ethics reemerged with a vengeance, however, in 1974, as a result of two incidents involving Prime Minister Tanaka. First was his strategy of seeking explicit endorsements and funding by various big businesses for specific LDP candidates in that summer's upper house elections.[31] Mass media and public criticism of this blatant "money politics" embarrassed the big businessmen, who were also dismayed by Tanaka's pressure tactics and the relatively poor performance of the party at the polls. (The LDP barely held on to its majority). This extravagant display of money politics appeared all the worse coming in the midst of spiraling prices, the nation's highest inflation rate since the immediate postwar years, and a drop of the growth rate to below zero.

Nevertheless, Tanaka might have held on to power had it not been for the second incident, which struck directly at him. In its November 1974 issue, *Bungei Shunju,* a high-quality monthly with a circulation of approximately seven hundred thousand, published the first of two articles on Tanaka's financial affairs, written by Takashi Tachibana (a freelance writer who had worked for the magazine formerly). The articles were masterpieces of investigative journalism with scrupulous attention paid to the facts. Tachibana detailed how Tanaka had raised and spent political funds, amassed a large personal fortune, and managed the financial affairs of the *Etsuzankai*. The articles did not accuse Tanaka of violating the law, but they did expose many highly questionable dealings, especially for someone in public office. One such practice was the creation of "ghost companies" *(yurei gaisha)*, without offices or employees, which existed largely on paper to hide and transfer personal income. Tanaka held several such companies, which traded frequently in real estate that was destined to become sites of government reclamation projects, power plants, and bullet-train rights-of-way. Kenji Osano, Tanaka's old friend who was to become one of Lockheed's channels to the prime minister, was one of his frequent partners in such dealings.

At first the Japanese press virtually ignored these revelations. The sluggishness of Japanese newspapers in developing issues of political ethics stands in sharp contrast to the zeal of the *Washington Post* and other American newspapers in their exposure of the Watergate incident. One significant difference in the cases, of course, was that no direct violation of the law was immediately apparent in the case of Tanaka's finances, while political spies had broken into the offices of the Democratic Party's National Committee at the Watergate. More importantly in explaining the contrasting behavior of the newspapers in the two countries, however, are the close ties that exist between politicians and reporters in Japan, compared to the more independent (even adversarial) relationship between the two in the United States. Japanese reporters have incredibly good access to politicians and government offices through press clubs and exclusive press conferences. They are reluctant to compromise this access by independent investigative reporting. Moreover, many Japanese reporters serve, or hope to serve, as political secretaries to influential politicians, a political ambition that can work to restrict the reporting of some news. In effect, the newspapers, however critical they may be at times of the government, are part of the political establishment; they will not take actions lightly that might shake the equilibrium of Japanese politics.

The Japanese press, however, was forced to jump into the fray on the issue of political ethics when in an interview before the Foreign Press Club Tanaka was subjected to intense questioning about the Tachibana articles. With this jolt from the outside, Japanese newspapers pursued the subject with vigor. Within a month, they were contributing to Tanaka's forced resignation from the premiership, demonstrating the potential strength of a truly independent press. The upshot of these events was Tanaka's replacement by Takeo Miki as prime minister and Miki's leadership in pushing through the National Diet reforms of the Public Office Election Law and Political Funds Control Law. The latter was designed to inhibit political corruption by providing for public disclosure of political funding and setting limits on the size of political donations. Less than five weeks after this law came into effect on 1 January 1976, the Lockheed scandal broke in Washington.

Structural Corruption and Scandal in the Lockheed Incident

One of the most fascinating and thought-provoking aspects of the Lockheed scandal is the apparently strong and sincere belief by Tanaka that he did nothing wrong. This, of course, was not the judgment of the public, which reacted with outrage to the revelations of the Church Committee, or of the Japanese law enforcement agencies and courts, which found Tanaka guilty of accepting bribes and wrongfully using his public office. These contradictory reactions reveal a fundamental dichotomy between the common sense of the public and the dicta of the political establishment. The key to understanding this dichotomy and to explaining when structural corruption becomes "scandalous" lies in the persistence of the elite character of Japanese politics.[32]

Despite the democratic reforms of postwar Japan and the catering to special interests and local constituencies by Japanese politicians, national politics in Japan remains to an extraordinary extent the private preserve of the professional political establishment. The public political parties are widely viewed as private households, controlled by and functioning on behalf of their members or special constituencies. The Japan Socialist Party is seen as a captive of public employee unions, the Democratic Socialist Party of private sector unions and their corporate management, Komeito of Sokagakkai, and the Japan Communist Party of its own top leadership. This does not mean that the opposition parties collectively fail to represent a broad spectrum of public interests. They do, but the public feels very much like outsiders in relation to the household matters of these parties. The LDP, of course, has a legitimate claim to being a catch-all party, but this does not negate its elitist character. National leadership appears to be a product of in-house LDP factional maneuvering rather than a response to public concerns. The persistence, and even growth, of Tanaka's power within the LDP in the years after the Lockheed incident is a case in point. Moreover, the very high cost of politics has narrowed the party's pool of candidates, which is increasingly filled by persons from established political families.

The Japanese public retains a good deal of cynicism regarding politics and politicians as a result of the high cost of politics, the closed character of the parties, and the backstage deals that set so much of national policy before public deliberations in the National Diet begin. Citizens are further disengaged from direct participation in national election campaigns, since stringent formal regulations on campaign activities combined with the near-universal expenditure of funds in excess of the legal limits make such involvement by amateurs a risky business. The public's cynicism about politicians and their disengagement from national politics constitutes one of the highest costs of the murky realm of political fund-raising to Japanese democracy. Another cost to democracy is the persistence of a huge gap between the world of the political professionals (politicians, bureaucrats, interest group leaders, and political reporters) and that of the public. In the former world, with its cut-throat competition for power, many politicians act on the understanding that anything not explicitly prohibited by law is permissible. In other words, accountability to the common sense notions or moral code of the public is minimized by the gap that separates political professionals from the public.[33] Tanaka's belief in his innocence was premised on the existence of this gap and on the assumption that he had done nothing that other politicians would not have also done if given the chance. Wherein was he mistaken? In other words, what made the Lockheed incident scandalous to the public rather than just another episode of "structural corruption," removed from public scrutiny and judgment?

The difference between routine collusive backstage dealings, in other words, "structural corruption," and scandalous behavior, I believe, can be understood by asking the question, "By whom was it done, for whom, and with what result for the public?" It should be noted that personal corruption, while far from rare in Japan, is dealt with harshly. "Dishonest graft," wherein political professionals are personally enriched at the public's expense, when exposed, can result in the end of a political or bureaucratic career. The Japanese are particularly intolerant of dishonesty of this sort among their meritocratic public bureaucracy.

In contrast, the Japanese public has been very tolerant of influence-peddling by its politicians, in effect by the sale of access to policymaking processes within the political establishment. Collusive activity in awarding government contracts in Japan is akin to what George Washington Plunkitt of Tammany Hall called "honest graft," which involves financial benefits for the recipients without direct cost to the public. As James Q. Wilson remarked about American politics, one might say of Japan, "that there has been a rather sharp decline in the amount of dishonest graft over the last 30 or 40 years, but probably much less decline in the amount of honest graft."[34] The persistence of "honest graft" in Japan is reinforced by the society's emphasis on preparing the groundwork (*nemawashi* or "binding the roots") for any transaction by the use of personal connections to arrive at a deal before a formal decision is made or announced.

Influence-peddling by politicians is tolerated and even expected within certain bounds by the Japanese public for additional reasons as well. Given the strength of the Japanese state, the pervasiveness of the bureaucracy, and the insulation and even secretiveness of government deliberations on policy prior to the formal legislative process, the access provided by politicians to the early formative stages of this process is a service highly valued by societal interests of all sorts. Japanese politics in the 1960s and 1970s developed a strongly distributive thrust when a multitude of interest groups learned how to use politicians as intermediaries to tap the resources at the hands of government. It was one of the greatest strengths of Tanaka and many of his conservative colleagues that their influence-peddling served redistributive goals, closing the regional gap in well-being and shoring up weak sectors of the economy from agriculture to retailing. Insofar as Japanese democracy puts less of an emphasis on participation and more on equality of well-being and equal treatment at the hands of the state, representation of the sort provided by Tanaka, despite his mode of staying "just on the inside edges of the law," has been accepted and rewarded by the Japanese public. Indeed, even when most of Tanaka's supporters in Niigata's Second District realized that he had stepped over the bounds of legality in the Lockheed incident, they forgave him. As one supporter put it, "If the father had not been a thief, we children would have died."[35] The rest of the country, however, were not his children and judged him more harshly.

In addition to its redistributive thrust per se, there is no doubt that the collusive activity of businessmen and conservative politicians and the special access that the latter provide to the bureaucracy have been a contributing factor to the building of social infrastructure and the conduct of industrial policy, both of which have had enormous benefits for the population more generally. One author distinguishes between the graft involved in capital formation and that involved in operating economies, arguing that the former is functional and perhaps necessary for national development, while the latter is detrimental in character.[36] The distinction is arguable, since trade-offs exist between rapid national economic development per se and the slower achievement of developmental goals through means that reinforce other values, including democratic participation and a different mix of public policies. Nevertheless, insofar as the distinction is accepted, it is clear that Japan's "structural corruption" has been a positive force for capital formation without introducing undue inefficiencies into the system.

Contrary to the view of William Safire and many others, the Lockheed incident was not just another case of endemic corruption. The incident was scandalous to the public because it violated the commonsense view in several fundamental ways. Consider the issue of "by whom" it was done. One of the key actors, whose name emerged in the very first exposure of the Church Committee, was Yoshio Kodama. His prominence in the incident raised bad memories of prewar times when right-wing extremists had an inordinate and disastrous influence on national policy. Do extremists and underworld elements still have entrée into the highest circles of national decision making? Such a situation, once exposed, could not be tolerated by the public.

Tanaka's link to Kodama was detrimental in itself; but the fact that he took the actions he did as prime minister was a further indictment. As the most prominent public figure in the country and its most visible leader abroad, the prime minister is expected to act in an exemplary way, more like a statesman than an ordinary politician. As one of Japan's most astute political analysts has expressed it, "The common sense of the public is not so anachronistic as to expect from a statesman the 'well and fence' of the past. But 'to refrain from putting your shoes back on in the melon field and to refrain from adjusting the crown under the plum trees'" is a commonsense virtue.[37] In other words, a politician need not be so clean as to sell all his personal assets and be left with only a well and a fence, but he should be wise enough to avoid suspicious behavior. Tanaka, of course, had already violated that maxim in the financial dealings that had led to his forced resignation in 1974. The public was ready to believe the worst regarding his actions when the Lockheed incident broke.

The scandal was exacerbated greatly by the "for whom" part of our question. Clearly, the action was for the benefit of Lockheed, a foreign company, and not for the good of Japanese society. Indeed, it was the worse incident of Japanese officials taking foreign bribes since the imperial navy succumbed to the solicitation of the German electric giant Siemens in 1914. Moreover, the related decision on the purchase of Lockheed's P–3c Orions rather than the domestic production of the next generation of antisubmarine warfare aircraft raised the further issue of who was making decisions regarding Japanese security matters. Needless to say, it was also an embarrassment to see how well foreign enterprises seemed to be able to pull the right strings to get the Japanese political system to work for them. Finally, the Lockheed incident was a case in which it was difficult to argue that there was any substantially beneficial result for the Japanese public, except insofar as satisfying President Richard Nixon's desire to support Lockheed might alleviate American pressure on Japan in other policy areas.

Conclusion

The Lockheed case illustrates the fact that Japanese liberal democracy, like any other, can draw lines in regard to what behavior constitutes a threat to legitimate government and what is tolerable, if not entirely desirable, behavior by the political establishment. Much of what Americans see as illegitimate conflicts of interest and collusion are tolerated in Japan. And there is a certain ambiguity as to what constitutes a bribe in a society in which gift-giving and reciprocity are customary. Clear violations of the law, personal enrichment through dishonest behavior, bureaucratic corruption, and unseemly behavior by national leaders, however, are seen by the public as detrimental to legitimate government.

It is important to reiterate, however, that the behavior of political professionals in Japan is often obscured by the one-party dominance of the government, by the related inadequate capacity of the national legislature to act as a check on much of what goes on behind the scenes, and by the ambivalence of the mass media toward upsetting the equilibrium of Japanese politics. The situation is exacerbated by the high cost of politics in Japan, which deepens public cynicism and perpetuates a gap between the world of politics and that of the ordinary people.

Nevertheless, the Lockheed scandal did reveal many bright notes for Japanese liberal democracy. The independence of the law enforcement agencies and the courts was exemplary. They were supported, of course, by the statesmanlike behavior of Justice Minister Inaba and Prime Minister Miki, who set a standard that the public may demand of future leaders. The potential contribution of the mass media as a guardian of public standards of legitimate government also was thrown into greater relief by the incidents of the mid-1970s involving Tanaka.

Finally, Tanaka's career must be viewed in a more positive light as well. Many of Tanaka's initiatives as a politician served to broaden the range of beneficiaries of government action, thereby contributing to a certain equalization of Japanese society that has been an important part of postwar democracy. His bold policy leadership vis-à-vis the bureaucracy demonstrated to other politicians and interest groups how they too could play a more active role in shaping public policy. There is a discernable shift among Liberal Democratic Party politicians from being mere intermediaries to becoming policy experts and innovators. There is no doubt that Tanaka has played an important role in bringing about a more pluralistic political system that is both segmented and inclusionary in character. It is no wonder that despite his faults he remains a folk hero in Japan.

NOTES

1. For an excellent interpretative essay on Kakuei Tanaka and the Lockheed scandal, see Chalmers Johnson. "Tanaka Kakuei, Structural Corruption, and the Advent of Machine Politics in Japan," *Journal of Japanese Studies* 12, no. 1 (1986): 1–28. Lockheed's worldwide efforts to sell its planes are detailed in David Boulton. *The Grease Machine* (New York: Harper and Row, 1978); and foreign corrupt practices of American multinationals, including Lockheed, are analyzed well in John T. Noonan, Jr., *Bribes* (New York: Macmillan, 1984), pp. 652–80.

2. Boulton, *The Grease Machine*, p. 137.

3. The events of the scandal are reconstructed here from contemporary accounts in the *Asahi shimbun* and the *New York Times* and Tetsuro Murobushi, *Oshoku no kozo* (The Structure of Corruption) (Tokyo: Iwanami Shoten, 1981), pp. 113–80. They have been

checked against Iwanami Shoten, *Kindai nihon sogo nempyo, Dai-ni ban* (A Comprehensive Chronology of Modern Japan) (Tokyo: Iwanami Shoten, 1984).

4. Johnson, "Tanaka Kakuei," p. 15.

5. For excellent detailed analyses of "structural corruption," see Tetsuro Murobushi, *Oshoku no kozo* (The Structure of Corruption), and Takashi Tachibana, *Tanaka Kakuei kenkyu: Zenkiroku* (Research on Kakuei Tanaka: A Complete Report) (Tokyo: Kodansha, 1982), volumes 1 and 2.

6. James Q. Wilson, "Corruption is Not Always Scandalous," in *Theft of the City: Readings on Corruption in Urban America,* ed. John A. Gardiner and David J. Olsen (Bloomington, Indiana: Indiana University Press, 1974), p. 30.

7. An excellent brief analysis of the strength of official bureaucracy in Japan is Chalmers Johnson, "Japan: Who Governs? An Essay on Official Bureaucracy," *Journal of Japanese Studies* 2, no. 1 (Autumn 1975): 1–28. For a more detailed treatment, see Johnson's *MITI and the Japanese Miracle* (Stanford: Stanford University Press, 1982).

8. Robert J. Smith, *Japanese Society: Tradition, Self and the Social Order* (Cambridge: Cambridge University Press, 1983), pp. 9–36.

9. Terry E. MacDougall, "Political Opposition and Local Government in Japan," (Ph.D. dissertation, Yale University, 1975), pp. 56–63.

10. This point is developed well in Johnson, "Tanaka Kakuei."

11. The classic and still useful study of *Koenkai* is Gerald L. Curtis, *Election Campaigning Japanese Style* (New York: Columbia University Press, 1971).

12. For a useful analysis of conservative brokerage politics in Japan, see Kent E. Calder, "Kanryo vs. Shomin: Contrasting Dynamics of Conservative Leadership in Postwar Japan," in *Political Leadership in Contemporary Japan,* ed. Terry E. MacDougall (Ann Arbor, Michigan: Michigan Papers in Japanese Studies, 1982), pp. 1–28.

13. On Kodama, see Boulton, *The Grease Machine,* pp. 45–61 and 239–52, and Johnson, "Tanaka Kakuei." For a systematic analysis of the role of the "fixer" in Japanese politics, see Richard Samuels, "Power Behind the Throne," in *Political Leadership in Contemporary Japan,* ed. Terry E. MacDougall, pp. 127–44.

14. The first decade of postwar Japanese politics, including the conservative merger, is presented in a richly textured analysis in Junnosuke Masumi, *Postwar Politics in Japan, 1945–1955* (Berkeley and Los Angeles: University of California, Center for Japanese Studies, 1988).

15. Asahi Shimbun, *Nihonjin no seiji ishiki: Asahi shimbun seiron chosa no 30-nen* (The Political Consciousness of Japanese: 30 Years of Asahi Shimbun Public Opinion Polls) (Tokyo: Asahi Shimbun, 1976).

16. Calder, "Kanryo vs. Shomin," pp. 7–8.

17. Terry E. MacDougall, "Asukata Ichio and Some Dilemmas of Socialist Leadership in Japan," in MacDougall, *Political Leadership in Contemporary Japan,* pp. 51–91.

18. Terry E. MacDougall, *Politics and Policy in Urban Japan* (New Haven: Yale University Press, forthcoming) discusses the evolution of postwar Japanese local politics and local-center political relations in detail.

19. Among the many useful studies of Tanaka's constituency-based politics, a particularly outstanding one is Masayuki Fukuoka, *Nihon no seiji fudo: Niigata san-ku ni miru seiji no genkei* (Japanese Political Climate: The Basis of Japanese Politics As Seen in the Third District of Niigata) (Tokyo: Gakuyo shobo, 1975).

20. This description of Tanaka's early years is based largely on Fukuoka, *Nihon no seiji fudo,* pp. 11–64. For a very useful account of Tanaka's career in English, see Calder, "Kanryo vs. Shomin" and also Johnson, "Tanaka Kakuei."

21. An analysis of the reasons for the dominance of the Yoshida School is Terry E. MacDougall, "Yoshida Shigeru and the Japanese Transition to Liberal Democracy," *International Political Science Review* 9, no. 1 (1988): 55–69.

22. For a brief English-language analysis of early postwar political scandals, see Masumi, *Postwar Politics in Japan, 1945–1955,* pp. 158–61 and 297–99. A more detailed analysis is contained in Muroboshi, *Oshoku no kozo,* pp. 1–114.

23. Tachibana, *Tanaka Kakuei kenkyu: Zenkiroku*, vol. I, p. 75 chart.

24. Bradley M. Richardson and Scott C. Flanagan, *Politics in Japan* (Boston: Little, Brown and Company, 1984), p. 183.

25. Fukuoka, *Nihon no seiji fudo*, pp. 43–52.

26. Seizaburo Sato and Tetsuhisa Matsuzaki, *Jiminto seiken* (Liberal Democratic Party Government) (Tokyo: Chuo Koron-sha, 1986).

27. Ronald J. Hrebenar, "The Money Base of Japanese Politics," in *The Japanese Party System*, ed. Ronald J. Hrebenar (Boulder, Colo.: Westview Press, 1986), pp. 55–79 and Takayoshi Miyakawa, ed., *Seiji handobukku '86 Oct* (Political Handbook, October 1986) (Tokyo: Seiji koho senta, 1986), p. 178.

28. For the most detailed accounting of these methods, see Tachibana, *Tanaka Kakuei kenkyu: Zenkiroku*, Vol. 1.

29. James Huffman, "The Idiom of Contemporary Japan XI," *The Japan Interpreter* 9, no. 4 (Spring 1975) : 505–15.

30. Hans H. Baerwald, "Japan: 'Black Mist' and Pre-electioneering," *Asian Survey* 7, no. 1 (1967) : 31–39.

31. Michael Blaker, *Japan at the Polls: The House of Councillors Election of 1974* (Washington, D.C.: American Enterprise Institute, 1976).

32. On the elite character of Japanese politics, see Richardson and Flanagan, *Politics in Japan*, pp. 162–216, 265–89.

33. On this gap between political professionals and the public, see also Jun-ichi Kyogoku, "The Common Sense of the Public and of the Political Establishment," *Japan Echo* 2, no. 1 (1975) : 13–24.

34. James Q. Wilson, "Corruption is Not Always Scandalous," p. 32.

35. As quoted in Richardson and Flanagan, *Politics in Japan*, p. 183.

36. James Q. Wilson, "Corruption is Not Always Scandalous," pp. 32–33.

37. Jun-ichi Kyogoku, "The Common Sense of the Public," pp. 20–21.

9 • Israel: The Lavon Affair

MITCHELL COHEN

It began but five years after Israel's successful, though bloody war of independence and it was a murky, intricate business. "Could a playwright have written a plot more complicated than this one was in real life?" asked the Jewish state's attorney-general in its final stages.[1] The "Lavon Affair" shook the foundations of the Israeli political system, leaving virtually no part of it untouched.

Widely known in Hebrew simply as *Ha-Parashah* (The Affair), it set Israel's founding father and first prime minister, David Ben-Gurion, against Pinhas Lavon, a man once considered his possible successor, and it resulted in an unbecoming decline in the former's political career and the abrupt end to that of the latter. The long-term consequences of the affair, which itself went through three stages beginning in 1954 and finally coming to a close in 1965, remain to the present day; the episode was symptomatic of a reshaping process then underway within the Israeli political world, and it involved political figures still prominent today.

The First Stage: A "Security Mishap"

In July 1954 a group of Egyptian Jews were arrested following ineffective attempts by them to sabotage British and American institutions in Cairo and Alexandria.[2] Seized as well were Israeli agents who were accused of recruiting them. This operation—in Israeli parlance *Esek ha-Bish*, the "Security Mishap"— apparently was designed to complicate Egyptian relations with the West by making it appear as if Egyptian militants had committed the acts.

The Middle East of the early 1950s provided the backdrop to these events. Britain, after years of tension with Egyptian nationalism, was negotiating with-

230

drawal from the Suez Canal Zone; the United States was pressing for an anti-Soviet alliance of Middle Eastern states, excluding Israel (whose existence was rejected by the Arab allies sought by Washington); and Egyptian leader Gamal Abdel Nasser was asserting his personal authority, two years after having led a successful military coup against King Farouq. Immediately following the fall of the Egyptian monarchy, Ben-Gurion, then Israel's premier and defense minister, declared before the Knesset (Israel's parliament) that his country desired "a free, independent, and progressive Egypt." Israel's "good-will," he asserted, was demonstrated by its unwillingness "to exploit Egypt's difficulty [with Britain] in order to attack her or take revenge upon her, as she did to us when our State was established."[3] Egypt had attacked Israel after Britain left Palestine and an independent Jewish state was declared in 1948. After its defeat, Cairo, in tandem with all its Arab allies, refused to sign a peace treaty. Relations between the two neighboring countries were marked by ongoing border tensions, including an Egyptian blockade of Israeli shipping through the Suez Canal (in defiance of United Nations Security Council resolutions and the clear intent of the 1949 armistice agreements), and restrictions on shipping to the Jewish state through the Gulf of Aqaba (which effectively blockaded Israel's port of Eilat). In these circumstances someone in the Israeli defense establishment ordered the activation of "Unit 131" in Egypt.

Unit 131 was part of an Israeli intelligence network established in 1948 solely for use in wartime. At the time of the "Mishap" it was under the authority of Aman, the Israel Defense Forces (IDF) intelligence branch. The Egyptian Jews in it, activists in Zionist youth movements, went into action on instructions from Avry Elad, an Israeli agent who had arrived in Cairo earlier in 1954 and who was the sole participant not arrested. The rest of the "Zionist Spy Ring" was tried in Cairo in December. It was a particularly tense moment for the Egyptian regime: Nasser's successful negotiations for British withdrawal from the Suez Canal (chastised by his foes as too concessive), his fierce repression of the fundamentalist Moslem Brotherhood after its attempt to assassinate him in October, and his November ousting of Mohammed Neguib, the popular general who had been the figurehead president since the revolution, all led to protests against the young Egyptian leader in parts of the Arab world. Thus while neither Cairo nor Jerusalem initially made much of what the Egyptians called "the Zionist plotters," by the time of the trial, the atmosphere and the circumstances had changed. The Israeli media denounced the events in Cairo as a show trial. In January six of the prisoners were given lengthy prison terms, two were acquitted, and two were sentenced to death. Nasser apparently was unmoved by appeals from Eisenhower, Nehru, and the pope, as well as by a secret exchange in which Moshe Sharett, who had been Israeli prime minister and foreign minister since late 1953, declared that "Many of us admire your brave idealism and tenacity of purpose and wish you the fullest success in attaining the emancipation of the Land of the Nile from the last vestiges of foreign domination and the initiation for the masses of the people of an era of social regeneration and economic welfare."[4] Moshe Marzouk, a Cairo physician, and Samuel Azaar of Alexandria were executed on 31 January 1955.

Soon afterward the defense minister of Israel, Pinhas Lavon, resigned explaining that this was due to a dispute with the prime minister over reorganizing the defense apparatus. There was no hint of any linkage to the Cairo events. However, behind closed government doors a furious dispute was taking place: Who gave the order for the Egyptian operation? The "Mishap" was clearly a political action because it aimed to disrupt international relations, but Sharett learned of its details only in October 1954, some three months after the fact.[5] Lavon vigorously denied having given the order, claiming that it was done by Military Intelligence Chief Benyamin Gibli, who in turn blamed Lavon.

The intricate tale of intrigue that soon unfolded, and which would have bemused Joseph Conrad or John Le Carré, must be understood against the broader background of developments in Israeli politics. David Ben-Gurion, the man who read Israel's declaration of independence in 1948, who led the country in its ensuing "War of Liberation," and who served, simultaneously, as first prime minister and defense minister, announced in late 1953 that he would temporarily retire to Sde Boker, a kibbutz in the Negev desert. However, the "Old Man," as he was known, was displeased that his party, the ruling social democratic party Mapai ("Israel Workers' Party"), designated his foreign minister to replace him. Sharett was a man of intelligence and talent, but he was not a commanding leader and the two men had serious policy differences. Briefly, Ben-Gurion believed in forceful, "activist" foreign and defense policies in response to Arab hostility, and he was skeptical about Sharett's belief in the possibility of reconciliation and his consequent emphasis on diplomacy. Ben-Gurion sought to sustain his policies by surrounding Sharett with Lavon as defense minister and two allied Ben-Gurion protégés, Moshe Dayan and Shimon Peres as, respectively, IDF chief of staff and director-general of the Defense Ministry.

The interpersonal dynamics and competition among these men virtually guaranteed difficulties. Lavon was a rising figure in the Labor movement, which had dominated Israeli (and before 1948 Zionist) politics since the early 1930s. A charismatic orator with an impressive intellect, he came to the defense ministry as a dove turned hawk. Desirous of proving his mettle in security affairs, Lavon inevitably found himself at odds with the more moderate and ever cautious Sharett. The new defense minister was seen by some as unpredictable, and his appointment to what was viewed as the second most important position in the government was opposed by several leading figures in his party, Mapai, as well as by the head of the Mossad (Israel's foreign intelligence service). Dayan and Peres were talented, politically ambitious young men who wanted the tenures of Sharett and Lavon to be as brief as possible. Sharett, Lavon, and the Dayan-Peres team composed what has been appropriately characterized as a "disturbed hierarchy" on virtually all levels.[6] In addition, Military Intelligence Chief Gibli had a checkered past because of his role in the "Tobianski affair" during the 1948 war. Then a senior intelligence officer, he had been a central actor in the summary trial and execution of an Israeli on charges of spying for Britain. Afterward he denied responsibility and his superior received the blame.[7]

Sharett established a secret commission to study the "Security Mishap" that was composed of two highly respected figures, former IDF Chief of Staff Yaakov Dori and Supreme Court Justice Itshak Olshan. The proceedings increasingly irritated Lavon and both Dayan (who was on a mission outside of Israel at the time of the "Mishap") and Peres gave what has been called "vindictive testimonies" against Lavon. Peres, theoretically Lavon's subordinate, sought to turn the hearing "from a challenge to the army intelligence division's competence and responsibility . . . into Lavon's trial."[8] Nonetheless, in the end the verdict of the Olshan-Dori Committee was inconclusive:

> To sum up, we regret that we are unable to reply to the questions put to us by the Prime Minister (Mr. M. Sharett). We are unable to say anything except that we have not been convinced beyond a reasonable doubt that the "Senior Officer" [Gibli] did not receive orders from the Minister of Defense; at the same time we are not certain that the Minister of Defense (Mr. P. Lavon) indeed gave the orders ascribed to him.[9]

With the backing of Ben-Gurion, who had been enraged when informed of the "Mishap," the Mapai leadership decided that Lavon would have to resign. It was compelled to reconsider after he threatened to make the matter public. He in turn demanded the ouster of Peres and Gibli and the restructuring of civil-military affairs so as to reinforce civilian authority over military affairs. This was refused by Sharett, who, had he accepted, would have faced the resignation of several leading military figures, apparently including Dayan. Lavon then resigned and Ben-Gurion returned as defense minister under Sharett, and he transferred Gibli elsewhere. In July 1955 Ben-Gurion replaced Sharett as prime minister, and the latter remained as foreign minister until he resigned in July 1956 in a policy dispute with Ben-Gurion. He was succeeded by Golda Meir, a Ben-Gurion stalwart, and Lavon was pacified later by his appointment as secretary-general of the Histadrut, Israel's powerful trade union federation.

These developments all occurred behind closed doors and would not have become a *cause célèbre*, but for the fact that Israeli intelligence discovered in 1957 that Avry Elad, the only agent who had escaped from Egypt and who was now in West Germany, happened to be friendly with the Egyptian military attaché in Bonn, who was also an intelligence agent and who just happened to have been one of the investigators at the Cairo trial. Elad was recalled to Israel, arrested, and tried secretly. Although it was not proven that he was a double agent, he was sentenced to a decade in prison for other security-related offenses. In the course of his trial, Elad declared that he had perjured himself at the Olshan-Dori Committee and had manufactured evidence at the suggestion of Gibli's assistant. (This led to Gibli's eventual dismissal). By 1960 Lavon, having received additional indications that forgeries had been used in 1955, now went to the prime minister, Ben-Gurion, and requested exoneration for the "Security Mishap." What had been a secret and internal government matter focusing on responsibility for a military/intelligence failure and confined to a small circle of officials rapidly turned into a very public political storm.

Stage Two: The Affair Goes Public

When Lavon asked to be cleared, Mapai was in the strongest position in its history, having won its largest plurality in the 1959 national elections. There were, however, serious strains within the party. A struggle for succession was underway; Ben-Gurion, though vigorous in his mid-70s, was beginning to show signs of tiring. Throughout the late 1950s he had championed the Tseirim (Young Guard) of Mapai, whose most prominent members were Lavon's foes Dayan and Peres. Both of them entered the Knesset in 1959 and became, respectively, agriculture minister and deputy defense minister. The Tseirim, who were in fact close to middle age by then, were in constant conflict with the aging "Veterans" of Mapai such as Finance Minister Levi Eshkol, Foreign Minister Golda Meir, Education Minister Zalman Aran, Commerce and Industry Minister Pinhas Sapir, and the Tel Aviv–based Mapai party machine known as the Gush (the Bloc). The premier's qualities as a national leader and personal fidelity to him among the various individuals and groupings in Mapai kept their rivalries within controllable bounds most of the time. The reopening of the Lavon Affair changed this.

Ben-Gurion responded to Lavon's demand for exoneration by insisting on his own neutrality. Not having accused Lavon, the premier averred that he couldn't clear him, and that to do so would be to incriminate others (Gibli in particular) without due process. "I am not an investigator or a judge," he declared.[10] The dissatisfied Lavon presented his case before the Knesset Security and Foreign Affairs Committee in early October 1960. In his testimony he insisted that he had been framed and that Dayan and Peres, though not involved in the mishap per se, had exploited it maliciously to undermine him. When this was leaked to the press, the "Lavon affair," as it now quickly became known, was transformed into the dominant issue of Israeli domestic politics. However, because of military censorship the details of the Cairo fiasco and the names of many of its chief actors were not published. Reading the daily newspapers, Israelis discovered that a "Security Mishap" had occurred, that Lavon felt he had incurred blame for it in a fraudulent manner, and that a variety of important figures (who were referred to by assorted euphemisms) were involved. "A storm has risen in Israel," stated former Premier Sharett, "a storm now raging in the press and the length and breadth of Israel's public life. What is now underway is not a process of inquiry, but a scandal factory."[11]

Lavon went on the public offensive, demanding rehabilitation, attacking Dayan and Peres, and insinuating that there had been a conspiracy against him in the top ranks of the military. Ben-Gurion, father of the army and mentor of Dayan and Peres, became increasingly restive and seemed to take Lavon's criticisms of the military personally. And as the premier's anger at Lavon grew, so too did his partisanship. "The Prime Minister deserves admiration for his deep feeling of responsibility for the good name of the army," declared one of the country's most prominent historians, Jacob L. Talmon, in perhaps the most trenchant and searing critique written during the affair. "However, it is very dangerous when someone in these circumstances presents a "the-army-and-I-are-the-same, or I am Defense-complex such as Louis XIV's 'L'Etat, c'est moi.'"[12] In short, Ben Gurion was accused of confusing the public and private realms, and this helped to undermine his authority. He began to lose his public image as the national leader above the fray, and he seemed to be waging a vendetta against Lavon. In the meantime, the Histadrut secretary general gained in public sympathy, although he became more and more shrill in his attacks on Ben-Gurion.

A "Committee of Seven" cabinet members was established to find a path out of the labyrinth, and while it was meeting in November and December 1960 the state attorney-general revealed that new evidence of alleged forgeries had been uncovered. The committee, whose moving spirit was Finance Minister Eshkol,[13] concluded that "on the basis of the material at its disposal," Lavon "did not give the direct order for the 1954 Security Mishap." It added that there was no need for further investigation.[14] Most of Mapai's leadership was relieved by this declaration because, fearful of a party split, it wanted to close the already prolonged and messy affair as quickly as possible. The cabinet accepted the Committee of Seven's report, but Ben-Gurion rejected it on the grounds that the committee was authorized only to make decisions on how to proceed and not to make judgments. In clearing Lavon, Ben-Gurion reiterated, it implied that someone else was guilty. In his view, personal, legal, and other issues were being confused and the only way to close the affair was by means of a duly constituted judicial investigation.

Lavon and his supporters rejected this suggestion, arguing that the events of 1955 were political, not legal, in character. He pointed out to the Mapai Central Committee in January 1961 that following the massacre of Israeli Arabs in the village of Kafr Qasim (during the 1956 war) a ministerial committee investigated and exonerated the IDF General Staff.[15] Why was this procedure valid then and not now, he queried? A strictly legal inquiry into a murder, he pointed out, can result in the release of a murderer due to a technical insufficiency of evidence. A public investigation, on the other hand, of something like the affair was more likely to reach a truthful and fair result. The conclusions of the Committee of Seven therefore ought to be accepted, he argued.[16] In the meantime, public pressures mounted and a group of distinguished intellectuals, organized by Hebrew University philosopher Natan Rotenstreich, declared publicly that Ben-Gurion's actions and specifically his attempt to preempt the cabinet's acceptance of the Committee of Seven's conclusions were a threat to democracy.

Ben-Gurion had not only rejected the Committee of Seven, but he tendered his resignation and made it clear to Mapai that it had to choose: Lavon or him. For the party leadership the choice was obvious because the Founding Father, whatever his foibles, was more important than Lavon. Moreover, the Histadrut secretary general's behavior, especially in his Knesset appearance and his attacks on the premier, displayed a disregard of party needs. Lavon was censured by the party central committee and, in a maneuver engineered by Eshkol, he was dismissed from his position at the Histadrut.

Although Ben-Gurion was politically victorious, he had been badly compromised. Having protested his principled advocacy of a judicial inquiry (which Mapai did not endorse) and having insisted that democratic process and the rule of law were the issues, his defeat of Lavon appeared to be a settling of scores through crude power politics. Observed Talmon,

Pinhas Lavon can hardly be classed among the saints, but the minute he was brought up before the forum of Mapai to account for his behavior in the "Affair" (while Mr. Ben-Gurion was not required to give any accounting) he became a symbol of the struggle for justice, decency, and liberal ideals. It is the way of History, with her fondness for Mephistophelian irony, to choose as symbols of higher values men who are not exactly charming.[17]

The "Old Man" remained premier, but relations with his party colleagues, most significantly the Veterans, were severely strained. Also, severe damage had been done to his ties with Mapai's coalition partners, some of whom now refused to rejoin a government headed by him. Mapai was compelled to call new elections and lost 10 percent of its vote. Ben-Gurion remained in office until the summer of 1963 when, discouraged and tired, he resigned and was replaced by Eshkol. But the affair was not yet over.

Stage 3: A Final Round

With Ben-Gurion's exit from the premiership (he retained his seat in parliament), Mapai and Israeli politics were dominated by the Veterans, specifically the new Premier and Defense Minister, Eshkol, and the Mapai "Troika" of Foreign Minister Golda Meir, Pinhas Sapir (Eshkol's successor as finance minister), and Education Minister Zalman Aran. Although the situation temporarily calmed, tensions remained between them and the Tseirim. Dayan and Peres felt isolated and on the defensive without their mentor. They resented, among other things, Eshkol's assumption of the defense portfolio along with the prime ministry, believing him less qualified than themselves. Eshkol, however, was loath to create circumstances akin to 1954–55 when the premier and the defense minister were rivals.[18] His judgment proved correct, as Dayan, capitalizing on his stature as the hero of the 1956 Sinai war, frequently criticized Eshkol's defense policies, although as agriculture minister this was hardly his public prerogative.

The Veterans sought to counterbalance their younger opponents through an electoral alignment—projected by some as the first step to a possible union—with the Ahdut ha-Avodah (Labor Unity) Party. Ahdut ha-Avodah was a left-wing nationalist force that had originated in a 1944 split in Mapai, and in its ranks were popular, dynamic figures such as Yigal Allon whom the Mapai Tseirim saw as future rivals for the nation's leadership in the event of a merger. The Veterans were decades older than Dayan and Peres and nature would eventually eliminate their rivalry. The same could not be said of Allon, who was, not incidentally, also a military hero (from the 1948 war).

The final phase of the affair was triggered by an attempt by Eshkol to reintegrate Lavon's followers, who had felt increasingly alienated from Mapai during Ben-Gurion's final period as premier, more fully into the party. From the beginning of the Affair, Eshkol doggedly sought to save his party from the morass enveloping it; hence in 1960–61 he was instrumental in the Committee of Seven's decisions; he opposed Ben-Gurion's call for a judicial inquiry, but he also engineered Lavon's ouster. Now he hoped to initiate a healing process. Lavon's backers were concentrated around the Min ha-Yesod (From the Foundation) group led by Rotenstreich. They published a journal of the same name, championed ideological reform within the party, and were preparing to renounce Mapai at a meeting at Lavon's Kibbutz Hulda when Eshkol sent them a reconciliatory letter in the spring of 1964. The decision to remove Lavon, Eshkol declared, was now just "so much history" and no longer had "any significance whatsoever today."[19]

This was sufficient to infuriate Ben-Gurion, who by then seems to have become convinced that Lavon, whom he referred to as "the hypocritical vulture" in his diaries, did give the infamous order.[20] Ben-Gurion insisted that Eshkol had no authority to reverse a party decision and that Gibli had never been able to defend himself. Eshkol, defending his "Hulda Letter" before the Mapai Secretariat, declared at once that he did not regret having proposed Lavon's ouster in 1961, and that his letter to Min ha-Yesod was sent "in the name of Levi Eshkol and on behalf of a large number of comrades—including a considerable section of the Party secretariat, but not on behalf of any official party forum and this was stated explicitly in the letter."[21] Ben-Gurion began a campaign to reopen the affair, demanding among other things, a Supreme

Court inquiry into the proceeding of the Committee of Seven. The latter, he was convinced, had engaged in "a miscarriage of justice" and this gave Israel's first premier "no peace since . . . the moral integrity of the supreme organs of the State" were, in his view, threatened in consequence.[22] Basing himself partly on research done by journalist Hagai Eshed, an ardent supporter of his, and two lawyers he had engaged to conduct an investigation while he was still defense minister, Ben-Gurion went to the justice minister and the state attorney-general in the fall of 1964 with his demands and evidence. The minister,[23] while rejecting an investigation of the Committee of Seven, thought the material pertaining to 1954 merited reexamination. Since Eshkol was the moving spirit behind the Committee of Seven, Ben-Gurion's maneuvering constituted a direct threat to the premier; in any event Eshkol adamantly opposed reopening the Pandora's box. In December he made use of a political weapon Ben-Gurion himself had oftentimes employed with great effect as prime minister. Eshkol resigned. His aim was clearly to quash the entire business and his maneuver succeeded: Mapai rallied to him, he reconstituted the government, and the affair was not officially reopened. In the meantime he found himself endlessly assailed in public by Ben-Gurion, who openly questioned his competence as premier.

It was at the Tenth Mapai Conference in early 1965 that matters came to a final head. Ben-Gurion sought to commit Mapai to a judicial inquiry and was rebuffed, although he attained some 40 percent support among delegates. Just as significantly, if not more so, Mapai voted for an electoral alignment with Ahdut ha-Avodah. Shortly thereafter Ben-Gurion announced that he would form his own list, Rafi (the Israel Workers' List), to contest the upcoming Knesset elections. This led to a split in the Tseirim, with Peres and a more reluctant Dayan among others following Ben-Gurion, while others remained loyal to Eshkol. The Ben-Gurion group was expelled from Mapai by a party tribunal, and Rafi fared poorly in the 1965 elections, obtaining a mere 7.9 percent of the national vote after a particularly vicious campaign. Ben-Gurion entered the political wilderness and his weak party could not press its views on the victorious Mapai. Of Israel's first premier one observer wondered, "How could Churchillian greatness suddenly appear in the guise of provincial pettiness, vindictiveness, and rancor?"[24]

The Lavon affair was finally over. Normalcy was reestablished, at least temporarily, but with two key actors—Ben-Gurion and Lavon—gone from stage center. In 1968 Mapai, Ahdut ha-Avodah, and Rafi amalgamated into the Israel Labor Party under Eshkol's leadership. Peres and Dayan joined (the former becoming its chairman in 1977), but the obstinate Ben-Gurion refused, forming his own "State List." He finally retired two years later and died in 1973.

The Israeli Political World and the Lavon Affair

Three key interrelated factors structured the Israeli political universe at the time of the Lavon affair: the country's defense problems, its parliamentary system, and the role of Mapai as the dominant political party. Israel is a self-consciously Jewish state that was established under conditions of siege following a century of intense anti-Semitism, which culminated in the Nazi slaughter of six million Jews. The Zionist movement, founded in the late nineteenth century, sought to respond to two thousand years of persecution by establishing a Jewish nation-state in which a long scattered and often refugee people would be able to defend itself. Independence came after a struggle against a British colonial administration, Palestinian Arab nationalism (whose chief proponent, Haj Amin el-Husseini spent World War II in Germany propagandizing for Hitler), and the armies of the Arab League, whose aim in invading the newly proclaimed state in 1948 was declared by its Secretary-General Azzam Pasha to be "a war of extermination and a momentous massacre which will be spoken of like the Mongolian massacre and the Crusades."[25]

Consequently, self-defense became central to Israeli political culture and national priorities. The tension between Israel's democratic character and its state security requirements is captured in the role of Ben-Gurion himself; he was not only premier, but was wartime leader, first defense minister, and the key figure in shaping the new state's armed forces. Furthermore, with tens of thousands of Jewish immigrants from dozens of countries entering the Jewish state in its first years, and with virtually all Israelis subject to compulsory army service, the IDF became an essential means for social integration and education, and a mediator between the individual, the state, and the society. "Our army," declared Mapai, "must serve as a school of civic good-comradeship and fraternity, a bridge between different Jewries and different generations. It is, and must remain, a unique army because it will be . . . the instrument of a unique enterprise of pioneering and state-building."[26] While the IDF is under the authority of the democratically elected representatives of the Israeli public, as a result of Israel's perpetual state of siege and Ben-Gurion's dual role, it and the entire defense establishment tended to function in a highly autonomist fashion, lacking, as one scholar has aptly noted, adequate institutionalized mechanisms through which to mediate the political-civilian and military spheres properly.[27] The 1954 "Security Mishap" illustrated the problems inherent in this situation, especially since it occurred when, for the first time, the prime and defense ministers were not the same individual.

Israel is a parliamentary democracy with a unicameral 120-member legislature. Long before statehood was declared in 1948, both the Zionist movement and Palestinian Jews possessed well-developed party systems. Indeed, political parties were involved in virtually every aspect of life. They operated within firmly established nonsovereign representative bodies, most importantly the World Zionist Congress (founded by Theodor Herzl as the "legislature" of the Jewish national movement in 1897) and the Asefat ha-Nivharim (an "Elected Assembly" of Palestinian Jewry founded in 1920). Elections to both were by proportional representation and the competing party lists formed "cabinets" composed of coalitions of parties to run the respective executives of the two bodies, the "Zionist Executive" and the Vaad Leumi (National Council). The Israeli electoral system, one of proportional representation, carried over these traditions and structures. The electorate votes for candidate lists drawn up by the parties and a given party obtains Knesset seats proportionate to the vote it receives. The party's candidate for prime minister is commonly the party's leader and heads its list. (Israel also has a president, but he/she is a ceremonial head of state elected by the Knesset and without significant power). To form a government, majority support within the Knesset is generally required. No party has ever received a majority in polling, and in consequence, coalition cabinets became the inevitable pattern. The leading party formed the government and reserved the most important ministerial positions—usually considered the prime, defense, foreign, finance, and education ministries—for itself, giving various other portfolios to the smaller parties required to sustain a vote of confidence. Coalition politics—often fragile coalition politics—have been a fundamental fact of Israeli political life. Until the 1977 national elections, Mapai (and its successor, the Labor Party) was always the leading party, usually governing in a "historic alliance" with the National Religious Party. The latter supported Mapai-Labor foreign and domestic policies, and in returned received ministerial appointments and concessions of particular concern to its orthodox constituents.

Mapai was founded in 1930 and within five years it had established itself as the dominant force in Zionism, a role it was to play for four decades. It was, as many students of Israeli politics have noted, a "dominant party," as defined by Maurice Duverger's classic study, *Political Parties*. It never achieved an electoral majority (either before or after statehood), but it clearly outdistanced its rivals over an extended period of time, and its "doctrines, ideas, methods [and] style" came to be identified in the minds of most Israelis with the heroic epoch of state-building and the attainment of statehood. Its dominance rested in part on the public's belief in its dominance,[28] as well as on Mapai's great mastery of political and economic organization. In the public's mind, Mapai was not only the party of government, but a force that could be depended on to pursue the national interest responsibly. Mapai's leaders were the nation's "founding fathers," and the party's central role in the struggle for independence, combined with its dynamic leadership in the 1948 and 1956 Arab-Israeli wars, joined to give it an almost unassailable stature. Furthermore, Mapai was the majority party in the Histadrut, the major nongovernmental public institution in the state. The Histadrut (the Confederation of Labor), founded in 1920, was (and is) a vast and well-organized enterprise of the workers' public, extending far beyond trade unionism to ownership of close to a quarter of the country's economy (through cooperative Histadrut enterprises) and the maintenance of a vast social welfare system, ranging from a health care system (Kaput Holim—the Sick Fund) to labor exchanges. In the pre-state period, Mapai and the Labor movement projected the Histadrut itself as the embodiment of a future socialist Jewish state. Mapai's control of this organization was a formidable political and economic asset.

Finally, in contrast to Mapai's strength, there was the initial weakness of its right-wing opposition. The Herut (Freedom) Party, led by Menahem Begin (the group was later the central component of the Likud bloc), was the most vociferous antagonist of Mapai, but the group was isolated by virtue of its long history of extremism. In the 1930s Mapai successfully defeated Herut's predecessor organization in a fierce fight for control of the World Zionist Organization. Begin's animosity to Ben-Gurion, which was both personal and political, had been especially displayed in public during the 1952 debate over proposed Israeli acceptance of West German reparations for Nazi atrocities against the Jews. Opposing this as "blood money" and seeking to exploit the issue politically and to turn it into a public scandal, the Herut leader helped foment a riot in front of the Knesset. Begin denounced Ben-Gurion as "that maniac who is now Prime Minister," and went so far as to warn ominously that should reparations from Germany be accepted "anything is permitted."[29] Such behavior contributed to the effective marginalization of the far Right in Israeli politics. Ben-Gurion habitually declared that he would serve in any government save one with Begin or the Communists.

Herut eventually legitimized itself by the 1970s, but its political standing in the 1950s and 1960s precluded it from playing a significant role in the Lavon affair—although it could only gain from the damage done to Mapai's image. The more moderate right-wing General Zionist Party (later the major component of the Liberal Party) was also unable to challenge Mapai's dominance, but it was considered, in contrast to Herut, as part of the political mainstream and had served in governments at various junctures. Such was also the case with the spectrum of smaller left-wing and religious parties, some of whom were frequent Mapai coalition partners. Because of Mapai's dominance, the main scenes of action during the affair—the Defense establishment, Mapai itself, the Histadrut—tended to exclude the opposition and smaller parties, with one major exception, Lavon's appearance at the Knesset Foreign Affairs and Security Committee. The parliament itself played mostly a secondary role and the Supreme Court hardly played a role at all, although some of its justices participated in government-constituted inquiries.

The Impact of the Affair

In the *Zeitgeist* of pre–Lavon affair Israel, the country's leader, dominant party, and military were often identified with the national interest and with each other because of their historical roles. There had been past political crises, but none had revealed leaders and institutions to be so caught up in intrigues and political back-stabbing, let alone intrigues and back-stabbing justified as the selfless pursuit of the national good. In the affair, Ben-Gurion seemed to have lost perspective, the defense and intelligence establishments were tarnished, and Mapai seemed unable to control the affair itself or its own internal rivalries.

Three premiers—Sharett, Ben-Gurion, and Eshkol—were involved in different phases of the affair. The prime minister of Israel is considered *primus inter pares;* as in many other parliamentary systems, however, the more forceful the individual premier, the more *primus* he or she becomes. Ben-Gurion's primacy as prime and defense minister from 1948 to 1953 and again from 1955 to 1963 was firm, but Sharett did not enjoy the same supremacy. Their differing statures had significant consequences. As head of the government, Ben-Gurion devoted little attention to daily party affairs, entrusting these to his loyalists in the Mapai leadership and especially the Gush party machine in Tel Aviv. (A major exception to this rule was his active promotion of the political fortunes of the Tseirim). Mapai's dominance was stable and despite chronic coalition crises between 1949 (the convening of the first Knesset) and 1965, the Knesset generally completed or came close to completing its four-year terms. (National elections were held in 1949, 1951, 1955, 1959, 1961, 1965).

Israel's perpetual state of war, Ben-Gurion's preoccupation with security, and his policy disputes with foreign minister Sharett helped to make the defense ministry the second most prestigious position in the government. Consequently the defense ministry took on an essential role in determining foreign policy, and the foreign minister often found himself constrained in policymaking, if not reduced to simply carrying it out. Ben-Gurion left daily defense ministry affairs in Peres's hands. Although tensions between the defense and foreign ministries, dominated respectively by Ben-Gurionists and Sharettists, eased somewhat when the staunch Ben-Gurionist Golda Meir became foreign minister in 1956, a pattern of institutional rivalry remained and reinforced the autonomy of the defense ministry and the IDF.

With Sharett as premier and foreign minister, Lavon as defense minister, Dayan as IDF chief of staff, and Peres as defense ministry director-general, problems were virtually inevitable. Both Sharett and Lavon were angered by IDF actions taken without their foreknowledge; the premier found himself surrounded by ambitious opponents who disagreed with his policies and wanted his demise; Lavon found himself in conflict with Sharett, Dayan, Peres, and Gibli (although the latter was originally his ally); Dayan and Peres felt that Lavon circumvented them improperly in daily ministry and army affairs; Peres resented restrictions on the freedom of action he had enjoyed previously under Ben-Gurion. Furthermore, Gibli as head of military intelligence ought to have been responsible first to the chief of staff (Dayan), who in turn was responsible to the defense minister. (It should be recalled that Dayan was out of Israel at the time of the "Security Mishap"). Hence in its daily operations, the government of Israel, its defense ministry, and its military forces were plagued by serious conflicts of authority and subordination, and a profoundly "disturbed hierarchy" existed between and within both civilian and military branches of the government. Nevertheless, after the "Security Mishap," only personal and not institutional changes were made, i.e., Lavon was removed. (Lavon's proposal on the verge of his resignation in 1955 for a civilian-military council to oversee the defense sector was rejected by Sharett and also by Ben-Gurion after the latter returned to the defense ministry).

The establishment of Havereinu (Our Comrades) was a significant innovation of the Sharett premiership. Composed of the Mapai cabinet ministers and the Histadrut secretary-general, Havereinu served as a "nonconstitutional executive body" of Mapai, which met regularly to determine policy. Mapai was always a strongly centralized political apparatus and Havereinu came into being because Sharett recognized that he lacked Ben-Gurion's authority and needed more collegial support among the party leaders. Furthermore, the party Secretariat had been expanded early in 1954, and this necessitated a smaller body for decision making on a regular basis. The sensitive nature of the "Security Mishap" itself made the establishment of a smaller forum imperative, as the affair could not be discussed in broader party bodies.[30] Thus party and national leadership took on a much more collective character.

With Ben-Gurion's return as prime minister and defense minister, the antecedent pattern reasserted itself, although Ben-Gurion maintained Havereinu, (which temporarily became Sareinu [Our Ministers] in the early 1960s when Lavon, the Histadrut chief, was excluded during the affair). The precedent of more collegial leadership was, however, to damage Ben-Gurion in 1960–61, because by refusing the cabinet's endorsement of the Committee of Seven's report, and by resigning to force Lavon's ouster, he looked less like a national and party leader in a democracy and more like a man unable to distinguish between himself, his party, and the state and its defense. In his resignation statement in January 1961, he stated, "All my life I have accepted the decisions of the majority, in the party, in the Histadrut, and in the government. But in security affairs, as I see them, there is only one thing for me—my conscience."[31] During Ben-Gurion's final two years as premier, with his authority in decline, the collective strength of the Mapai Veterans, led by Eshkol and the "Troika," was asserted. When Eshkol became prime minister, the party had a truly collegial leadership, despite a substantial concentration of power directly in his hands. Like his predecessor he was both prime and defense minister, but unlike Ben-Gurion, he functioned as both government and active party leader. He retained both portfolios until the eve of the 1967 war when he was compelled to yield the Defense Ministry to Dayan.

There was, however, an even broader context of internal Mapai developments and conflicts. The tension between the veterans and the Tseirim was not only a generational clash, but an institutional and ideological conflict as well. In particular question was the relation between the state and the Histadrut. With its cooperative economy, social welfare networks, and trade union apparatus, the Histadrut was originally seen by the Labor movement as the embodiment of the future socialist Jewish state. Once the British mandatory regime was replaced in 1948 by a sovereign Jewish state with a Mapai prime minister, the place of the Histadrut within Israel had to be determined. Ben-Gurion pressed a policy of *mamlakhtiyut,* a term that may be roughly rendered into English as statism (*mamlakha* means kingdom in Hebrew). This policy asserted the primacy of the state over all "particularistic" segments of Israeli life. For example, in defense policy this entailed abolishing the pre-state, politically affiliated Zionist military undergrounds and unifying them into the IDF; similarly, *mamlakhtiyut* aimed to unite the politically and/or religiously oriented educational "trends" of the pre-state period into a single state education system (this was only partly achieved). *Mamlakhtiyut* entailed transferring many of the Histadrut's functions to the state. At the Eighth Conference of the Histadrut in 1956, Ben-Gurion warned that the Histadrut was "neither the state's rival nor competitor, but its faithful aide and loyal supporter." He insisted that "Every service benefitting the entire public should be under state control."[32] While the Histadrut's water company and system of labor exchanges were nationalized with little Mapai or Histadrut opposition, the same was not the case with its health system, Kupat Holim. This health system covered some 75 percent of the population and was available only to Histadrut members. It thus served as a powerful incentive for joining the Labor confederation.

Dayan and Peres championed *mamlakhtiyut* and took up cudgels against the Histadrut—Kupat Holim in particular—and against the Veterans of Mapai, whom they accused of fidelity to outdated socialist ideas and undemocratic methods of running the party. Clearly, weakening the Lavon-headed Histadrut's power and that of the Mapai Veterans was politically advantageous to Dayan and Peres, who, thanks to Ben-Gurion, obtained "safe spots" on the 1959 Mapai Knesset list.[33] In their political rise, Dayan and Peres came from a base outside the party per se—the state and military apparatuses—and thus were relatively independent from the party Veterans, the Gush, and the Histadrut, all of whom they freely and very publicly assailed. Also, in security-conscious Israel, Dayan and Peres were able to flaunt their backgrounds in defense, which they contrasted with that of the Veterans, whose primary achievements were in domestic and economic matters. The personal rivalry between Lavon and the Dayan-Peres duo increasingly was transformed into a question of *mamlakhtiyut* versus the Histadrut and the historical voluntaristic socialism of the Labor movement. Simultaneously the Mapai Veterans, threatened by Dayan and Peres, became closer to Lavon.

While the Veterans and Lavon rarely had objected in the past—in fact had assisted in implementing—*mamlakhtiyut*, after Lavon came into open conflict with Ben-Gurion he launched a public attack on "étatism." The argument that *mamlakhtiyut* undermined the Labor movement by nationalizing Labor institutions and by replacing socialist with statist-nationalist politics was a criticism long made of Ben-Gurion by members of smaller left-wing parties, Mapam and Ahdut ha-Avodah. Now Lavon and Mapai intellectuals such as Rotenstreich and the Min ha-Yesod group claimed that Ben-Gurion's statism undermined pluralism in Israeli society by encouraging an exaggerated faith in, and also a dependence on, the state.[34] Consequently, while the Lavon affair did not generate them, it crystallized and threw into sharp relief a host of problems and conflicts: the relation between the civilian and defense establishments, the relation of the state and the Histadrut, those of the Veterans and the Tseirim, the party and its leader, and others. As Ben-Gurion became a partisan in the affair, party cohesiveness began to unravel. Even in internal party elections for the Mapai caucus of the El Al (National Airlines) branch of the Histadrut Clerical Workers' Union, there was a competition between a "Mapai Center Loyalist" list, and a "Histadrut Loyalist List."[35]

The extent to which the outcome of the affair was determined within the upper echelons of Mapai and not within formal government bodies is one of its striking features, though hardly surprising given the nature of the Israeli political universe. The cabinet, however, did play a crucial role, particularly through the ministerial Committee of Seven, but it is necessary to bear in mind that the cabinet (and the committee) were dominated by Mapai. When Ben-Gurion in effect discarded the cabinet endorsement of the Committee of Seven's report, the ensuing crisis—the threat of the premier's resignation—was resolved by Mapai (by ousting Lavon). Similarly, Ben-Gurion's onslaught in 1964–65 was resolved by the Mapai conference and the Rafi split. Despite Ben-Gurion's demands for judicial inquiries, and despite the roles played by various respected judicial figures, the direct role of the judicial system per se in the affair was minimal. Indeed, between 1955 and 1960 Ben-Gurion did not pursue the affair through judicial or any other means. The ouster of Lavon was an internal Mapai matter; Ben-Gurion's 1964–65 quest for a judicial inquiry commission was defeated by political means.

What then of the Knesset? Israel's government is responsible to the Knesset, but here again Mapai's dominance and party discipline minimized the role of the parliamentary body. It was clear that Mapai wanted to resolve the scandal within the party and not in forums where the opposition could derive political capital from it. The Lavon affair only became a matter of parliamentary scrutiny when Lavon appeared at the Knesset Defense and Foreign Affairs Committee in the fall of 1960. This committee, perhaps the most prestigious of the ten standing committees in the Israel parliament, actually has a minimal role in decision making. (This too was a result of Ben-Gurion's efforts to give the defense sector autonomy and of his own role as a combined prime minister and defense minister). However, the committee receives privileged briefings, and while it includes some opposition members, participation in it is restricted (the Communist Party has always been barred from it, for instance).

Lavon committed three major transgressions of the "rules of the political game" in 1960. His appearance before the Knesset committee was a major violation of customary Mapai behavior. The party expected its members, and especially its leaders, to resolve such matters in party forums. Going to the Knesset was in retrospect the first of Lavon's steps on the path to political defeat. Second, Lavon, in his testimony and elsewhere, cast aspersions on the nation's military elite. In doing so he carried his battle into previously sacred, and therefore politically dangerous, terrain (and, as we have noted, Ben-Gurion took this personally). Finally, his testimony at the committee was leaked to the press, something that had never happened before and that was assumed to have been due to him or an associate. By such actions, combined with his often intemperate verbal assaults on the premier (including an initial refusal to invite Ben-Gurion, the organization's first secretary general, to address the Histadrut's 40th anniversary celebrations) and attacks on "statism," Lavon contributed mightily to his own political ruin. What is significant, however, is that his downfall was determined within Mapai, even though the 1954 Mishap was a government matter and although his undoing came through his ouster from a nongovernmental position as secretary general of the Histadrut.

The Press and Public Arena in the Affair

"The citizen of Israel," remarked Talmon, "is beginning to feel a dangerous duality: on the one hand there are governmental bodies, subject to public review and working in the open, and on the other, secret activity, intrigues, and plots of an almost underground character twisting and redirecting whatever is done through accredited channels."[36] Certainly this comment by a historian accurately reflected a disturbing reality that was exposed through the Lavon affair, and it captures why the affair was an affair, a scandal that went far beyond the simple question of "Who gave the order?"

If a party is dominant because it is so regarded by the population, then it is self-evident that a major scandal within it is bound to be consequential. This is especially so when, as in Israel, the party leader is virtually a national monument. The affair occasioned what one scholar calls an "unprecedented upsurge of independent public opinion."[37] Whereas there had been volatile public issues in the past, the dominant status of Mapai (and of Ben-Gurion himself) had contained them. The Lavon Affair in 1960–61 engendered intense friction within the ruling party itself and spawned new ramifications. The press entered the fray with vigor, students formed a "Committee to Defend Democracy," and after the letter by prominent intellectuals chastising the premier was issued in January 1961, efforts by Ben-Gurion's backers in the Mapai machine to counter the criticism with their own group of writers and academics were unsuccessful. Many intellectuals who had previously had great access to and had cooperated with Ben-Gurion and the national leadershp now played a new, harshly adversarial political role.[38] Furthermore, faced with an antagonist of Ben-Gurion's stature and power, reshaping public opinion became an obvious goal for Lavon and his supporters. They actively sought to use the press to this end. It was this struggle that Ben-Gurion ultimately lost, even though he defeated Lavon politically. Finally, the affair not only occasioned a broader role for the Israeli press and a new level of public discourse. In addition, the defense establishment, with which Ben-Gurion had so closely identified himself and that previously had been an untouchable terrain for public debate, was its focus.

Television did not come to Israel until 1968, and until 1965 when the Israel Broadcasting Authority was established, radio was under the direction of the prime minister's office. It was politically censored during the Lavon Affair.[39] So the affair was played out primarily in newspaper debates. While the country, as a nation of immigrants, had well over a dozen dailies in several languages, the most important were those in Hebrew, and also the English-language *Jerusalem Post*. Israel's press was—and is—a free one, but it functions in a country at war, and that inevitably brings with it constraints and military censorship. Shalom Rosenfield, former editor of the daily *Maariv*, has detected an almost "'conditioned' reflex of preferring the national interest over purely professional considerations" in Jewish journalists, dating from long before statehood.[40] This was rooted in a siege mentality produced by the long history of anti-Semitism and the vicissitudes of the Arab-Israeli conflict. Rosenfeld points to the state of war, the economic boycott conducted by the Arab states against the Jewish state and its trading partners, Israel's sense of responsibility for Jews throughout the world, and Israel's large minority of Arab citizens (who are assumed by many Jews to be a potential fifth column) as factors producing ongoing dilemmas for the (Jewish) Israeli journalist.[41]

When many of the Israeli newspapers were founded (mostly in the 1920s and 1930s), they were part of the Jewish struggle for statehood; they championed the Zionist leadership and were progressively in conflict with the British authorities. A Reactions Committee of editors was established during the mandate period to provide ongoing coordination in response to censorship and political events. With independence, the "authorities" were no longer the British enemy but rather a Zionist government. The Reactions Committee became the Editors' Committee and had a complex relationship with both the government and the military censor. It met frequently with Ben-Gurion and top officials for briefings, including privileged ones. It is noteworthy that committee members occasionally felt that they were being made privy to classified information—which bound them to secrecy—for political rather than security reasons. Editors requested at times not to be briefed so as to avoid having their hands tied.[42]

The Editors' Committee reached a formal, though voluntary, agreement with the defense establishment (with origins in an arrangement between the Reactions Committee and pre-state Haganah Zionist military underground) on the terms of military censorship. It was an attempt to balance the democratic principle of a free press with security needs. According to this agreement, the goal of military censorship was solely to prevent publicizing information deleterious to state security. Article 5 stipulated that censorship would "not apply to political affairs, opinions, commentaries, or assessments, unless these contain classified security information, or unless such information may be inferred from them."[43] Editors voluntarily submitted materials they deemed potential security hazards and received lists from the military indicating those problematic subjects needing to be checked. A mechanism was also established to resolve disputes between the editors and censors through a tripartite and confidential tribunal composed of one representative each of the editors, the military, and the "public" (usually a lawyer). The IDF chief of staff had the prerogative of accepting or rejecting its conclusions.[44]

It should be stressed, however, that this is an arrangement, not a law, and it is only applicable to those media that are officially party to it. Thus it is not a legally institutionalized aspect of democratic process. Furthermore, various publications, ranging from Herut and Communist ones in the 1950s to more mainstream ones in the 1980s, were and are not signatories, and therefore they were and are not protected by the agreement. Thus they are potentially subject to severe restrictions, which the government has at its disposal based on laws initially enacted by the British mandatory authorities before 1948. The government ultimately has, in the words of a senior news editor at Israel Radio, "legal weapons the likes of which cannot be found in any important democracy in the world."[45] On the other hand, in the eyes of most Israelis, their democracy has been taxed by circumstances unlike those elsewhere. We see here how a tension between democratic principles and perceived *raison d'état*—in particular security of the state—has been an ongoing reality of Israeli political life.

In 1954–55, the nature of the "Security Mishap," the Israeli connection to the Cairo trials, and the specific circumstances of Lavon's resignation were censored, although the fact that some sort of investigation tied to Lavon was underway leaked through the press. In 1960–61 it was an entirely different story. In the aftermath of Lavon's Knesset appearance, the affair became, as we have noted, a *cause célèbre*. However, because it was a delicate security matter involving top intelligence officials, the Israeli public found its dailies reporting through code words; at issue was who gave the order for "The Security Mishap," with no explanation of the mishap. The public knew that Lavon had something to do with it, but that an unnamed "senior officer" and an unnamed "third man" (respectively Gibli and Elad) were also involved. Even after Lavon publicly mentioned Gibli by name at a January 1961 Mapai meeting, the press only identified " . . . i." Lavon complained that censorship was used politically against him. Apparently almost all specific details pertaining to the affair were censored, without explanation from the censor. Substantial tensions ensued as editors and journalists began to sense the censorship decisions were not being made on security grounds alone.[46] At the same time, some journalists and newspapers assumed an open role of advocacy. Journalists found themselves in the midst of a complex constellation in which they had to juggle not only the demands of the censor and the expectations of major figures in the affair who were leaking information to them, but their own professional rivalries; it was increasingly difficult to determine what a newspaper's competitors did or didn't know and would and wouldn't publish.[47] Finally, many of the details and much speculation that was censored in the Israeli press did appear in foreign newspapers, some of which, ironically, were available in Israel. (The censor apparently believed that allowing Israeli papers to print such information or rumors would legitimize them.) Thus a peculiar situation evolved in which the Israeli public had to turn to the foreign press to find out aspects of a major Israeli scandal; the head of the Israeli Students Association at one point protested this situation by publicly reading materials from the French to fellow students at a conference.[48]

The affair gave rise to an outpouring of books, pamphlets, and articles; indeed, the polemics continue into the 1980s. Journalists Eliahu Hasin and Dan Horovitz published a pro-Lavon account as early as March 1961, simply called *The Affair*. Ben-Gurion himself later authored a self-defense and Hagai Eshed, who was hired by Ben-Gurion while he was still in office to examine the affair (and therefore had access to secret materials) published a controversial account that was severely criticized by the distinguished Hebrew University professor, Yehoshua Arieli, in a book ominously entitled *The Conspiracy*. Ben-Gurion's 1964 attempt to reopen the matter was largely based on Eshed's work, which pointed a finger at Lavon. Ben-Gurion sought to make the book available before the 1965 Mapai conference, but the censors (who worked under the authority of the defense minister who was by then Levi Eshkol) edited out almost half of it, and sought to restrain publication on the grounds that since Eshed wrote it while in the employ of the defense ministry, it was state property. However, the edited version and summaries of it began appearing in the press, in particular in *Ha-arets* and *The Jerusalem Post*, in late February 1965. (The cabinet expressed public regret but did not press any charges). A fuller version of Eshed's highly polemical account, which in his words aimed "to accuse and to defend someone," was published in 1977 and received vigorous criticism. Ironically, its publication was in part made possible because of Labor's electoral defeat by Ben-Gurion's historical rivals; the Likud, led by Begin, had obvious political reasons for relaxing censorship of information on the Affair.[49] In 1980 yet another account of the events of 1954 appeared, this time, however, by the former head of foreign intelligence, Iser Harel, under the even more ominous title *Anatomy of Treason*.[50] Some of the initial restraints on revealing the affair's details were lifted in 1971, after Prime Minister Golda Meir attended the wedding of one of the former Cairo prisoners, all of whom had been released to Israel in the late 1960s through prisoner exchanges. The censorship issue was briefly reignited in 1975 when three of the former prisoners appeared on Israeli television and indicated that Dayan, who was defense minister between 1967 and 1974, had blocked publication of their account of the "mishap" for political reasons.[51]

In brief, the Israeli newspapers at various stages played informative, sensationalist, and advocacy roles during the affair. Despite censorship, they were crucial in getting information to the citizenry and also to many politicians. The advocacy role during the final two stages of the affair (1960–61 and 1964–65) was tied to—but did not automatically reflect—the division of Israeli newspapers between those that are independent and those that are politically affiliated. *Maariv* and *Ha-arets*, both independents, played particularly notable roles in the shaping of public opinion. Most of the *Maariv* editors were supporters of Begin's right-wing opposition. Although the paper had endorsed many government positions in the past, it was self-evident that a weakening of Mapai and Ben-Gurion would help Herut. *Maariv* had virtually no Ben-Gurion supporters within its top staff. In 1960-61 it backed Lavon's rehabilitation and opposed his removal from the Histadrut. In 1964–65 it opposed reopening the affair and backed the "de-Ben-Gurionization" of Israeli political life. *Ha-arets*, the country's most sophisticated daily, was (and is) a liberal-centrist paper (its editor-in-chief, Gershom Schocken, was long involved in the small Progressive Party), and it had been notable for its criticism of the Mapai establishment. During the affair it supported Ben-Gurion and his call for a judicial inquiry, and opposed Lavon and later Eshkol. It supported the creation of Rafi and the champions of *mamlakhtiyut* in Mapai against the veteran socialists and the Histadrut. However, in contrast to *Maariv*, a broad spectrum of opinion appeared in its pages.[52] One scholar has noted that as a result of the advocacy role of the two papers in the Affair, their functions were not too different from that of party newspapers. The *Jerusalem Post* took a pro-Ben-Gurion position. *Davar*, the

Histadrut (and therefore *de facto* a Mapai) daily took a pro-Lavon stance, as did the left-wing papers and indeed public opinion as a whole.[53]

Aftermath

"How are the mighty fallen." It was with this biblical passage—David's lamentation upon learning of the deaths of Saul and Jonathan—that one of the polemics of the affair was closed.[54] For its two major protagonists, the affair spelled the end of their political careers. Ben-Gurion, state-builder and former premier, went into the political wilderness; Lavon, once his possible heir, a former defense minister and former Histadrut chief, was effectively barred from having a political future. The ramifications of the Affair were, however, much more than personal, although the political system per se was unchanged and no significant institutional or structural reforms came in its aftermath. Ben-Gurion, after all, rejected Lavon's suggestions for such reorganization in 1955 and the "Old Man," along with Peres (director-general of the Defense Ministry from 1953 to 1959, deputy defense minister from 1959 to 1965, defense minister from 1974 to 1977) and Dayan (chief of staff of the IDF from 1953 to 1958, defense minister from 1967 to 1974) had seen Lavon himself, rather than institutional relations between the political system and the private sectors as the essential problem.[55] Premier Eshkol did make an attempt to address this issue. This effort, however, was limited and in the days before the June 1967 war, with the Arab world mobilized on Israel's borders and openly proclaiming hostile intentions, Eshkol was compelled to yield the defense portfolio to Dayan.[56]

The most significant transformations subsequent to the Lavon Affair took place in the Israeli party system, and especially in the role of Mapai. On the one hand, changes were not immediately reflected in coalition-building. Despite Ben-Gurion's difficulties in cabinet formation in 1961, the backbone of the government—the "historic alliance" between the dominant Mapai Party and the National Religious Party—remained intact for another decade and a half. On the other hand, if a party's dominance depends in part on the public's perception of its dominance, then the Lavon affair was one important step in the process that subverted the status of Mapai and the Labor movement—a process that ultimately culminated in the victory of Begin's right-wing opposition in 1977. Indeed, identification with the right wing quadrupled from 8 percent (1962) to 16 percent (1969) to 23 percent (1973) to 28 percent (1977) to 32 percent (1981) while identification with the Left and the moderate Left displayed the reverse fate, dropping from 31 percent (1962) to 25 percent (1969) to 22 percent (1973) to 18 percent (1977) to 17 percent (1981).[57]

A wide variety of factors, of which the Lavon affair was but one, brought about these changes. In fact, the Lavon affair itself is perhaps best viewed as a symptom rather than as a catalyst of transformations then already underway. Continual warfare, especially the traumas of the 1967 and 1973 wars, the rise of terrorism by Palestinian Arab organizations, and Israeli isolation and vilification in the international arena, especially at the UN, made the ultranationalist and xenophobic message of Herut more plausible to many Israelis. Also, Israel underwent a significant demographic change as a result of large-scale immigration of Jews from Arab lands into the country in the 1950s. Their mistreatment in Arab countries made many of them receptive to the message of Herut.

These immigrants tended to be more religiously oriented than the secular Labor movement and they had not experienced the "heroic age" of state-building under Mapai leadership. Perhaps most importantly, the paternalism of the Labor establishment toward them and a sense that it was not sufficiently open to them led to many resentments and a sense of political alienation that was eventually translated into new voting patterns. In addition, the decline of the charismatic Ben-Gurion undermined Mapai's appeal and status among these new Israelis, a possibility *Ha-arets* pointed to as early as February 1961.[58]

Mamlakhtiyut, which demoted the Labor movement to a secondary position in Israeli society (rather than identifying the nation's interests with those of Labor, which had been Mapai's original political strategy) raised significant questions for the dominant party's identity. This was partly played out during the affair in the conflicts between the Veterans and the Tseirim. Indeed, the 1960–61 outbreak of the affair, seen against the consequences of *mamlakhtiyut*, may be viewed as the beginning of the end of the "historic Mapai," both in its public image and in the party's own practices. For one thing, the fact that the political and professional rise of Dayan and Peres took place despite the party organization indicated a weakening of the latter's strength and also raised questions about its ability to develop its own young leadership from within. The "parachuting" (as it was called) of military figures into top political positions, and the circumventing of party mechanisms, became an ongoing feature of Israeli politics, and not just in Mapai, which illustrated a significant change in party power. Furthermore, Mapai had proven itself incapable of containing the 1960–61 crisis and eventually suffered the (Rafi) split. This fracturing led to the decline and a split in the Gush machine, and an exit from the party of many distinguished figures, not the least of whom was Ben-Gurion, who was busily engaged in public excoriation of Eshkol.

That Mapai was victorious and Rafi soundly defeated in the 1965 elections made it appear that Mapai's dominance had been sustained and "normalcy" reestablished. But this was only the case in the short run. The crisis that preceded the 1967 war, in which Eshkol was perceived as indecisive in the face of the military mobilization of the Arab world, led to Dayan's appointment as defense minister and the formation of a National Unity Government, which admitted Herut into the halls of power for the first time. This conferred a new legitimacy on Begin's party, which from the mid-1960s was successfully constructing a broader right-wing front through an electoral alliance (Gahal) with the Liberal Party.[59] In mid-1973 this effort was extended by the formation of the Likud. Mapai broadened its own front by amalgamating with Ahdut ha-Avodah and Rafi to form the Israel Labor Party in 1968. While this brought under one roof Mapai and the two major groups that had split from it (Ahdut ha-Avodah in 1944 and Rafi in 1965) the new party was much less cohesive than the historical Mapai. It increasingly became what Otto Kirchheimer called a catch-all party.[60] Labor formed an electoral alignment with the left-wing Mapam Party in 1969.

Thus within a decade after the end of the Lavon Affair, Israeli politics had moved away from a dominant party system and toward a competitive one, characterized by two major blocs, each composed of left- or right-leaning parties. In its first years, particularly under Golda Meir's leadership (from 1969 to 1974), the Labor Party was more of a federation than an integrated party. The three factions, the former Mapai, Ahdut ha-Avodah, and Rafi, were allotted representatives on party institutions according to a key based on pre-unification strengths. This helped maintain factionalism and inner party competitive tensions, and conjured the constant specter of a shattering of the party. Each faction effectively had veto power over the party as a whole, and the frequent result was internal immobilism. Ironically, unity led to no substantial electoral benefits either.[61] The 1973 war, which began with a surprise attack against and devastating losses for Israel, greatly tarnished Labor's image, and led to the resignations of Meir and Dayan. The former was replaced by Itshak Rabin, but only after a bitter contest with Rafi's Peres. It is striking that neither of the two chief contenders for the premiership were from the ex-Mapai faction and neither rose through Mapai ranks. Former Chief of Staff Rabin, although he was not identified with any faction, was closest to the old Ahdut ha-Avodah, whose Yigal Allon had been his commander in the 1948 war and who became his foreign minister. With Peres as his defense minister, conflicts were predictable.

Rabin rose through army ranks, Peres through the defense and state establishment, and Allon through the kibbutz movement and the Palmach (the pre-1948 left-wing shock troops of the Zionist underground). Although Pinhas Sapir was the finance minister, it was now clear that the route to political leadership was no longer necessarily via the old Mapai establishment. Furthermore, in all the major parties military figures had become increasingly prominent. (In Labor, this was yet one more consequence of the generational battle between the Veterans and the Tseirim).

As prime minister, Rabin paid little attention to internal party affairs and with the death of Sapir, the ex-Mapai faction within Labor increasingly dissolved. In the meantime the relations between the premier, the defense minister, and the foreign minister echoed those of the 1954–55 period. This was especially reflected in animosity and competition between Rabin and Peres, with the latter undermining the former in ways reminiscent of the relations between Sharett and Lavon. A relatively minor financial scandal in the spring of 1977 forced Rabin to step aside and Peres became party leader shortly before Labor finally lost its political power as yet another split from Labor (creating the Democratic Movement for Change) helped lead to the victory of the Likud that year. At the same time, the National Religious Party, whose own "Young Guard" had been enthralled by the reconquest of lands that had been part of ancient Israel in the 1967 war, and which had consequently been transformed more and more into a militant religious nationalist force, ended its historic alliance with Labor and joined the Begin-led government. The 1981 elections resulted in a virtual stalemate between the two chief blocs, although Begin in the end was able to inch out Peres for the prime ministry; in 1984 the election results forced the two major blocs into a national unity government because neither had sufficient strength to form a government on its own.

The political world—or at least much of it—in which the Lavon affair took place had been fundamentally reshaped. Israel's democratic political system securely reproduced itself, but this was not the case with the party system or the Jewish state's political culture. Labor's dominance was gone and the Labor Party, now led by Peres, was a very different party from the Mapai of 1960. (In fact its leadership contained a large proportion of former Rafi adherents.) However, the salient new reality in Israeli politics was that two major blocs now competed in elections, with each having the possibility of victory. The Lavon affair itself was not the cause of the transformation of Israel from a dominant into a competitive party system, but it was one link in the chain, both for its consequences and for what it represented.

NOTES

I wish to express my gratitude to Yoram Peri for his invaluable comments on earlier drafts of this essay.

1. The statement was made by Moshe Ben-Zev, quoted in Hagai Eshed, *Mi natan et ha-horaah?* (Who Gave the Order?) (Jerusalem and Tel Aviv: Edanim and Yediot Ahronot, 1979), p. 9.

2. The following account is based on a variety of published materials. The reader should bear in mind that some of the facts of the affair are still very much in dispute and not all materials pertaining to it have been made public.

3. "Israel Welcomes the Egyptian Revolution," Statement to the Knesset by Prime Minister Ben-Gurion, 18 August 1952, in *Israel's Foreign Relations: Selected Documents 1947–74*, M. Medzini (Jerusalem: The Ministry for Foreign Affairs, 1976), p. 294.

4. Quoted in Gideon Rafael, *Destination Peace: Three Decades of Israeli Foreign Policy* (New York: Stein and Day, 1981), p. 38.

5. Rafael, *Destination Peace*, p. 37.

6. See Alouph Hareven, "Disturbed Hierarchy: Israeli Intelligence Failures in 1954 and 1973," *Jerusalem Quarterly* no. 9 (Fall 1978): 3–19.

7. Hareven, "Disturbed Hierarchy," p. 9.

8. Amos Perlmutter, *Military and Politics in Israel* (New York and Washington: Praeger, 1969), p. 88.

9. Quoted in David Ben-Gurion, "Truth Above All," *Jerusalem Post*, 13 January 1961.

10. David Ben-Gurion, *Israel: A Personal History* (New York and Tel Aviv: Funk and Wagnalls, and Sabra Books, 1971), p. 607.

11. Quoted in Ben-Gurion, *Israel*, p. 617.

12. J. L. Talmon, "The Lavon Affair—Israeli Democracy at the Crossroads," *New Outlook* 4 (March–April 1961): 25.

13. Its head was actually Justice Minister Pinhas Rosen.

14. "C'ttee Finds Lavon Didn't Give Order," *Jerusalem Post*, 22 December 1960.

15. During the 1956 Egyptian-Israeli war Israeli Arabs from the village of Kafr Qasim were shot by the IDF upon returning from work in violation of a curfew of which they had not been informed. Eight Israeli soldiers were tried by a military court and two officers received lengthy sentences, which were, at a later date, reduced.

16. "Lavon: Further Probe a Danger," *Jerusalem Post*, 13 January 1961.

17. Talmon, "The Lavon Affair," p. 24.

18. See Nathan Yanai, *Party Leadership in Israel* (Ramat Gan: Turtledove Publishers, 1981) p. 47.

19. "Prime Minister's Letter to Lavon Group," *New Outlook* (May 1964): 56.

20. Michael Bar-Zohar, *Ben-Gurion: A Biography* (New York: Delacorte, 1977) pp. 306–7.

21. "Eshkol's Statement," *New Outlook*, (May 1964): 56–57.

22. Ben Gurion, *Israel*, p. 695.

23. The Justice Minister was then Dov Yosef.

24. Shlomo Avineri, "Israel in the Post–Ben-Gurion Era: The Nemesis of Messianism," *Midstream* 11, no. 3 (September 1965): 16.

25. Howard M. Sachar, *A History of Israel* (New York: Alfred A. Knopf, 1976) p. 333.

26. *Our Stand: The Program of Mapai* (Tel Aviv: Mapai, 1949) pp. 8–9.

27. See Yoram Peri, *Between Battles and Ballots: Israeli Military in Politics* (Cambridge and

New York: Cambridge University Press, 1983) p. 281. This trenchant study is the best in the field.

28. See Maurice Duverger, *Political Parties,* (London: Methuen, 1964) pp. 307–8. Also see Alan Arian and Samuel Barnes, "The Dominant Party System: A Neglected Model of Democratic Stability," *Journal of Politics* 36 (August 1974): 562–614. Ariel Levite and Sidney Tarrow, "The Legitimation of Excluded Parties in Dominant Party Systems: A Comparison of Israel and Italy," *Comparative Politics* 15, 3 (April 1983: 295–328) Yonathan Shapiro, "The End of a Dominant Party System," in *The Elections in Israel 1977,* ed. A. Arian (Jerusalem: Jerusalem Academic Press, 1980).

29. "200 Hurt as Police Defend Knesset from Herut Riot," *Jerusalem Post,* 8 January 1952.

30. Peter Y. Medding, *Mapai in Israel: Political Organisation and Government in a New Society* (Cambridge: Cambridge University Press, 1972), p. 123.

31. "The Lavon Affair: 1954–1964," *Jewish Observer and Middle East Review* 13 (December 18, 1965): 14.

32. David Ben-Gurion, "Ha-Histadrut ba-Medinah" (The Histadrut in the State), in *Ha-Veidah ha-shminit shel ha-Histadrut* (The Eighth Conference of the Histadrut) (Tel Aviv: The Histadrut, 1956), p. 73. For an extensive analysis of the *mamlakhtiyut* and its implications for the Labor movement, see Mitchell Cohen, *Zion and State: Nation, Class, and the Shaping of Modern Israel* (Oxford: Basil Blackwell, 1987).

33. Since in Israel's electoral system of proportional representation a party list obtains a percentage of seats in the Knesset equal to the percentage of the vote it wins, "safe spots" are the highest ones on the candidate list drawn up by the party and ensure an individual's election to the Israeli parliament.

34. See especially the essays by Lavon and Rotenstreich in *Kovets Min ha-Yesod* (Min ha-Yesod Collection) (Tel Aviv: Amikam, 1962). An abridged version of Lavon's essay is in English as "A Chosen People and a Normal Society," *New Outlook,* February 1962.

35. "'Affair' Rears Head in Union Branch Poll," *Jerusalem Post,* 11 December 1960.

36. Talmon, "The Lavon Affair," p. 27.

37. S. N. Eisenstadt, *Israeli Society* (London: Weidenfeld and Nicolson, 1967), pp. 331–32.

38. See Michael Keren, *Ben-Gurion and the Intellectuals: Power, Knowledge, and Charisma* (DeKalb, Illinois: Northern Illinois University Press, 1983).

39. Michael Brecher, *The Foreign Policy System of Israel* (London: Oxford University Press, 1972), p. 189 n.2.

40. Shalom Rosenfeld, "Newspaper Editor's Dilemmas," *Jerusalem Quarterly* (Fall 1982): 115.

41. Ibid., pp. 100–101.

42. Rosenfeld, "Newspaper Editor's Dilemmas," pp. 104–5.

43. Ibid., p. 102.

44. Rosenfeld, pp. 102–3. For an in-depth analysis of these matters, see Dina Goren, *Sodiyut, Bitahon, ve-hofesh ha-itonut* (Secrecy, Security, and Freedom of the Press) (Jerusalem: Magnes Press, Hebrew University, 1975).

45. Mose Negbi, "Paper Tiger: The Struggle for Press Freedom in Israel," *Jerusalem Quarterly* 39 (1986): 18. Negbi provides a bitterly critical analysis of the Israeli press establishment and the status of the press.

46. Goren, "Sodiyut," pp. 207–8.

47. Ibid., p. 207.

48. Ibid., p. 208. Some of the foreign press speculation, particularly in the Arab world, was outlandish and even ludicrous. The east Jerusalem *Falastin* told its readers that the "Security Mishap" in question was a smuggling ring that was pilfering and then selling food from the IDF. According to this fantastic account, when Lavon captured the chieftains of this band—none less than Moshe Dayan and Shimon Peres—Ben-Gurion forced Lavon to resign to protect his protégés. "Arab Versions of the Affair," *Jerusalem Post,* 22 October 1960. The *Post* was summarizing a *New York Times* article.

49. See Hagai Eshed, *Mi natan et ha-horaah?* (Who Gave the Order?) (Jerusalem: Edanim, 1979) p. 9. For a strident critique of Eshed's early account, see Yehoshua Arieli, *Ha-Knuniya* (The Conspiracy) (Tel Aviv: Kadima, 1965) especially pp. 9–15. See also Eliahu Hasin and Dan Horowitz, *Ha-Parashah* (The Affair) (Tel Aviv: Am ha-Sefer, 1961), and David Ben-Gurion, *Devarim Ka-havayat-am* (Things as They Are) (Tel Aviv: Am ha-Sefer, 1965).

50. Iser Harel, *Anatomiyah shel beqidah: 'Ha-Adam ha-Shlishi' ve-ha-mapolet be-mitsrayim 1954* (Anatomy of Treason: The 'Third Man' and the Collapse of the Israeli Spy Network in Egypt 1954) (Jerusalem: Edanimi, 1980).

51. Terence Smith, "The 'Lavon Affair' is Revived in Israel," *New York Times*, 30 March 1975. Their account did appear however, with a preface by Golda Meir herself, and is available in English as *Operation Susannah*, as told to Aviezer Golan by Marcelle Ninio, Victor Levy, Robert Dassa, and Philip Natanson (New York: Harper and Row, 1978).

52. My description of *Maariv* and *Ha-arets* is culled from Hanan Kristal, "Emdot politiot shel ha-itonut ha-yomit ba-'Parshat Lavon,'" (The Political Positions of the Daily Press in the 'Lavon Affair'," in *Medinah, Mimshal, vi-hasim beinleumiyim*, no. 6 (Fall 1974).

53. Ibid.

54. Arieli, *Ha-Kenuniyah*, p. 178.

55. See Peri, *Between Battles* pp. 238–39.

56. This separation of the prime minister and the defense minister has since become a continuous feature of the Israeli cabinet.

57. Asher Arian and Michal Shamir, "The Primarily Political Functions of the Left-Right Continuum" in *Politics and Society in Israel*, ed. Ernst Krausz (New Brunswick and Oxford: Transaction Books, 1985) pp. 162–63.

58. Kristal, "Emdot . . .," p. 87.

59. Mapai's move toward alignment with Ahdut ha-Avodah and the defeat of Ben-Gurion and the Tseirim also encouraged the Liberals to align with Herut in Gahal. The Tseirim preferred a Mapai alliance with the Liberals to one with Ahdut ha-Avodah. As opposition parties Rafi and Gahal often cooperated with each other.

60. See Otto Kirchheimer, "The Transformation of the Western European Party Systems," in *Political Parties and Political Development*, ed. Joseph LaPalombara and Myron Weiner (Princeton: Princeton University Press, 1966).

61. This is argued forcefully in Yossi Beilin, *Mehiro shel ihud: Mifleget ha-Avodah ad milhemet yom ha-kipurim* (The Price of Unity: The Labor Party until the Yom Kippur War) (Ramat Gan: Revivim, 1985).

Conclusion: Appreciating Scandal as a Political Art Form, or, Making an Intellectual Virtue of a Political Vice

JOHN LOGUE

> Politics, *n.* The conduct of public affairs
> for private advantage
> —Ambrose Bierce

The development of a new subfield of political science is usually cause for despair among informed laymen. Another field of intrinsic interest, they complain, will be obscured by jargon and require an advanced knowledge of statistics.

Political scandology, we promise you, will be an exception to the usual practice of political science. The appeal of corruption, money, murder, sin and sex in the service of politics, and vice versa, will not be concealed by neologisms. Avarice, lust, greed, envy, the hunger for illegitimate power and similar human preoccupations that fueled the scandals described in the preceding chapters will retain the names that we recognize. Christine Keeler and Mandy Rice-Davies will not be reduced to correlation coefficients.

Scandology focuses on the pleasure of politics as a spectator sport. Its appeal is that of the best political gossip: the corruption of power not rumored but made manifest. What is more stimulating to the political juices than finding a favorite political enemy mired in some thoroughly discreditable affair? What is more pleasant than to see one's erstwhile opponent laid low by some uniquely newsworthy act of hypocrisy? Political scandals are fun, and political scandology should be too.

There is, however, an element in scandology that goes beyond the vicarious thrill of witnessing the fall of those who perverted public service for private gain or who have twisted the instruments of law into tools of illegality. Scandal has not only a prurient interest, but it can also be used as a tool to understand the institutional configurations that permit it and the political cultures that tolerate it. Scandals are a recurring illness in the democratic body politic. What can we learn about the organism from analyzing them and the way the political system responds? It is characteristic of the chapters in this volume that the authors combine the spice of scandal with structured analysis to use the fact of scandal, and of the political systems' responses to scandal, to cast substantial light on fundamental historical, structural, and cultural factors in the politics of nine liberal democracies. As Stephen Bornstein, who regards scandals as pathologies, notes, "In politics as in medicine, pathology can teach us some interesting things about normal anatomy and biology."

In their introduction, Andrei Markovits and Mark Silverstein argue persuasively that political scandals can only occur in liberal democracies. The caprice, arbitrariness, violation of the rule of law, abuse of power, and blatant pursuit of personal benefit of and by political leaders that characterize the scandals examined in this volume would, after all, not be scandals at all in classic tyrannies or leader-centered authoritarian regimes, which are defined by the expectation that their leaders will behave in precisely such a fashion. The scandals discussed in this volume are anomalies; they represent clear violations of the expected limits on the behavior of leaders in relation to the led. In many of the world's political systems both historically and currently there are no such limits on leaders. Hence, there can be no scandals—or, alternatively, the regime itself is a scandal.

Our theme, then, is a classic one: how are the governors to be restrained? At issue is the question of restraining the individual leader from acting outside the checks of law, custom, and at least in these nine cases, the party system. It is a problem as old as the institution of political leadership. That problem is resolved in liberal democracies by the combination of rule by law, the creation of institutional checks, and "the institutionalization—almost sanctification—of due process" that Markovits and Silverstein so well describe in their introduction to this volume.

Historically successful predemocratic regimes prescribed self-restraint on the part of leaders that restricted their abuse of power. This was codified in idealized form in the elite cultures of aristocracies of birth (Britain) or merit (the Imperial Chinese bureaucracy and perhaps that of Meiji Japan), which ruled by right of their superiority. Values of honor, obligation, and stewardship and respect for the limits laid down by common law and practice checked the wise. The less wise were unchecked; they perished in assassinations, caused civil wars, or became tyrants. Until the very recent past, one could meet in liberal democracies a sense of obligation to serve in politics among an aristocracy of birth that permeated the way others approached politics as well. Consider the comments of LeRoy Percy, Senator from Mississippi and heir to the culture of the planter aristocracy of the Delta, "A man's job is to make the world a better place to live in, in so far as he is able—always remembering that the results will be infinitesimal—and to attend to his own soul." The two were obviously intertwined. After losing his seat in 1912, Percy wrote one supporter, "I do not expect to shirk any duty that comes my way. . . . If I can keep this small corner of the United States in which I reside, comparatively clean and decent in politics and fit for a man to live in, and in such condition that he may not be ashamed to pass it on to his children, I will have accomplished all that I hope to do."[1] The occasion for this reflection was Percy's loss to James K. Vardaman, one of that breed of Southern demagogues who raised the combination of populism and racism to a fine art.

Traditional conservatism in liberal democracies grew out of the tradition of politics as obligation. The self-restraint that accompanied this tradition seems to have fallen into abeyance as conservative parties' leadership has ceased to be the preserve of those who shared such values. The idea that leadership might require self-restraint is obviously foreign to many of the conservatives described in this volume. Consider the Italian Christian Democrats involved in the P–2 Masonic Lodge, Tanaka and his Liberal Democratic Party associates in Japan, or Nixon's White House. The only exception is the British Conservative Party in Robin Gaster's portrayal: Defense Minister Profumo's most scandalous behavior was not his fling with Christine Keeler but his lying about it to his peers. Alone among the protagonists of our scandals, Jack Profumo has done penance.

The leaders of some of the parties of the Left in liberal democracies have been constrained by other factors. Some clearly were driven by an almost religious devotion to socialist ideas. That required a degree of personal austerity that precluded personal enrichment. Some labor and socialist parties were so well organized that they controlled their leaders instead of vice versa; their leaders were directly responsible to an organized community. But those strictures, too, have gradually relaxed as European socialist parties have lost the elan of the mass movement and the driving vision of social transformation. Their leaders, too, have become politicians among politicians and are not immune to the temptations of money or power.

The concept of political leadership as an obligation prescribed by ideology, by service to a movement, or by *noblesse oblige* was as foreign to demagogues like Vardaman as to the cast of characters in Watergate, the Flick affair, the AKH and Lockheed scandals, the Lavon affair (except, possibly, Lavon himself), not to mention the multitudinous Italian scandals graphically described by Judith Chubb and Maurizio Vannicelli. The absence of a concept of political obligation runs like a red thread through the scandals of this volume. With the obvious exceptions of President François Mitterrand and Defense Minister Charles Hernu in the Greenpeace affair, these men and women are self-seeking. They have used public office to private ends in a fashion suitably described by the term "scandal."

Distinguishing the Scandalous from Politics as Usual

What constitutes the common denominator that leads the authors to consider the very diverse phenomena that they describe to be political scandals?

That they are political is clear enough, and that they are scandals as we would use the term in everyday language is plausible as well. But is everyday use analytically adequate? Let us start by asking what these scandals have in common.

A more unlike collection of activities grouped under a common rubric is difficult to imagine. In the Italian cases, we have avarice of heroic proportions combined with the mafia, murder, and what is little more than garden variety patronage in a patron-client system; all involve private gain from positions of public trust. In the AKH and Lockheed scandals one sees evidence that extravagant venality knows no cultural bounds. The Flick affair involves huge amounts of money and there is substantial opportunity for private gain, but much (most?) of the money was passed on by its recipients to their respective parties. In the *Spiegel* affair, there is no private gain; instead a defense minister uses the powers of state to pursue a personal vendetta. In the Watergate, there is a clear abuse of power to prevent the replacement of current officeholders by their opponents. The object of the Lavon affair remains unclear; that it was used in the pursuit of power is, however, abundantly clear. The Royal Canadian Mounted Police seems no more than overly zealous in its pursuit of domestic sedition; the FBI matches that with monotonous regularity and none dared call it scandal. The Profumo affair is deliciously juicy, but it is hard to see it today as much more than an anachronistic Victorian morality play with overtones of farce. In the sinking of the *Rainbow Warrior,* not only is there no private gain, one can advance a reasonably strong argument that those involved acted to fulfill their public obligations as they saw them, albeit in an illegal fashion.

What is their common denominator?

One common denominator is what they are not: these are not the grubby scandals of city hall or urban machine. There are no inflated contracts for fencing school yards, fixed speeding tickets, or shoddy materials used in public buildings here. These are front-page scandals and cover practically the entire gamut of what we might call "high scandals"—sex, sabotage, espionage, murder, the mafia, million-dollar bribes, national security, and extraordinary abuses of power.

But what analytically useful common denominator do they have?

I thought, when I began to read these chapters in manuscript form, that the defining characteristic of the political scandal was its confusion of the public and private spheres. Had I attempted an inclusive definition at that time, I would have tried something like "scandals involve the crass intrusion of private interest into the conduct of public business." Scandal bridges the separation of public and private spheres that Markovits and Silverstein consider essential to the vitality of liberal democracy; indeed they judge that separation to be the distinguishing characteristic of the liberal democratic state. More specifically, I think that my definition would have focused on what I would call "the gross violation of cultural and legal norms that limit the use of positions of public trust for private purposes."

This sort of definition may be uncomfortably relativistic for the morally inclined, but realism has some analytical virtues. Clearly the use of office for individual gain is not in itself scandalous—or, if it is, politics is scandalous by definition, for few seek office for exclusively altruistic reasons. *Noblesse oblige* motivates few modern politicians. Ideology motivates more of them, especially in movement parties in their radical early years; these politicians, however, do not figure in this volume's scandals. Our cast of characters here are rational, materially self-interested individuals par excellence; they seem to have been drawn to politics by the pay, the patronage, and the other individual benefits of power.

There is, of course, a threshold at which self-interested behavior in positions of public trust does become a scandal. Theft from the public till, the regulator's shaking down the regulated, or the taking of direct payment while in government for the performance of favors would generally trigger that description. Those activities fit the category that the Tammany Hall philosopher, State

Senator George Washington Plunkitt, some eighty years ago designated "dishonest graft." Plunkitt, like most of us, righteously frowned on such behavior.[2]

The problem is determining where that threshold lies. To continue to use Plunkitt's categories, the problem is distinguishing dishonest graft from "honest graft." His definition of honest graft—"I seen my opportunities and I took 'em"—accurately describes the behavior of a substantial number of office holders. "Every good man looks after his friends," says Plunkitt. "If I have a good thing to hand out in private life, I give it to a friend. Why shouldn't I do the same in public life?"

I'll grant that the distinction between the scandalous, dishonest graft, and the normal, honest graft, may be difficult to grasp for ordinary mortals. You almost have to be a lawyer to understand it.

Let me give an example. When I was growing up in Texas a substantial portion of the lawyers in the state legislature, as ill-paid a body as ever refused to tax corporations, were on retainers from corporations to provide legal services should those ever be needed. Their services weren't needed, but their votes were. Giving lawyers retainer fees wasn't buying votes—it was merely doing business with friends. Unless the recipient wasn't a lawyer, of course. The unfortunate servants of the people who were farmers or union officials or teachers couldn't accept similar gratuities without inviting indictment for bribery.

The saddest case I remember was that of a nonlawyer, a country type in the Texas House who recycled his unused office funds into a pick-up truck. A used pick-up truck mind you. That was obviously a scandal, and he went to the pen.

The money scandals that figure in this volume are, of course, of a different magnitude. The Flick affair, the Lockheed scandal, the AKH–General Hospital scandal, and the various scandals tied to the P–2 Masonic Lodge involved millions or tens of millions. As the scope of government has grown, so has the scope of potential corruption.

What really distinguishes the scandalous act from the normally self-seeking is its blatant violation of community norms of what Markovits and Silverstein call the community's *conscience collective*. This may seem to make the definition of scandal to be as much in the eye of the beholder as is obscenity, and to raise the same awful problems of determining community standards. Who would want to be forced to operationalize a definition of that?

Let me offer an operational shortcut that is, incidentally, the genuine common denominator of the scandals discussed in this volume: concealment.

All of the actors in these chapters were sufficiently aware that they were overstepping either community norms or the law that they all sought to conceal their actions. The Flick, Greenpeace, Watergate, Lockheed, P–2, and AKH cases involved obvious illegalities. Strauss, in acting in his official capacity out of personal spite, and Profumo in his choice of such an indiscreet bedmate and in lying to his colleagues, overstepped community norms among their peers. The Lavon Affair is less clear in its basic facts, but its concealment was virtually absolute; it was, in fact, its total secrecy that enabled Lavon's opponents within Mapai to use the affair to force him into the political wilderness.

Moliere put it neatly in *Tartuffe:* "It is public scandal that constitutes offense. . . . to sin in secret is not to sin at all." Moreover, it is the fact of concealment that enables us to distinguish genuinely scandalous behavior in politics from the merely incompetent, simply stupid, or stubbornly wrongheaded acts that seem to be almost as commonplace as honest graft. Genuinely scandalous behavior is known by the actor to be sufficiently dangerous that he or she makes serious efforts to conceal it. The merely incompetent, stupid, or wrongheaded actor, by contrast, often takes pride in publicly proclaiming responsibility for the disaster in making. Having had the nature and scope of the catastrophe amply demonstrated by events, such individuals are more likely to announce proudly that "We must stay the course" or "This lady's not for turning" than to adopt the obviously more sensible course of dissociating themselves from the failed policy, which, if at all possible, should be attributed to the opposition. Or one can always attribute it to the "mysterious malicious forces" to which French Defense Minister Hernu initially ascribed the sinking of the Rainbow Warrior or to those even more mysterious "occult powers" that Chubb and Vannicelli mention in the Italian context.

Scandals belong to the genre of political morality plays that feature the calamities of failed leadership. But unlike the folly of leaders—the stubborn pursuit of a disastrous policy despite the evidence[3]—and unlike political tragedy—the fall of a political giant through hubris—the rest of us are not pulled into the fall of our political leaders in scandal. Scandal is not the systematic policy of a repressive government and it is impossible in systems that elevate the caprice of the leader to the policy of government. In the scandal, the leader does not proclaim his folly to the multitude nor challenge the gods; instead the leader pursues his private ends, using the veil of secrecy (frequently under the guise of national security) to conceal his violation of the law, of the public trust, and of the political norms. Unlike folly and tragedy, scandal contains elements of farce. The scandal replaces the limits that law and custom place on the leader with the triumph of the individual leader over his contraints in unexpected, abnormal, indeed implausible fashions. Scandals shock not only because of the violation of public trust, but also because of the whimsical improbability of finding that the Japanese prime minister has been bought by a foreign corporation, of catching the president of the United States up to his ears in a third-rate burglary, or discovering the British defense minister in bed with the mistress of a Soviet naval attaché. One has to suspend disbelief at the picture of the former national security adviser sneaking off to Iran with a Bible and a cake from President Reagan for the Ayatollah Khomeini, or the Iran-Contra conspirators simply misplacing the Sultan of Brunei's $10 million contribution, which was deposited in the wrong Swiss bank account. And would anyone really believe that Lockheed would ask for receipts for bribes or that Nixon would tape record the cover-up of Watergate for posterity? These are the sorts of plots editors turn back to the authors of potboilers as too outrageous to hold the reader's interest.

Political Culture, Parties, and Scandals

What are the roles of cultural and structural factors in making some liberal democratic systems more scandal-prone than others? Particularly what is the relation between scandal and the party system, which appears in each of the nine cases, despite the very different natures of the parties and party systems in question?

It is clear from the above that what is a scandal is a question of political culture. In the Italian case, for example, the mere sale of influence does not qualify as a scandal unless you sell to the mafia or the Red Brigades. In the Japanese case, it seems to have become so standard, in large measure because of the high costs of Japanese elections, that Terry MacDougall speaks of "structural corruption," and former Prime Minister Kakuei Tanaka was convinced that his receipt of $2.1 million from Lockheed did not constitute wrongdoing. In the American case, however, that sort of thing does constitute scandal, as several of Mr. Reagan's former aides also discovered. In the Profumo case in Britain a quarter of a century ago, or in the Hart case in the United States in 1987, extramarital sex ended promising political careers; in Denmark it is not even cause for comment. Political culture governs even the acceptable uses of ill-gotten gains. In the Flick case, many party members saw no scandal because the politicians who received the money passed it on to their parties; had they kept it, it would have been a scandal indeed. There may be little perplexity, incidentally, about why Italian scandals leave few traces: many are not seen as scandals at all. Much of the *partitocrazia* that Chubb and Vannicelli describe is, at worst, honest graft, and more a custom than an aberration.

It is hard to avoid noting the role that parties play in all the cases studied. Austria, Canada, France, Great Britain, Israel, Italy, Japan, the United States, West Germany—there is no major scandal without party. This obviously attests to the central role of parties in liberal democracies. It also attests to the failure of parties to control their leaders. Leaders have become independent actors, as contemptuous of party as of law and due process in their pursuit of self-interest. The party is their vehicle for personal advancement; they jettison it when that seems opportune. The behavior of President Nixon that Silverstein details epitomizes this political independence of party.

What is surprising under these circumstances is the frequent failure of the opposition parties to exploit the scandal for partisan advantage. In the *Spiegel*, Profumo, and Watergate affairs, the opposition utilized its opportunities, but the results were limited. The Lockheed and Lavon affairs had more of the character of an internal party struggle within the Liberal Democrats and Mapai, respectively, than a conflict between parties. Tanaka actually strengthened his position politically within the Liberal Democratic party and among voters in his constituency after his conviction. In most of the Italian cases, in the Flick case, the AKH scandal, and in the Greenpeace affair, the opposition pulled its punches. May I suggest that the reason was that the presumably scandalous behavior in these latter cases was in less sharp violation of community norms? The most striking case is France, where Bornstein quotes one opposition RPR dignitary as saying "what we are denouncing, really, is that the operation was a failure."

A substantial number of the cases of ineffective party opposition occurred in countries with either dominant parties (Israel, Italy, Japan) or collusion between oligopolistic parties (Austria); German politics in the Flick Affair shows some of the latter characteristics. Such arrangements unquestionably encourage stability in party government, but they remove the check on scandal that a competitive party system could be presumed to offer. The failure of the opposition to attack lowers the political costs of scandal, reducing the likelihood of control, and increasing the likelihood that the opposition will be drawn in as well, as was in fact the case in the Flick and AKH affairs.

What is worthy of consideration is not only the ubiquitousness of both honest and dishonest graft in some countries but also the absence of both in others, when both countries would seem to share similar political cultures. On the surface, for example, it is puzzling why the Austrian and the German Social Democrats have their full share of financial scandals—the German *Neue Heimat* affair is surely much more a scandal from a socialist point of view than the Flick affair, because it severely damaged cooperative housing, which was a major institution of the labor movement—while their Scandinavian colleagues are virtually free of such embarrassments. I doubt that culture is a sufficient explanation. Instead, I suspect that it is structural variables: the leaders have much closer contact with the led in the Scandinavian labor movement, and that tends to reinforce the limits on the misbehavior of the leaders.

Institutional Checks on Scandals

The realist's immediate response is that the fact of scandal proves the inadequacy of institutional checks. "Power tends to corrupt," said Lord Acton, "and absolute power corrupts absolutely." Though liberal democracies' structures prevent the absolute corruption of absolute power, they are susceptible to the regular partial corruption that the case studies in this volume detail. The checks of law, the courts, investigatory commissions, and exposure in the press prevented none of the scandals described. Presumably they did prevent others. Recollect that part of our definition of scandal involved the fact that it was an abnormal intrustion of the private into the public realm.[4]

The institutional checks on the scandals in this volume were applied after the acts had occurred. Prosecutors brought charges. Courts heard the cases, exposing in an august public form the avarice, venality, and simple lawlessness of leaders. Promising careers in politics were cut short, or, like that of Franz Josef Strauss's, at least briefly interrupted. New careers on the lecture circuit were created. Investigating commissions returned mammoth reports. Newspapers upped their circulations, and prying journalists won prizes. Of the principal figures in the scandals, only former Japanese Prime Minister Kakuei Tanaka served time in jail; he remained the kingmaker within his own party, however. Lesser actors were more severely and more frequently punished.[5] And comparable scandals subsequently recurred with regularity.

Indeed, some seem even more bizarre. An agent of the Canadian Security Intelligence Service, created to assume the security functions of the discredited Royal Canadian Mounted Police, was convicted of planting bombs. South of the border, the revelations of the Iran-Contra affair left Watergate enthusiasts gasping in admiration, but—at least as of this writing—the Reagan administration successfully contained the scandal by placing the entire responsibility on an expendable subordinate; the explanation that Oliver North was running his very own, independent foreign policy was grotesque, but seemingly acceptable to the public.

What is striking in these cases is their general lack of long-term impact. Those that are financial scandals produce some tightening of the rules, but since the initial scandals involved violations of the then-extant rules, some skepticism about the effectiveness of extirpating greed in politics with new rules may be warranted.

Scandals involving abuse of power had, if possible, even fewer consequences. Strauss, who distinguished himself in the *Spiegel* affair not only by use of government power to pursue a personal vendetta against that newsweekly, but also by his asking favors of dubious legality from Franco's police, subsequently became the Christian Democratic candidate for the chancellorship and continued to dominate Bavarian—indeed at times even federal—politics. In the United States, the Republican Party lost the 1976 election after Watergate by a narrow margin, but recaptured the White House in the subsequent election in 1980. In terms of scandal, the Reagan administration seemed intent on proving Marx's dictum that history repeats itself as farce. The most serious institutional reform occasioned by the scandals analyzed was Canada's creation of a new security agency from the personnel of the old, which, not surprisingly, continued the abuses that had characterized its predecessor, although, as Reg Whitaker notes, without the Mounties' aura of legitimacy. Only in Israel did scandal produce long-term changes, but these, as Mitchell Cohen details them, had to do with the fragmentation of Mapai as its leaders fell into open warfare over Lavon, its consequential failure to recruit new voters, and the exploitation by the Right of the opportunity to win power. One need not be particularly cynical to regret the replacement of Mapai's occasional scandal with the folly—as Tuchman uses the term—of Menachem Begin and Herut in Lebanon and on the West Bank.

The limited impact that scandals have had in institutional terms stems from their nature. They are, by and large, not institutionalized abuse. The RCMP was, and Canadians found an institutional, albeit inadequate, answer. Nor do scandals generally involve systematic political abuses. But most of the scandals are aberrations: implausible, peculiar, and occasionally bizarre acts by individual leaders, who are as different in their abuses of power as they are different in personality. The individualization of the scandals that bear their names reflects their uniqueness, not generic characteristics.

National Security and the Anatomy of Scandal

Markovits and Silverstein remark in passing that while "paranoia is a fact of political life," it is only in liberal democracies that "fears for the national security appear inevitably to trigger political scandals." National security does figure in every scandal in this book in some fashion, except the Austrian hospital scandal and the Flick Affair.

How it figures, however, is another story. Throughout these case studies the invocation of national security serves two purposes. The first is to justify the concealment of the scandal itself. The "national security" argument has, after all, become the primary acceptable ground in liberal democracies for a government to deny its citizens knowledge of what it is doing in their names. When the threat is real, as in the cases of Israel or FLN terrorism in Quebec, few will question the argument, including the victims. Pinhas Lavon waited years to seek vindication. The Canadian New Democrats, regular targets for RCMP investigation, preferred not to castigate their persecutors, Whitaker says, because "We don't want to look like a bunch of Pinkos." In point of fact, however, national security was not really at issue in any of the cases except, conceivably, the Lavon Affair. It was invoked merely to conceal the peccadilloes of politicians or their more blatant abuses of power.

The second purpose is that "national security" is in fact the standard reason for the suspension of due process and procedure and, indeed, legality in liberal democracies. It is not surprising to find security agents and agencies involved in the Watergate, Greenpeace, *Spiegel* and the P–2 affairs; their actions in these presumably illegitimate capacities were identical to their actions in presumably legitimate capacities at other times. The fineness of the line between legitimate and illegitimate suspension of due process, procedure, and law is clearest in the RCMP affair, where the security agency itself became the scandal.

Asking why security agencies act in this manner is like asking why tigers eat meat; it is their nature. Asking why the RCMP's actions were a scandal while the comparable acts of the FBI are not, however, leads us back to an analysis of political culture. Whitaker's use of the term "peaceable kingdom" to describe Canada has some validity; in the United States, by contrast, paranoia has been raised to a matter of principle. Lester Pearson was denounced to the U. S. Senate Internal Security Cmmittee as pro-Soviet and Pierre Trudeau was briefly barred from entry into the United States under the McCarran-Walter Act; the Canadians considered both sufficiently reliable to serve as prime ministers.

In short, national security serves both to legitimize the systematic violation of process, procedure, and, often, law carried on by security agencies in liberal democracies and to justify the concealment of the capricious violations of process, procedure, and law that are at issue in most of these scandals. In the latter case, Samuel Johnson's characterization truly does apply: patriotism is the last refuge of a scoundrel.

The Scandal as Purification

Markovits and Silverstein suggest that the ritual of scandal and punishment serves as a means of legitimation in liberal democracies. They serve to "build support for the system by concretizing its overall legitimacy. . . . The rituals of political scandals and their resolutions take the abstract values of liberal democracy and make them tangible and visible. They reaffirm for the citizenry that the process does work. . . ." Is this a case of finding a silver lining in every cloud? Or can scandals that destroy citizens' confidence in individual leaders actually strengthen their confidence in the liberal democratic system?

The evidence demonstrated in these essays is ambigious. Some scandals seem to delegitimize. Aline Kuntz finds an undermining of governmental legitimacy through Strauss's abuse of power and an undermining of the party system through the Flick affair. Chubb and Vannicelli clearly see Italian scandals as pernicious. Anton Pelinka judges the AKH scandal to be one of the causes for the decline of *both* major parties relative to their minor competitors. MacDougall notes the degree of public cynicism that results from the fact that Japanese politics is awash with corporate cash. Silverstein is skeptical that the structural reforms caused by Watergate will preclude similar abuses; indeed he offers the Iran-Contra Affair as a postscript. And Whitaker finds the replacement of the Mounties' secret police functions with a new agency, the CSIS, to be ineffective; the new agency seems as scandal-ridden as the old. It is hard to see much greater legitimacy for any of these liberal democracies in the aftermath of their responses to the scandals described and easy to argue the opposite.

In the French case one can make a plausible argument that scandal legitimized: it legitimized the socialists as nationalists, as a party that puts France first. The weakness of the opposition's attack on the issue, at least in my interpretation, stems from its acceptance of the legitimacy of the government's illegal actions. I'm not certain that legitimation via illegality is desirable. Bornstein does not mince words; he describes scandals as pathologies.

One may argue that the purifying potential of these scandals was lost in the failure to punish their perpetrators adequately. Had the punishment fit the abuse of power, perhaps their results would have been different. Certainly the Watergate scandal reaffirmed Americans' conviction that the rule of law was prefereable to the rule of capricious men—despite the fact that the scandal's central actor, Richard Nixon, has enjoyed a prosperous retirement while his subordinates went to jail. There are limits to *lèse majesté*, even for American democrats. The episode made press, voters, and politicians far more vigilant in their defense of democratic procedures. There is nothing like the violation of democratic rules to increase our appreciation of them. "Democracy is the worst form of government," Winston Churchill once put it, "except all those other forms which have been tried from time to time."

As rites of purification, scandals and their resolutions leave much to be desired. To prescribe scandal as a cure for the abstractness of the virtues of liberal democracy is as dubious as prescribing leeches for physical ailments. Like leeches, scandals are not fatal, but they are likely to leave the patient a bit shaky. So let us not dignify them too much by ascribing to them too salutary a role. Because scandals are person-centered, they do not necessarily undercut the legitimacy of democratic systems. Punishing the person expeditiously and appropriately will almost certainly legitimize the system itself. But that is hard to do, for the very reason that scandals revolve around abuse of power. Those in a position to abuse power are also in a position to avoid punishment.

Comparative Scandology

Case studies of scandals in nine liberal democracies suggest some conclusions more concrete than those sketched above.

First, while political scientists cannot easily define what a scandal is, its participants instinctively know when their behavior is scandalous. They demonstrate that through their frantic efforts at concealment. Though their efforts may ultimately fail, the attempt at concealment is, like hypocrisy, the tribute that vice pays to virtue.

Second, each country gets the scandals it deserves. Some cultures find sex scandalous, so they are plagued with licentious politicians. Other systems set a premium on money in the election process. Not surprisingly, so do their politicians. Those political cultures that are most fearful of opponents foreign and domestic yield bizarrely paranoid scandals. The scandal expresses in an abnormal and personalized fashion a more general characteristic of the political culture.

Third, scandals are not an aberration. They are too numerous and too frequent to be that. I doubt that scandals can accurately be described as pathological, as Bornstein suggests; all nine systems seem to live well with endemic scandal. Rather than a pathology, they may be more accurately seen as normal—like pollution in industrial societies or contaminated water in Third World countries. We do not particularly like them—indeed, they nearly outrage us—but we can live with them. They may simply be a cost of maintaining a liberal system in which politicians are more likely to be concerned with individual advancement and self-promotion than feel any strong sense of obligation.

Ideology may provide some immunity and so may political education in a movement party, but that immunity is neither universal nor permanent, as witness the involvement of Austrian and German Social Democrats in financial scandals in those countries.

Fourth, scandals may or may not lead to greater system legitimacy. It depends upon the effectiveness of the response. Trying to resolve scandals by punishing the guilty produces little legitimacy unless the effort is successful. That occurs too rarely. Nixon's being forced from office did legitimize the courts, Congress, and, above all, the press. The punishment visited on Profumo proved that the Conservative Party can police its own. But has the response to the Austrian, German, French, Italian or Japanese scandals legitimized those systems? The answer, I fear, is negative. Punishment was slow, ineffective, or altogether absent. The fact of scandal disillusioned some, including some of the followers of the discredited leaders; the failure to respond appropriately disillusioned others. Only cynics found their faith reaffirmed. Still, the pursuit of the perpetrators of scandal does encourage the vigilance vital to maintaining liberal democracy.

Finally, while it is hard to argue that scandals have many redeeming virtues for the political system, they do make politics a more interesting spectator sport. What is, after all, the babble of recent candidates compared to the charms of Donna Rice or Christine Keeler? Television evangelist turned Republican presidential candidate Pat Robertson seems more human now that we know that God has a statute of limitation on the sinfulness of premarital sex. And the fact that one hundred officials of the Reagan administration either had been indicted or were under investigation surely appeals to the Guinness-Book-of-Records sentiment in each of us. Let us make an intellectual virtue of a political vice and learn to appreciate the scandal as a political art form.

NOTES

1. William Alexander Percy, *Lanterns on the Levee: Recollections of a Planter's Son* (New York: Alfred A. Knopf, 1941), pp. 75, 152.

2. William Riordon, *Plunkitt of Tammany Hall,* original edition 1905 (New York: E. P. Dutton, 1963), pp. 3, 5–6.

3. Cf. Barbara Tuchman, *The March of Folly: From Troy to Vietnam* (New York: Alfred A. Knopf, 1984).

4. The line is difficult to draw. In the Japanese case, the interpenetration of the private and public spheres renders ambiguous the boundary between normal politics, which is well-greased by monumental infusions of corporate cash, and the truly scandalous. Tanaka, his voters, and his faction within the LDP did not find his behavior to be scandalous at all. His opponents, the press, and the courts held a different view.

5. Two of the Italian figures, Roberto Calvi and Michele Sindona, died under exceedingly odd circumstances, but practically the only agency not suspected in their deaths is the law.

Contributors

Andrei S. Markovits. Department of Political Science, Boston University; and Center for European Studies, Harvard University.

Mark Silverstein. Department of Political Science, Boston University.

Stephen E. Bornstein. Department of Political Science, McGill University.

Judith Chubb. Department of Political Science, College of the Holy Cross.

Mitchell Cohen. Department of Political Science, Bernard M. Baruch College and the Graduate Center of the City University of New York.

Robin Gaster. International Monetary Fund, Washington, D.C.

Aline Kuntz. Department of Political Science, University of New Hampshire.

John Logue. Department of Political Science, Kent State University.

Terry MacDougall. Department of Political Science, Boston University.

Anton Pelinka. Department of Political Science, University of Innsbruck.

Maurizio Vannicelli. Department of Political Science, College of the Holy Cross.

Reg Whitaker. Department of Political Science, York University.

Index

Accame, Falco, 150n
Acton, Lord, 261
Adenauer, Konrad, 159, 160, 162n
Agnew, Spiro T., 20
Ahdut ha-Avodah Party, 236, 243, 249–50, 253n
Ahlers, Conrad, 151–52, 159
AKH scandal, 166–69, 256, 258, 260; factors in, 181–84; political impact of, 177; ramifications of, 184–88
Allgemeines Krankenhaus. *See* AKH scandal
All Nippon Airways (ANA), 195, 197–98
Almond, Gabriel, 138
Alon, Yigal, 250
Alpert, Carl, 21
Alternance, 116–17
Ambrosiano bank, 137, 141
Andreotti, Giulio, 128
Androsch, Hannes, 167–69
Annales school, 2
Anti-Semitism, 237–38
Aran, Zalman, 234, 236
Archer, Jeffrey, 78
Ashida, Hitoshi, 215
Astor, Bill, 66
Augstein, Rudolf, 151, 152
Austria, 183–84; cabinet of, 178–79; civil service in, 177–81; consociational democracy of, 166–88;

constitutional rules of, 169–71; fascism in, 183; federalism in, 181–82; government of, 177–81; Grand Coalition of, 179–81; institutions of, 181–84; judiciary in, 177–81; "new middle class" of, 186; parliamentarism in, 171–77; political parties in, 181–83, 184–86; postwar reconstruction of, 166; Second Republic of, 181
Austrian Constitutional Court, 180–81
Austrian National Council, 170–71, 179, 181; structure and power of, 172–77
Austrian People's Party, 175, 179–80, 182, 183
Azaar, Samuel, 231

Baker, Howard, 20
Barre, Raymond, 10, 119n
Barzel, Rainer, 153, 161, 164n
Barzini, Luigi, 142
Bauer, Franz, 167
Begin, Menachem, 29–40, 249–50, 262
Ben Barka, 111
Ben-Gurion, David, 230–31, 233–37, 240; Begin and, 239–40; book on Lavon affair by, 246–47; Lavon affair, effect of on, 248–49; power